MW00561008

NEW DIRECTIONS IN GERMAN STUDIES

Vol. 13

Series Editor:

Imke Meyer

Volumes in the series:

Vienna's Dreams of Europe

Culture and Identity beyond the Nation-State

Katherine Arens

Bloomsbury Academic
An imprint of Bloomsbury Publishing Inc

B L O O M S B U R Y
NEW YORK · LONDON · OXFORD · NEW DELHI · SYDNEY

Bloomsbury Academic
An imprint of Bloomsbury Publishing Inc

1385 Broadway	50 Bedford Square
New York	London
NY 10018	WC1B 3DP
USA	UK

www.bloomsbury.com

BLOOMSBURY and the Diana logo are trademarks of Bloomsbury Publishing Plc

First published 2015

© Katherine Arens, 2015

Library of Congress Cataloging-in-Publication Data
Arens, Katherine, 1953- author.
Vienna's dreams of Europe : culture and identity beyond the nation-state / Katherine Arens.
pages cm. -- (New directions in German studies ; volume 13) Includes bibliographical references and index.
ISBN 978-1-4411-4249-8 (hardback) -- ISBN 978-1-4411-7021-7 (paperback) -- ISBN 978-1-4411-1823-3 (e-ISBN; ePUB) -- ISBN 978-1-4411-7560-1 (e-ISBN)
1. Vienna (Austria)--Intellectual life--19th century. 2. Vienna (Austria)--Intellectual life--20th century. 3. Austrian literature--Austria--Vienna--History and criticism. 4. Austria--Civilization. 5. Austria--In literature. 6. Group identity in literature. 7. Group identity--Austria--History. 8. National characteristics, Austrian. 9. National characteristics, European. I. Title.
DB851.A76 2015
943.6'1304--dc23
2015011009

ISBN: HB: 978-1-4411-4249-8
PB: 978-1-4411-7021-7
ePub: 978-1-4411-1823-3
ePDF: 978-1-4411-7560-1

Series: New Directions in German Studies

Typeset by Fakenham Prepress Solutions, Fakenham, Norfolk NR21 8NN
Printed and bound in the United States of America

Contents

Acknowledgments

The studies in this volume represent over a decade of work dedicated to the straightforward but never simple observation that "Austria" and "Germany" have never been the same culture, no matter how many scholars of "German" literature have taken that cultural unity as a given for over a century. My goal here is unreachable but none the less necessary: to make a case that only a variety of *germanophone cultures* can ever be the objects of investigation for *Germanistik* and *German studies* in all of their forms.

The literatures and cultures of earlier political forms of today's "Austria" are heavily interwoven among several different languages (from the Latin that joined the Holy Roman Empire's elite with that of the rest of Europe to the Italian, Magyar, and Slavic languages characterizing the Austrian and Austro-Hungarian Empires—and the translation conduits that exist today). The earlier political forms of today's "Germany" have a more complicated provenance, for the Federal Republic, like the Empire that came into being in 1870/71, has always been an assemblage of different nation-states, each germano-phone, with Prussia asserting pride of place; not only the Berlin Wall, but other trade, passport, and political boundaries had divided them from each other for most of their existences. The present constellation of the FRG has been the longest-lived of these assemblages, and it too has arguable roots as a single "culture," since the German Democratic Republic had its own culture for at least two-thirds of the era since the end of World War II. To study "German" culture—*germanophone cultures*—is thus a puzzlement, a perpetual bewilderment, not just a puzzle with a single solution.[1]

My thanks are due to the many conference audiences who followed me on my meandering journey through this puzzlement and who have helped me find what I present here: a fundamental distinction within

---

1 See "For Want of a Word" (1999) for the argument I made introducing the concept as necessary for German studies.

germanophone cultures between national identities, a willingness to define one's own culture with reference to Europe and to consider it as attached not to a central authority, but rather to public discussion and debate. The cultural identity politics suggested here follow historical associations and points of reference, rather than the evolution of a nation-state and its ideas; networks, not national-genetic determinism, are my focus. The germanophone Austrian culture that I pursue here retains that reference point; it has allowed me to engage stimulating colleagues in many venues. I cannot thank all of them enough for their attention and consideration, nor can I acknowledge them individually.

A small number of individuals are, none the less, particularly significant for the project's genesis. First among them is Clifford Albrecht Bernd (now retired from the University of California, Davis), former president of the Grillparzer Society of America, who invited me to participate in his society's conference on "The Other Vienna" in 1999 and helped me begin to correlate public spaces with public education and literacy; a second invitation from the Grillparzer Society, at a conference hosted by Franz Szabo (Habsburg historian *extraordinaire*) at the Wirth Institute at the University of Alberta, continued my Grillparzer-sponsored musings and allowed me, in 2004, to explore alternative approaches to nationalist identity politics. Bernd must be acknowledged in his long-term role of mediating between Austrian and North American scholars, and for his ethics in honoring both traditions with the best scholarly work.

These conferences also brought me the pleasure of meeting and learning from William C. Reeve (Queen's University), the finest of North American Grillparzer specialists. The International Herder Society allowed me, in 1998, to take up the comparisons between Lessing, Herder, and Sonnenfels that appear here in greatly altered form; I acknowledge particularly Sabine Gross as an intellectual center for that organization. The long-term editor of the *German Quarterly*, James Rolleston (Duke University), provided me with many opportunities to clarify my own theoretical premises, over many a conference discussion.

The Austrian Studies Association (formerly: Modern Austrian Literature and Culture Association) and its yearly conference have been important sounding boards for various of these ideas; I single out David Luft (Oregon State University) and Robert von Dassanowsky (University of Colorado, Colorado Springs) as generous, always critically astute colleagues who combine the best in scholarship with professionalism and dedication beyond the call of duty. It is also at the ASA that I had the opportunity to meet Imke Meyer (University of Illinois at Chicago) and watch her develop into a major force in our profession, an elegant mind and spirit; I thank her for her help with this volume, her generous commentary, and her constant attention to the needs of the fragile community of Austrianists in the US.

Closer to home, the University of Texas at Austin has granted me research support to a degree generous in this day and age. At early phases of this project and again as it was nearing completion, the University Research Institute provided me with one-semester research grants (2002 and 2008), and the office of the Dean of Liberal Arts two single semesters with teaching leaves (2001 and 2007). These grants were critical in making possible not only this volume, but also two others that I had the folly of working on simultaneously. I thank them for their trust in me and hope the wait was worth it.

Leah Ross, cinematographer extraordinaire, helped make this possible at a crucial time; I thank her for her generous attention and for her unquestioning support. Carlos Amador (now Michigan Technological University) has offered an astute critical ear as I tried to sort out Catholic cultures and to think beyond the limits of current theory; his friendship and support has made this possible in many ways that cannot be enumerated. Janet Swaffar (University of Texas at Austin) has been an inimitable source of inspiration and support for this project and many others. She is the colleague, editor, and friend that we all need and rarely find, and I am grateful for her help, now as always—I couldn't have done it without her, and I dedicate it to her as poor return on a long-term collaboration. Finally, William Russell continues to make all of this possible by being there, always and without reservation.

Introduction: Austria as a Challenge to Europe

Cultural studies in this new millennium have focused on the legacies of colonialist–imperialist nationalism in an era of global capitalism, decolonization, and the increasing number and scope of global communication networks. Jürgen Habermas' *Structural Transformation of the Public Sphere* (*Strukturwandel der Öffentlichkeit*, 1962, translated 1989) has been a touchstone for scholars interrogating the often-devastating relations of state capital, mass and official cultures, and identities that are the hallmarks of the modern era, its media, and its cultural identity politics.[1] Scholars of culture whose intellectual homes are in Western Europe and the anglophone often prefer to question how dominant governmental forces marginalize non-hegemonic groups, threaten minority cultural positions, and set national and capitalist interests into collusion.

Nation-states, their infrastructures, and the flow of capital have thus become the dominant heuristics used by scholars to track the West's ideologies, values, and identities, and to further the critiques of Europe's Enlightenment begun in Horkheimer and Adorno's *Dialectic of the Enlightenment* (*Dialektik der Aufklärung*, originally 1944 but revised for the now standard 1947 edition). Yet after a half-century of this optic, these scholars' analyses often seem formulaic or resolutely Western:[2] in

---

1 Because of the limitations of Horkheimer's discussion of the public sphere, particularly his reluctance to concede any positive function to it, I will use "public space(s)" in this volume to refer to sites in culture intended for public use—that is, under control of public law rather than by individuals. Similarly, I will use "nation" to refer to a cultural entity that may or may not correspond with a state as a political entity. When they converge, I will often use "nation-state."

2 For a discussion of how discussions of nineteenth-century European imperialism do not adequately frame germanophone nations, see Katherine Arens, "Said's Colonial Fantasies: How Orientalism Marginalizes Eighteenth-Century Germany" (2004).

their accounts, Europe's imperial states have brought little to the globe except ethnic nationalism, colonialism, ecological destruction, forced migration, and suppression of global diversity. They have done so in the interests of a purportedly global "reason" that all too often, through its preferred tool of instrumental reason, justifies genocide and exploitation of individuals and whole cultures of *others*.

Despite such compelling moral and ethical narratives, the scholars who produce such accounts of Europe do not serve their causes well, from historical points of view. They persist in conceiving the region in radically presentist terms, often those derived from Horkheimer and Adorno. They map the histories and interests of post-Enlightenment nation-states using benchmarks drawn from their own, tendentious evaluations of an Enlightenment equated with the dominant Western empires and take their conclusions as foregone. In consequence, the maps they produce are framed by concepts heavily conditioned by the Cold War's post-1945 and post-Cold-War maps of Europe. Even the purpose and morality of post-1989's new "united Europe" is framed over and against the supposedly more fundamental identities of its nation-states.

Thus, for instance, as the German Democratic Republic (GDR) fades into historical memory, the German Federal Republic (FRG) can frame the event as a celebration of a return to some kind of historically attested normalcy—Germany has purportedly recovered its identity as a whole and intact European nation-state. The Federal Republic's persistent image of the German Democratic Republic construes it as a typical hostage of Soviet aggression, a narrative which has given the FRG an identity as a nation with a clear political destiny since the late 1940s: the West's bulwark against Soviet aggression and the chaos of not-Europe. When that GDR victim state emerged from the political and social colonization of Ronald Reagan's "evil empire," so the story goes, it did so in an apotheosis of Western values, especially free market capitalism and the purportedly universal democratic participation of its citizens in a unified Europe.

Unfortunately, such a narrative works principally to orient the direct political action of a nation-state like the FRG, still hoping to overcome its mid-twentieth-century lapse of commitment to such European values. It may not be the most suitable heuristic for scholarly work on topics other than treaty history. None the less, from a cultural viewpoint, concepts like "German reunification" used in the political rhetoric framing such events carry with them assumptions about geopolitical and cultural normalcy that are extremely tenuous. Such heart-warming stories of restoration occlude the fact that the newly "whole" German nation after 1989 actually has had through history only a short track record as a centralized nation state. At the outside, in a very generous calculation, it had been a state for just over a century (since its unification and emergence in 1871, leaving aside concerns about its shifting state forms and borders in the Weimar Republic and the Third Reich that might make its run closer to fifty years, at best). Moreover, that initial unified German *Reich* of the 1870s was also a different kind of state. It had emerged against a background of Prussian leadership—a regionalism that its own leadership worked hard to overcome as they created the national fiction of the *Reich*. When the GDR was "returned" to the West, then, that same region and its people (sometimes archly called "Red Prussians" during the Cold War, in reference to Soviet militarism) were strictly relegated to a secondary position within the new state. Berlin was, of course, restored as a capital but, as accounts go, it was rapidly colonized by Western capital in the form of real estate developers while East Germans lost jobs, rights, and title to lands expropriated by their one-time leaders, sold off to capitalists by the *Treuhandanstalt* after 1990, or even reclaimed by "refugees" from the West.

Such deformations of historical memory about the maps under-lying national and European consciousness are indeed the stuff of current scholarship, but scholars of germanophone cultures (not just the culture of the Federal Republic in one of its late twentieth-century forms) must, I believe, now question accounts like Horkheimer and Adorno's or the current narratives of reunification. I have elsewhere made the case for the use of *germanophone cultures* rather than *German culture* to describe the object of investigation for those scholars in "German studies," given that "Germany" has never had a culture with a single center.[3] Here, I want to extend my optic to show what might be gained by looking beyond the heuristic of the nation-state that has never really served precise scholarly understanding of "German culture," particularly in its pre-World War II forms. Austria's "idea of Europe" strictly allows for germanophone culture to be associated with history other than that of a Germany whose identity was fluid at best, completely artificial or strategic at worst.

The German language was, after all, never the property of either a single culture (in this sense, a "nation") or a single state (as a political entity). As just intimated, today's "Germany" has neither the legal,

---

3   See Katherine Arens, "For Want of a Word: The Case for Germanophone" (1999), for the details of this argument. Given that germanophone cultures never united under a single dominant region, using the term "German literature" or "German culture" naturalizes a twentieth-century political configuration as the basis for culture—a complete political mis-assessment of the political situation in the nineteenth century. For exemplary examples of how scholarship responds to contemporary pressures, see Thomas Wallnig, Johannes Frimmel, and Werner Telesko, eds, *18th Century Studies in Austria, 1945–2010* (2011).

the cultural, nor the political provenance attributed to a nation with a relatively consistently evolving political identity—there simply is no narrative about the material forms of "German culture" that would justify taking "Germany" as the reference point for studies of the origin and evolution of today's "German culture." The Baltic, the Holy Roman Empire, Switzerland, Luxemburg—and even Texas, Philadelphia, or Milwaukee—have legitimate claims to participating in a *network* of cultural sites where German was used in various ways over decades or centuries as the language of their national elites or of coherent group identities in them. Thus to follow Horkheimer, Adorno, and Habermas into analyses of the German Enlightenment as the origin of Europe's modern nation-states is at best tendentious and at worst dangerous: a blatant falsification of political, economic, and historical data on many levels. Scholars of Europe in the current generation have none the less retained their favored models that relate culture to political decolonization and recolonization by nation-states, wars, and repression, as they analyze the consequences of French and British decolonization, the fall of the Third Reich, the break-up of the Soviet Union, British devolution, and German reunification.

In this volume, I will, in a set of case studies, challenge such scholarly foibles on two grounds. The first is historical, deriving from the case of "Austria" as another of Europe's "colonial empires," one mostly forgotten because history is always written by the victors. The second is theoretical, arguing that a national culture that need not be defined primarily in terms of an ethnic national monoculture, nor in terms of a state with centralized politics.

In historical terms, the Austria that emerged as one of Europe's neutral states after World War II is the heritor of an imperial lineage of much greater scope (historically and geographically) and consistency than Germany's Prussia, and one with a potentially greater claim to be seen as a colonizing power.[4] Yet its imperial heritage is anything but simple. The Holy Roman Empire that existed from 962 CE until Napoleon dissolved it in 1806, the Austrian Empire that succeeded it until the Austro-Hungarian compromise of 1867, and the Austria-Hungary that existed until 1918 were all elements in a chain of "Austrias" that lie behind today's small Austria. Each of those state forms can be straightforwardly reclaimed as a stratum in the evolution of germanophone culture(s) in Europe, even as they foreground political dreams of imperial control rather than images of ethnic and cultural pluralism and humanist morality. All these Austrias more or

---

4   See the volume edited by Johannes Feichtinger, Ursula Prutsch, and Moritz Csáky, *Habsburg postcolonial: Machtstrukturen und kollektives Gedächtnis* (2003), for various discussions about Austria's colonial identity.

less shared a common location—usually Central Europe and the core landholdings of the imperial and royal house of Habsburg, known in other languages as the *domus Austriae* or *Casa de Austria*. However, they never enjoyed the luxury of an official name, an official language in the singular, or a single dominant culture. Instead, they had a ruling family, a self-declared moral duty to protect Europe, cultural networks that reached across national groups and languages in various ways (some more benign and others virtually genocidal), and a marginally flexible approach to ethnicity and language by assuming stable multi-lingualism (with German leading, but never acknowledged as the exclusive dominant).

Geographically, the Habsburgs ruled the first empire on which "the sun never set" (they used the image) when they joined under a single uneasy leadership the Netherlands, Spain (and its colonies in the Americas), and great swathes of today's Central Europe. Intellectuals, politicians, and merchants born onto the map of this "European" empire with its global reference points acknowledged their need to work transnationally in all their undertakings. They would likely find the post-1989 political map of Europe to be familiar, including its gradual expansion eastward, just as they would its problems of multi-culturalism, migration, and language politics. After all, 1989 not only "reunified" Germany in the imagination of politicians and historians of culture, it also revived in the region something that might be called the "Habsburg successor states": the national map of Central Europe and the Balkans that had some borders forcibly drawn by outside allies in 1918 and then again after 1945. These realignments created and recreated ethnic-national states (ignoring other options) out of regions often shared among many groups with historic rights and experiences.

The fact that each of these states had multiple ethnic groups in them has emerged, quite naturally, as the central problem of the Balkans for scholars and critics, just as it had for politicians of the nineteenth century. Habsburg intellectuals of earlier eras, however, rarely tried to solve that problem (as the GDR problem was solved by the FRG) by declaring a single normative monoculture. Central Europe, they would have assured us, has never been a monoculture in language, ethnicity, religion, or any of the other dimensions assumed to be critical for the development of national and individual identities. To be sure, that statement would never have included the assumption of absolute cultural and historical parity, nor of civil equality, as today's politicians claim is necessary and "real" in a democratic state.

I have already touched upon this point as requiring twentieth-century scholars of "German" culture to reframe their subject of investigation in the plural, as *germanophone cultures*. But now I would extend this *aperçu* further into the reality of theory-building, to require that Europe's nation-states be rethought as anything but state monocultures. The Europe defined by the passing of the Cold War and the Iron Curtain—the Europe of NATO and the first member nations of the European Union—is not the only Europe carrying forward some kind of Enlightenment legacy, and its rationalities need not only be understood as driven by the political forces of capitalism and imperialism. They represent jurisdictions with borders that have multiply shifted and populations who have been massively redefined by the two world wars and multiple diasporas unleashed by twentieth-century politics.

Many intellectuals from the historical incarnations of Austria have maintained in their work a different definition of European culture, one centered on Austria, as the *Sol Austriacus* image on the cover of this volume suggests.[5] Yet this Austria was simply central to *Europe* itself and its culture. Europe, rather than its constituent parts, was and is often their reference point for many of these intellectuals' discussions, the basis for their mental maps of their identities and cultures. The points of their compass point North and South as often as they do East and West; national borders and ethnic borders are rarely aligned with political borders or with durable, historically attested nation-states in the ways that today's scholars prefer to assume. Moreover, that Europe, as we shall see, often is understood in terms of moral and ethical logics rather than instrumental ones, and as a common inheritance in culture rather than as national property or nation-defining ethnicities. That is, the *nations* themselves, and not just individuals opposing them, are often seen as asserting moral purposes with longer-term historical definitions.

When the Empire of Austria (earlier, as the Holy Roman Empire, and later, as Austria-Hungary) imagined itself in the eighteenth and nineteenth centuries, it did so without the luxury of centralization and a univocal cultural mission—its central mission was to act as a military boundary against a non-Christian Ottoman Empire. To the "modern" nation-states of Europe defined after the French Revolution and in some part revoked after the Napoleonic era, that "Austria" seemed conservative, almost feudal. That Habsburg state was caught up in an on-going balancing act of interests (political, ethnic, military, and cultural), and so it had never been able to centralize and rationalize its populations with the vehemence of Napoleon's France, nor become imperial on the basis of external holdings as did England with its colonial money. This empire's fall after 1918, when centrifugal forces had free rein, argued that it none the less had some kind of force as an identity in the region.

---

5   The image was made in 1698 (Cod. 8617 fol. 3r, Austrian National Library).

Remember that the Austro-Hungarian Empire did not fall solely because of internal tensions (which many historical accounts assumed); it was politically dismembered by outside forces, just at the moment when it was poised to model European federalism.[6] Even after its devolution, however, Austria remained (and remains today) an identifiable cultural sphere within Europe, no matter its persistent identity as a one-time colonizer of Balkan territories with some of the familiar mechanisms of imperial domination at its beck and call. That memory of "domination" has always been overblown, however. The Habsburg army was famously unable to win battles; it did not have the money to buy off particular ethnic and class interests; it accommodated—often poorly, but at least officially— multilingualism, regional interests, class mixing, religious variations, and public utilities in many regionally important cities, not just its capital.

Not surprisingly, then, many public voices in today's Austria remember that the European nations were not all colonial (or not in the same way), that their country's own imperial–colonial era ended in 1918, not later, and that their own sense of Europe's major cultural and political divides traced a sharp North–South axis rather than today's East–West dominant. Post-World War II Austrian politicians from both Left and Right have used their nation's neutrality as their reference point to think beyond (or around) the East–West divide of the Cold War, as a third way monumentalized in one way in Vienna's UNO-City, the world's third center (after New York and Geneva) for the United Nations. "Austrian" writers (some, like Peter Esterházy or Claudio Magris, writing in languages other than German) now confront reunited Europe in full acknowledgment of the fact that, for years, the most common name in the Viennese phone book was *Prohashka* and that any number of Habsburgs (not just their citizen-subjects) never spoke German. Such intellectuals are also often living legacies of Austro-Hungary, writing as some of the "ethnic Austrians" whose own heritages mix nationalities, ethnic identities, and traditions, including ancestors from the Balkans and beyond. Others are living heritors of the names of the noble families serving the *Casa de Austria* for hundreds of years and now serving the new states of Western Europe.[7] They live

---

6   A standard history of Austria is Robert A. Kann's *A History of the Habsburg Empire, 1526–1918* (1980).

7   Several members of Austria's hereditary nobility took on significant roles in post-1989 Europe. See, for example, Stefan Lütgenau, *Paul Esterházy 1901–1989: Ein Leben im Zeitalter der Extreme* (2005), who saw his family holdings through the twentieth century, until they became a public legacy for Hungary in the form of what in the US would be termed a national park.

out and meditate on the everyday ethical consequences hidden behind necessary choices of political and historical narratives; they use their voices to launch public discussions of alternate ways of thinking about pasts and futures.

On all fronts, then, "Austrian" intellectuals have access to a different map of Europe and its nation-states than is familiar to the West defined by today's Western powers—a map that advertising experts once marketed as being "in the heart of Europe" and centered on the Vienna now branded as "different" or "something else" (*Wien ist anders*). The Austria of its own intellectuals calls for interpretive paradigms outside the mental strictures imposed by the maps of the (post)colonial national imperia and nation-states theorized as the cores of nineteenth- and twentieth-century Europe.

Such acts of public representation sponsor Austria's identity-fantasies or dreams in the present. They also are clear challenges to more recent scholarly work, since they speak to their own publics out of a European framework about their national inheritance, not as representing domestic legacies alone. They also raise the question of the morality of national representation, offering challenges to a current cultural scholarship defined by nation-states.

Before we move on to what that "Austrian Europe" may be used for, it is useful to first ask what that dream of Europe looks like in practice, as a narrative supporting historical memory and today's politicized identity politics. A particularly whimsical version of that story is found in a volume celebrating Austria's millennium, compiled to include living heritors (fossils?) of some of its identities. *Sonne über Österreich* can help to orient us to that map of Austrian dreams, even as it begins to point to what might be at stake in imagining (or reclaiming) different maps on which to base our historical and scholarly stories about (post-, non-)national identities and cultures.

The persistence of *Mitteleuropa* in memory (but not in Austria)

> Europe is a continent of many languages, peoples, and states, each with its own history and traditions. If, despite all that, Europe forms a cultural unity, it is because we Europeans all draw life from the same roots ... (Nikolaus Lobkowicz)[8]

---

8   All translations in this volume are by the present author unless otherwise indicated. "Europa ist ein Kontinent vieler Sprachen, Völker und Staaten, von denen jeder seine eigene Geschichte und seine eigenen Traditionen ist. Wenn Europa dennoch eine kulturelle Einheit bildet, so deshalb, weil wir Europäer alle aus denselben Wurzeln leben ..."

The fall of the Berlin Wall was of course an impressive twentieth-century media event, in Europe as well as for those audiences worldwide praising the American mission defined by Ronald Reagan. They saw in the pickaxes tearing at the bricks in front of the Brandenburg Gate the triumph of the West's national identity over the "Evil Empire" of the Soviet Union and the recovery of Central Europe, *Mitteleuropa*, from its domination. Unfortunately, that political photo-op began a series of events that inadvertently eclipsed another anniversary: Austria's 1996 millennium, the celebration of its thousand-year existence as a more or less continuous political entity: "In the year of Our Lord 1996, we are called to celebrate 1000 years of Austria. How? Why? Because in a document received by the Bishop of Freising, an estate named 'Ostarrici' is named" (Kuehnelt-Leddihn, 20).⁹ The rhetoric of that millennial celebration allowed Austria to recall and restate a memory of Austria that the Cold War had suppressed—a memory not of *Mitteleuropa* (a term reflecting the political logics inherent in the Cold War) but of a European idea that had existed much longer than twentieth-century European powers often wished to remember. The historical narrative of this Austria was instead grounds for an identity—a dream?—with distinctly greater historical provenance, which in the country's millennial year was dutifully enshrined on its stamps and coins, reflected in many acts of public self-imagining about what Austria meant at the end of the twentieth century.

A textual celebration of that anniversary, *Sonne über Österreich* (Sun Over Austria), does confirm how odd that choice is of the year 996 CE as the linchpin for acts of public memory and history-telling about Austria's official identity and politics. Otto von Habsburg (1912–2011), then heir-presumptive to the vanished Habsburg throne, blesses this tale with his presence and political legitimacy in a brief introduction, entitled "1000 Jahre Ostarrichi-Urkunde" ("1000 Years of the *Ostarrichi Charter*"), which marks the volume with a certain conservatism. The origin of this Austria is very distinct and empirical, yet in Habsburg's account it is *textual*. Reflecting widely accepted facts, Habsburg outlines how historical memories of Austria and its legitimacy as a political entity are based on an entity summoned into being by a word in a document rather than by dreams of noble battles, conquests, or land grants. A territory whose borders are today forgotten, the name of *Ostarrichi* appeared in a legal document 1,000 years ago. In consequence, the lineal descendants of its inhabitants will celebrate various *real* political entities that derive their provenances from it (Habsburg,

---

9   "Wir werden in diesem Jahr des Herrn 1996 aufgefordert, ein tausendjähriges Österreich zu feiern. Wieso? Warum? Weil in einem Dokument ein Gut, das der Bischof von Freising erhält, 'Ostarrichi' genannt wird."

"1000 Jahre," 9–10). That document, republished in the *Monumenta Germaniae Historicae*, bears the seal of Kaiser Otto III; that territory is renamed *Austria* in Latin about fifty years later, in a donation document sealed by Konrad III (Morsak, 37).

A less comfortable truth hidden behind this account is the fact that the document happens to reside in Munich. None the less, one might also consider it particularly fitting that Austria's millennium is celebrated with reference to a document, given that its last incarnation, the Austro-Hungarian Empire, never did have a simple, legal, country name. "Austria-Hungary" was a commonplace designation for the last political incarnation of the Habsburg territories, not its official name, but its leader was never simply "Emperor of Austria." His actual title was much longer: "Emperor of Austria, Apostolic King of Hungary, King of Bohemia, of Dalmatia, of Croatia, of Slavonia, of Galicia, of Lodomeria, and of Illyria, King of Jerusalem, and so forth, Archduke of Austria, Grand Duke of Tuscany and of Cracow ..."—a title which continues on for lines. This Austria is thus what Erik von Kuehnelt-Leddihn calls a "millennium-old forgery" in his essay in this celebratory volume ("Gedanken über eine tausendjährigen Fälschung," 19–27).[10] The political entity thus was first recognized as a name in a document, but without defined borders—and ended with a run of hundreds of years that left politicians and intellectuals of all stripes defining their projects in reference to the at best partially recreatable borders of a political entity with no legal name. None the less, *Sonne über Österreich* expressly and confidently embraces this fluid political entity behind today's Austria to celebrate Austria as a truly European state, paradigmatic for the latter twentieth century.

Yet their celebration is not only political. Making their case on another level, the authors in this book reduplicate its contents in five languages: German, Hungarian, Italian, Croatian, and Czech, enacting the kind of "cultural unit" defined by Nikolaus Lobkowicz in the quotation above. This amalgam celebrates one particular cultural vision of Austria, definitely not the Central Europe or Austria of today's historians, as a part of a Europe which is almost a mythical geographical entity whose soul lies outside the nightmares of nationalism:

> Two meanings of "European" must from the first be distinguished. In the first sense, which I will call anthropological, the meaning of "European" includes all cultures where are marked in significant ways by Europeans. ... In a second sense, which

---

10 Jacques Le Rider discusses this older image of *Mitteleuropa* in *Hugo von Hofmannsthal: Historismus und Moderne in der Literatur der Jahrhundertwende*, in a chapter entitled "Die österreichische Idee eines Mitteleuropäischen Reiches."

I will call socio-cultural, only things that happen in Europe can
be called European – on a continent whose politics, science and
technology seems to be becoming planet-wide, even as it demonstrates its singularity ... (Lobkowicz, 33)[11]

This shared (but ultimately imaginary) Europe is a cultural and
political unit offering its inhabitants and supporters dreams of a transnational life world (Dilthey's term), conceived beyond the limitations
of any single national identity known today. Such dreams clearly also
ground a laconic statement made by Otto von Habsburg and rescue
it not as part of the individual hubris of an heir-without-a-throne,
but rather as a potentially legitimate projection of this region's plural
identity into the political sphere: "Austria was not meant for small-
state machinations" ("Österreich ist nicht für Kleinstaaterei gemacht"
["1000 Jahre," 9]).

Woven through the essays in *Sonne über Österreich* is, however, that
extremely political, millennium-old definition of Austria: a bulwark
against the end of civilization. That Austria found its high point in
1683, in Christian Europe's military defense against the Ottoman
Empire on the heights of Vienna's Kahlenberg. It resurfaces in today's
dreams of united Europe:

Europe was always Austria's goal. ... Austria will realize itself
within united Europe. It has found a new mission.

Thus there remains for Austria, after its first millennium, the
task of cooperating, in proven ways (and in memory of a great
tradition), according to old Austrian principles, with a Europe
that will bring us all peace and security. (Habsburg, "1000
Jahre," 10)[12]

---

11 "Zwei Bedeutungen von 'europäisch' müssen zunächst unterschieden werden.
   Im ersten Sinn, den ich hier als anthropologisch bezeichnen will, umfaßt die
   Bedeutung von 'europäisch' alle Kulturen, die maßgeblich von Europäern
   geprägt worden sind. ... In einem zweiten Sinn, den ich sozio-kulturell nennen
   möchte, ist europäisch nur, was sich in Europa tut, auf einem Kontinent,
   dessen Kultur zwar auf dem Wege über die Politik, die Wissenschaft und die
   Technik planetarisch zu werden scheint, der aber dennoch Eigentümlichkeiten
   aufweist ..."
12 "Europa war für Österrich immer ein Ziel. ... Österreich wird gerade im vereinigten Europa sich selbst verwirklichen. Es hat eine neue Mission gefunden.
   "So bleibt für Österreich nach dem ersten Jahrtausend weiterhin die Aufgabe,
   in bewahrter Art und Weise, nach den alten österrischischen Grundsätzen—
   unter Erinnerung an eine größere Tradition—weiter an jenem Europa
   mitzuwirken, das uns allen Frieden und Sicherheit bringen wird."

To be sure, this image is just as much a falsification or dream as is any
other national identity narrative (see Hobsbawm and Ranger), but it is a
particularly bold one, interesting for its claims to European hegemony.
Yet that Austria is not necessarily widely disseminated today, no matter
its appeal to its politicians and pundits: when Kuehnelt-Leddihn
surveyed current Austrians about their own memories of crucial
moments in history, he found that their memory of history has been
radically reduced to an inventory of events like 1683, all used in current
tourism as publicity, voided of almost all historical specifics.[13]

Readers familiar with Austrian history cannot fail to have noticed
that these interpreters of Europe bear names of lineages deeply
entwined with the imagined Austria of which they speak, hence
representing a conservative vision of historical legitimacy and change.
Still, they betray a willingness to rethink the relationship of their
Austria to Europe, preserving historical verities as they reinterpret
the salient moments in their narratives. Their Austria is imagined as
a historical moral duty, a litmus test for the "European idea" of others
sharing their continent. The familiar Habsburg "motto" AEIOU ("Allen
Ernstes ist Österreich unersetzlich" [Kuehnelt-Leddihn, 22]), says Willy
Lorenz, has another meaning in a moral geography of Europe: "in
all seriousness, Austria is irreplaceable." The Habsburg crown lands
are central to Europe's dreamwork, because they have always been
what English speakers might identify with Shakespeare's "coast of
Bohemia": the borders of civilization and center of its legal negotiations, vaguely situated somewhere just beyond known land. It is an
Instanz, a central power, with a historical mission to fulfill in controlling
"the Turk" and the Reformation alike. That central power, in turn,
rested on a functional logic centered around the emperor:

> Without the Habsburgs, the ruling house of Austria, Austria
> would not only never have possessed Czernowitz, Ragusa, Milan,
> Freiburg, Lausitz (45 kilometers from Berlin), Belgium, Trieste,
> or Lublin, but rather would have only reached the train station
> restaurant at Attnang-Puchheim. (Salzburg was the most recent

13 It is also significant for the argument of a dream-map of Europe that I am
pursuing here that he remarks on the limited images of history perpetrated by
the French, British, and US historians who write the history of Europe, whom
he claims are "Atlantic" historians (Kuehnelt-Leddihn, 20), many of whom
don't even read German, let alone the other languages of the Europe that could
include the land beyond Vienna's *Gürtel*. In his estimation, remedies do not
come from inside Austria, either, since neither current inhabitants of Austria
nor historians trace the history of a region that became the Ostmark, then the
"Alpen- und Donaugau" (Kuehnelt-Leddihn, 21), ignoring the fluid situations
of his current millennium.

Habsburg acquisition. During Mozart's lifetime it did not yet belong to Austria.) (Kuehnelt-Leddihn, 22)[14]

This imagined Austria has created new iterations of Europe's map, just as the 1698 "Sol Austriacus" does when it maps Austria onto the center of a globe with its European face turned toward us. The Austria on that oddly effaced globe is "evidently" a different kind of world, a "multinational, multiconfessional Danube monarchy" (Haselsteiner, 159), defined as a state of mind rather than a state.

Just as importantly, these voices acknowledge the need for a different approach to understanding that Austria, "a cultural-historical, cultural-typological, cultural-morphological, comparative-synoptic approach" (*kulturhistorischer, kulturtypologischer, kulturmorphologischer vergleichend-synoptischer Betrachtungsweise* [Haselsteiner, 160]). They do not posit this imperium as a *Gesamtkultur* or a universally applicable one, but rather one with many different centers, each linked multiply with other points within and outside it, hosting multiple narratives reflecting its "truth," and reinforced by clear, mobile lines of power extending across ephemeral internal boundaries (and not just capitalist ones).

To assume otherwise would be a kind of cultural imperialism of the sort that Karlheinz Auchenthaler explores when he addresses "Austrian literature" as a construct that all too often gets leveled into German literature, in an essay entitled "Not Everything Written in German is German Literature." That title is borrowed from the 1995 Frankfurt Book Fair, which was, he asserts, one of the first times that Germans asked such a question about Austria, despite the intensive self-questioning in the 1960s and 1970s by Austrian writers on "cultural imperialism" in literary histories (Auchenthaler, 174), especially the "germanization" of Austrian artists (Auchenthaler, 180). Austrian writers have long compared historical traditions with specific regional cultural politics (most notably, the century-old commonplace brought into focus by Herman Broch of Austrian culture as Baroque (Auchenthaler, 176). Such self-critical reflections also have accompanied Austria's political evolution since the end of World War II and the enforced neutrality imposed in its 1955 *Staatsvertrag* (Auchenthaler, 179), putting it outside NATO's Europe.

---

14 "Ohne Habsburg, der Casa Austria, würde Österreich nicht nur nie Czernowitz, Ragusa, Mailand, Freiburg, die Lausitz (45 Kilometer vor Berlin), Belgien, Triest oder Lublin besessen haben, sondern hätte gerade nur das Bahnhofsrestaurant von Attnang-Puchheim erreicht. (Salzburg war die jüngste habsburgische Erwerbung. Zu Lebzeiten Mozarts hat es noch nicht zu Österreich gehört.)" (Kuehnelt-Leddihn, 22)

From first to last, therefore, *Sonne über Österreich* documents not only a strand of Europe's imperial histories that has largely been lost to today's critics, but also points to necessary methodological debates about where Europe starts and ends and how to think about it. Notably absent from it are explanations referring to the Cold War's "Central Europe" (*Mitteleuropa*), or to abstract flows of capital or law. Instead, the volume stresses concrete networks of people and objects, maps of real spaces, and appeals to functional or moral purposes to define nations. To be sure, one cannot deny that these authors have their own imaginary globes and power networks (perhaps even the kind of crypto-monarchical cabal posited by Andrei Codrescu in his recent *The Blood Countess*, a novel about the Hungarian Queen Elizabeth Báthory [1560–1614]).

Sonne über Österreich none the less is an appropriate introduction to the persistence of dreams about Austria as Europe. The political and conceptual dislocations initiated by World Wars I and II have been particularly cruel to the image and significance of a region of Europe that has persisted as a ruling hegemony in various forms from *Ostarrichi* to the Republic of Austria. The guardians of past politics who are represented in this odd volume offer glimpses of a historical truth—almost a history written by a subculture—that has almost been forgotten alongside their current agendas: in its various incarnations, Austria-as-Europe, portrayed from the outside for almost two centuries as a failing nation-state, remained a significant reference point in and for Europe and its politics (cultural and otherwise). Their Austria is not the lost empire that needed to be rescued by the allied West because of its inability to modernize, an image dominating in the latter twentieth century even before the Cold War, at least since Rebecca West gave it its classic formulation in *Black Lamb and Grey Falcon: A Journey through Yugoslavia* (1940)—a volume that set the image of Austria's Balkans into stone for the twentieth century.

Rebecca West's Austria was not a patchwork of failing states, but rather an empire that collapsed under its own weight as it sank out of historical view. The authors of *Sonne über Österreich* would recognize the centerpiece of West's account (the region's political crisis after 1918), but they would note her insufficient attention to other regional and transnational factors, including history, shared experience, and traditions of interaction and interdependence (sometimes hostile and fraught), that were just as critical to Europe in 1940 and beyond. The Austria of *Black Lamb and Grey Falcon* offered images of imperial and aristocratic decline that persisted in the major works of history on Austria and its successor states throughout the twentieth century, such as Robert Kann's *History of the Habsburg Empire, 1526–1918* (1980). This Austria appears as an entity doomed to fail, with no reason to exist beyond its own hunger for power as it dominated (or even decimated) nationalities under its control.[15] And, of course, its culture was also cast as decadent, an image set into stone by Carl E. Schorske, with his *Fin de siècle Vienna: Politics and Culture* (1981). The magisterial political histories of the once-Habsburg regions outside Austria, often written by exiles from Central Europe or their children, start from the assumption that earlier forms of "Austria" need to be understood first of all as an obstacle to national self-determination (never yet realized, but arguably happening after the fall of the Soviet Union and the realignments in the Balkans).[16]

Sonne über Österreich is thus simply only one of many documents that call for a rethinking of that Procrustean bed narrative of scholarship on Europe since the First World War and Rebecca West's great study: that European politics and culture are most clearly defined in terms of nation-states. This scholarly tenet that nation-states are the appropriate framing for twentieth-century history remains active even today, where the isomorphism between languages, ethnic groups, cultures, and national borders has been called decisively into question—such entities are at best "imagined communities" (Benedict Anderson's fabled term), called into existence to support dominant ideologies and hegemonies.

The present volume aims at thinking beyond the nation-state, at recovering another kind of historical identity narrative central to the amorphous entity identified under names from *Ostarrichi* to the Republic of Austria. Such alternate identity narratives emerge clearly and repeatedly in the work of major intellectuals in this region, not only in crypto-monarchist tracts like *Sonne über Österreich*. Thinking through nation-states, the modern historiographical habit provides a narrative about *Europe* that has always been central to the one-time Habsburg regions' identity discourses, often in lieu of the national narratives that remain the provenance of the region's many subcultures that have since sought to establish nation-states guaranteeing them cultural-political

---

15 The many struggles for national identity in the Habsburg states have been the subject of much recent scholarship, mainly in terms of the growth of ethnic nationalism through language and family politics in the final decades of the Empire—a tradition opposite to what I trace here. See particularly Pieter M. Judson and Marsha L. Rozenblit, eds, *Constructing Nationalities in East Central Europe* (2005); Pieter M. Judson, *Guardians of the Nation: Activists on the Language Frontiers of Imperial Austria* (2006); and Tara Zahra, *Kidnapped Souls: National Indifference and the Battle for Children in the Bohemian Lands, 1900–1948* (2008).

16 The most noteworthy of these histories may be Norman Davies' *God's Playground: A History of Poland* (1982), and Peter F. Sugar and Péter Hanák, eds, *A History of Hungary* (1990). For the persistence of the Cold War optic in "German" literary history, see Katherine Arens, *"Geister der Zeit*: The Allies' Enlightenment and German Literary History" (2003).

hegemony.[17] In this region whose history extends from *Ostarrichi* to the Republic of Austria, many voices have had equal recourse to an identity narrative that defines them as *Europeans*, not ethnic-nationals. It may be objected that this identity narrative is an upper-class or elite memory today but, as I will demonstrate below, it remains broadly intelligible within the region, even to publics who might not be able to adduce facts in surveys (and not only to germanophone publics[18]).

This geographic entity—Austria, Austria-Hungary, the Holy Roman Empire, Austrian Empire, Habsburg Empire, the Republic of Austria—has been aware of its own historical–cultural dreamwork for a millennium, as it negotiated its position in Europe in full awareness that nation-states are transitory (they, not England, were the core of the first, later lost, Empire on which the sun never set and beyond). Moreover, the reference point of "Europe" in historical identity politics is not necessarily confined to hegemonic narratives in the region; as the examples below will attest, it was broadly available to many *public spaces* there. By "public spaces," I mean a very specific kind of cultural organization—absolutely *not* the Frankfurt School's "public sphere" (*Öffentlichkeitssphäre*, a term which explicitly refers to state hegemonies and capitalism), nor the idea of mental maps as cultural reference points[19] locating specific national identity politics (popular in recent

---

17 I use the term "subculture" here advisedly, with an explicit bow to Dick Hebdige, Stuart Hall, and the Birmingham School of Cultural Studies. In Dick Hebdige's version (1979), a subculture expresses a different, critical object of scholarly interest: a group whose identity relates to the dominant culture, in referencing its objects and discussions, but which is doing so in a spirit of self-redefinition in resistance to that culture (by what is often termed "resistant consumption"). In another sense, the term is parallel also to Gilles Deleuze and Félix Guattari's defintion of a minor literature (or *minoritarian*, as a better translation might be, reflecting the aspect of voluntary affiliation with the group). See *Kafka: Toward a Minor Literature* (1986), for a description of that literature.

18 For views of this cultural space that reach beyond its germanophone regions, see Ana Foteva, *Do the Balkans Begin in Vienna?* (2014), which originated in a 2009 dissertation from Purdue University; Nikola Petković, "The 'Post' in Postcolonial and Postmodern: The Case of Central Europe" (Diss., University of Texas at Austin, 1996); and Agnieszka Barbara Nance, "A Nineteenth-Century Polish 'Invented Community': Galicia as a Nation without a State" (Diss., University of Texas at Austin, 2004).

19 The idea of "culture" and its relation to national history has been theorized in various ways that do not directly apply here since I am arguing for a tradition working against nationalism. Most familiar is Katie Trumpener, *Bardic Nationalism* (1997), which ties cultural origins to nation-building imperial projects. Michael C. Carhart, in *The Science of Culture in Enlightenment Germany* (2007), traces the origin of the term. I use "culture" here more loosely, as a network of connections across which products of culture are shared and the history of those sharings.

discussions of Central European identities, like Larry Wolff's *Inventing Eastern Europe* [1994] or Maria Todorova's *Imagining the Balkans* [2009]).

Instead, I define a public space as a space for discussion supporting a constellation of cultural referents extending throughout defined regions (contiguous, continuous, or discontinuous but networked). That space can have multiple forms in any era and support multiple discussions, but it is distinguished by its ability to support coherent discourses that can be intelligible to many parties; that space can be occupied by discourses configured in various ways by emergent or established interest or participant groups (community, national, or otherwise identified). The cultural referents that are the waypoints in these discourses are more than master signifiers. Instead, they comprise a repertoire of comprehensible vocabularies/languages, logics of explanation, and stories that individuals and groups can deploy to discuss, represent, argue, or refute issues of the day—not on the level of official or hegemonic cultures, but as intelligible alternatives, proposals, expressions of heretofore unrepresented or unrepresentable issues, or discussions in minoritarian, evolving voices.[20] That is not to say that hegemonic figures cannot use public spaces—the examples presented in the chapters that follow are most often texts written by figures who may indeed be considered hegemonic in one domain of culture or another. However, speaking in public spaces, in these discourse networks, need not be the equivalent of public sphere speech, nor need it present formulations of issues that are automatically hegemonic.[21] Instead, these public spaces that sponsor moments of public meaning-making need to be seen as enacting public representation and identities *en procès*: on trial and in process, as the French term allows us to ambiguate.[22] The discourses and discussions produced, in turn, often represent improvisations or enactments of what today is called *glocal* meaning production (wherein *global* issues take on *local* forms), sponsored by a culture and its forms of association (communities, professional guilds, online or corresponding communities, etc.).

"Europe" is such a reference point for the various discourses through which constellations of meaning are given form in the chronologically and geographically random spaces encompassed in the historical names from *Ostarrichi* to the Republic of Austria. It is neither

---

20 "Minoritarian" refers here to Gilles Deleuze and Félix Guattari's idea of a minor literature; see *Kafka: Toward a Minor Literature* (1986), for a description of a literature that offers a different reading of the space of culture than the dominant—not opposing it, but differently positioned within it.

21 In current parlance, that public speech might best be characterized as "glocal": a global set of possible enunciations, only realized locally, never in its full extent.

22 Julia Kristeva uses this dual meaning as she redefines the subject in Lacanian terms. See the chapter entitled "The Subject in Process," in *Polylogue* (1977).

a mapped space, nor an imagined community or myth, nor a reality, but it is always a referent that leads beyond the nation-state and into different visions of what a culture can mean.

Austria's Europe of the imagination: A public space *en procès*

In the chapters that follow I will offer vignettes from this Austrian tradition of speaking about Europe in various forms of public speech—dreams, if you will, that intellectuals and politicians, mostly in Vienna, use to conceive of themselves, their audiences, their cultures, their issues, and their nation(s). I do so not in order to reify an "Austrian culture" that would simply correct one historical error by introducing another, or to argue Austria or its imagined Europe as having real geographical limits. Instead, I want to challenge scholars of Europe to consider how, since the Enlightenment, Austrian texts often present a very different evaluation of Europe and its cultural networks than their counterparts.

The strategy I propose is thinking about Europe in patterns that dominant historiographies of culture marginalize. To do so highlights not hegemonic cultures or their opponents, but cultures in the process of becoming, in moments of change and transformation. For close to a millennium, texts from this tradition document how writers have meditated on issues using reference points other than the ethnic nationalism, capital, and monolingualism that figure prominently in theories of Western nation-states, their politics and cultures. The point of this challenge to today's scholarship is strictly practical. These almost forgotten alternative models for identity and culture narratives open vistas on how today's scholars might theorize public representation and identity politics differently than simply as a legacy of nation-states, state colonialism, and capitalism. Just as importantly, it allows us to conceive of multiple public spaces in constant mutation, rather than a monolithic public sphere, and to recapture voices at various distances from hegemonic power without overgeneralizing their compliance with or resistance to it.

A strange multilingual volume like *Sonne über Österreich*, of dubious political pedigree (but impeccable lineage), cannot justify a redefinition of scholarly practice. None the less, its example provides testament that Austrian intellectuals have indeed thought beyond the nation-state and with reference to different maps of the globe than scholars of imperial-colonial Europe use. These essays embrace the paradox of an empire—or, better, an imperial space—that was only ever conditionally hegemonic, often multilingual, and sometimes colonial.[23]

---

23 Recent scholarship in Austria has explored the idea of the Austro-Hungarian Empire as having internal colonies of ethnic others. See, for example, Endre

The series of case studies that follow this introduction are conceived to introduce the implications of this alternative framing of Europe as a trope challenging scholarly conventions of today's cultural studies (and particularly in "German studies"). Cultural studies based around the nation-state today are ideologically marked by resistance to global imperialism as defined around the colonial legacies of Great Britain and France; they are motivated by critiques of the global capital associated with them. Yet they often fail to explain cultural phenomena that *require* accumulations of capital or collective action to bring them into existence, sometimes outside of official hegemonies. Michael Hardt and Antonio Negri have opened this question in one way in their epochal *Empire* (2000) when they speak about imperial formations rather than just historically attested empires. The examples included here complement *Empire* in documenting intellectuals' attempts at building new forms of collective consciousness and identities within a state that need not ever emerge as part of national culture, but which can serve to define subcultures or minoritarian cultural identities for underrepresented points of view and groups. That is, these cases acknowledge that identity politics within the modern nation-state have more points of origin than in state power alone and show how that politics functions more flexibly for various groups within the nation-state—in public spaces that come into existence or prominence to highlight certain issues.

To evolve models tracing a multiplicity of cultures within the nation-state is critical, since too simple assumptions about the functions of ethnicity, language, and culture within political hegemony simply will not capture the dynamics of a historical space like Austria's. This historical space is layered with cultural remnants from not one, but at least two millennia (since the Danube basin was already a space for Roman colonization); its capital and cultural center (one of several, but a dominant one) is a Vienna that was long the greatest of multilingual cities (with a population over two million in 1910, with over a third of them of Slavic or Hungarian origin), yet which has been relegated in our contemporary cultural histories to museum status as part of a backward, dying, Catholic empire. The cases offered here document intellectuals working in an imperial center asserting rights and prerogatives rather differently than Hohenzollern Prussia, Bourbon France, or Hanoverian/Saxe-Coburg and Gotha Great Britain. They point to historical and cultural reference points (transnational and European, if not global) as critical to understand identity politics within the

Hars, et al., eds, *Zentren, Peripheren und kollektive Identitäten in Österreich-Ungarn* (2006); Johannes Feichtinger, Ursula Prutsch, and Moritz Csáky, eds, *Habsburg postcolonial: Machtstrukturen und kollektives Gedächtnis* (2003), and Wolfgang Müller-Funk, Peter Plener, and Clemens Ruthner, *Kakanien Revisited* (2002).

nation. After all, writers and intellectuals often dream beyond the borders imposed on them, depending on how they see their own identities interpolated onto or existing on global networks -- just as an important reference point for analyses in a post-national era, as it was in pre-national Austria-Hungary, for example.

Each case study highlights how a writer can use public space to host discussions about local identities while referring to both a nation-state and a larger map of Europe. Thereby they are enabled to investigate not the politics of a single identity position, but rather the multiple identities available within any culture. Each case also illuminates aspects of Austria's struggles with change and modernization of its culture since the eighteenth century, as engaged intellectuals who sought to articulate how their publics fit into an evolving Europe and at what civic and moral costs. Additionally, many of these intellectuals sought to engage their publics through their eras' mass media (usually the theater, but also in public essays and manifestos), either in the long nineteenth century (the cases in Part One of this text), or the twentieth (Part Two). The results were texts presenting mediated and sometimes provisory public discussions critical of historical master discourses, addressing *what* needs to be done in their worlds. Because so many of them have either never been translated or are unfamiliar outside of Austria, the cases will quote liberally from the originals to show how very consistent their historical reference points are.

This volume's first chapter tracks two of the most famous germano-phone intellectuals of the Enlightenment, as they spoke to the public in the form of aesthetic letters: Gotthold Ephraim Lessing and Joseph von Sonnenfels, prominent in studies of Enlightenments in Berlin/Hamburg and Vienna in the late eighteenth century. These two sets of letters constitute a dialogue about newly emerging national theaters, particu-larly as mass media. Setting the terms of the dialogue, as would become conventional in German intellectual history, Lessing aligns himself with an emerging cultural nationalism that would come to be associated with German Classicism. Taking up the form of the serial public letter as used by Lessing (but never directly in contact with him), Sonnenfels reframes Lessing's assumptions to align his public with the imperatives of a broader European vision. Sonnenfels' cultural perspective on the theater is expanded in Chapter 2, as Austria's most famous nineteenth-century dramatist, Franz Grillparzer, fashions another dialogue with the aesthetics of the era. Seen biographically, Grillparzer's philosophical opposition to the increasingly dominant paradigms of aesthetic-national leadership familiar from Weimar Classicism and Romanticism eventually led him to withdraw from the public culture of Vienna's stages. Yet he, too, picks up threads of that era's conversation about the purpose of national theater—creating in it a public, transnational, and historically literate space of discussion, educating its audiences into critical perceptions about the hegemonies dominating their lives rather than inculcating fixed ideologies. These two chapters together show what was at stake in defining spaces for public speech that were not identical with the public sphere of the nation-state.

The third chapter continues the recovery of a theater tradition that stresses public speech and discussion instead of the production of national culture. Its subject is a theater tradition flourishing in Vienna from the eighteenth century on: the Viennese *Volkstheater* (literally: people's theater, although often translated "folk theater"), which had analogues in the *commedia dell'arte* and the European comedy tradition that includes Beaumarchais, Marivaux, Congreve, and Sheridan. Two plays from opposite ends of the nineteenth century, one by Grillparzer and one by Johann Nestroy, exemplify these germanophone social-critical comedies that help audiences ask questions whose answers may foster the transformation of individuals and their public discussions. These plays (in origin crossing borders between a state-supported theater and a commercial one) outline well-defined challenges to emerging national hegemonies and their increasingly instrumentalized public spheres. That is, they speak from *within* the class positions of their audiences to critique both the state and its citizens, to educate rather than to propose new ideologies.

In Chapter 4, that ability to bring an audience to question emerges as a central intellectual strategy defining the Biedermeier era, the name given to Austria's bourgeois nineteenth century.[24] This chapter reads public works of visual art in different media alongside the highly visual prose of the artist-novelist Adalbert Stifter to argue commonalities between their construction of public spaces and that of the contemporaneous theater. Like the plays discussed in the two prior chapters, these works are structured to provoke their audiences to participate actively in making sense of multiple perspectives. How these works appeal to their audiences suggests a public interested in change and politics in ways that may not be revolutionary in the classic sense, but which are none the less profoundly engaged with the identity and state politics of everyday life.

Part Two of this volume skips to the twentieth century, and to intellectuals inheriting this tradition of public critique and discussion. Two

---

24 Note that germanophone cultural historians also refer to the era as the *Vormärz*, explicitly labeling it as falling before Europe's 1848 revolutions and outside its political consciousness. "Biedermeier" was originally a pseudonymous author of poems published in *Fliegende Blätter* that reflected the petit bourgeois mentality of the mid-century; it was not used to designate the epoch until about 1900.

Austrian authors co-opted by the German canon are here reread as acting on a map of germanophone Europe and of an extended European culture. Their dreams might be utopian, but they express experiences under threat as nationalism fragments the Europe they were born into in largely nonsensical appeals to shifting national borders. Conventional scholarly images portray Hugo von Hofmannsthal as a conservative moving towards an Austrian ethnic nationalism and Arthur Schnitzler as a playwright of sex and decadence. Those stereotypes are here challenged because they use traditional European theater genres (under the rubric of "the Viennese folk theater") to enact similar interrogations of contemporary culture for audiences facing political dislocations and loss of voice on the map of Europe.

The final two chapters take the problem of public critique using the image of Austria-in-Europe to post-World-War-II Austria, as the Cold War gradually yields to the purportedly new ideal of the European Union and a unified continent. The *Vienna Group* (*Wiener Gruppe*), led by h. c. artmann, and their literary heritor, Peter Handke, still use the critical traditions of the *Volkstheater* and emphasis on public discussion sketched in earlier chapters. Essays by Otto von Habsburg, and Handke and Milo Dor, document, however, how that space for critical engagement can still be framed more explicitly in relation to a realigned, post-Wall Europe dominating smaller regional and national sites in new ways. They suggest that narratives of Europe beyond the nation-state open contemporary political discussions to whole new dimensions of moral responsibility for its (ab)uses of histories in the nationalist mode.

These case studies thus exemplify my claim that scholars who overlook European cultural references in their work on national cultural sites overlook networks and identity narratives less tightly controlled by abstract forces of capital and governmentality than the Frankfurt School and scholars of coloniality and post-coloniality would prefer to assume. Let us now move back over two hundred years, to a moment in the age of Revolutions where two prominent intellectuals and theater critics seek to define their respective publics on a map of Europe under stress by the forces of history. Let us begin to explore a site of culture where the Enlightenment was critical and communitarian rather than instrumental, and where acts of public speaking implicated moral obligation by individuals, not just acts of government.

Part One
An Austrian Imperial Europe

The Habsburg territories of the late eighteenth and nineteenth centuries were the seat of an empire that had existed for over 800 years, at the heart of the geopolitical shifts that would soon form modern Europe.

Under Charles V as the Holy Roman Emperor, the House of Habsburg in 1520 had held the largest empire in the world (ruling properties including New Spain). Europe's electors, however, forced a split in the house, creating an Austrian branch of the house, which continued the family's almost unbroken possession of the throne of the Holy Roman Empire. Yet that Empire had been under attack since the Protestant Reformation, and so Habsburg culture had already been dislocated within Europe, at the outbreak of the Thirty Years War (1618), when the court shifted its seat from Prague to Vienna. Its fortunes declined even more precipitously, as the Spanish branch of the family gradually died out, a process culminating with the 1700 death of Charles II, Spain's last Habsburg ruler, and the ensuing War of the Spanish Succession.

At the same time, the leadership of germanophone culture was called into question by the Seven Years War (1756–63). Prussia hoped to profit from the comparative weakness of Austria and the Holy Roman Empire, as it sought to expand and to consolidate territories into something more like a modern nation-state.[1] The results of this conflict between Prussia and Austria redrew the maps of Europe and the world, but it did not facilitate the emergence of a united or centralized germanophone cultural sphere: the Peace of Paris gave England the French possessions in Africa, India, and North America; the Peace of

---

1   The great powers (Austria, France, Russia, and the *Reichsfürsten*) allied against the upstart (Prussia, aided by England, and Hannover). But then Russia pulled out of the coalition because Elizabeth II died; England pulled back from full support of its allies; and Austria's long two centuries of military defeat began after it failed to vanquish Prussia's armies and partition its territories.

Hubertusburg gave Silesia to Prussia and guaranteed the borders of Prussia and Austria. In consequence, an alternate set of political and social forces, the specter of a German empire under Prussia (and hence Protestant) opposing the Catholic Holy Roman Empire under the Habsburgs, materialized to reconfigure the space of Central European identity in other ways, as traditional alliances dividing Catholic and Protestant princes took on new financial and political urgency under pressure from the great colonial powers of England, France, and Russia.[2]

The house of Habsburg was saved by the Pragmatic Sanction of 1713, which allowed for female succession to the throne. This resolution was also accidentally prescient: at the death of Charles VI, he left only a female heir: Maria Theresa. When it came down to her actually inheriting these extensive European holdings, France, Prussia, Saxony, and Bavaria objected to the proclamation they had once supported, leading to the War of the Austrian Succession in 1740, a world war that was to last until 1748, and the Treaty of Aix-la-Chapelle.

Ultimately, Maria Theresa and the House of Habsburg survived as a continuous entity, losing Silesia to Prussia. She also managed to reclaim the throne of the Holy Roman Empire for her husband, Francis 1, in 1745, by bartering a conquered Bavaria back to its traditional ruling family. The House of Habsburg (now officially Habsburg-Lothringen, since Francis was of the House of Lorraine) was again the center of a successful dynasty. Vienna had become the imperial seat only at the start of the Thirty Years War in 1618, after the Defenestration at Prague signaled the need to move the government out of Bohemian territories. With Habsburg power now reasserted, Vienna was poised to evolve into a European capital city and culture center.

The story of "modern" Austrian culture begins in that Vienna, a city entangled with recurring political and cultural threats—from France, Prussia, and Russia, in turn. These empires were all bent on expansionism into traditional Habsburg territories but would achieve these goals only with the end of World War I.

Historic Austria's first major milestone of its modern era came in the second generation after Maria Theresa's long reign (1740–80). Her two sons succeeded her on the throne, first Joseph II (1765–90, originally as co-regent of Austria with his mother) and then Leopold II (originally Grand Duke of Tuscany, then Holy Roman Emperor from 1790 to 1792). Leopold's son Francis assumed the throne and then became

---

2   The definitive history of Austria is Robert A. Kann's *A History of the Habsburg Empire, 1526–1918* (1980). A brief treatment of the situation is Joachim Whaley, "Die Habsburgermonarchie und das Heilige Römische Reich im 18. Jahrhundert."

Francis II of the Holy Roman Empire. Yet the Holy Roman Empire's days were numbered once Napoleon declared himself Emperor and began to consolidate his new European Empire, and so, as Napoleon's imperialist politics led to the destruction of the Holy Roman Empire in 1806, Francis was declared Emperor of Austria in 1804 (now Francis I), a throne he held until 1835. Surviving these geopolitical transitions was achieved in no small part because one of Maria Theresa's daughters was Marie Antoinette of France, and one of Francis' daughters was the Marie Louise married to Napoleon.

The Habsburgs of the eighteenth and nineteenth centuries typically had many children and married them off well, following traditions back to the later Middle Ages. "AEIOU" was the house's unofficial device, introduced by Frederick II (1415–94), and variously interpreted as:

1 *Alles Erdreich Ist Österreich Untertan*: All the world is subject to Austria.
2 *Austria erit in orbe ultima*: Austria will be in the world to the end.
3 *Austriae est imperare orbi universo*: Austria is to rule over the whole world.

This "Austrian" culture around 1800 still had such imperial claims and saw itself as part of Europe, a player among the great powers. What that meant to the citizens of this empire, however, was quite different than the "imperial ideas" present in absolutist Russia, enlightened absolutist, militarist and largely Protestant Prussia, Catholic France (to say nothing of the older empires centered on England or Spain, whose ruling dynasties were replaced by foreign families). Most critically, the Habsburg court was *in* Vienna, and in many ways *part* of Vienna. That court played a role in public culture in ways that courts in Versailles, Potsdam, or St. Petersburg were not because of their distance from city centers, and that a constitutional monarchy with a foreign ruling family like England's Hanoverians could not be.

Most particularly, Vienna's court and public shared many spaces, some sponsored by the court and others emerging as commercial ventures. The most important theater, the *Burgtheater*, supported itself by presenting performances to the court, then repeating them for the general public, for example. Ballet, opera, and serious theater were cultivated there, and not just as playgrounds or brothels for the rich and titled (as was all too often the case in Paris and St. Petersburg; Italy's various capitals may have been exceptions to this rule). Many music performances in Mozart's era were subscription concerts, held in noble houses but not quite as socially restricted as salons often were— the events were ticketed. Just as importantly, public theaters existed outside the old city walls, not as subject to regulation or patronage as were London's—there were no moments of iconoclasm in Vienna to shut theater doors, and the tickets were priced for the groundlings as well as the elite. Critically, these theaters were not only popular, they cultivated performers and playwrights who would enter the "Austrian canon," not just passing entertainments; their directors looked to Europe's theaters for inspiration and material, and their audiences expected the best in comedy and music.

Let us now turn to that public space as represented by its most visible participants, especially in Vienna, and acknowledged as a site for public speech about the state of their own culture: the state minister and theater censor Joseph von Sonnenfels (1732–1817), professor turned *literat*; the civil servant and dramatist Franz Grillparzer (1791–1872); actor–playwright in the comic traditions, Johann Nestroy (1801–62); and writer, painter, and school superintendent Adalbert Stifter (1805–68). These names form the canon of Austrian greats of the long nineteenth century, constant reference points for all later Austrian culture through today.

Outside their cultural homeland, however, and particularly in the history-writing about "German" literature that dominates scholarship since World War II, these authors are all too often dismissed as naïve and apolitical because they accept voices from beyond their respective Austrias without calling definitively for revolution, as playwrights from Schiller to Hebbel would. None the less, these texts remain hallmarks for the public voice and public space of Viennese and Austrian culture, real or imagined, from their creation up through today, because they document the existence of, or at least their authors' hopes for, a public capable of exercising critical capacities and judging their own and their nation's place on Europe's stage. Sonnenfels, Grillparzer, Nestroy, and Stifter were not interested in acting as harbingers for a future, more utopian version of the nation they lived in. Instead, their voices call for public discussions about culture and politics on a European historical scale, finding in such discussions hopes for a more engaged, enlightened public discussion about shared lives, historical memories, and present experiences.

One Letters to the Ruling Class: The Public Spaces of Enlightenment

In a famous letter to Friedrich Nicolai, Gotthold Ephraim Lessing expressed his frustration about freedom of thought in his Berlin:

> For once, let someone in Berlin try to write about things as freely as Sonnenfels had written in Vienna; let someone try to tell the elegant Court Rabble the truth, as he had done; let someone appear in Berlin to raise his voice for the rights of the oppressed, against plunder and despotism, as now is happening even in France and Denmark: and you will soon experience which European land is the most enslaved up to the present day.[1]

Lessing here points to a fact all too often ignored in German cultural history, and which the case of Austria brings to the fore: that the age of Enlightenment and revolution came to various germanophone regions under different circumstances, into different social structures, and with different results for what has come to be called the public sphere and its institutions.[2] In the late eighteenth century, Austria was already part of a different Europe than were Prussia and other germanophone regions.

---

1 Cited Kiesel, 622–3:
   Lassen Sie aber doch einmal einen in Berlin versuchen, über andere Dinge so frei zu schreiben als Sonnenfels in Wien geschrieben hat; lassen Sie es ihn versuchen, dem vornehmen Hofpöbel so die Wahrheit zu sagen, als dieser sie ihm gesagt hat; lassen Sie einen in Berlin auftreten, der für die Rechte der Untertanen, der gegen Aussaugung und Despotismus seine Stimme erheben wollte, wie es itzt sogar in Frankreich und Dänemark geschieht: und Sie werden bald die Erfahrung haben, welches Land bis auf den heutigen Tag das sklavischste Land von Europa ist. (August 25, 1769)
   Note that Lessing at the time was being courted for a position in Vienna (Hadamowsky, 295).
2 A significant exception to this is Hans Erich Bödeker, "Raisonnement, Zensur und Selbstzensur," which is at great pains to differentiate patterns of what he

After the Protestant Reformation, the germanophone world received the Enlightenment late for very pragmatic reasons: almost two centuries of wars.[3] Like Lessing, many authors of the second half of the eighteenth century understood that working in Protestant Prussia with its new military status and its salon-driven culture meant something very different than working in an increasingly bureaucratized Catholic Vienna with a conscious cultural relationship to Europe.[4] Neither Berlin nor Vienna had the urban culture that had supported and disseminated the Enlightenment in France and England. Home of the Habsburg chancellery only since 1618, Vienna would emerge as a major city only after Napoleon; Berlin's salons lay apart from the court,[5] which had moved to Potsdam. Both Habsburg and Hohenzollern rulers, moreover, used censorship to achieve their aims. Lessing's reference to Joseph von Sonnenfels thus signals how world politics remained a potent force in the dissemination of Enlightenment ideals in Prussia and Austria as rival public spheres.

Beyond its political significance, the connection between the two intellectuals is, in fact, more significant than Lessing's off-hand remark might at first suggest. Between 1759 and 1765, Gotthold Ephraim Lessing began the seminal series of *Briefe, die neueste Literatur betreffend* (Letters Concerning the Most Recent Literature). In 1768 and 1769, the Austrian bureaucrat and court official Joseph von Sonnenfels (1733–1817),[6] acknowledging his debt, took the form over to offer his own

---

calls "aufklärerischer Kommunikation," especially with respect to issues like censor regulations (see 189ff.).

3   After the wars associated with the Reformation which engaged all of Europe, one had the Thirty Years War (1618–48), which enacted a relatively stable compromise to the religious wars begun after the Protestant Reformation, assigning a religion to a country according to the religion of its rulers.

4   As Benedict Anderson would conceive it, "German" culture had no clear new "imagined community." The German cities that had been prominent in the Renaissance (Augsburg, Nuremburg, Cologne) were, in fact, in fiscal and population decline. In the eighteenth century, Hamburg and Frankfurt grew, while Vienna was experiencing a first true wave of urbanization that would take hold decisively after Napoleon. See Etienne François, "Villes d'Empire et Aufklärung," for a more detailed discussion. See also Werner Rieck, "'Fast mit jedem Jahr wächst meine stille Bewunderung des großen Mannes': Friedrich II. im Urteil Herders," especially 295–6, which documents a more general interest in comparing the absolutist rulers of Vienna and Berlin.

5   For an account of the role of salons in Berlin see Deborah Hertz, *Jewish High Society in Old Regime Berlin.*

6   Scholars on the Austrian Enlightenment and scholars on the German Enlightenment do not share an optic on what canonical literature is, especially since many Austrian intellectuals of the eighteenth century were critical of Prussia and of Goethe's program in Weimar.
    For an introduction to Sonnenfels, see the introduction to the reprint volume

parallel set of letters on culture, his *Briefe über die wienerische Schaubühne* (Letters on the Viennese Stage), just at the time he saw an advertisement for the *Hamburgische Dramaturgie*. These two sets of aesthetic letters, one each directed at Berlin and Vienna, adapt Enlightenment ideals to two different contexts, expressing the two authors' very different senses about the needs and strengths of their respective publics, and the nations that they represented.

Today's germanophone literary history favors the ultimate winners and their nationalist voices (Prussians and other German Protestants) in valorizing the significance of Lessing's work.[7] Yet Vienna's role in Enlightenment culture can be argued as a specific alternative approach to a modern nation state in a European context. The comparison between Lessing's and Sonnenfels' public letters makes the case for a regional model for understanding the Enlightenment's dissemination beyond England and France into rival political spheres. What Lessing and Sonnenfels say about the role of art in establishing a national culture confirms that a shared language by no means implied the existence of a shared German cultural identity, or a shared notion about what a nation-state should be.

These Enlightenment intellectuals both engaged with their generation's project of improving the nation through art and cultivating a national elite outside of the hereditary nobility. Lessing particularly is known as an exponent of a national literature. Both authors agree that a "German" national culture is necessary but disagree about what that culture and the German stage disseminating its ideals should be.

---

of the *Briefe über die wienerische Schaubühne*, and Roland Krebs, "Une Revue de L'Aufklärung viennoise." See also Hubert Lengauer, "Zur Stellung der 'Briefe über die wienerische Schaubühne' in der aufklärerischen Dramentheorie," for an introduction to his aesthetics, and Roger Bauer, "'Luxus' in Österreich: Joseph von Sonnenfels zwischen Jean-Jacques Rousseau und Adam Smith."

Lessing scholarship is close to oceanic, because he has been cast in literary history as one of the few hegemonic literary voices in German literature. For an overview of his scholarly reputation, see Barbara Fischer and Thomas C. Fox, eds, *A Companion to the Works of Gotthold Ephraim Lessing* (2005). Critical is that there is little or no work on what his choices in locale for employment imply—analyses of German Enlightenment culture focus on ideas and aesthetics rather than practical politics. When authors of the eighteenth and early nineteenth centuries move to Vienna, they drop off the map of German cultural history, in no small part because moving usually implies a conversion to Catholicism.

7   For another vision of the literature of this era, see Herbert Zeman, "Die österreichische Literatur und ihre literaturgeschichtliche Darstellung vom ausgehenden 18. bis zum frühen 19. Jahrhundert." A different version of the comparison made here was included in Katherine Arens' "Translators Who Are Not Traitors: Herder's and Lessing's Enlightenment," *Herder Jahrbuch/Herder Yearbook*, Vol. 5 (Stuttgart: J. B. Metzler, 2000), 91–109.

For Lessing in Hohenzollern Prussia, that national culture is distinctively non-French and indigenous to Protestant Germany; intellectuals, as representing a new nobility of spirit, will bring new intellectual leadership to that state. For Sonnenfels, in contrast, Habsburg Austria was less reticent about borrowings from French culture, if those borrowings contributed to the well-being of the public. Sonnenfels was thus more inclined to define a national culture as a regional one based on social and political interaction, where Lessing believed in ideas and intellectual leadership to secure a national culture.

These two related but antithetical visions of germanophone culture document the existence of a war for the intellectual leadership of their nations. Just as Lessing and Sonnenfels brought their ideas of a national culture to their readers in differing ways, one can recapture the sense that Central Europe adapted more than one Enlightenment, each deriving from the Imperial centers of France and England. This comparison requires scholars of germanophone cultures to move beyond stereotypes based on the fiction of an emerging "German" culture-nation and to open up more nuanced questions about regional public institutions and identities as implementation of Enlightenment ideals and the aesthetic education of a new public that is the acknowledged program of Weimar Classicism.

The sources and their publics

Perhaps the finest formulation of Enlightenment aesthetics in German is found in the *Letters Concerning the Most Recent Literature* (*Briefe, die neueste Literatur betreffend*, 1759–65), outlining an aesthetic program now identified as the dominant in German Enlightenment aesthetics. These letters appeared in a moral-aesthetic review, the *Bibliothek der schönen Wissenschaften und der freien Künste*, edited by two of the most prominent of Berlin Enlightenment intellectuals, Moses Mendelssohn and Friedrich Nicolai. Although he would write the first series of *Letters*, Lessing actually shared the anonymous authorship of the series with them (and, later, with others), but he was early suspected to be the sole author and has always received credit for the letters' tone and reach.[8] The most famous of the series now is #17, advocating the primacy of English models over French ones for German theater; the

---

8   Scholars now believe that Lessing wrote one sixth of the whole corpus (55 out of the 332 pieces published between January 1759 and July 1765. In a later review, Johann Gottfried Herder reported about their impact in another important intellectual periodical, the *Teutschen Merkur*, in October 1781: "Von diesen war *er* Urheber und Vater: der Ton in ihnen war *sein* Ton … Hier ist deutsche Geist und Freiheit, ohne Schwärmerei und Ausgelasseheit … Lessings Urteile hat die Zeit bewährt. Was damals scharf hieß, nennt man jetzt recht; was hart schien, ist jetzt … billige Wahrheit …" (830).

issues it broached were taken up by Lessing again in a second series of equally important essays, the *Hamburg Dramaturgy* (*Hamburgische Dramaturgie*, 1767 to 1769). The letters' distinctive polemic tone made them much admired as a visible success *d'estime* or *de scandale*. On March 10, 1761, Johann Heinrich Gottlob v. Justi even wrote to Friedrich II, trying to get the letters banned:[9]

> The public, however, is so far removed from approving of the unseemly, impolite and unrestrained behavior of these writers toward all worthy and famous scholars, that all reasonable people should rather treat them with justifiable abhorrence. Every one shows their antipathy by using a certain expression to refer to the writing's author, which honor and discretion forbid me from recording here. (Lessing, 828)[10]

It is no wonder, then, that several notable series of aesthetic-polemical letters explicitly claimed these *Letters* as their models, given their visibility and popularity in certain circles.

Joseph von Sonnenfels' *Letters on the Viennese Stage* (*Briefe über die wienerische Schaubühne*), written in 1768 and 1769, were the most significant response to Lessing. Writing from Vienna, Sonnenfels followed Lessing in his concern about the development of a German national culture through the medium of a national theater, understanding that the theater was the era's mass medium, as theaters were

---

9   A considerably less polite reaction is that by Johann Geog Hamann to Lindner, July 20, 1759: "Die Briefe die neueste Literatur betreffend, die ich mit so viel Vergnügen gelesen, als man einem Patienten kaum zutrauen kann, der seinen Arm in der Schärfe trägt. Sollte aber wohl das Publikum von *Richtern* und *Kennern* dergl. Einfälle billigen, die gar zu deutl. verraten, daß nicht der Mann, an den diese Briefe gerichtet sind sondern der Schriftsteller ein solcher temporair Invalide ist, der seine eigene lange Weile vertreibt—und seine gesunde Urteilskraft zur Lust oder aus eigennützigen Absichten, wie die Bettler, zum Krüppel macht. Kein Bergmann wird durch diese Briefe gebessert werden; der ist zu tumm sie zu lesen; kein Wieland an seinem guten Namen viel verlieren, vielleicht dadurch für sich und seine Leser oder Anhänger gewinnen—kein Philosoph einem Witzling mehr zutrauen als einer privilegierten Akademie" (Lessing, 827).

10 "Das Publikum aber allhier ist so weit entfernt, das ungesittete, unhöfliche und zügellose Betragen dieser Schriftsteller gegen alle verdienstvolle und berühmte Gelehrte zu billigen, daß sie vielmehr von allen vernünftigen Leuten allhier mit gerechten Abscheu beleget werden. Jedermann gibt diesen Abscheu durch einen gewissen Ausdruck zu erkennen, womit man die Verfasser dieser Schrift bezeichnet, den aber die Ehrerbietung mir nicht erlaubet hierher zu setzen."

opened to a new ticket-buying public.[11] Moreover, both argued that
such a theater needed German dramatists who would write in German,
free themselves from French models, and turn towards English models,
especially to Shakespeare and to his contemporaries (e.g. Nicolas
Rowe). This new theater also needed improved norms for acting,
declamation, and production, as well as a standard language currently
lacking in the regional germanophone worlds. Finally, both believed
that a theater that enlightened the minds and morals of a nation had
to have actors who lived up to respectable standards of conduct, and
who thus had actual livelihoods guaranteed to them, as members of a
standing stage rather than traveling troupes.

From the first, however, regional differences about the role and
implementation of such mass media *vis-à-vis* a public emerged
when theory met practice. The Enlightenment's attention to drama
had first come to the German-speaking world over a group of
Swiss aestheticians; its first great monuments were Bodmer and
Breitinger's *Discourses of Painters* (*Diskursen der Maler*, 1721–3)
and Gottsched's *Critical Poetics* (*Kritische Dichtkunst*, 1730). The
Zurich which had political calm and the luxury of a stage fostered
these aestheticians who had enacted a public ritual exorcism when
Gottsched drove *Hanswurst* (Punch) from the stage, signaling the
end of Baroque poetics on the German-language stage and the
introduction of a new, more literary stage. Driving Hanswurst out
signaled that the popular improvisational theater of the *commedia
dell'arte* had to yield to a regulated stage with fixed texts and trained
or at least professional actors. But Gottsched had distanced himself
from this program by 1740 because French and German norms and
sensibilities often clashed in Switzerland, where new demands for a
German poetics fought the general popularity of French rationalism
and its classical French stage. The center of German culture was
moving elsewhere.[12]

After 1750, Lessing weighed into this fray from an increasingly
important Berlin with a considerably more German and nationalist
cultural mission. Lessing had already edited and contributed to the
Berlinische priviligierte Zeitung (until 1755); and he pursued the Berlin
public in the later *Letters* until July 1760. His engagement with Berlin

---

11 For an outline of theater history in the era, see Hilde Haider-Pregler,
    "Entwicklungen im Wiener Theater zur Zeit Maria Theresias." See also Helmut
    W. Lang, "Die Zeitschriften in Österreich zwischen 1740 und 1815," for an
    overview of his publishing situation.
12 I will not deal with this aspect of the conflict here, but this conflict for theater
    space was also necessarily a religious conflict. Growing Swiss Calvinist icono-
    clasm played no small part in the gradual suppression of certain forms of
    theater, just as growing conservatism in Lutheranism did in Sweden.

coincides with the local branch of the Seven Years War, the Third Silesian War (1756–63), in which Prussia, supported by England, resisted Austria's attempts to recover Silesia. By October 8, 1760, Berlin was fully engaged in war and Austrian troops occupied Berlin; at the end of the war, Lessing lost his job as secretary to General Tauentzien, freeing him to try his fate as house critic for a newly founded theater in Hamburg instead of Prussia.

The *Letters Concerning the Newest Literature* are specifically marked as implicated in the war effort, which Lessing cast as a war for national identity, carried out on an aesthetic front. The set has a contemporary frame, indicating that an anonymous critic of the current Berlin literary scene purportedly addressed them to a friend in the army, a fictitious "Herr von N.," an officer wounded in the battle of Zorndorf (August 25, 1758, a notable Prussian victory).[13] To be sure, fictive letters were nothing new in Europe, not since Montesquieu's 1721 *Lettres persanes*; Lessing and Nicolai had themselves both used the form in earlier works. Yet these *Letters*, first published on "Den 4. Jenner 1759," are explicitly framed for Berliners at war:[14] "He wrote to some of his friends in Berlin and asked them to help him fill out the gaps in his knowledge of the newest literature that the war had caused" (Lessing, 30).[15] Through this mouthpiece, Lessing declares his own war on the poor art and scholarship of a city that deserved better.

The Berlin that the *Letters* describe was "rich enough in marvels, just not in educated marvels" (Lessing, #1, 31).[16] The war had chased all the muses out of the city;[17] what remained was somewhat lacking: "If I cannot name for them a single new *genius*, I can only list very few works of authors who are already familiar that are worthy of being

---

13 The fictitious situation was in this sense prescient: the fictitious Prussian officer was patterned on the poet Ewald von Kleist, who actually was wounded on August 12, 1759, and died shortly thereafter in Frankfurt an der Oder.

14 The series is, however, not tightly conceived, and the framing narrative tends to be lost for pages as Lessing interjects what are actually formal essays, broken into installments seemingly only by space conventions. Note that Wilfried Zieger, in "'Doch ich vergesse mich. Wie gehört das alles zur *Zelmire*?'," offers one of the very few text-based discussions of Lessing's argumentation strategies in the *Letters*, as a key to his critical polemics.

15 "Er schrieb an einige von seinen Freunden in B**[erlin] und ersuchte sie, ihm die Lücke, welche der Krieg in seine Kenntnis der neuesten Literatur gemacht, ausfüllen zu helfen."

16 "reich genug an Wundern, nur nicht an gelehrten Wundern."

17 "es ist eine alte Klage, daß das allzunahe Geräusch der Waffen, die Musen verscheucht. Verscheucht es sie nun aus einem Lande, wo sie nicht recht viele, recht feurige Freunde haben, wo sie ohnedem nicht die beste Aufnahme erhielten, so können sie auf eine sehr lange Zeit verscheucht bleiben" (#1, 31).

maintained with those deeds of posterity" (Lessing, #1, 31).[18] Most obviously, the city lacked learnedness: those men of letters (*Gelehrte*) who remained in the beleaguered capital were of poor caliber, too many of them simply translators who behaved like tradesmen of poor quality:[19] "Erudition, as an *industry*, is at least in satisfactory shape among us. [...] our translators are still working without a care in the world" (Lessing, #2, 32).[20] Where the truly *learned* should improve the public, these translators, editors, and essay-writers make frequent and unforgivable factual, linguistic, aesthetic, and historical mistakes. Such scholars and translators cannot accomplish the enlightenment of the German public as they should (as Lessing repeats later in this series and in the *Hamburgische Dramaturgie*). Lessing's fictive aesthetic reporter has begun a war against the intellectual mediocrity and scholarly inadequacy that characterized what should have been a cultural center.

A decade later, Joseph von Sonnenfels' Vienna was not a city at war, and so his *Briefe über die Wienerische Schaubühne* (1768 in book form) would cater to a different imperative and a different public mood. His fifty-six tightly scripted *Letters* began publication at the end of 1767 (perhaps in response to an early announcement for Lessing's *Hamburgische Dramaturgie*, but using the *Letters* as a model). Sonnenfels' Vienna had been a capital and center of government for just over a century. The city had had a standing theater since 1710, albeit one that was not open to the public for its palette of performances (including Italian opera, ballet, and declamation); in 1741, a second house opened for public performance to subsidize that *Hoftheater*. The issue of a national culture thus had a very real reference for Sonnenfels: performances in the walled city, in noble salons, and in the various *Vorstadtbühnen* (theaters outside the city walls, less regulated than patent theaters) supported many of the performing arts, including the vibrant music scene that Mozart would seek out at the end of the century. In addition, Vienna had its own unique form of German-language drama, the classical Viennese comedy or *Volkstheater*, a theater in the critical improvisational tradition featuring *Hanswurst*, Harlequin, or Punch, a comedic resistor like Figaro.

---

18 "[K]ann ich Ihnen auch nicht ein einziges neues *Genie* nennen, kann ich Ihnen nur sehr wenige Werke schonbekannter Verfasser anführen, die mit jenen Taten der Nachwelt aufbehalten zu werden verdienten."

19 Lawrence Venuti will underscore Germans' growing preference for translations that emphasize foreignness of the source text, in an era when the English were valorizing fluent translation; see *The Translator's Invisibility*, especially chapter 3.

20 "Wenigstens ist die Gelehrsamkeit, als ein *Gewerbe*, unter uns in noch ganz leidlichem Gange. ... unsere Übersetzer arbeiten noch frisch von der Faust weg."

Sonnenfels was by any measure one of Lessing's *learned*, despite his reputation for later scholars as a petty bureaucrat: he was for his public lawyer, philologist, *Hofrat*, and professor.[21] Before publishing his aesthetic letters, Sonnenfels had for seven years already lent his voice to the cause of Viennese theater reform, starting in the moral weekly *Die Welt* (1762–3), then as editor of and contributor to the twice-weekly *Der Mann ohne Vorurtheil* (September 23, 1765–7), the most important Viennese moral review. Like Lessing and Gottsched, his goal was to "literarize" the theater, to drive out improvisation, low jokes, witches, superstition, and the like, and to replace them with a "regular" or "regulated" (*regelmäßig*) theater furthering public morals and education.[22] He considered the theatrical repertoire (both comedy and tragedy) as a tool spreading public values and morals (*eine Schule der Sitten* [Sonnenfels, 363]); he considered actors as professionals who could and should be held responsible for their conduct and example.[23]

Where Lessing's Berlin had lacked the muses, Sonnenfels' Vienna thus had a relatively thriving public arts culture, due to general public interest and the consistent patronage of the upper classes. It is thus no wonder that Sonnenfels understood what a theater aimed at both entertainment and education (*Unterhaltungs- und Bildungstheater*) could do as a mass medium. Where Lessing had been concerned about the

---

21 Sonnenfels' family had Central European roots back to the seventeenth century (including some from Prague, and one ancestor who was *Oberrabbiner* of Berlin). His father was a Jewish Orientalist of small means who had converted in 1735; Maria Theresa ennobled him in 1746 as "von Sonnenfels," and by 1757 he was appointed official court translator for Hebrew. His son Joseph (b. c.1733, d. 1817) studied philosophy and philology at the university of Vienna (1745–9), ultimately mastering nine languages. Between 1754 and 1756, he studied law, and then joined other professors in founding the "Deutsche Gesellschaft" (1761), a society at the center of Viennese Enlightenment. He was responsible for Josephine legal reform (abolition of torture), and for language reform (that is, for the establishment of a standard besides the regional dialects). A 1763 professorship for "Polizei und Kameralwissenschaft" led him to the position of theatre censor from 1770 on; between 1794 and 1796, he was rector of the university; he died as *k. k. Hofrat* and President of the *Akademie der bildenden Künste*.
22 Note, too, that Sonnenfels' discussion of the Viennese popular theater is referred to as the "Hanswurststreit," referring to the era 1748–1770 in which new ideals of the theater were actively being tested against the huge popularity of competing comic actors. See W. E. Yates, *Theater in Vienna*, 8ff., for a brief recapitulation of the issue; Reinhard Urbach, *Die Wiener Komödie und ihr Publikum*, for a readable overview of the theater history; and Yates and McKenzie, eds, *Viennese Popular Theater*, for a recent collection introducing major issues on the dramaturgy of the *Volkstheater*.
23 "Der Komödiantenstand gilt ihm als Beruf mit besonderer Verantwortung für die Öffentlichkeit" (Sonnenfels, 364).

relative unavailability of German-language plays, however, Sonnenfels saw a theater that could draw on foreign models, even French ones, while serving "our nationality" and the development of a moral public. By "nation," however, Sonnenfels was not appealing to an ideal vision of a single ethnicity: "our nation" was a multilingual empire, whose German speakers were as yet underrepresented in its culture. His "nation" was a public sharing experience and values (a culture, not just a language, or several languages). The theater that was to improve the Viennese public was not necessarily nationalistic in the modern sense, even while it tried to appeal to its audience through both the mind and the senses (a point that Schiller would echo).

Not all German speakers in Europe, however, conceded Vienna's superiority. While Lessing was admired and even feared[24] for his attempt to reform authors and German drama, Sonnenfels' fervor led him to be mocked in a 1767 play in the very genre he tried to reform, the satirical *Volksstück: Der auf den Parnaß versetzte grüne Hut* (*Hanswurst's Green Hat Transposed to Parnassus*). Moreover, the Berlin Enlightenment did not appreciate either the Viennese theater (because of its roots in Catholic and purportedly non-German Baroque and Jesuit traditions) or Sonnenfels' attempts to reform it. Later, in Berlin's *Letters on the Newest Literature* (#203), Nicolai would provide what became literary history's prevailing opinion about the Viennese theater (in the context of two book discussions, one on aesthetics and the other a tragedy):

> Yes, one will find that, among the large cities in Germany, Vienna is the least able to bring the German stage to perfection. Austria has not yet given us a single author who would warrant the attention of the rest of Germany; good taste (at least as concerns the German language) is there scarcely in its infancy, scarcely at the level where Saxony and Brandenburg already were around the year 1730. (cited Sonnenfels, 360)[25]

---

24 A letter from Johann Georg Sulzer to Bodmer on May 19, 1759, underscores the power in that voice: "Aber, wer Lessing u.s.f. beleidigt, der hat sich unversöhnliche Feinde gemacht" (Lessing, 827). Wilfried Barner, in "Autorität und Anmaßung," is at pains to prove how Lessing established his prestige by choice of interlocutors (see 25ff.).

25 "Ja, man wird finden, daß unter allen großen Städten in Deutschland Wien am aller ungeschicktesten sey, die deutsche Schaubühne zur Vollkommenheit zu bringen. Oesterreich hat uns noch keinen einzigen Schriftsteller gegeben, der die Aufmerksamkeit des übrigen Deutschlands verdient hätte; der gute Geschmack ist, (wenigstens was das Deutsche betrifft) daselbst kaum noch in seiner ersten Kindheit, kaum noch da, so Sachsen und Brandenburg schon um das Jahr 1730 waren."

Nicolai's opinion did not stop Lessing from acknowledging Sonnenfels' comparatively greater freedom of expression, even in a purportedly backward culture. Still, like the proverbial "rest of Germany," he was not interested in Viennese theater as viable in "German culture."

From the start, then, Lessing and Sonnenfels speak to audiences with very different possibilities and expectations. Lessing's Berlin was wounded, just as the fictitious Herr von N. who received Lessing's *Letters* was: it was a disrupted civil space that at times allowed for little real commerce in ideas and Enlightenment, and which was threatening to lose its identity under occupation by foreign powers (either by armies or by authors). This needed a new, enlightened cadre of scholars to bring the traditional ruling classes to their senses and into a new world. In contrast, Sonnenfels was writing to a city that had a functioning theater featuring music, opera, and ballet from across Europe (the Viennese theater even had one of the early eminent ballet masters in Noverre [Sonnenfels, 7]).[26] All these arts did not necessarily speak German, but they did speak to a public that included not only the traditional ruling classes, but a new public with the ability to visit the theaters and the taste to evaluate performance quality.

Thus where Lessing addressed his letters to a wounded young poet, to a would-be voice of genius, Sonnenfels would choose a very different fictional interlocutor. Sonnenfels' letters were purportedly "aus dem Französischen übersetzt" ("translated from the French"; title page); in them, the Viennese public meets a 1767 business traveler (not a soldier) writing home to Paris about Vienna: "Vienna is completely like Paris" (Sonnenfels, 3)[27]—by no means a true statement, but at least not a complete parody.

Moreover, where Lessing's letter-writer found a society disrupted by war and a false economy of misused scholarship, Sonnenfels' anonymous Parisian traveler found scholars aplenty in Vienna, yet ones who were excluded from high society in an unfortunate way (Sonnenfels, 4).[28] In this Vienna, the *learned* exist, but just are not allowed to mix in the "best" circles of society, from noble circles (*die Kreise des Adels* [Sonnenfels, 5]). Domestic equivalents of Voltaire, Sonnenfels asserts, will not develop if intellectuals are judged by their clothes and shown the door: "But generally, German scholars are nothing but scholars. The sciences and grace in social intercourse are considered characteristics that are incompatible with each other"

---

26 For a history of the ballet in Vienna, including a description of Noverre's status, see Riki Raab, "Das k. k. Hofballett unter Maria Theresia."

27 "Wien gleicht … Paris vollkommen."

28 "Ich habe, wie Sie mich kennen, mich in allen Gesellschaften nach den Gelehrten dieser Stadt umgesehen; ich fand keinen."

(Sonnenfels, 6).[29] Sonnenfels' Vienna has the scholars that Berlin lacked, but they are not allowed to perform as part of society, as part of the nation—they are not considered an elite.

Lessing bemoaned the lack of intellectual leaders in Berlin; Sonnenfels, in contrast, sees in Vienna a cosmopolitan theater and public that is beginning to enjoy a range of theater and music on the European level, performed in good taste and even improved from their sources:

> I find myself in the land of marvels. A serious music theater *without castrati*, music *without Solfegiettos*, or as I would rather call it, *gargling*, a French poem without pathos and flightiness—with this three-fold marvel, the theater next to the Palace has been reopened. I would like to add a fourth thing, perhaps by no means the smallest among them: the *prima donna* is *a born German*. (Sonnenfels 10)[30]

Sonnenfels reflects European norms for performance, even as he acknowledges local improvements on them. The learned in his city may not have access to the ruling classes, yet the public theater spaces do bring together the best in Europe, as this letter-writer insists. At the performances in the new theater, he finds an increasingly broad audience—a peacetime public of emerging taste, pointing to a new era of national development: "These observations will sometimes lead me to the spectators, and to sentiment and even to the spirit of the nation itself" (Sonnenfels, 6).[31]

The role of the *learned* and their audiences in each state is thus different. For Lessing, the *learned* are leaders of their audiences: they are the monitors of correct language, correct values, and aesthetic superiority, or else they victimize their audiences.[32] For Sonnenfels, the

---

29 "Überhaupt aber sind [die deutschen Gelehrten] sonst nichts als *Gelehrte*. Die Wissenschaften und Grazie des Umgangs werden als Eigenschaften, die miteinander unverträglich sind, betrachtet."

30 "Ich befinde mich in dem Lande der Wunderwerke. Ein ernsthaftes Singspiel *ohne Kastraten,*—eine Musik *ohne Solfegieren*, oder wie ich es lieber nennen möchte, *Gurgeley*—ein wälsches Gedicht *ohne Schwulst und Flitterwiz*—mit diesem dreyfachen Wunderwerke ist die Schaubühne nächst den Burg wieder eröffnet worden. Noch wohl ein viertes habe ich Lust hinzuzusetzen, und es ist vielleicht nicht eben das kleinste: die erste Sängerin eine *geborene Deutsche*."

31 "Diese Betrachtungen werden mich manchmal auf die Zuschauer, und auf das Gefühl, und den Geist der Nation selbst leiten ..."

32 Rudolf Vierhaus, in "Kritikbereitschaft und Konsensverlangen bei deutschen Aufklärern," makes the point that the kind of public debates that this would involve was part of the process of enlightenment (81). Klaus L. Berghahn, in contrast, says such debates led Lessing away from more important issues:

learned are to be part and parcel of the society that attends all manner of theatrical performances. Where Lessing insists on a public who will learn from writers and men of letters, then, Sonnenfels wants artists and the learned to enter into a conversation with the public and the elite that sponsor them. He wants the formation of a public that rivals Paris in its reputation for taste and *Bildung* (self-formation).

Roger Chartier, in "The Man of Letters," draws several contrasts between the salon culture of Paris and the print and periodical culture of Berlin. The learned in German discussed in the framework of periodical publications, rather than in salons, and "their close connections with men who held posts and offices in the service of the state or who sometimes participated directly in the bureaucracies constructed by absolute (on occasion, enlightened) German princes" (Chartier, 164–5). Masonic lodges in Berlin were also important extensions to public space for communication. Critically, such spaces allow for the development of a public outside the direct control of the absolutist states.

Chartier does not, however, consider other germanophone cities of the era. Still, his point helps to illuminate another difference between Vienna and Berlin: Lessing's Berlin is indeed a land of periodicals, with the learned elite trying to join with the traditional ones in leading the nation toward Enlightenment. In contrast, Sonnenfels evaluates the position of the learned as part of an extended social space guaranteed by institutions, including theaters and salons. If his nation is to be improved, public debate and public discussion are necessary, especially in spaces where audiences of various estates mix.

In an extreme sense, then, Lessing is advocating the development of an intelligentsia to lead his Berliners into high culture. In contrast, Sonnenfels hopes to form a public with taste, one that integrates high and popular culture and the best of European arts and letters, no matter their ethnic-national origins. Yet to function for this public, these arts must be naturalized to the local norms—opera with "German" divas, so that the arts become part of indigenous society.

Translations and "German national culture"

While Lessing and Sonnenfels agree that a German national culture is necessary, they disagree as to what that German culture should be. For Lessing, that national culture is distinctively non-French, and most particularly indigenous. For Sonnenfels, however, that culture may not be French-national or French-language, but it can be *Wälsch*: French

"Über die Polemik gegen Gottsched versäumte er, Grundsätzlicheres über Shakespeare zu schreiben; statt sich über den Lyriker Dusch zu ärgern, hätte er Klopstock mehr Aufmerksmakeit widmen können …" (180).

in inspiration, but not necessarily connected to the recent state of the French nation. The ethnicity of an artwork or artist (like the political nation-state in which it originated) is not in and of itself indicative of quality or relevance to an emerging nation. Lessing's "German culture" is thus quite literally at war with foreign influences, while Sonnenfels' Vienna is trying to build an aesthetics that is national (indigenous to the life of the nation) but not isolationist, solely germanophone, or ethnocentric. What these differing ideologies imply for a German national culture comes into high relief in Lessing's and Sonnenfels' varying evaluations of how translations can serve the development of public taste and national culture.

Not surprisingly, Lessing uses translation and translators to underscore his point about the learned and their lacking potential for intellectual leadership. His example is what he considers a botched translation of Pope by Johann Jakob Dusch, a poet who had criticized *Miss Sara Sampson* (Lessing, 832). Over several pages, Lessing rehearses a litany of errors in Dusch's work, from the word level up, suggesting that he lacks *Wortverstand*, the basic ability to comprehend the text he purportedly translated (Lessing, #2, 34). Lessing considers a bad translator like Dusch particularly dangerous to public intellectual health because he is active. He had not only mis-translated Pope, but also Gay's fables, thus ruining a second English poet (*verdorben* is the verb [Lessing, #3, 34]); his next victims were Bolingbroke's letters on the use of history (Lessing, #3, 36): "So many lines, so many inexcusable mistakes" (Lessing, #4, 37).[33] Dusch shows no discrimination or ability, but he exemplifies any number of "learned day-laborers" (Lessing, #3, 36) who lack language skills, writing talent, and discrimination *vis-à-vis* their audience. They just translate for money.[34] Lessing substantiates his charges by quoting badly-translated passages and then critiquing them by offering his own improved versions. He also insists that the translator be a scholar who knows the history and culture of the text he translates and who can bring the text to his audience.[35]

Lessing thus denies that translations can be used to improve the public, given that there are few or no good ones on the German market.

---

33 "So viel Zeilen, so viel unverzeihliche Fehler."

34 "Unsere Übersetzer verstehen selten die Sprache; sie wollen sie erst verstehen lernen; sie übersetzen sich zu üben, und sind klug genug, sich ihre Übungen bezahlen zu lassen. Am wenigsten aber sind sie vermögend, ihrem Originale nachzudenken. Denn wären sie hierzu nicht ganz unfähig, so würden sie es fast immer, aus der Folge der Gedanken abnehmen können, wo sie jene mangelhafte Kenntnis der Sprache zu Fehlern verleitet hat" (Lessing, #4, 36).

35 Lessing's example is a translator who errs because he did not know the books of the Bible (Lessing, #4, 39).

If, he argues, all the libraries of the world were destroyed and we had retained only such poor translations, we would never know what had been lost. Such disreputable scholarly behavior must be avoided at all costs, and critics interested in the public good must correct the problem,[36] "because the damage that they cause is indescribable" (Lessing, #7, 42).[37] Texts from other contexts cannot be copied or translated into the present without reflection and critique because they rest on foreign norms that have been used to create texts manufactured according to artificial aesthetic recipes rather than art, texts with "[t]oo too many ingredients for a single purgative!" (Lessing, #5, 40).[38] However, foreign texts, understood in their foreignness by scholars, can indeed be of value in forming an indigenous culture—once they are naturalized on his terms. Lessing's vision thus stresses scholarly and critical leadership by writers and translators of taste who learn from foreign texts, but do not emulate them without reflection.

Sonnenfels sets the act of translating into a very different social context. His case study is not a set of published texts, but rather the variety of play translations that appear on the Viennese stages because a season's bill in a standing theater demands a constant flow of new material (a situation Lessing will confront in Hamburg, as well). Like Lessing, Sonnenfels sees the essential incompetence of translators who do not even realize that French drama isn't what it once was:

> Translating, and translating, to be sure, does not yet create for a nation its own theater; especially where the work proceeds so spryly, and the choices are decided so unfortunately. The *grammarian* with his laurel-leaved and non-laurel-leaved shoulders descended with violence upon the French: and the French are precisely the least appropriate models that they could have used to practice on. (Sonnenfels, 173)[39]

---

36 When Christoph Martin Wieland offered what Lessing considers a terrible translation of "De rerum natura," in a tone of "pietischtischen Stolz" (Lessing, #7, 43), Lessing again accuses him of destroying public trust. Note that Wieland was a slightly younger competitor of Lessing who had enjoyed patronage when Lessing lacked it.

37 "Sie haben Recht; dergleichen schlechte Übersetzer, als ich Ihnen bekannt gemacht habe, sind unter der Kritik. Es ist aber doch gut, wenn sich die Kritik dann und wann zu ihnen herabläßt; denn der Schade, den sie stiften, ist unbeschreiblich."

38 "Zu viel, zu viel Ingredienzen für *ein* Vomitiv!"

39 "Uebersetzen, und Uebersetzen heißt freylich noch nicht einer Nation ein eigenes Theater schaffen: besonders wo die Arbeit so rüstig vor sich geht, und die Wahl so unglücklich ausfällt. Der *Grammatiker* mit seinen belorberten und unbelorberten Schültern fiel mit Gewalt über die Franzosen her: und die Franzosen sind gerade am wenigsten die Modelle, nach denen sich hätten üben sollen."

Moreover, just because a play has been translated does not mean that it will work for its intended audience: it can remain foreign in concept and expression. In consequence, a drama that has a claim to national status cannot only suit the German language; it must also suit the audiences and national actors (*Nationalschauspieler* [Sonnenfels, 176]). To be sure, many actors are lazy and do not want to be challenged by more difficult but rewarding materials; yet bad literature only reinforces such lazy habits, since poor and alien text is hard to memorize, while good text is easier to memorize and present naturally (Sonnenfels, 201–2). Actors, then, and not scholars, are the first best critics of drama translations.[40]

Sonnenfels' alter ego does not, however, say that plays chosen to be translated or presented should cater to the taste of those actors or to the masses (*Haufen* [Sonnenfels, 205]). He is not violating Lessing's call for historically and rhetorically correct translations. But Sonnenfels assesses a translated text in terms of its social function, not only its function as text. Therefore, a "good" play or play translation becomes so because it works in the theater, bringing together the text, the performance, and the audience's expectations and experience about what makes a complete impression. That is, the translated drama is responsible not only to scholarly norms of correctness and coherence, but also to the social and institutional criteria of the theater, as its public knows it. The translator of a theater text has greater responsibility than one of other text types because it has to be spoken:

> [H]e must therefore work not just as someone who understands the language, he must work as someone who knows the stage and must himself, in a certain sense, be an actor, in order to be able to heighten the rest pauses in speech, the words on which spoken emphases must be laid, the transitions, the concluding fall of speech—in order to be able to order theatrical phrases into the kind of symmetry that facilitates expression, to link what went before with what follows into a relationship made necessary by the context of the action and the ordering of dialogue (Sonnenfels, 207–8)[41]

---

40 Since Sonnenfels speaks of plays as offering a coherent social experience rather than simply replicating some past time, it means that translators (and writers) are again justified in asking actors for help in naturalizing their materials to local needs (Sonnenfels, 211).

41 "[E]r muß also auch nicht als ein blosser Sprachverständiger, er muß als ein Kenner der Schaubühne arbeiten, und muß selbst, in einem gewissen Verstande, *Schauspieler* seyn, um die Ruhepunkte der Rede, die Worte, worauf der Nachdruck der Rede gelegt werden muß, die Uebergänge, die Schlußfälle der Reden, um eine theatralsche Periode in derjenigen Symetrie ordnen zu

Sonnenfels' translator is thus responsible not only to the history of the text and to the world of the text, as Lessing's was, but also to the audience and its present sense of the stage. Both believe that successful translations are as difficult to produce as are original works, and that they should not simply contribute novelties borrowed from foreign sources.

However, Sonnenfels then defines successful plays in nuanced terms. Each genre of play has its own logical and emotional center, its own truth. Shakespeare is the model for history plays, because he brings the "complete life" of a person onto the stage and lets it play out (Sonnenfels, 220). In contrast, a character play must revolve around an individual's personal traits to unify that person's actions and dialogue.[42] The coherence of any artwork has to be anchored in a proper, place- and class-appropriate use of language.[43] That language must be understood as a social phenomenon, correlated with the audience's experience, and not as an exercise in ideal style—what Sonnenfels calls the "language of civilized social intercourse" (*die Sprache des gesitteten Umgangs* [Sonnenfels, 283]). A play can only be credible if it speaks to its audience, in terms understood by that audience.

Sonnenfels thus agrees with Lessing that foreign language and stylistic conceits can be a danger to their local audiences, but only Sonnenfels sees the advantage of contact between conceptual worlds, that "our language" can be enriched through the contact:

All words violating good tone in social intercourse also offend in dialogue. [...] I am not quite as averse to neologisms, used judiciously. We are so in need of words for social intercourse, so needy—but we cannot acquire the words before we are familiar with the matter itself. We so lack certain silly expressions, free turns of phrase, idioms, and commonplaces of social intercourse; and yet it is only these which prevent circumlocution or drawn out exchanges, and which the French possess in great number.

könneň, wie sie den Ausdruck befördert, erhöht, mit dem vorhergehenden, und dem was folget, in derjenigen Beziehung steht, welche der Zusammenhang der Handlung und die Reihung des Gesprächs nothwendig machet."

42 "Ich sehe hier nicht auf den poetischen Karakter der Sprechenden: die vollkommene Uebereinstimmung desselben, das ist die Einheit des Karakters, ist ein unwandelbares Gesetz der *Handlung und des Gespräches*" (Sonnenfels, 272).

43 "Ist der Innhalt des Schauspiels eine Begebenheit in einem Hause, wie man es zu nennen pflegt, von *höheren* oder *mittleren Stande*: so kömmt *allen* Personen ein gewählterer, feinerer Ausdruck zu; derselbe Anstand, der in den Handlungen der Personen von Erziehung wahrgenommen wird, muß auch über ihre Reden verbreitet werden" (Sonnenfels, 282).

Which dramatic writer could enrich our language from that source, without drawing too near to the genius of language, without speaking French in German, without translating literally, but by copying through analogy? (Sonnenfels, 287)[44]

In consequence, Sonnenfels identifies problems as arising not when his German audience confronts the French language or dramas originally written in French, but rather when an author offers them an unconsidered mix of social or conceptual forms.[45] If a mixing happens (of language, or of language levels), then the work loses focus, coherence, and the ability to expand an audience's experience and knowledge: it is a detriment to learning.[46]

From Sonnenfels' perspective, then, translations can improve an audience. Each time a dramatic form is made to work in German, Sonnenfels explains, new language is created, and a new set of concepts is opened to the audience, potentially broadening their experience.[47]

---

44 "Alle *Wörter*, welche im Umgange wider den guten Ton verstossen würden, verstossen auch im Dialoge. ... Dem *Neologismus* mit geziemender Mässigung bin ich nicht so ganz abgeneigt. An Wörtern zu dem gesellschaftlichen Umgange sind wir so dürftig, so dürftig—aber die *Wörter* konnten uns auch eher nicht zu Theil werden, als wir mit den *Sachen* bekannt wurden. An gewissen törichten *Ausdrücken*, freyen *Wendungen*, *Redensarten* und *Sprückwörtern* des Umgangs fehlt es uns so sehr; und doch sind es nur diese, welche wir dem *Weitschweifisten*, dem *Gedehnten* der Unterredung bewahren, und worinnen die Franzosen einen so großen Vorrath vor sich haben. Welcher drammatische Schriftsteller, ohne dem Genie der Sprache zu nahe zu treten, ohne im Deutschen zu französieren, ohne wörtlich zu übersetzen, sondern analogisch nachzuahmen, unsre Sprache von daher bereichern könnte."

45 "ein Schriftsteller muß sich einer idealen Sprache bedienen, und man ist darinnen nicht immer glücklich,weil man Schöpfer seyn muß. Die *Leichtigkeit* artet oft in das *Hagere*, die *Lebhaftigkeit* in das *Gekünstelte* aus: was eine artige Sprache werden sollte, wird eine *gezierte*, eine *kostbare*: die Wendungen sind *gesucht*, die Periode *zerstückt*, die Wörterordnung *unnatürlich*; die ganze Rede *gedrechselt*." (Sonnenfels, 283–4)

46 "Der Gang der Periode des Dialogs schlüßt allen Wohlklang, alle Symetrie der Wörter, alle völleren Schlußwörter, alles Maß des Ohres aus. Was in einem Aufsatze, dessen Bestimmung ist, *gelesen* zu werden, was da eine Schönheit ist, wird hier ein Fehler, wo nur *Gespräch* vor den Augen liegen muß. Die Nachlässigkeit ist der Schmuck, worinnen diese Schöne nur allein gefällt. Es ist schon sonst irgendwo gesagt worden, daß alld *Bindewörter*, welche der *Ton* des Schauspielers, oder seine *Gebehrde* ersetzen kann, im Dialoge überflüssig sind: nicht nur überflüssig, sondern *fehlerhaft*; denn sie legen dem Talente des Schauspielers eine Schwierigkeit im Weg: ..." (Sonnenfels, 288)

Note that he uses the same criterion about wholeness for his ballet criticism as well, especially "unity of action" (see 298, 299, 304).

47 "Das heißt in eigentlichen Verstande das Gebiet derselben erweitern ... So

The writer who can open such a new world may indeed be a genius. More critical is that a play needs good (plausible, natural) dialogue (Sonnenfels, 243) and a coherent plot (*Handlung*), not just a sequence of events (*Gang* [Sonnenfels, 245]). However, even that kind of genius needs to convey to the audience a coherent experience, based on logic, whether the plays are comedies or tragedies (Sonnenfels, 262). If plays do not satisfy this norm, the results will be damaging to the audience, which is the likely result of foreign theater texts brought to the state as replicas rather than rethought adaptations (Sonnenfels, 261).

Here, then, is the point at which Sonnenfels looks decisively beyond the boundaries of his national culture as part of a larger world. He insists that translations, like other importations from foreign cultures, can serve the audience and that audience's world, if they accommodate local customs (Sonnenfels, 233). Lessing, in contrast, argues for translations as successful (coherent, historically correct) replication of alien worlds rendered comprehensible to local norms, but not necessarily made part of them. That is, Lessing supports the integrity of a text as representing a world of ideas, while Sonnenfels supports the integrity of an audience's world experience, invoked by a text from a foreign source. Lessing is the textual scholar and critic appealing to his audience's reason, where Sonnenfels argues the stage as an inclusive institution of public formation through experience.

Lessing's learned men of letters need not appeal to the "court rabble" (*Hofpöbel*) since they are trying to build a new, more rational republic of letters through genius. Writers or translators who flatter the existing order rather than live up to that fiat are traitors; they will not improve German culture since that culture does not presently exist in the public sphere. Sonnenfels' thinking is less utopian and more pragmatic, as he advocates the extension of forms of sociability (even those of the upper classes) to create new forms of public discussion. Through translation, he can show his public how other times and places may engage in a coherent public discussion.

Through their evaluations of translators, then, both Lessing and Sonnenfels position their public intellectuals. Lessing's good translator is the equivalent of an indigenous poet, making texts (their history, philology, and content) accessible to an audience who should learn from them. Sonnenfels' translator is the facilitator for a public discussion, learning from the audience and actors (in the case of drama) and profiting from a well-ordered theater institution. Both expose their audiences to the world, but only Sonnenfels believes that the forms of expression and communication that translators naturalize onto the

---

verstehe ich es, eine neue Sprache erschaffen: und solche Neuerungen sind das Vorrecht des Genies …" (Sonnenfels, 235).

German stage can profitably be naturalized for his domestic audience. Sonnenfels has seen translators do their jobs for improving the public space of the theater, and he understands how the theater experience, with its performance of social relations as well as history, character, or other ideas, can improve the public climate for nuanced discussion. Lessing is interested in naturalizing foreign texts so that their ideas become clear to his readers, who must judge their value for their own nation; Sonnenfels believes that foreign texts can and should bring new worlds of experience to their readers that can be integrated into their world to expand it—a considerably more positive evaluation of the potential value of texts from elsewhere in Europe indigenous culture.

National theaters and the creation of new public spaces

Sonnenfels and Lessing agree that German-language texts and a mass medium (printing or theater) are necessary for public improvement, even when they disagree about the nature of that improvement. Yet when Sonnenfels and Lessing describe their ideal German stages, they are also describing a German *nation* emerging in public space, not necessarily a German *state*.

Only Sonnenfels, not Lessing, discusses the stage as an effective public forum for performance, not just as a place to present a text. Where Lessing decried French clerical orators' use of persuasion as a deformation of textual authority, Sonnenfels is willing to valorize Gluck's music as a way of articulating a particularly clear, persuasive, and distinctive human experience. Performing such music publicly will improve first the performers themselves, and then the audience, just as a drama might: "[C]omedies with music will also always make a stronger, longer-lasting effect; and I would almost like to say that they would be capable of forming *actors* for the opera stage" (Sonnenfels, 24).[48] Any form of theater can be good for a nation's mind and spirit when it contributes an image of a new whole, a new world, or a familiar world clarified or rendered logical in new ways, as part of a performance satisfying an audience's experience while extending its vision. Thus an author must produce a text that represents the public's best taste (Sonnenfels, 63), while the actors must contribute their own taste and judgment to turn that text into a successful performance (Sonnenfels, 69).

This contrasting assessment is not a one-time divergence between these two critics; they discuss the drama throughout their respective series of letters to similarly divergent ends.

---

48 "Seine *Singspiele* werden auch immer in der Aufführung eine stärkere, eine anhaltendere Wirkung machen; und ich möchte beynahe sagen, sie werden der Opernbühne *Schauspieler* zu *bilden* fähig sein."

Lessing's discussions about the German national theater are familiar as representing a new aesthetics of the drama, especially in #17 of the *Letters* (February 16, 1759), when he first turns his full attention to the importance of the German theater as the instrument of Enlightenment. It is noteworthy for the present context that these improvements are couched as an attack on a rival critic:

> "No one," say the authors of this library, "will deny that the German stage owes a great portion of its initial improvement to Professor Gottsched."
> I am this no one; I completely deny it. One might have wished that Mr. Gottsched had never interfered with the theater. His purported improvements actually concern unnecessary trivialities, or they are actually exacerbations. (Lessing, #17, 70)[49]

In Lessing's view (which became the dominant view in German literary history from the late nineteenth century on), Gottsched had erred by trying to improve the German theater using translations from the French. Not surprisingly, Lessing felt there was nothing natural about such borrowings, and that Gottsched had done less for the German theater than he had for his own reputation:

> Gottsched laid his curse on extemporizing; he had Harlequin ceremoniously driven out of the theater, which itself was the greatest harlequinade that was ever played; in short, he did not so much want to improve our old theater as to be creator of a completely new one. And what kind of new one? A Frenchified one; without investigating whether or not this Frenchifying one was appropriate for our German way of thinking. (Lessing, #17, 71)[50]

Lessing's charge against Gottsched is familiar, but his reference to the "German way of thinking" has a different resonance, when one

---

49 "'Niemand, sagen die Verfasser der Bibliothek, wird leugnen, daß die deutsche Schaubühne einen großen Teil ihrer ersten Verbesserung dem Herrn Professor Gottsched zu danken habe.'
Ich bin dieser Niemand; ich leugne es gerade zu. Es wäre zu wünschen, daß sich Herr Gottsched nienals mit dem Theater vermengt hätte. Seine vermeinten Verbesserungen betreffen entweder entbehrliche Kleinigkeiten, oder sind wahre Verschlimmerungen."

50 "[Gottsched] legte seinen Fluch auf das extemporieren; er ließ den Harlekin feierlich vom Theater vertreiben, welches selbst die größte Harlekinage war, die jemals gespielt worden; kurz, er wollte nicht sowohl unser altes Theater verbessern, als der Schöpfer eines ganz neuen sein. Und was für eines neuen? Eines Französierenden; ohne zu untersuchen, ob dieses französierende Theater der deutschen Denkungsart angemessen sei, oder nicht."

compares it to his descriptions of the critic's task. Lessing's German theater is marked here as a kind of theater of the mind, not a theater of performance, as Sonnenfels' was. Foreign texts cannot serve this nascent German mind except as exemplars for scholars, never directly. Just as translation is a matter for scholars, so, too, is the choice of which foreign texts might be used on the stage. Lessing's public must be protected from plays that cannot suit them, just as they were from bad scholars.

Foreign exemplars, accordingly, should be chosen carefully, preferably from countries with historical affinities to German culture (hence less foreign, in an absolute sense). Thus Lessing's ideal German theater would be based on the English theater rather than the senti-mental-aristocratic theater of France; it would do better for its audience in showing the more natural (to Germans), genial world of Shakespeare than the courtly one of Corneille and Racine. Moreover, that ideal German theater should foster rational thought in the audience, a theater that is rational, manly, and tough-minded—everything that French culture was not, in his familiar assessment.[51] Lessing will cast Shakespeare's *Othello* as a product of genius, while Voltaire's *Zayre* resulted from a cultural ideal that tried to seduce through artifice rather than to educate (Lessing, #17, 72). Similarly, Voltaire's work would only inspire a public to the artifice of an unnatural court culture, never to the insight that genius can offer into a culture with a full worldview.

Sonnenfels would concur that *Othello* is a fine play, but he would be far from denying genius or cultural relevance to Voltaire—he is less interested in national provenance than in quality. In consequence, Sonnenfels investigates how great plays from any culture serve their public, and what kind of world representation, logic, and standards for performance and acting would make the plays work more naturally and profitably for his local audiences. Sonnenfels' theater geniuses are not only text authors, and not only German; they can be any author or performer who can teach the audience (Sonnenfels, 17). Voltaire's theater thus must be considered one kind of genius among others. But authors are not alone in this power: Noverre's contribution to the ballet can raise public taste in ways parallel to those used in any tragedy.[52] Yet, in music, French music is inferior to that of Willibald

---

51   "daß wir mehr in den Geschmack der Engländer, als der Franzosen einschlagen; daß wir in unsern Trauerspielen mehr sehen und denken wollen, als uns das furchtsame französische Trauerspiel zu sehen und zu denken gibt; daß das Große, das Schreckliche, das Melancholische besser auf uns wirkt als das Artige, das Zärtliche, das Verliebte; daß uns die zu große Einfalt mehr ermüde, als die zu große Verwickelung etc." (Lessing, #17, 71).

52   "Und nicht allein gute Stücke, auch vortreffliche Ballette werden das Vergnügen des Publikums vollkommen machen ..." (Sonnenfels, 345).

Gluck (another of Vienna's finest [Sonnenfels, 18]). In a similar vein, overblown acting is as bad a theatrical phenomenon as any play based on bad logic. A *Histrio* is not an actor (*Schauspieler* [Sonnenfels, 15]); singers must also act well to offer a plausible and comprehensible performance (Sonnenfels, 22).

That Sonnenfels also has constant recourse to concepts of taste as well as logic is also indicative of his broader social and historical approach to the theater. Discussions of taste are more familiar to scholars of the English and French eighteenth centuries, where they are taken to reflect the influence of the upper classes on the public. Yet in the Viennese context, Sonnenfels attributes taste to a greater public—as a set of reactions by audiences of all estates to a performance that corresponds to experience. "Taste," therefore, is defined as a kind of knowledge sustained within a group as part of its public face and ability to process experience, and not as a mere superficial style or class marker.

Sonnenfels concurs with Lessing that a national stage needs better dramaturgy (Sonnenfels, 30), better plays, and better playwrights (31); that harlequin should indeed be banished if he won't learn fixed text (29); and that better actors are necessary.[53] Not surprisingly, Sonnenfels' "good playwrights" include not only Lessing himself, but also Corneille and Voltaire, in their own contexts (Sonnenfels, 32). Here, Sonnenfels justifies his approval of such European dramatists: Corneille and Voltaire served their own publics with a kind of enlightenment, and with good sense conveyed in verses, as their public understood the form. Fine writers in the style of their day, they did not use bad language, but only some language and style elements that do not work for the present audience (Sonnenfels, 35).[54] Their supposed "errors" reflect different publics, at different times.

French models are thus not abhorrent to Sonnenfels, as they were to Lessing—they just represented different social constellations. A writer's nationality does not excuse a basic lack of knowledge of how poetry or prose works to meet an audience's needs and expectations (Sonnenfels, 37). A dramatic writer's work must instead be judged on how he uses the forms of language to achieve an effect on an audience, within a nation's norm of expression—it must speak to the theater audience *as part of a national community of expression*, not simply within

---

53 And not only for their declamation: "Mein Prüfstein der Schauspieler und Schauspielerinnen ist immer der Zwischenraum, wenn sie nichts so sprechen haben ..." (Sonnenfels, 27).

54 These were: "unedle, müssige Verse, das, was wir unkorrekte nennen; und sogar hie und da Flitterwiz, wahre Concetti."

the conventions of a theater.[55] In consequence, the language and logic
of a play cannot be the only criteria against which its soundness is
measured. Not just theatrical intertextuality, but other institutional and
social-cognitive criteria from a nation's history and habits also figure
into making a "good" play, for even the best language cannot save a
play when a writer peoples the stage with boring characters or when
that writer's play is performed by ham actors (Sonnenfels, 41).

In drawing these distinctions, Sonnenfels uses the kind of historical and
scholarly acumen that Lessing would demand from his critics. Sonnenfels,
like Lessing, can compare easily two German versions of a play and judge
their relative excellence (Sonnenfels, 48). Ultimately, however, Sonnenfels
will analyze good *theater* in the form of well-performed plays, where
Lessing prefers to judge good *play texts*, delivered by actors who submit
themselves to them. Thus only Sonnenfels will appreciate how good farce
influences the public (offering *Scherzen*—jokes—and not *Fratzen*—pratfalls,
low humor [Sonnenfels, 62]). And as a scholar, he will supplement a
discussion of Molière with a scholarly presentation of Goldoni, who
improved Italian drama and standards of comic acting, transforming the
commedia dell'arte into a bourgeois theater (Sonnenfels, 57).[56]

Lessing is, in fact, Sonnenfels' paradigm for a comic playwright:
"But the gentleman has earned a bit more than passing praise. German
theater writers should always study his *Minna* rather than our French
plays!" (Sonnenfels, 78–9).[57] Unlike the allegedly poor plays deriving
from older French norms, Sonnenfels realizes Lessing's excellence in
drawing characters for the modern era (Sonnenfels, 83), but he pays
Lessing a backhanded compliment that stresses his abilities as a writer
rather than his dramatic sense: "To his discredit, *Lessing* has taken
up such thin story material that he had to be *Lessing* to find in it the
material for five acts" (Sonnenfels, 86).[58]

---

55   "der poetische Wohlklang der deutschen Gedichte müsse in einer gewissen
     edleren Ordnung der Rede gesucht werden, die von der prosaischen dadurch
     abgeht, daß sie die Begriffe, auf denen der Nachdruck ruhet, wie ein klugen
     Maler die Hauptperson seiner Handlung, stark ins Gesicht bringet ..."
     (Sonnenfels, 38).
56   Note that Sonnenfels offers a very comprehensive scholarly overview of theater
     history—including the history of acting, dance, and music theater. And he
     valorizes virtually the same group of good German playwrights as Lessing
     does, including J. E. Schlegel, Cronegk, Gellert, Weisse, and others. These are
     the authors whose plays he judges as not always good, but always useful for a
     study of the theater (Sonnenfels, 203).
57   "Aber der Mann verdient ein wenig mehr als einen obenhinfahrenden Lobstrich.
     Die deutschen Theaterdichter möchten immer lieber seine *Minna*, als unsre
     französischen Stücke studieren!"
58   "*Lessing* hat eine so magere Geschichte zu seinem Vorwurfe gewählt, daß er
     Lessing seyn mußte, um darinnen den Stoff zu fünf *Aufzügen* aufzufinden."

Sonnenfels does believe that German national theater had not yet emerged, but he points to a different cause for that state of affairs. The problems of the stage have less to do with a lack of natural genius in germanophone authors than with social deficiencies in German circles. German society simply does not offer models for certain patterns of language and knowledge:

> Although Germany already possessed theatrical writers who have dared to their own honor to approach the drama, it has continuously lacked theatrical language, at least a language for the finer comedy. The cause thereof can be discerned. The inter-locutors of finer comedy, or, more properly, of the *noble comedy* are absolutely people drawn from better society, persons of rank, persons of breeding, persons from the great world: their tone is the tone of social intercourse, the tone of the better-bred world which also extends itself to the servants and maidservants who in French plays often speak with insufferable wit. Does Germany up to the present moment have a real language of great society? Is it at all possible that at every court, in every capital city, at the seat of such well-bred intercourse, in every gathering that only French is spoken? […] Thus the German actually has no theater language because he has no language for social intercourse; […] the lack of a better-wrought social jargon. (Sonnenfels, 99–100)[59]

In short, Germany lacks a certain kind of theater language (particularly the language for comedy). Where Lessing believed that a genius could create a language and thus a society through the theater (a top-down model), Sonnenfels stresses instead that theater form will only seem natural if it is understood by a society that recognizes how it addresses

---

59 "Obgleich Deutschland bereits theatralische Schriftsteller aufzuweisen hat, die sich mit Ehre an das Drama gewaget haben; so mangelte es ihm bis itzt doch beständig an einer theatralischen Sprache, wenigstens an einer Sprache für das *feinere Lustspiel*. Die Ursache davon läßt sich angeben. Die Zwischenredner des feineren Lustspiels, oder eigentlicher, des *edeln Komischen* sind überhaupt Leute aus besseren Gesellschaften genommen, Standspersonen, Personen von Erziehung, Personen aus der großen Welt: ihr Ton ist eigentlich der Ton des Umgangs, der Ton der artigeren Welt, der sich bis auf die *Bediente* und *Mädchen* hinab verbreitet, welche in unseren französischen Stücken sogar oft unausstehlich witzig sprechen. Hat aber Deutschland bis auf diese Stunde eine eigentliche Sprache der großen Gesellschaft? ist es sogar möglich, daß sie jemals dazu gelange, da an allen Höfen, in allen Hauptstädtern, dem Sitze des sogenannten artigen Umgangs, in allen Versammlungen durchaus französisch gesprochen wird? ... Eigentlich also hat der Deutsche keine Theatersprache, weil er keine Sprache des Umgange hat; ... den Mangel eines bearbeiteteren gesellschaftlichen Jargons."

them.[60] A germanophone culture must therefore be a coherent society before it can support an improved culture.

Significantly, Sonnenfels again finds in Lessing the single exception to his rule of deficiency among germanophone authors. Lessing represents the cosmopolitanism and fine expression of a social elite, he believes, offering dramas firmly based on a well-ordered society:

> Lessing is the only one who breathes in broader circles, and his plays show the powerful influence of such local advantage principally in the singularity of his language: it is the fine language of the cosmopolitan who lets the connecting words and transitions simply go, because they can be replaced by tone: he does not parse his expressions aesthetically, but is content with leaving his thoughts half expressed and the other half to be discovered, out of the assurance that he speaks with people who will guess them correctly. (Sonnenfels, 102)[61]

This assessment of his personal style is probably precisely the opposite of what Lessing would have liked to hear. Sonnenfels praises Lessing for relying on the existence of a particular social stratum for the effect of his plays, while Lessing would have insisted that his plays, like any good ones, were simply following the inner logic of a particular situation and its appropriate means of expression—that they were well-constructed dramas. Lessing would not concur that the audience's knowledge of a social situation makes a play comprehensible. Sonnenfels believes that the public needs to hear the language of such "men of the world" in order to engage a new and larger vision of the world that this language communicates. Through Sonnenfels' Lessing, the public will learn about a new situation, not just a set of ideas in the abstract; Lessing himself would stress his personal abilities to clarify the situation.

For Sonnenfels, therefore, the theater is meant to offer the public not an ideal, but a coherent image of a group's experience and of the

---

60   This is, interestingly, a comment that Austria's great dramatist of the twentieth century, Hugo von Hofmannsthal, echoes when he comments that the German language lacks a language of social mediation (his point in "Wert und Ehre deutscher Sprache").

61   "*Lessing* ist der einzige, der in einem weitern Umkreise athmet, und seine Stücke zeigen den mächtigen Einfluß dieses Lokalvortheils hauptsächlich in dem Eigenthümlichen seiner Sprache: es ist die feine Sprache des Weltmanns, der in Wendungen und Uebergängen ungezwungen, die Bindewörter fahren läßt, weil sie der Ton ersetzen kann: der seinen Ausdruck nicht ästhetisch zergliedert, sondern zufrieden, den Gedanken halb gesagt zu haben die andre Hälfte errathen läßt, aus Zuversicht, daß er mit Leuten spricht, die ihn errathen werden ..."

language needed to negotiate that experience. When there are not enough domestic playwrights to model such language and its society then the theater will need to use translations, especially translations of authors like Corneille, Molière, and Lope de Vega. Yet these translations need to be presented on a well-regulated stage as adaptations that overcome the distance of time and language and speak within their audience's society; their translators must not follow the original form of a play, an arbitrary standard of accuracy to measure their translations against, but they must rather reinforce the play's logic and coherence for the intended audience (Sonnenfels, 104). Where Lessing (in the *Dramaturgie*) points to the unities of time and place as critical in making plays seem probable in logical terms, Sonnenfels believes that a play must be critiqued not only *vis-à-vis* its logic, but also, in different ways, as material for the actors and the audience—as a performance. Concomitantly, simply correcting logical, language, or performance flaws in "bad" performances will not necessarily make a good play.

Thus any plan aimed at improving a theater must attend to more than a play's logic structure:

> An enlightening criticism, one which is useful to the writer, the actor, and the spectator, is perhaps not that strict, implacable one that never lightens its brow to smile upon a young genius and lead his timid steps with love … (Sonnenfels, 124)[62]

In "enlightening criticism," critics must be careful not to stifle beginning authors, and to help actors figure out how to behave, especially when they try to overact to compensate for otherwise poor plays. In this way, critics can help performance and the play texts to be mutually illuminating for the audience, and the genius of the text heightened through the performer's genius. Sonnenfels thus wishes to improve an existing audience by improving an existing theater and encouraging it to reflect a broader, more coherent vision of society. Such improvement, however, is a challenge that can only be met within public space, using public institutions and accommodating their needs, not simply under the leadership of a genius whose text will itself carry the messages of Enlightenment to an audience. In consequence, Sonnenfels takes on the theater as a *local* project of enlightenment.

What Sonnenfels will argue instead is that the history of the local audience must be respected as a theater is improved. In his world, the

---

62 "Eine *aufklärende Kritik*, welche dem *Schriftsteller*, dem *Schauspieler*, dem *Zuhörer*gleich nützlich ist: vielleicht nicht jene strenge, unerbittliche, welche nie die Stirne aufheitert, um einem jungen Genie zuzulächeln, und seine furchtsamen Schritte mit Liebe zu leiten …"

Viennese *Volkstheater* (folk theater, the theater of Punch, Hanswurst, and Kasperl) had an inherited form that requires adaptation to improve a newer generation. Considered historically, some plays of the original *Volkstheater* did indeed affect their audiences as powerfully, authentically, as any national theater must do:

> thus it was wisely decided to call the language of his neighbors to aid, and to preserve unfalsified the purity of the Austrian dialect. Hanswurst thus spoke in the dialect of a person from Salzburg, or Bavaria, if you will; and even this idea seemed droll: the Austrian farmer found the dialect of the Salzburger or Bavarian farmer amusing. ... One must not forget that the German theater was opened principally for the diversion of the more common citizen, because the court, the nobility, and others of the "right set" there had the most opulent French operas, which were very often given free at court ... (Sonnenfels, 313)[63]

However, the *Volkstheater* must also be updated to remain relevant. The actors who had, over generations, played *Hanswurst* in his various incarnations (Staberl, Kasperl, and others) adapted the original stock characters to contemporary performance standards. In this way, each showed a kind of genius: "They were not only actors, but also prolific writers, but the most prolific among them, whose poetic vein seemed inexhaustible, was Kurz [the Hanswurst actor Bernadon]" (Sonnenfels, 314).[64]

When Bernadon used stage machinery to play Hanswurst, did jokes and pantomimes, and extemporized, the audience loved it, and so it was right for the time—he had improved performance standards. However, his successor, Hafner, concentrated more on advancing comedic writing, toward "the apotheosis of the Green Hat"—an improvement of the character who was known for wearing a green hat as his stock costume (Sonnenfels, 319). In Sonnenfels' opinion, the

---

63 "so war es weislich gedacht, die Sprache seiner Nachbarn zu Hülfe zu rufen, und die Reinlichkeit des österreichischen Dialekts unverfälscht zu erhalten. Hanswurst sprach also in der Mundart eines Salzburgers, oder Bayern, wenn sie wollen: und auch dieser Einfall schien drollicht: der österreichische Bauer fand die Mundart des Salzburger, des bayerschen Bauern lächerlich. ... Nicht zu vergessen, daß die deutschen Schauspiele hauptsächlich für den Zeitvertreib des gemeineren Bürgers eröffnet waren; denn der Hof, der Adel, und was sonst sich des gens, comme il faut zu nennen pflegt, hatten die kostbarsten und prächtigsten wälschen Opern, welche sehr oft vom Hofe frey gegeben ..."

64 "[Sie] waren nicht allein Schauspieler, sondern auch fruchtbare *Dichter*; aber der fruchtbarste unter ihnen, und dessen Ader unerschöpflich schien, war *Kurz*" [the Hanswurst actor Bernadon].

subsequent generation, his own, was now ready to redefine itself away from the French and Italian performance norms of the *commedia dell'arte* in its finest form, away from improvisation, and toward a more literary theater. To realize this goal, however, requires not only German plays, but also good translations that suit the audience.[65]

What Sonnenfels advocates as the basis of a national theater, then, is a new form of theater, supported by a new theater criticism, not just a new set of correct plays monitored by scholars. This theater will contribute to the enlightenment of the nation if it keeps contact with the public, improving taste while accommodating the best of its habits and its historical experience:

> The most pleasant, most instructive, innocent amusement for the citizens of a state is indisputably a well-regulated theater. If this theater is national, it will make the prevailing vices and follies worthy of scorn and laughable: thus these amusements will be raised still further, and even the lowest citizen comes to know the true Good and Beautiful; good taste spreads throughout the entire nation. (Sonnenfels, 344)[66]

The phrasing of this recommendation has a deliberate ambiguity in it: the German version, "die herrschenden Laster und Thorheiten," cannot help but suggest both "the prevailing vices and follies" and "the vices and follies of the rulers." None the less, "men of talent and science" will use the national theater to stage their dreams of improved human realities—tragic or comic, historical or current, conveyed as dramatic or operatic or balletic. Through these performances, a public of taste and good sense will evolve, one that learns through its pleasures and its senses as well as through its mind (Sonnenfels, 344).

Sonnenfels thus ties the health of the nation and the enlightening potential of the theater together much more closely than had Lessing, representing that nation as a community rather than a classroom. Where Lessing believed that a national theater would be formed by texts written by geniuses and performed by actors who would not get in their way, Sonnenfels believed in a more collaborative approach to improving public space. Lessing's theater would be purged of foreign

---

65 It is indicative that, among the new plays, Sonnenfels liked the adaptation *Julie* (from *La nouvelle Helöise*) that Lessing hated (Sonnenfels, 325).

66 "Das angenehmste, das lehrreichste, das unschuldigste Vergnügen für die Bürger eines Staates, ist unstreitig eine wohleingerichtete Schaubühne. Ist diese Schaubühne national, macht sie die herrschenden Laster und Thorheiten verächtlich und lächerlich: so wird diese Vergnügen um desto mehr erhöhet, und auch der niedrigste Bürger lernt das wahre Gute und Schöne kennen; der gute Geschmack verbreitet sich auf die ganze Nation."

influences in order to evolve its own voice.[67] Sonnenfels' would work
to naturalize and improve on these norms for the betterment of the
present community. No wonder, then, that Lessing's letters were
addressed to a poet-aristocrat fighting a battle for Prussia's future
independence from the European powers, while Sonnenfels' alter ego
was a fictional business traveler, writing Viennese taste onto a map of
Europe whose center had, in the last generation, been Paris.

These comparisons are not exceptions. Throughout the balance of
the *Letters*, for instance, Lessing evaluates the theater by presenting its
plays, critics, and translators as guarantors of the public's culture and
knowledge. His audience's enlightenment is to proceed cognitively
rather than theatrically or emotionally. He will, in consequence, reject
texts written with overblown sentiment (his example is Wieland),
or those using sentimental-religious rhetoric (following models like
Pope), for instance, to impose feelings on the reader, prescribing what
they should feel rather than educating them. For the same reason,
Lessing condemns Wieland's defense of France's clerical orators, those
"virtuosos" using physical eloquence (*körperliche Beredsamkeit*) that
they had learned from actors (Lessing, #13, 56–7).[68] These cleric-orators
work on the audience's will without fostering their understanding,
and so cannot further Enlightenment or *Bildung*, let alone inculcate
religion. Instead, anyone who is to be enlightened must exercise mind,
body, and his own abilities in expression. The genius author will set
the terms of that confrontation to lead his public into the battle for
enlightenment.

Sonnenfels, too, continues throughout his *Letters* as he had begun
them. Because Sonnenfels remembers that the essence of theater is
performance, not just the text, he is considerably more comfortable than
Lessing was with affect as part of education, taking into account what
an audience will see in them and experience from them. Sonnenfels
is not implying that an author must cater to the audience, but rather
that a play must appeal to the heart of the nation as well as to its mind
(Sonnenfels, 166), both its imagination and its reason (Sonnenfels, 277).

---

67 This pedagogical imperative, guided from above, also pervades the *Hamburgische
Dramaturgie*, which appeared in 120 installments between May 1, 1767 and July
20, 1767, then on April 19, 1768 and Easter, 1769. This set of essays tried to
reinforce through criticism the founding of a standing theater in Hamburg
that should improve German minds and morals. Again, however, Lessing will
discuss comparatively little about specific performances, but much about bad
plays, bad translations of plays, and inappropriate aesthetics (thus he rereads
Aristotle's unities as logical criteria).

68 "Er [Wieland] ist ein erklärter Feind von allem, was einige Anstrengung des
Verstandes erfordert, und da er alle Wissenschaften in ein artiges Geschwätz
verwandelt wissen will, warum nicht auch die Theologie?" (Lessing, #13, 59).

In contrast to this appeal to enlightenment through the group, Lessing argues primarily for an individual's learning through reason, and only secondarily through sense or social experience. As he sees it, even the best-understood and best-constructed exempla from the past can only be guidelines for the education of individuals, albeit necessary ones: "Historical knowledge of things that have transpired cannot, through any exertion of genius whatsoever, be produced or invented; the senses and memory must be engaged before one can use wit and judgment" (Lessing, #11, 54).[69] Where Lessing stresses the importance of individual wit and judgment, however, Sonnenfels has to include the actor and affects, as well.

The comparison between Sonnenfels and Lessing thus documents that the germanophone Enlightenment dreamed of at least two different national theaters: one, a theater of the enlightened mind, and one for an enlightened public—a theater of genius; and a second that can all too easily be remembered as a theater of bureaucrats. Just as critically, for Lessing, "national" meant indigenous, while Sonnenfels used the term to mean "relevant to the national community." While both insisted that foreign texts need to be made accessible to their respective nations, Lessing was skeptical about what a foreign text could bring, unless it was translated up to the standards of an independent work of art; Sonnenfels looked to the cultural spaces of Europe for whatever texts might be used to enlighten his audience, his nation of many estates and professions.

The Enlightenments of Europe
The comparison of these two sets of letters, one patterned consciously on the other, demonstrates weaknesses in any cultural histories that do not account for the historical moments in which texts were written and for the public they are designed to serve. These letters document the *transnational* phenomenon of the Enlightenment in germanophone cultures and how it rests on at least two competing visions of the nation-state, its public, and their educations, two different ideas about what was at stake with the Seven Years War. Lessing's vision was elitist, intellectualized, almost romantic in its insistence on individual agency and leadership; Sonnenfels' was more historically grounded, based on a vision of a progressively more open society and the institutions that support it. (The latter is, moreover, a vision that persists in Central Europe to this century, a more postmodern vision, while the

---

69 "Die historische Kenntnis der *geschehenen* Dinge aber kann durch keine Anstrengung des Genies heraus gebracht oder gefunden werden; die Sinne und das Gedächtnis müssen hier beschäftigt sein, bevor man Witz und Beurteilungskraft gebrauchen kann."

former conforms to Western modernism.) Critically, these two visions of society also posit different grounds for personal identity and agency.

Sonnenfels' reforms had to be transacted via the existence of a "standing theater" that had been part of the dominant class' cultural consciousness in Vienna since 1710 and which had created shared media experiences extending across class lines. Lessing, in contrast, was looking to figure out what kinds of public expression and public utilities would become available to him, as he ultimately moved away from the unsatisfying cultural politics of the rising Prussian Empire to Hamburg, with its more clearly bourgeois consciousness. The former was thus trying to modernize the ruling classes of the Habsburg empire's dominant elite culture, perhaps to include a rising bureaucratic class (not quite noble, yet not bourgeois), while Lessing was placing his bets on a bourgeoisie more clearly planning to be its own ruling class (or at least as an educated elite whose influence would be little contested), as this scholar clearly schemed to marginalize or at least to circumvent older ruling classes and their emphasis on society and sociability.

These two writers did recognize that each operated in a different context of Enlightenment, as Sonnenfels' comments on Lessing and Lessing's statements about Vienna, cited at the start of this chapter, both reflect. Yet Lessing's statements have a very distinct motivation that must also be factored into our assessment of his overall program in undervaluing Vienna. On April 11, 1769, a letter from Bode to Klopstock indicates that Vienna was trying to hire Lessing, since he was looking to leave Hamburg, perhaps moving to Rome for the latest of his job changes (cited in Kiesel, 941–2). Nicolai feared such changes and wrote to Lessing on August 19: "As part of freedom of thought, the freedom to write must be there, and in Vienna, where one is not permitted to read most English writing and a part of the French corpus, ... a thinking mind must breathe constrained air" (Kiesel, 620), adding that books printed outside Austria are banned there.[70]

Lessing's response above sharply counters Nicolai's presumptions. Directly preceding the passage cited above is another reference to Vienna: Lessing had no serious objections to moving to Vienna, just as he had earlier expressed interest in Rome. Had he gotten a position in Vienna, however, his goals might have shifted radically, given his clear careerist instincts. Nicolai will not be put off as he persists in questioning the viability of Vienna. On August 29, Nicolai pushes again:

---

70 "Zu der Freiheit zu denken, gehört doch wirklich die Freiheit zu schreiben, und in Wien, wo man fast alle englische und zum Teil französische Schriften nicht lesen darf, ... muß ein denkender Kopf doch etwas eng atmen."

I want to hold every good opinion about Vienna, but do not just rely on Sonnenfels alone! If he utters a few truths to minor nobility, he none the less kowtows ever more deeply to the high nobility, and especially with respect to anything the Empress does. (Kiesel, 625)[71]

What Nicolai resists is the "learned slavery" (*die gelehrte Sklaverei*) he associates with a city like Vienna, where books are confiscated—the true heart of a publisher and bookseller coming out. Lessing lets the matter drop thereafter, according to existing letters. He will not have to deal with Sonnenfels, or with that "high nobility" that Nicolai fears. But a bookseller's fears do by no means adequately characterize what kinds of public speech were possible in that city. Sonnenfels *was* himself the official state censor and, as in any censorship situation, there were clear leaks and clear channels of public communication possible, despite official reactions. The theater remained one of them, as we shall see in subsequent chapters.

This comparison of public letters confirms that even these players recognized different Enlightenments within germanophone Europe and understood that which one would triumph would remain a matter of contestation. Methodologically, they require scholars of those germanophone Enlightenments to consider what, in fact, the "nation-states" posited in them might actually have been, and how to capture that. Lessing seems to be strictly anti-aristocracy, looking for his new public in a class of educated readers who will dissent from the current hegemonies; Sonnenfels, in contrast, looks to the map of Europe and all its estates, aristocratic or not, when he seeks a space of critical consciousness and sharing to improve the nation from within. These competing theories of Enlightenment thus correlate with images about ruling classes, drawn by engaged intellectuals within different German-speaking regions, each offering blueprints for what they would consider cultural politics *par excellence*, solidly rooted in the soil gained from Europe's realignments in the eighteenth century.

What this initial analysis suggests, however, needs to be further nuanced, as do the polemics of each Enlightener, since each speaks locally, not globally. Geographically speaking, the city of Berlin was divided from its court in Potsdam; Vienna's cultural life revolved around its palace and court theater, the many performance spaces in great houses that on occasion sold tickets to events, and its commercial

---

71 "Ich will von Wien gern alles Gute glauben; aber berufen SIe sich nur nicht auf Sonnenfels! Wenn er dem niedern Adel ein Paar Wahrheiten sagt, so bückt er sich zugleich desto tiefer von dem höhern Adel, und vor allem, was die Kaiserin tut."

theaters outside the city wall. Culturally, official Berlin was indeed "Frenchified," given the waves of Huguenot immigrants welcomed by the court for their skills, and who remained a significant and distinct presence there through the nineteenth century. Access to the Leipzig book trade gave entrepreneurs like Nicolai more economic freedom than authors in other germanophone regions may have had, but little, if any, access to political power. State bureaucrats like Sonnenfels had more rules to follow, especially when foreign books were censored, but in practice, they also had theaters and newspapers under official protection as well as under official scrutiny—they had a reliable public space in which to operate, even if that space was regulated (at times even censored). Nicolai was very wrong about Sonnenfels' access to only lower nobility, unless he was referring to face-to-face communications, because publications would find their way to a greater public that knew how to read around restrictions and how to decode the serious criticism in humor.

As the culture of absolutism was yielding to historical circumstances in both germanophone cultural spheres, Lessing felt he needed to declare war to recapture the bedrock of his own culture, while Sonnenfels could let a Parisian business traveler point out that freedom for public discussion was good for his nation. The *Letters on the Newest Literature* intended to spark a cultural revolution and the birth of a new German nation, realizing its own inner principle as a nation (even a nation-state) with its own exclusive identity within Europe. The *Letters on the Viennese Theater*, in contrast, argued for the evolution of a culture whose borders were open to Europe's influences, showing that a germanophone high theater could assert itself next to (but not necessarily to the exclusion of) other European influences and add to a conversation reaching across national and state borders. Lessing's original *Letters* declared war on Europe in the name of the future German nation-state, while Sonnenfels' response advocated a nation of culture that would put a new language on Europe's cultural map.

Two Extending Europe's Enlightenment: Why Grillparzer Resists Weimar

Joseph von Sonnenfels posited that Enlightenment was a project for a community, not just for individuals, and for Europe, not just for a single nation-state. Yet another Habsburg civil servant, playwright and archivist of the *Hofkammer* (exchequer), Franz Grillparzer (1791–1872) is the literary artist who actually played out that imperative on the Viennese stage. Grillparzer was the most visible dramatist at Vienna's *Burgtheater* for the generation of the Napoleonic Wars and the years leading up to 1848, but he, like Sonnenfels, remained a civil servant (a court librarian).[1] His life was conducted on terms that Kant would have recognized, with his official post as representative of a private use of reason, and his plays as examples of public speech opening questions about the evolution of Austria and its ruling classes.

In the literary histories that equate germanophone literatures in the plural with German literature in the singular, Grillparzer has been cast as an epigone of the Weimar Dioscuri Goethe and Schiller, one whose work in verse does not live up to Goethe's standards, who wrote no theory, and whose history plays do not live up to the political claims of Schiller's work. At best, he appears as the Habsburg dynasty's house playwright. In that position, such scholars continue, his verse

---

1   The best overview of recent scholarship on Grillparzer is found in Marianne Henn, Clemens Ruthner, and Raleigh Whitinger, eds., *Aneignungen, Entfremdungen: The Austrian Playwright Franz Grillparzer (1792–1872)* (2007). The main source for publications on Grillparzer in German is in the *Jahrbuch der Grillparzer-Gesellschaft* (tables of contents online at http://grillparzer.at/gesellschaft/jahrbuch/index.shtml) (accessed May 15, 2015); it is not presently indexed in the *MLA International Bibliography*. A short, partial version of the present argument was published in German as "Die Klassik als Tyrannei der Moderne: Wie Grillparzer Weimar widersteht" (2007–8).

lacks the verve of philosophical calls for freedom and revolution like Schiller's, and Goethe's sense of technique and poetic decorum in verse dramas. These histories forget that the dramas of Goethe and Schiller do not belong in the same framework as Grillparzer's. Despite their exemplary verse forms, the Weimar dramas were often conceived for reading before performance (an assertion straightforwardly confirmed by the impossible lengths of many of Schiller's most famous monologues). Moreover, for financial reasons, the authors of these plays often sought audiences on other germanophone stages, while civil servant Grillparzer needed only to address those of his Vienna, a very different public space than Goethe's Weimar (or Lessing's Berlin and Hamburg).

Just as the last chapter pursued the differences between Sonnenfels' and Lessing's projects, the present discussion will pursue how and why Grillparzer worked in conscious opposition to Weimar Classicism's definitions of the structure and purpose of the stage as central to evolving national cultures.[2] Grillparzer preferred a critical theater to a revolutionary one, and dramatic literature that spurred the public to reconsider the relation of history to its present affairs and situation within Europe. Concomitantly, he refused the equation of author with a critical authority that was so prominently defended by the author-critics of Weimar Classicism and Jena Romanticism.

To engage his public dramatically and politically, Grillparzer brought to Vienna a diverse body of plays inspired by European theatrical traditions, not only the Shakespearean models favored by Goethe and Schiller. He found tools to engage his audiences in sources like Calderon, Lope de Vega, Roman comedy, and French classicism (its mythological approach, not its poetic meter).[3] When he felt he had lost his audiences to a rising tide of ethnic nationalism, he withdrew from the Viennese stage. None the less, after his "retirement" as a dramatist, he continued to write a series of masterly historical dramas for the desk drawer, plays that have emerged as critical masterpieces, still performed today in Vienna because of their relevance as critiques of public consciousness about rulers, hegemonies, and especially gender roles.

---

2   A short version of this material was presented as a speech in a special session on "What does it mean to write for Vienna in the *Vormärz*?" sponsored by the International Grillparzer Society and the Modern Austrian Literature and Culture Association at the MLA Convention, San Francisco, CA, December 29, 1998.

3   The same can be said of his rare fictional prose pieces: he wove intense discussions of the situation of Poland into his novellas, *The Cloister of Sendomir* (*Das Kloster bei Sendomir*; see Arens, "The Fourfold Way to Internationalism: Grillparzer's Non-National Historial Literacy" [2007]) and of urban poverty into *The Poor Fiddler*.

A comparatively small body of critical prose pieces, only some of which were published, illuminates Grillparzer's redefinition of art as fostering not only education, but also critical discussion in public space.[4] These relatively unfamiliar texts connect his overt rejection of Weimar Classicism to his original extension of the *Ancients and Moderns* debates of the late Enlightenment: his decision to appeal to a particular vision of the public and its capacity for critical intelligence, based on history, but addressing present needs.[5] Where Lessing, Weimar Classicism, and Jena Romanticism highlighted the role of the artist as leader in creating a work for its readers or viewers, Grillparzer argues for a theater that sets the writer, audience/readers, and the artwork on an equal footing within critical cultural public dialogues about the present ("Zur Literaturgeschichte [Zweite Fassung]," XIV, 167). In these drafts and fragments, then, Grillparzer claims the importance of public spaces that are less class-bound than England's and nowhere near as repressed as Berlin's (as Lessing and Nicolai had insisted was the case, in their essays written before the Carlsbad decrees and Chancellor Metternich's post-Napoleonic cultural censorship).

Most critically, that the public space that Grillparzer extends to the stage is not the property of a national elite of artists reveals the politics of a future nation-state. In these short texts Grillparzer shows us instead the approach to politics and history of a practicing writer who is neither a prophet nor a seer, and whose work hopes to spur the public to critical engagements with its present and with the great political master narratives of their age.

The poet, the critic, the scholar: Redefining public enlightenment

Like most intellectuals in the so-called "age of Goethe," Grillparzer knew the aesthetic issues associated today with Weimar Classicism and Jena Romanticism: how an artwork interacts with an audience, how it should be constructed and staged, and what kind of education or enlightenment—*Bildung*—might result from that encounter. Yet his stage is not the "moral institution" defined by Schiller,[6] but rather an extension of public political space, aimed at fostering critical discussions that will improve his nation's culture through an address to a collective rather than individuals alone.

---

4   These materials were collected in the *Prosaschriften*, volumes XIII and XIV in the *Sämtliche Werke*, ed. A. Sauer.

5   For a useful account of that debate as reflecting a battle for the custody of the spaces for aesthetic and political discussions, see Joan E. DeJean, *Ancients Against Moderns* (1997).

6   From Schiller's 1784 essay "The Stage Considered as a Moral Institution" ("Die Schaubühne als eine moralische Anstalt betrachtet").

Grillparzer shares a point of departure with contemporaries like Schiller and Schlegel: Immanuel Kant's work on aesthetics and cognition. Yet Grillparzer disputes philosophy's right and ability to assess art in all its dimensions. As he notes in an 1835 essay:

> German philosophy had scarcely completed its great revolution at Kant's hand and won consistency and a place in its first fully developed form, when, seemingly in a revolutionary fashion, it also began to extend its usurpations to neighboring and ivory-tower areas.—From which, however, Kant himself must be excepted. Never has a philosopher spoken more appropriately about the fundamental questions of art than he, and if what he said did not always further art, then the cause for that lies only in the fact that art can absolutely not be furthered from the standpoint of philosophy. ("Über den gegenwärtigen Zustand der dramatischen Kunst in Deutschland [Fortsetzung]," XIV, 81–2)[7]

The philosophical aesthetics of artists purportedly following Kant must by definition fail to address the conditions for the production and reception of art. Each discipline has its own place, and its own historical imperative:

> Whoever neither knows nor feels the Beautiful is a fool; whoever feels it, an enthusiast; whoever knows it, a philosopher of art; whoever tries to execute what he feels and knows of it is a dilettante; whoever executes it, an artist. ("Brief über den Dilettantismus," XIV, 42)[8]

This description echoes assumptions familiar throughout eighteenth-century Europe in dividing disciplines from each other. Even though Grillparzer's artist is likely to be sensitive to philosophy's definitions of what is "natural" to each art (including terms like fantasy, feeling, and sensitivity), his actual task is to render an ideal palpable for an

---

7   "Die deutsche Philosophie hatte kaum durch Kant ihre große Umwälzung vollbracht, und in ihren ersten Ausbildungs-Formen Bestand und Platz gewonnen, als sie auch, ziemlich revoluzionär anfing, ihre Usurpazionen über benachbartes und weltfremdes Gebiet auszudehnen.—Wobei jedoch vor allem Kant selbst ausgenommen werden muß. Nie hat ein Philosoph aneignender über die Vorfragen der Kunst gesprochen als er, und wenn, was er sagte, nicht künstlerisch förderlicher war, so liegt die Ursache nur darin, daß aus dem Standpunkte der Philosophie die Kunst überhaupt nicht zu fördern ist."

8   "Wer das Schöne weder weiß noch fühlt ist ein Tropf; wer es fühlt, ein Liebhaber; wer es weiß, ein Kunstphilosoph; wer, was er davon fühle und weiß auszuführen strebt, ein Dilettant; wer es ausführt, ein Künstler."

audience, to enact, embody, or perform an idea drawn from history or experience in his chosen medium (for Grillparzer, the stage).

Grillparzer insists that the artwork also requires its audience to do more than empathize with or understand it as a representation of the artist's insight. An artwork may indeed educate or form its audience, but that is not enough. As Grillparzer sees it, the audience does more than be engulfed by the experience of a representation:

> The Palladium of spiritual formation is unhindered communication. Feeling, in contrast, is the expression of the particular existence of the individual; it dies with each individual, and is new-born with each. I can just as little assume the feeling of another as change persons with him, and to give up one's own way of feeling means as much as denying one's individuality, annihilating one's self as an individual. ("Über den gegenwärtigen Zustand der dramatischen Kunst in Deutschland [Fortsetzung]," XIV, 85)[9]

That is, the artwork will be able to form the individual spirits of its audience only if it spurs acts of communication within a group, in the context of its real historical experience.

Grillparzer's description of education through art moves beyond those common to the European Sentimentalism of the eighteenth century, which had itself evolved to counterbalance rationalism: a work that evokes sentiment does not necessarily engage the mind. At the same time, Grillparzer is not simply espousing the *Bildungsideal* of the age of Goethe, the idea of self-formation through a work of art that leads its audience beyond the constraints of the here and now. He will not accept that the artwork stems principally from the artist's individuality or insight because, by definition, that work must communicate with its audience, and hence is constrained by the limits of what can be communicated by it. Just as an individual cannot simply react to a work to be educated, the artist and his work cannot be cut off from the kind of understanding held in common by his audience as a group. Grillparzer valorizes the artwork as instantiating action in a *shared* public space; that space becomes an *immediate reality* for an audience that engages with it as a representation of national culture,

---

9   "Das Palladium der Geistesbildung ist die ungehinderte Mitteilung. Das Gefühl dagegen ist der Ausdruck der besonderen Existenz des Einzelnen; es stirbt mit Jedem, und wird mit Jedem neu geboren. Ich kann eben so wenig das Gefühl eines Andern annehmen, als die Person mit ihm tauschen, und die eigne Art zu fühlen aufgeben heißt so viel als seine Individualität verleugnen, sich als Mensch vernichten."

individualized but not created by the author's skills and sensibilty. Essentially, Grillparzer denies the correlation between *Bildung* and genius that was the hallmark of Weimar Classicism, and especially of Schiller's theater.

In "Göthe und Schiller" (1836), Grillparzer amplifies his description of what an artist does. An artist who crafts a representation out of his own individuality creates an artwork that is probably antithetical to the education of its audience. On the other hand, when an artist emulates another's work, copying a style or borrowing an ideal, the result will not be any better. The works of a poetic genius like Goethe may be excellent in themselves, but copying his works as "classics" of a genre or his ideas as ideals is antithetical to the idea that art educates an audience. In Grillparzer's estimation, Goethe is a past master, not an exemplar for current art production. A later artist may imitate how he handled genres, but never his impact, because both the situation and audience experience have changed. Yet that kind of emulation has become the norm for germanophone writers of Grillparzer's era: "The confusion of Goethe with his school or with a categorical understanding of what he was, or with what his imitation might bring forth, is the source of all misunderstandings about this perhaps greatest of all Germans" ("Göthe und Schiller," XIV, 87).[10] Goethe's genius may only be considered exemplary *as it shows a way to start a conversation with an audience*, not because his talent is unique. What a later artist can learn from Goethe is a pattern of communication with an audience, but not how to communicate with his own, present audience whose situation and concerns differ from those in Goethe's Weimar.

Grillparzer will generally approve of Goethe for his talent, but he seldom, if ever, approves of Romanticism, as he notes most overtly in "Über den Gebrauch des Ausdrucks 'romantisch' in der neueren Kunstkritik" (1819). His day's art needs to take up the problem of representation in more concrete terms than Romanticism does, because the movement all too often fails to make ideas visible to the audience. Romanticism generally espouses a formalist aesthetic of the mind that can initiate an "annihilation of the corporeal" (*Vernichtung des Leiblichen*) rather than an illumination of real historical experience (XIV, 28):

The astounding direction of the newest taste for art in Germany may very easily be explained by the convergence of two facts: historical, even analytic-scientific knowledge of what was

---

10 "Diese Verwechslung Göthes mit seiner Schule oder Gattung dessen was er war, mit dem was seine Nachahmung hervorbrachte, ist die Quelle aller Mißverständnisse über diesen vielleicht größren aller Deutschen."

excellent in art in earlier times, joined with our own impotence. Those setting the tone among us are what Jean Paul calls feminine geniuses. These cases lack neither in receptivity nor in love for the beautiful, but only in the strength to form it and to externalize it, outside of one's self. ("Über den Gebrauch des Ausdrucks 'romantisch' in der neueren Kunstkritik," XIV 27)[11]

That expression, "outside of one's self," is critical to Grillparzer's assessment of art as communication with an audience; he assesses Romanticism as unable to produce what very much later will be called an "objective correlative" of an idea.[12]

Artist-critics like Schiller and the Romantics may know more about literature in an abstract way than the public does, but the public, the *audience*, must be the actual judge of art's success or failure, exercising its "healthy human understanding." Weimar Classicism and Jena Romanticism had thrown this opportunity away, from Grillparzer's point of view. Their hubris was probably understandable, given that Goethe and Schiller lived in small cities. Yet the consequence was an art unresponsive to the public's needs; these authors simply were not attuned to a real conversation with an audience able to assess or evaluate their representations (*Darstellung* ["Zur Literaturgeschichte (Zweite Fassung)," 169]). The critic- and genius-driven aesthetics of Grillparzer's day had embraced the excess of literary scholasticism, rather than audience participation:

Even as those philosophers immediately following Kant, along with the Brothers Schlegel, first took up a dismissive tone and began to overestimate themselves, their innovation remained principally in the circles of scholastic dust, and touched the nation little. More permanent was the effect that August Wilhelm Schlegel caused, the book of Mme. de Staël, *de l'Allemagne*. It was the first sign of recognition from abroad, where it struck with the force of a natural need satisfied, because unbearable French

---

11 "Die wunderliche Richtung des neuesten Kunstgeschmackes in Deutschland läßt sich sehr einfach erklären aus dem Zusammentreffen zweier Tatsachen: historische, ja analytisch-wissenschaftliche Kenntnis des vor uns gewesenen Vortrefflichen in der Kunst, verbunden mit eigener Impotenz. Die Tonangeber unter uns sind, was Jean Paul weibliche Genies nennt. Da fehlt es weder an Empfänglichkeit noch Liebe fur das Schöne, aber an Kraft, es zu gestalten und außer sich hin zu stellen."

12 Mullan provides a good account of why Grillparzer's aesthetic was incompatible with Romanticism (Mullan, 1979, 5ff.), with reference to his philosophical sources, especially with Kant (with Bouterwek and Schopenhauer).

suppression had begun to shake its national spirit awake. ("Zur Literaturgeschichte [Erste Fassung]," XIV, 137)[13]

This new generation of philosophically driven theory brought into existence a new literature that was too abstract, full of "monstrosities" (*Monstruositäten*) that did not speak to audiences (XIV, 138). Philosophical aesthetics, normative poetics monitored by critics, and literary history[14] alike had become tools for imposing self-censorship and self-abnegation on a culture, helping to destroy current talent and to falsify links between art and its audiences ("Zur Literaturgeschichte [Zweite Fassung]," XIV, 169).

In this critique of German Classicist and Romantic aesthetics, Grillparzer extends eighteenth-century norms in a different way, following neither the British path of emphasizing taste nor the Weimar one stressing genius as the source of aesthetic revelation. In a real sense, he has taken a position on the *Ancients and Moderns* debate, asking whether or not a modern author can achieve what the ancients had. An author like Goethe clearly can, when he takes up older genre forms and makes them live for the present audience. None the less, his success must be evaluated not philosophically or in terms of normative aesthtics, but as public acts of communication, structured in particular aesthetic forms—and there even he can fail, given how little direct contact he had in Weimar with diverse, literate audiences.

In another essay, Grillparzer identifies what it means for an author to use historically attested genres to affect his public. Austrian actor-playwright Ferdinand Raimund (1790–1836) becomes his example of a writer who speaks to his contemporary audience through his expertise in a particular genre (the modernized *Volksstück*). Raimund takes up a traditional form of drama to craft a "revival of the idea" inherent in them (he uses *Belebung* ["Ferdinand Raimund," XIV, 94]) and to spur the audience to actively participate in understanding the play's themes:

The public has written as much into [one of Raimund's plays] as he himself had. His half-unconscious gift was rooted in the spirit

---

13   "Selbst als die unmittelbar auf Kant folgenden Philosophen nebst den Gebrüdern Schlegel zuerst den Ton des Absprechens und der Selbstüberschätzung anschlugen, blieb die Neuerung doch größtenteils im Kreise des Schulstaubes und berührte die Nazion wenig. Schon nachhaltiger wirkte, durch August Wilhelm Schlegel veranlaßt, das Buch der Mad. Stael *de l'Allemagne*. Es war das erste Zeichen der Anerkennung von Seiten des Auslands und wirkte mit der Stärke eines befriedigten Bedürfnisses, da die unleidliche französische Unterdrückung den Nationalgeist wach zu rütteln angefangen hatte."

14   The only viable form of literary history would document contemporaneous evaluations of authors ("Zur Literaturgeschichte [Zweite Fassung]," XIV, 167).

of the masses, and if the uncomprehending eagerness of well-meaning friends had not ripped him away from his maternal soil, we would still have had what we had, and what all Germany lacked: a true theater of the people, in the best sense of the word. ("Ferdinand Raimund," XIV, 95)[15]

Raimund's tragedy was personal, in that he lost faith in the public who had helped him find his voice and impact. When he committed suicide, Austria lost a chance at a "theater for the people." None the less, Grillparzer casts Raimund as a success, because he gave comedy the impact customarily associated only with tragic drama. His vibrant comedies encouraged the audience to (re)think their habitual reactions to experience, allowing them to experience a mix of catharsis and *Bildung* that challenged their *ideés fixes*.

The contrast between Grillparzer's evaluations of Goethe and Raimund necessarily rests on the question of how nations and nation-states correlate with culture. Grillparzer addresses this issue in differentiating "German" from "Austrian" literature. Critically, "German" does *not* refer, in Austria, to anything but a language. In Grillparzer's usage, "German" is a political term for a nation-state and its purported ethnic identity, not a reference to the culture of a space identifiable as a distinct nation. Thus in "What Distinguishes Austrian Authors from Others?" ("Worin unterscheiden sich die österreichischen Dichter von den übrigen?," 1837), Grillparzer summarizes advantages that Austrian authors enjoy over German ones: "Modesty, healthy understanding of people, and true feeling" (XIV, 96). These virtues develop in Austrian writers like Raimund because they have a nation to work within—an audience with a shared culture that can ground both understanding and debates. In contrast, Germany's authors, particularly the Romantics (what he calls the "Schlegel school"), have little access to such a national culture. Despite their claims of being an artistic vanguard—or perhaps because they are lazy or lack talent—Grillparzer finds their texts willful and insensitive to the audience (*Unverschämtheit* [XIV, 96]). The result is the "present decline (*Verfall*) of German literature" ("Gutzkows Nero," XIV, 90). In consequence, Grillparzer affirms Goethe's decision to reject Romanticism, because a work of art should offer a complete and compelling experience to

---

15 "[D]as Publikum [hat] eben so viel daran gedichtet als er selbst. Der Geist der Masse war es in dem seine halb unbewußte Gabe wurzelte, und hätte der unverständige Eifer gutmeinender Freunde ihn nicht aus seinem mütter-lichen Boden losgerissen, wir hätten noch immer was wir hatten, und ganz Deutschland fehlt, ein eigentlich volksmäßiges Theater im besten Sinn des Wortes."

its public, which a writer guided by a philosophical formula or who tolerates an aesthetics of scraps cannot produce.[16]

Grillparzer's distinction between Austrian and German authors also applies to Germany's philosophically minded art criticism, which tends towards brooding speculation (*Grubelei*), no matter that its practitioners often had clear advantages in education over their Austrian peers.[17] Philosophical speculation about art cannot improve public taste, because it tends to establish inflexible, artificial categories describing art production and artworks (*Schubfächer*) ("Über den gegenwärtigen Zustand der dramatischen Kunst in Deutschland [Fortsetzung]," XIV, 82). Philosophical categories apply to logic, not to real experience or to art itself: "[I]t is the task of philosophy to bring nature to a unity of spirit; the striving of art, to produce in nature a unity for the spirit" ("Über den gegenwärtigen Zustand der dramatischen Kunst in Deutschland [Fortsetzung]," XIV, 83).[18] In fact, a science or systematic philosophy of art is rarely, if ever, positive: it may create canons or exempla, but not art. In this sense, even Schiller's insistence that art is the product of a "free play of the imagination" appears to Grillparzer as a limiting affectation, since it excludes other representations of experience.

Instructive in this context is an unfinished parody piece about *Iliad* translations, the "Parody of a Translation and Commentary on the Iliad" ("Parodie einer Übersetzung und Erklärung der Ilias" [Sommer 1816]). Grillparzer agrees that the original text has indeed been transformed

16 Grillparzer even echoes Goethe's evaluation of "the Romantic" as "das Kranke": "Eben daher kommt der gegenwärtig vorwaltende Hang zum sogenannten Romantischen, zu jenem Ahnen, Sehnen und übersinnlichen Schauen, für das es in der Natur überall kein Gegenbild gibt. Alle großen Meister aller Zeiten von Shakespeare und Milton bis Göthe waren mehr oder weniger plastisch, weil eben dieses plastische, gesonderte Hinstellen mit scharfen Konturen, als das schwerste in der Kunst, nur dem kräftigen Meister gelingt und deshalb auch seines Strebens Hauptziel ist. Die Formlosigkeit, welche ein Hauptingrediens der sogenannten Romantik ist, war von jeher ein Zeichen eines schwachen kränkelnden Geistes, der sich selbst auch seinen Stoff zu beherrschen nicht vermag" ("Über den Gebrauch des Ausdrucks 'romantisch' in der neueren Kunstkritik," XIV, 27).
17 "Da laß uns denn nicht verkennen, daß das übrige Deutschland an wissenschaftlicher Bildung und Östreichern weit voran steht. ... Nun haben sie aber bei all ihrem Vorgeschrittensein einen unglücklingen Hang zur *Grübelei*, der sie oft um den besten Gewinn bringt. Die Grübelei unterscheidet sich aber von dem Denken darin, daß Letzteres die Gründe des Vorhandenen aufsucht, aber zuletzt demütig vor den unauflöslichen Grundfakten stehen bleibt, an denen es eben so wenig eine Befugnis zu zweifeln hat, als an sich selbst, das dieses Selbst eben auch ein unerklärliches Grundfaktum ist" (II, 98).
18 "Denn es ist die Aufgabe der Philosophie die Natur zur Einheit des Geistes zu bringen; das Streben der Kunst, in ihr eine Einheit für das Gemüt herzustellen."

into a germanophone variant. Unfortunately, the translator has worked
with no sense of audience, but only according to scholarly formulae,
as the volume's subtitle confirms: "First, transferred out of the original
Greek *Idiomate in linguam Germanicam* and illustrated and illuminated
with moral, grammatical, political, and historical annotations" (XIII,
85).[19] Literary historians and scholars—Grillparzer mentions Gervinus
and Menzel—do similar damage to literature in following formulae
about how history is represented in texts ("Waldfräulein von Zedlitz,"
XIV, 112). No wonder, then, that Grillparzer's 1844 review of Gervinus'
famous history of literature is utterly dismissive. Gervinus is particularly odious because he does not see how poetry works as literature,
or how it worked in the past, in different cultural contexts—he simply
reduces it to abstractions about history and society which cannot
educate readers sufficiently ("G.G. Gervinus," XIV, 117).

In the 1817 *Vorrede* to the published version of one of his greatest
plays, *The Ancestress (Die Ahnfrau)*, Grillparzer demands that the public
judge his work ("Vorrede zu dem Trauerspiel *Die Ahnfrau*," XIV, 4).
That statement should be read neither as an idle claim, nor as a conventional trope of modesty, but as a fundamental belief: a play is a public
form of art that must function for that public, with the artist working to
create that connection. In his 1818 dedication to the published edition
of his classical tragedy, *Sappho*, he does defend the author's own voice.
He notes that he published it without the changes others made in it
as it was being produced; his goal was to preserve it as his, as "the
representation of *my* idea" of how the audience could be touched (*die
Darstellung meiner Idee* [XIV, 25]). He wished only to write plays that
worked for his audiences through their dramatic effect and content:

> I wish neither to be an author, nor to be called one, nor to become
> a member of the honorable guild, nor to make a name for myself
> from short reports from newspaper correspondents or from
> theater reviews, nor bare my teeth against anyone who dares to
> touch that shaky house of cards, nor to lecture every malicious or
> foolish soul who sets out to battle against me in the daily papers.
> ("Widmung des Trauerspiels *Sappho*, XIV, 25)[20]

---

19 "Zuerst aus dem ursprünglich Greichischen *Idiomate in linguam Germanicam*
    transferiertet, und mit Moralisch, Grammaticalisch, Politisch und Historischen
    Anmerkungen illustrieret und erhellet."
20 "Ich will kein *Schriftsteller* sein und heißen, will nicht zünftig werden in der
    ehrsamen Gilde, will mir keinen Namen bauen aus Korrespondenzartikeln und
    Theaterberichten und dann die Zähne blecken gegen jeden, der das wackelnde
    Kartenhaus antastet, will nicht jedem Hämischen oder Narren Rede stehn, der
    gegen mich in einem Tagesblatt zu Felde zieht."

Such personal antipathy to critics and to authors relying on abstract aesthetic norms runs throughout the essay fragments, in terms which echo the eighteenth century's damnation of rule-bound poetics (*Regelpoetik*) as fundamentally detrimental to the cause of literature. Yet he makes those connections in full recognition that his own era is, unfortunately, addicted to such abstractions—the direct result of being trapped in a post-Goethe, post-Lessing, and post-Schiller generation.

Yet the failure of Classicism and Romanticism for the present generation of writers is not necessarily the fault of the prior generation: they failed aesthetically because Germany's external circumstances, especially its politics, placed them in a state of powerlessness (*Kraftlosigkeit*). A "Bruchstück aus einem Literaturblatt vom Jahre 1900" (1835), a parody of a future encyclopedia article writing about his era's art, clarifies the relation of geopolitics to the production of literature:

> The state, conditions of law, demagoguery, religion, the objectively true—all posit themselves as the subject of poetry in place of the comfortable ideals that had earlier delighted the Germans, as if in a dream; and even where an ideal was held to be possible, any intent of realizing it was placed far beyond our abilities to do so by an arrogant, overwrought age that cast it in terms so superlative, that all of Germany soon resembled a madhouse, in which the madmen screamed in chorus, while the simpletons in each cell acted out their nonsense. (XIII, 112)[21]

The age of Goethe and Schiller had brought world literature to Germany. Unfortunately, the diversity of that literature, combined with a lack of public, blinded that nation's artists: they lost—or surrendered—their own voices and conversations to abstract assessments of masterpieces from different eras and nations.[22] Hegel again sanctioned this blindness in the Romantic generation, because his theories understood the

---

21 "Staat, Rechtsverhältnisse, Demagogie, Religion, das objektiv Wahre setzten sich als Gegenstände der Poesie an die Stelle der gemütlichen Ideale, die früher die Deutschen träumerisch entzückt hatten; und selbst wo sich das Ideale erhielt, ward es durch die Anforderungen einer hochmütig überreitzten Zeit so in die Superlative getrieben, die Vorsätze liefen so der Ausführungs-Fähigkeit voraus, dass bald ganz Deutschland einer Irrenanstalt glich, in der die Tollen im Chorus schrien, indes die Blödsinnigen zellenweise dummes Zeug treiben."

22 "Die Meisterwerke aller Zeiten und Völker waren durch Übersetzungen allgemein zugänglich und der Gegenwart und sich selbst unter einander so nahe gebracht worden, dass das Licht-Meer von Vortrefflichkeiten Blödsichtige notwendig blenden musste" (XIII, 112).

imminent only as an "absolute generality" (*absolute Allgemeinheit*)[23]—
an error by "if not one of the sharpest thinkers, then certainly one
of the greatest sophists of all times" ("Zur Literaturgeschichte [Erste
Fassung]," XIV, 140]).[24]

Grillparzer thus shares Sonnenfels' definition of art as a potentially
political conversation engaged in public spaces. What he adds to the
earlier discussion is an explicit condemnation of Weimar Classicism
and Romanticism as hindering art within the context of a nation—
these movements will not help a cultural community come to terms
with its current experiences and history. Even more importantly,
Grillparzer has extended eighteenth-century definitions of art as part
of a social process, rather than following Classicism into its definitions of the artist as leader, or Romanticism's equation of art as an act
of prophetic disclosure of values. Instead, Grillparzer affirms art as
central to public enlightenment because it can focus and create experiences for audiences who, he hopes, will engage with it to raise their
own consciousness about issues, be they local, political, or otherwise
historical in origin.

While such claims may sound utopian, they rest on Grillparzer's
analysis of genres—especially on the space of the theater as a kind of
mass medium. Grillparzer explains in great detail a playwright's use of
theater genres in the service of public discussion. What he had adduced
as contrasts between Austrian and German art emerge in this context as
indices for what theater genres can do in creating public spaces of the
sort he requires for improvement of the national community.

Drama as public deliberation

As Grillparzer summarizes in "Über das Wesen des Drama" (1820),
the drama as a mass medium has a particular mission in fostering the
education of the public. It is a playwright's goal to create a distinctive
meeting point of ideas and reality by constructing a representation

---

23 As Grillparzer writes in "Schreiben Gottes an den Bürgermeister Hirzel in
Zürch" (1839), "Ihr Freund und Lehrer Hegel glaubt auch an mich, ja er
beweist mich, wobei er mich aber zur absoluten Allgemeinheit macht. Mein
Herr Bürgermeister Hirzel! Ich bin nicht die absolute Allgemeinheit, so wenig
Sie selbst etwa die Bürgermeisterwürde in Zürch, sondern der wirkliche
Bürgermeister sind" (XIII, 121). He repeatedly rejects "Hegelei" for its use of
abstractions (XIII, 122). Roger Bauer, "Grillparzers Aufklärung," summarizes
this rejection as a "Hang zum Theoretisieren und zum Spekulieren" (76).
Günter Schneider, in "Grillparzer und die Spätaufklärung," points out that
Grillparzer's rejection of Hegel's abstraction resembles that of philosopher
Bernard Bolzano.

24 Hegel: "wenn nicht einer der schärfsten Denker, doch gewiß einer der größten
Denkkünstler aller Zeiten."

(*Darstellung*) through use of a genre. The form prescribed by a genre helps render that representation intelligible to the audience. Poetry represents only an individual creative fantasy. In contrast, "[t]he essence of drama is strict causality, because it is supposed to make something palpable, as if it really happened" (XIV, 30).[25] Moreover, dramatic representation rests on two logics: "the laws of necessity, that is, nature, and [...] the laws of freedom"[26]—frameworks that explain history in terms of natural verisimilitude and comprehensible human choice. Grillparzer's definition of drama thus explicitly precludes plots using a *deus ex machina*, a "machine," or other external clockwork devices (*Triebfedern*) to motivate the action artificially ("Über das Wesen der Drama," XIV, 30).

If genre facilitates communication and comprehension, it also enables public discussion about the experiences represented in each distinctive logic. Grillparzer moves art from the affective dimension into the cognitive one by insisting that art rests on formalized patterns of communication (narrative strategies or types) facilitating public understanding. As such, Grillparzer casts art as existing in a cognitive and rhetorical space, with its messages instantiated in a representation that enacts a kind of contract between the artist and the audience about what experiential truths are relevant to the situation. Neither party controls either the work or the exchange, and hence both are formed or educated by the relationships created by the artwork. In the case of the drama, that exchange happens in the particularly public space of the stage, facilitated by a text that structures shared experience according to its inherent logic(s) and made experientially real in new ways in a performance—by being made palpable, effectively credible, and present to the audience, which is then called upon to engage in public acts of judgment. This is anything but Schiller's ideal of the stage as a moral institution or of art as free play of the imagination, because Grillparzer stresses the stage as an alternate kind of reality to be experienced, not as a space of ideas alone.

In fact, Grillparzer follows not Weimar, but rather European tradition in describing the structure of drama in terms drawn from prevalent readings of Aristotle. Yet he also modifies (modernizes?) those inherited traditions to accommodate an audience with a different sense of history and of the logic of everyday life. Perhaps his most intense intervention is his redefinition of the ancient poetic ideal of "fate" as an external force impinging on human life. To maintain the

---

25 "Das Wesen des Drama ist, da es etwas Erdichtetes als wirklich geschehend anschaulich machen soll, strenge Kausalität."

26 "Nach dem Gesetze der Notwendigkeit d. i. der Natur, und nach dem Gesetze der Freiheit."

force of fate as a principle for tragic drama while modernizing what it means to individuals, Grillparzer distinguishes two kinds of fate, one attached to the rules of causality applying in nature (*Verhängnis*, destiny or providence), and the other (*Schicksal, fatum*), more a question of individual or group decision and will: "Fate is nothing more than providence without vision, I would like to call it *passive* providence, in opposition to the active one, that is posited as modifying nature in favor of the law of freedom" ("Über das Wesen der Drama," XIV, 31).[27]

Grillparzer also recasts fate as something cognitive, something *posited* by individuals as existing externally, not as genuine divine intervention or as a fluke of nature revealing new, previously unknown laws. He notes: "One [critic] finds in the Greek concept of fate merely a necessity of nature, another the punishing justice of the world, a third a force acting in hostile terms" ("Briefe literarischen und artistischen Inhaltes," XIV, 15).[28] In his reading, the key to drama is its origin in a reading of facts that are *understood* by the characters as representing "fate." But in Aristotle's original context, "fate" meant something completely different:

And thus it is also that the Greeks called fate the unknown quantity (= x), which lies at the base of the appearances of the moral world, whose cause remains hidden to our understanding, whether or not we immediately become aware of its effects. The whole concept was simply an outflow of that striving, inborn in the human spirit, to find a ground for that which is grounded, the striving to establish causal connections among the appearances of the moral world. ("Briefe literarischen und artistischen Inhaltes," 16)[29]

Fate thus is redefined as a human process of cognition, will, and decision based facts framed by history and derived from experience.

---

27 "Das Schicksal ist nichts als eine Vorhersehung ohne Vorsicht, eine *passive* Vorsehung möchte ich sie nennen, entgegengesetzt der aktiven, die, als die Naturgesetze zu Gunsten des Freiheitsgesetzes modifizierend, gedacht wird."

28 "Der Eine findet in dem Fatum der Griechen bloß eine Naturnotwendigkeit, ein zweiter die strafende Weltgerechtigkeit, ein dritter eine feindselig einwirkende Macht."

29 "Und so ist es auch, die Griechen nannten Schicksal die unbekannte Größe = x, die den Erscheinungen der moralischen Welt zu Grunde liegt, deren Ursache unserm Verstande verborgen bleibt, ob wir gleich ihre Wirkungen gewahr werden. Der ganze Begriff war lediglich ein Ausfluß des dem menschlichen Geiste angebornen Strebens dem Begründeten einen Grund aufzufinden, des Strebens, ein Kausalitätsband unter den Erscheinungen der moralischen Welt herzustellen."

Since "fate" is thus actually defined by humans, it will take a different form in each era, even while the abstract concept will persist essentially forever, "bis ans Ende der Welt" (XIV, 17). The Christians of his era will call that unknown quantity God, thereby quieting their curiosity. The drama starts its conversation with its audience by *enacting* the consequences of decisions within a particular world and its prevailing conventions *of morality*, not just logic—it appeals both affectively and logically by requiring acts of judgment based on the audience members' personal experience, not just on norms.

Taking the drama as an act of representation helps Grillparzer open up differences between various stage genres, in terms of both their innate logics of representation and how typical conflicts are structured around character types. For example, the *Trauerspiel* (a modern germanophone form of the traditional *tragedy*) plays off freedom and necessity in its representational logic, to show a figure's individual choice and its consequences. That logic of choice, in turn, differentiates the *Trauerspiel* from the classical tragedy, in which endings are typically more drastic and affectively negative than the former's "lifting of spirit because of the victory of freedom" ("Über das Wesen der Drama," XIV, 31).[30]

Familiarly, Aristotle defined the tragedy as evoking "fear and pity" in the audience. Grillparzer adds a more modern restatement of that goal, stressing that it moves the audience to more than affective responses. He believes that the tragedy aims at moving the audience to reflect on the human condition, on the necessity

> that humans recognize the nullity of the earthly; see the dangers to which the best are subjected and to which they often succumb; that, while steadfastly protecting the right and true for themselves, they regret the errors of their fellow men, never ceasing to love those who fall, even as they punish them, because every disturbance of eternal law must be annihilated. Love of mankind, patience, self-recognition, *purification of the passions through pity and fear*, will be effected by such a tragedy. The drama will continue to play itself out in the inside of people after the curtain falls, and the apotheosis of the law that Schlegel claims to see crudely visible on the boards and in the tatters of the stage will be directed resplendently onto the quietly

---

30 "Die Erhebung des Geistes, die aus dem Siege der Freiheit entspringen soll, hat durchaus nichts mit dem Wesen des *Tragischen* gemein, und schließt nebstdem das Trauerspiel scharf ab, ohnes jenes weitere Fortspielen im Gemüte des Zuschauers zu begünstigen, das eben die eigentliche Wirkung der wahren Tragödie ausmacht."

vibrating circles of the agitated spirit. ("Über das Wesen der Drama," XIV, 31–2)[31]

Critical is the fact that *das Rechte*, the right or just thing that plays itself out in the tragedy, derives from the audience's sense of logic and moral logic used to negotiate an understanding of a situation; it is not an issue of absolute or transcendental values or justice. When an audience engages with a situation represented in a tragedy, it will explore the purported inexorability of fate in the sense it understands that term. Yet in the modern version of that genre, the audience will find there not a straight-line logic of cause and effect between fate, failure, and punishment, but a complicated nexus of partial causes and decisions. Thus Grillparzer defines tragedy as exploring the logic of the world known to the audience, at moments when a character becomes entwined with greater forces from outside his own sphere.[32]

Here, Grillparzer's evaluations of Weimar Classicism emerge as a charge that Goethe and Schiller essentially avoid history in order to embrace abstracts. Schiller's historical tragedies show individual kings and queens making history by choosing and fulfilling their destinies; Grillparzer argues more modestly and consistently that an individual's choice interacts with history on a larger scale, beyond what

---

31 "daß der Mensch das Nichtige des Irdischen erkennt; die Gefahren sieht, welchen der Beste ausgesetzt ist und oft unterliegt; daß er, für sich selbst fest das Rechte und Wahre hütend, den strauchelnden Mitmenschen bedaure, den fallenden nicht aufhöre zu lieben, wenn er ihn gleich straft, weil jede Störung vernichtet werden muß des ewigen Rechts. Menschliebe, Duldsamkeit, Selbsterkenntnis, *Reinigung der Leidenschaften durch Mitleid und Furcht* wird eine solche Tragödie bewirken. Das Stück wird nach dem Fallen des Vorhangs fortspielen im Innern des Menschen und die Verherrlichung des Rechts, die Schlegel in derber Anschaulichkeit auf den Brettern und in den Lumpen der Bühne sehen will, wird glänzend sich herablenken auf die stillzitternden Kreise des aufgeregten Gemüts."

32 Present critics also see that this implies a unique performance style, as well. For instance, Urs Helmensdorfer comments on how an actor is engaged in delivering Grillparzer's verse ("Die Kunst, G. zu sprechen"):

Grillparzer sprechen heißt: Grillparzer spielen, seine Figuren sein. Seine Buchstaben sind nur ein Teil des Mediums, in dem der Dichter gestaltet. Die Mündlichkeit der Rede, das Werden der Gedanken, das Geben und Zurücknehmen der Worte, die Pausen im Fluß der Rede, die Durchlässigkeit der Worte für andere Mittel des Ausdrucks -- all dies unterscheidet Grillparzers szenische Dichtungen von dem Gedicht, das zwar vorgetragen werden kann (mit mehr oder weniger Gewinn), das aber schon gelesen alles ist, was es sein kann.

Die Szene ist für Grillparzer nicht das Schafott der Dichtung, sondern ihre Voraussetzung. ... Er schreibt nicht *für* die Darsteller, ... er gestaltet *mit* ihnen. (151)

an individual might be able to recognize as the truth of a particular situation. Thus the tragic stage represents a world of choices made or denied, brought forth for the audience to read and evaluate as a choice conditioned by the conventions of a particular historical time and place—by what we are taught to understand by history, philosophy, and religion:

> With this foreknowledge and feelings, step before our stage and you will understand what we want. *True acts of representation have no didactic purpose,* Goethe says somewhere, and the artists among you will salute him for that. The theater is no house of correction for rogues and no primary school for the immature. ("Über das Wesen der Drama," XIV, 32)[33]

Grillparzer's emphasis here is on the tragedy as an act of *Darstellung*, a representation of the larger whole in which a physically present reality exists.[34] Grillparzer sees the tragic playwright as addressing immature members of the audience, exhorting them to test their most favored truths (such as religion and philosophy) against the tragic hero's choices and against the assumptions of the world represented.

Grillparzer rewrites other elements from traditional Aristotelian aesthetics just as aggressively as he has fate, in two "Briefe literarischen und artistischen Inhaltes" (XIV, 11). The Greek chorus, for example, is not necessarily religious in any modern sense of the term; it took the form it did simply because of the era's overriding religiosity, a social value transformed into a formal aesthetic requirement, which might differ in other contexts.[35] In general, then, tragedy is best defined not as a specific form, but rather as a conversation about fate engaged within a particular historical context, appealing to the emotions and the human understanding of its audience:

---

33 "Mit diesen Vorkenntnissen und Gefühlen tretet vor unsere Bühne und ihr werdet verstehen was wir wollen. *Die wahre Darstellung hat keinen Didaktischen Zweck,* sagt irgendwo Göthe, und wer ein Künstler ist wird ihm beifallen. Das Theater ist kein Korrekzionshaus für Spitzbuben und keine Trivialschule für Unmündige."

34 In the "Brief üben den Dilettantismus" (1826), he summarizes: "Jede Kunst liegt in der vollkommenen *Darstellung* der mehr oder weniger vollkommenen Idee; und dies zwar so sehr, daß nur darin ihr charakterisctischer Unterschied von der Wissenschaft zu suchen ist" (XIV, 42).

35 "[D]er Chor war da ehe eine Tragödie war und keinem der Dichter aus der ältern Zeit stand es frei, sich seiner zu bedienen oder nicht. Er war ein festbestehender, von seinem Willen unabhängiger Teil seines Vorwurfs" ("Briefe literarischen und artistischen Inhaltes," XIV, 12).

The concept of fate is for us not the fruit of conviction, but rather one of dark foreboding. In all other kinds of poetry, the poet speaks, what he says is *his* opinion, and for that reason, a modern epic based on the idea of fate would be an absurdity. In drama, the characters who act will speak, and thus it lies within the poet's power to stage his characters, to direct the storm of their passions so that the idea of fate must arise in them. As a word is expressed, or the idea quickened, a bolt of lightning strikes at the soul of the observer. Everything that he has brooded about in painful hours, heard, presaged, and dreamed, becomes alive, the dark powers awake, and he plays along with the tragedy. ("Briefe literarischen und artistischen Inhaltes," XIV, 17)[36]

"Fate" was indeed the material of tragedy in the ancient world, and it remains so in the new. Yet if the older definition of fate is maintained in the present, the resulting drama will be a "machine," a mechanistic reappropriation of the ancients' sense and experience of religion that does not particularly speak for or to contemporaneous audiences.

The contemporary tragedy cannot be based on concepts from philosophy, history, religion, or the like, because, as abstracts, they would simply be functioning as "machines": "Religion in the pulpit, philosophy at the lectern, the human being with his comings and goings, errors and crimes on the stage" ("Briefe literarischen und artistischen Inhaltes," XIV, 19).[37] Each era's fate will reveal itself to its spectators through its particular mechanism, whether it be providence, psychological decision-making, religion, or chance. For Grillparzer's era, the tragedy's form represents a world with no single chain of causality; its content is the audience's immediate world of experience and the narratives that explain it. Each such narrative is by definition incomplete, and so the audience must fill the unaddressed dark spots in

---

36 "Der Begriff Schicksal ist bei uns nicht eine Frucht der Überzeugung, sondern der dunklen Ahnung. In allen andern Dichtungsarten spricht der Dichter selbst, was er sagt ist *seine* Meinung, und daher wäre ein auf die Idee des Fatums gegründetes neueres Epos ein Unding. Im Drama sprechen die handelnden Personen, und hier liegt es in der Macht des Dichters ihre Charaktere so zu stellen, den Sturm ihrer Leidenschaften so zu lenken, daß die Idee des Schicksals in ihnen entstehen muß. Wie das Wort ausgesprochen, oder die Idee rege gemacht worden ist, schlägt ein Blitz in die Seele des Zusehers. Alles was er hierüber in schmerzlichen Stunden ausgegrübelt, gehört, geahnt und geträumt, wird rege, die dunklen Mächte erwachen und er spielt die Tragödie mit."

37 "Religion auf die Kanzel, Philosophie auf den Katheder, der Mensch mit seinem Tun und Treiben, Freuden und Leiden, Irrtümern und Verbrechen auf die Bühne."

it, drawing on their own experience of the present (*Gegenwart*) ("Über den gegenwärtigen Zustand der dramatischen Kunst in Deutschland," XIV, 74).

Overall, Grillparzer redefines the tragedy (and the *Trauerspiel* as its variant form) to claim the theater as a public space that engages the audience to clarify what history and tradition have obscured—to engage in an active discussion confronting historical inheritance with the truth and experience of its current day. He thus also claims the theater as a public space in which a culture's master narratives are to be questioned—a political space.

The drama of politics: Stories in public spaces

Today's critics have been slow to acknowledge Grillparzer's politics, in no small part because they still prefer to conceive Grillparzer as a Habsburg apologist, opponent, or hagiographer who never chooses to *lead* his audience into revolutions against the historical misdeeds of ruling powers.[38] However, one might more properly stress how Grillparzer engages his audience in political critique by bringing them to reconsider Habsburg history in light of their own definitions of fate and morality, their experience of the present, and the traditional narratives that they still impose on the present. In this sense, Grillparzer's audiences can become actively politicized without having clearly determined political ideas imposed on them from the stage. Moreover, their politicization will be heavily intertwined with their own lived experience and with the narratives of history though which these experiences are read:

Whosoever wants to apply history correctly has to discriminate new conditions from the old core; they should not overlook new connections made with old constituent parts. That is not easy; a

---

38 Grillparzer's personal politics are never covert. In an essay on Metternich, he notes: "Man halt den Fürsten Metternich ziemlich allgemein für einen großen Staatamann. Ich war nie dieser Meinung" ("One fairly generally considers Prince Metternich for a great statesman. I was never of this opinion"; "Fürst Metternich," XIII, 164). His analysis of Metternich's position takes a larger view on the position of Austria in Europe, including facts like Turkey's importance to the economy ("Fürst Metternich," XIII, 168), a fact that Metternich ignores when he makes judgments about Greece. All in all, Metternich seems to be "led by women" ("Fürst Metternich," XIII, 174). Grillparzer is no more charitable about the Catholic church. In "Der Kirchenstaat" (1846), he recommends that the Church needs to move to Sicily to have its own place, outside of Rome, in order that there be a proper separation of church and state—"Scheidung der Obliegenheiten" (XIII, 193). He presumably would have welcomed the disappearance of the Papal States.

person who knows history need not necessarily be someone who understands the world. ("Preußische Konstitution," XIII, 183)[39]

History plays into all public discussions in this way. Even a document like the "Preußische Konstitution" (1844) should be understood as more than a representative of its genre. To grasp it, readers must approach the document in relation to the group's current experience and sense of history (XIII, 182).[40] Yet a caveat is in order: historical understanding may itself be deformed, especially by national sentiment. For instance, relying on German history as a guide may not be productive, because German history is neither well-written, nor well thought through. Grillparzer feels that the histories of other nations may offer better examples (XIII, 185).

Grillparzer is explicit that all historical narratives are fictions, based on politics seeking to create too-simple realities; his example is the Czech nationalism he discusses in "Professor Palacky" (1849). In Bohemia, as he tells the story, Czech patriots learned their nationalism "from German lecterns," allowing them to expound the unnatural pretense of an ethnic-national identity (XIII, 217). The historical and experiential reality of the Czech nation is more complex than such fictions would have it: the Czech lands evolved their own national culture in a place occupied by more than one ethnicity and more than one language.[41] A nation is defined by experience, not by language, and so a hereditarily bicultural region may evolve a culture based on two languages.

In "On Languages" ("Von den Sprachen," 1843), Grillparzer notes that nationalist political claims only compound such difficulties of understanding; his example is Hungarians' unnatural attempts to force the Slavs to learn Magyar, a language alien to their experience:

---

39 "Wer die Geschichte richtig anwenden will, muß aus den neuen Umständen den altern Kern heraus erkennen, und über die alten Bestandteilen die neue Zusammenfügung nicht übersehen. Das ist nicht leicht und ein Geschichtkenner ist deshalb noch kein Welterfahrner."

40 As an aside: he thinks it would be lovely if the Prussian king would grant his people a good constitution, since then the Austrians would get one in an attempt to keep up ("Preußische Konstitution," XIII, 181).

41 "Es sind jene eigentlichen Tschechen, verständig natürliche Menschen, die ihre Sprachen reden, weil sie eben ihre Muttersprache ist, aber auch nichts dagegen hätten, sich einer andern zu bedienen, wenn sie zufällig zehn Meilen weiter rechts oder links geboren wären. Sie wissen, daß die Sprache allerdings ein hohes Gut des Menschen ist, daß aber sein Wert in dem besteht, was er denkt und will, nicht in den Lauten, in denen er beides ausdrückt. Sie wissen, daß jajrhundertalte Verhältnisse sich nicht auf gutdeutsch durch ein läppischen Enthusiasmus über Nacht aufheben lassen, und daß Gleichberechhtigung nicht eine und dasselbe ist mit Gleichgeltung" ("Professor Palacky," XIII, 218).

"The Magyar language will never be to the country what Latin was" (XIII, 179).[42] Yet again, he refuses to define a national culture as either monolingual or hereditarily monoethnic. Both Czech and Hungarian cultures actually share a so-called German stratum in history because they were educated in German (XIII, 179–80). If such historical facts are denied, a culture and its texts will be misunderstood, and its political discussions further obscured by fictions (XIII, 179).

Chief among such fictions is nationalism, which Grillparzer considers at best a fashion (*Mode der Nazionalitäten*), at worst a contagious "childhood illness" that nations need to recover from (*Kinderkrankheit*; XIII, 180). When Grillparzer uses the term, he refers to a politics that equates a nation and its culture with an ethnic and monolingual state-form or governmental entity. The purportedly different nationalities warring for precedence in the Austrian Empire are actually related cultures, as they would realize if they would only come to their senses about their significant shared ground of experience:

> with changes of fashion, the now lampooned humanity may again reassume its earlier rights, and one will see that the best that the human being can be is being a human being, whether he wears an *Attila* and speaks Hungarian, or goes around in an English morning coat and French hat, despite his German language. ("Von den Sprachen," XIII, 180)[43]

Eighteenth-century intellectuals like Johann Gottfried Herder had defined a culture as a group sharing experience and history. Grillparzer stresses rather that culture is a shared set of *interpretations* of that shared experience. Any such narrative of experience, even an official history, must be interrogated, because it will always suppress alternatives.[44]

Grillparzer makes this point more gently in the form of parody, and in more than one essay. "News from Our Correspondent in the Land of the Iroquois" ("Korrespondenznachrichten aus dem Lande der Irokesen" [1820]) parodies texts that trumpet "true national sensibility, true popular education, true life of the fatherland" (XIII,

---

42 "Die magyarische Sprache wird dem Lande nie das werden, was die lateinische war."

43 "mit Umschlag der Mode wird die jetzt verspottete Humanität wieder in ihre frühern Rechte treten und man wird einsehen, daß das Beste was der Mensch sein kann, eben ist, ein Mensch zu sein, ob er nun einen Attila trägt und ungarisch spricht, oder trotz seiner deutschen Sprache in einem englischen Frack und französischen Hut einhergeht."

44 Lorenz points out that Grillparzer writes "Werke mit übernationaler Thematik … die essentialistische Kategorien wie Volk, Nation, Geschlecht und Rasse in Frage stellten" (41).

90).[45] This parody of travel literature shows how politics flattens out understanding through the use of too-simple narratives that foreclose alternate interpretations of past events. In the "Quandaries of a State Servant at the Death of His Land's Prince" ("Verlegenheiten eines Staatsdieners beim Tode seines Landesfürsten," 1835), Grillparzer creates a very double-voiced text about political narratives. His bereft, subservient civil servant prays for a new spiritual guide to replace his dead master as he reveals his dependence on various narratives that intertwine spiritual and secular authority (XIII, 115–18).

Contemporary critics have taken up Grillparzer's approach to historical truth as plural and somewhat nonpolitical by referring to his "nemetic concept of history" (*nemetische Geschichtsauffassung*), a term drawn from Herodotus to define history as an ethical narrative (Bachmaier, 89). Instead of revealing truth or recording memories, a history in this framing functions as a "form that builds tradition" (*Form der Traditionsblldung* [Bachmaier, 90]). Such a narrative form, in turn, will condition the free will and arbitrary judgments (*Willkür*) of individuals adhering to it, interpolating them into a community (Bachmaier, 91). History orients an era's principal "collective subjects" to the preferred meanings of its past and present (as *Kollektivsubjekte* [Bachmaier, 92]). These subjects are *not* absolutely determined to share a single interpretation of historical facts, but the master narratives they live with gives them reference points as options facilitating communication within their community.

Grillparzer would add that such narratives might even need to be censored. As he notes in "Über die Aufhebung der Zensur" (1844): "Should there thus be censorship?—Yes, if it is good. But since good censorship is not possible, bad censorship more damaging than none, then rather *no* censorship; but only for that *reason*" (XIII, 187).[46] Censorship might, in theory, facilitate Enlightenment if it helped individuals and groups to reject the "false and base" (*falsche und schlechte* [XIII, 188]), while propagating the good.[47] Good censorship would remind the group about its best assumptions and practices, to

---

45   "[Ä]cht nazionaller Sinn, ächt volkstümliche Bildung, ächt vaterländisches Leben."

46   "Es soll also eine Censur bestehen?—Ja eine *gute. Da aber eine gute Censur nicht möglich ist*; eine schlechte aber verderblicher als keine, darum *keine*; aber nur *darum*."

47   "Nicht bloß in literarischen, in vielen andern Dingen wird die persönlichte Freiheit im Wege der Prävenzion zum Wohl Aller und mit allgemeiner Billigung beschränkt. Das Tragen heimlicher Waffen, an sich unverfänglich, ist untersagt. Der Verkauf vieler Stoffe, Künsten und Gewerben unentbehrlich, aber in verkehrter Anwendung dem Menschenleben als Gift verderblich, findet sich heilsamen Einschränkungen unterworfen" (XIII, 189).

further a group's *self-censorship*. As he points out in "Aufrufe aus der Revoluzionszeit" (1848), however, the group usually exerts its own self-censorship because it has appropriate narratives to guide it: "by happy instinct discover[ing] the right by itself, everywhere" (XIII, 201).[48]

Thus Grillparzer's public space is more than just political space; it is also a space for an individual's choice of moral action with respect to the group and practical responsibilities. Walter Seitter notes that moral action rests on a group's shared, but not necessarily uniform, ethical-historical narrative, which exerts an ethical pull on its subjects as they judge their experiences (*Werthorizont* [Seitter, 47]). What Hans Höller calls "history in the I" (*Geschichte im Ich* [59]) consists of narratives that represent issues like war, history, and kingship in forms that help individuals understand new experience and extend old understandings in ways accessible to the group.

This is Grillparzer's definition of national politics: a critical re-experiencing and reevaluating of traditional narratives about history, morality, and the "truth" of experience. That politics lives outside a government or law code, in a space of public discussion sustaining and renewing the different interest groups participating in it.

Culture beyond the nation-state

Joseph von Sonnenfels' battles against "German" culture have clearly found their echo in Grillparzer's widely scattered theoretical contributions about art, the nation, and the theater as a necessary medium for educating new national classes. The politics of governments in the nation-states of Europe remain abstract and far removed from the average citizen if there is no medium making those politics real to them. In consequence, both agree that the health of the nation depends on its theater because that institution can stage discussions about what we call today the master narratives of a state—the various narratives recording a people's evolving experiences and concerns, which need constant revaluation for relevance to existing circumstances.

As we have seen, Sonnenfels described the space for such public discussion in his paper dialogue with Lessing. A generation later, Grillparzer was even more explicit about the dangers of an emergent German national culture claiming leadership on the basis of narratives about its *raison d'état*, unmatchable past, and utopian futures. Together, these two early canonical voices in Austrian culture claim the authority of public space for the drama and define it as a profoundly moral space of public discussion, a place for collective critique and

---

48 "[W]as soll man einem Volke sagen, das durch einen glücklichen Instinkt überall das Rechte selbst herausfindet!"

decision-making. A nation's culture is an abstract; it acquires its real existence in its people's actions and judgments, preserved (often tendentiously) in its master narratives.

A civil servant like Sonnenfels, Grillparzer knew what was at stake in positing a national culture as a shared space of experience rendered comprehensible by its narratives, especially when it becomes the ground of a state's political identity. Both agreed that the artist (playwright) should be responsible for making visible the consequences of action within the collective, using the stage as a mass medium fostering discussion about how inherited narratives condition present moral choice and practical action. Moreover, both understood that a national elite could stand outside that national culture or choose to reify it, to the detriment of that culture's ability to innovate. The playwright would find the tools to accomplish that mission within Europe, in Europe's various stage genres, from plays based on myth and fairy tales, through comedies and tragedies. Each form instantiates *different conversations* with the audience, brings different facts onto the stage, and calls for different acts of judging. Sonnenfels would have recognized Grillparzer's *Burgtheater* as a literate European stage, bringing narratives about the Habsburg state to its audiences for their evaluation.

Both these Viennese intellectuals felt that Germany's contemporaneous artist-critics were trying to force a new national culture into existence, in a context not rich enough to bring one forth naturally. The artists of Classicism and Romanticism demonstrated a willful self-imposed blindness about the relation between a culture and its art and eagerly accepted abstract theoretical falsifications like "the phantom of folk poetry" to define national culture ("das Phantom der Volkspoesie" ["Zur Literaturgeschichte [Erste Fassung]," XIV, 143]):

All of a sudden one discovered that the German nation was ur-poetic, even though the poems that were found (with the exception of the enigmatic *Nibelungenlied*) bore the traces of their foreign origin clearly and openly on their brows. One postulated antediluvian, mastodon-ichthyosauric folk epics, or at least fragments of them, that were merely compiled by a middle-high-German pedant who thus brought forth the extraordinary by mechanical means. The folksongs that were made by no-one were blamed on the unformed masses, and from then on one needed only the people and a couple of pedants to render any poetic gifts superfluous. ("Zur Literaturgeschichte [Zweite Fassung]," 165)[49]

---

49 "Es fand sich auf einmal, daß die deutsche Nation eine urpoetische sei, obgleich die aufgefundene Gedichte, mit Ausnahme des rätselhaften Nibelungeliedes, den fremden Ursprung eingeständlich und offen an der Stirn trugen. Man

Weimar Classicism, particularly Goethe, had produced some great art, but its aesthetic theories ultimately led to Romanticism's disastrous abstractions. The result was dire, for the cause of a germanophone literature was dire: "and thus we have only failed masterworks, instead of enjoyable art products" ("Über Genialität," XIV, 146).[50]

Their national–determinist art criticism and history purveyed negative, abstract judgments about what is purportedly "natural" to the nation, and so they have, in Grillparzer's estimation, destroyed any hopes for a germanophone national culture, which they sacrificed to the cause of an artificial national elite: "the whole formation of the German nation in the last 20 years was a false one" ("die ganze Bildung der deutschen Nazion in den letzten zwanzig Jahren war eine falsche" ["Zur Literaturgeschichte [Erste Fassung]," XIV, 136]). The "foreign" became anathema to that "elite," a limitation that cost the stage dearly by robbing it of options for initiating public critique.

From the point of view of today's literary history, Grillparzer lost his battle to discredit Weimar Classicism and Romanticism and define dramatic literature as part of critical public discussion rather than in relation to genius and national elites. He became perhaps the last germanophone dramatist resisting the narrower nationalist and bourgeois tastes dominating the latter nineteenth century in Europe. Until his end, he advocated for a broader integration between authors and audiences and rejected the explicitly nationalist stages descended from Weimar Classicism or Europe's Romantic movements. They had indeed banished Hanswurst, purportedly for reasons of taste but actually to support state interests represented in history tragedies and morality fables. Europe's repertoire of dramatic genres had gotten

----

postulierte antediluvianische, mastodontisch-ichthyosaurische Volksepen, oder doch Fragmente derselben, die nur ein mittelhochdeutscher Pedant zusammengesetzt und so das Außerordentliche auf mechanischem Wege hervorgebracht hatte. Die Volkslieder, die niemand gemacht hatte, wurden der rohen Masse in die Schuhe geschoben und man bedurfte von nun an nur das Volk und ein paar Pedanten um jede poetische Begabung überflüssig zu machen."

50   "und so haben wir denn lauter verunglückte Meisterwerke, statt genießbaren Kunstprodukten." His own era is in a difficult situation, under pressure from this history-in-the-making, given that Goethe's era is still vividly present in memory: "Diese Glanzperioden haben nämlich für die nächste Zukunft etwas Gefährliches. Nazionen von Geschmack und gesundem Urteil sind von der Vortrefflichkeit des Vorhergegangenen so durchdrungen, daß sie in der genauen Nachahmung das einzige Heil sehen und so allgemach in leeren Formalismus geraten; indes Völker, denen jene Eigenschaften im mindern Grade eigen sind, meinen das Vortreffliche zu haben, das sie nur besitzen, und sich gedrungen fühlen darüber hinauszugehen" ("Zur Literaturgeschichte [Zweite Fassung]," XIV, 161).

poorer and less willing to engage its public as mature and capable of critique.

By 1848, Grillparzer expressed the opinion that the audience for drama had actually been better twenty years previously: "We had in Vienna, fifteen or twenty years ago, an admirable public. Without excessive education, but gifted with practical understanding, proper sensibility, and sensitive imagination, it gave itself over to impressions without reservation" ("Über das Hofburgtheater," XIV, 122).[51] That "practical understanding" included awareness of both genre conventions and history on a European stage, and the willingness to take in new experiences and subject them to fresh analysis or critique.

Over the course of the nineteenth century, we know today, the Viennese *Burgtheater* did gradually become the kind of theater intended to build or educate the national elite, as later proponents of national theaters throughout Europe would insist. But Grillparzer still conceived of that theater differently than Weimar had, as something more public and open to political literacy rather than nationalist cultural politics. As Sonnenfels also would have advocated, that theater should not seek to inculcate judgments of taste and morality purportedly reflecting "eternal values"; it ought to educate the public about how to ask new questions, rethink traditional narratives, and engage with their present experience—to act as politically mature agents of culture. Just as importantly, that theater needed to use theater genres from across Europe to accept that challenge, so that its potential as a medium creating public space and opinion would not be restricted by the limitations of a particular nation-state.

Grillparzer was disappointed with the Viennese stage by the middle of the nineteenth century, but that stage had not become as narrow as he had feared. Vienna remained home to a deep vein of European comedy that cultivated a social critical optic. Grillparzer shared with what has come to be known as the *Wiener Volkstheater*, the Viennese Popular (Folk) Theater, an interest in the critical evolution of a theater public. Despite Grillparzer's pessimism, Austrian authors, especially its comic playwrights, continued to claim a space for a national culture not controlled by a national elite. This theater cultivated an ability to mix what later would be called high and popular culture so that it could remain relevant to an audience of mixed class origin and varied political leanings. Grillparzer argued that the theater could sponsor

---

51 "Wir hatten in Wien vor fünfzehn oder zwanzig Jahren ein vortreffliches Publikum. Ohne übermäßige Bildung, aber mit praktischem Verstande, richtiger Empfindung und einer erregbaren Einbildungskraft begabt, gab es sich dem Eindrucke unbefangen hin."

public discussions with political edge; the plays addressed in the next chapter exemplify how a Viennese theater audience could still find a public space for critical commentary on the master narratives of their lives—in comedy.

Three   Revolution from the Prompter's
         Box: Rewriting Public Dreams
         of Political Morality

The space for public critique that Sonnenfels described as part of
his dialogue with Lessing included models from European cultures;
Grillparzer claimed the theater as a force for critical public discussion.
Since their eras, the Viennese stage fulfilled their expectations by
cultivating a distinctive theater genre that still retains its place
within the city's public culture. The classical Viennese *Volkstheater*
(popular theater), a descendent of the *commedia dell'arte*,[1] continued
to represent the European tradition of comic theater banished from
"legitimate" germanophone theaters in favor of "well-regulated"
theatrical texts. Literary historians pursuing germanophone culture
from the German point of view assume that the Hanswurst debate
was settled in the eighteenth century in favor of the drama genres
preferred by Goethe and Schiller, but Hanswurst's banishment was
by no means absolute, particularly not in Vienna, where such
purportedly low comedy existed alongside serious drama, even at
the *Burgtheater*.[2]

---

1   A first attempt with this material was initially presented under the title
    "Revolution from the Prompter's Box: Grillparzer and Nestroy in Vienna" at a
    session sponsored by the *Grillparzer Gesellschaft* at the annual convention of the
    Modern Language Association, San Francisco, CA, December 29, 1998.
2   The scholarship on the Viennese theater is heavily dependent on the work by
    Otto Rommel (1880–1965), who established the canon for the genre in a series
    of 48 volumes under the title of *Österreichischen Klassikerbibliothek* (1908–14), and
    his standard history of the theater, *Die Alt-Wiener Volkskomödie: Ihre Geschichte
    vom barocken Welt-Theater bis zum Tode Nestroys* (Vienna: Anton Schroll, 1952),
    as well as working with other editions and biographies after the Second World
    War (most notably, the first Raimund and Nestroy editions). He was, however,
    at great pains to sever the history of that theater from European traditions,
    making it something original to Austria.

German theater history has been made poorer by critics' insistence on isolating the *Volkstheater*—like many other performance-based traditions—from Europe's contemporaneous theater context, and from the unique public space it offered its audiences. The Viennese *Volkstheater* comes from the great European comic and music-theater traditions, familiar today from Shakespeare's comedies, the Italian *commedia dell'arte*, Italian comedy in the hands of renowned authors like Goldoni, English comedy, and the court-centered French comedy of Marivaux, as well as from later forms like vaudeville, melodrama, and music theater down through the operetta and the opera of the World War I era.[3] It finds a parallel in puppet theater (from Punch and Judy on), and in the work of twentieth-century playwrights across the continent, such as Pirandello and Tom Stoppard.

From the German Classicist point of view combated by Grillparzer, Hanswurst had to be banned from the theater, since he violated

---

3   That the roots of the Viennese theater reach back to other European traditions is noted by the secondary literature on the *Volkstheater*, but, probably still following Rommel, that connection is considered genealogical, and so is rarely brought to bear on interpretations of contemporaneous performance and textual practices.

For general introductions to the Viennese theater (including its later incarnations) and to Nestroy, see: Peter Cersowsky, *Johann Nestroy, oder Nix als philosophische Mussenzen* (1992); chapter 1 (69–89) is on *Der Talisman*; Thomas Schmitz, *Das Volksstück* (1990), an overview of the genre in general terms, including music theater, as late as Brecht; Gerd Müller, *Das Volksstück von Raimund bis Kroetz* (which favors the twentieth century, although it does include Raimund, 1979); and Herbert Herzmann. *Tradition und Subversion: Das Volksstück und das epische Theater* (1997).

Jürgen Hein's *Johann Nestroy* (1990) is typical in underplaying the degree to which the *Volkstheater* worked in the European tradition, even as he documents Nestroy's roles (27ff.) and genre distinctions (63). Hein prefers play-writing traditions to performance ones: "Als ein Problem, stellt sich die Notwendigkeit, zwischen dem Schauspieler und dem Dramatiker zu unterscheiden, ohne entwicklungsgeschichtliche Momente aus den Augen zu verlieren" (9).

Acknowledgment of the *Volkstheater*'s Italian connections can be found in: Wolfgang Proß, "Das Konzept des Populären in Italien und sein Einfluß auf das deutschsprachige Theater des 18. Jahrhunderts"; and the connection to French vaudevilles is in Jeanine Charue-Ferrucci, "Du Roman populaire au 'Volksstück': L'adaptation par Nestroy de la louvelle de Michel Raymond: 'Le grain de sable.'"

In a similar vein, Roger Bauer, in "'Volkstheater' et 'Nationaltheater'," juxtaposes these theaters with older court theaters. The contemporaneous Viennese response to the genre is found in the work of Joseph von Sonnenfels, discussed in Jean-Marie Valentin, "J. von Sonnenfels et le peuple." The genre persists into the twentieth century, as documented in Hugo Aust, Peter Haida, and Jürgen Hein, *Volksstück*, which offers a comprehensive account of the forms, including a discussion of Lessing versus the Hanswurst character (61ff.) and how authors like Marivaux were translated into German (63).

tragedians' ideal of a well-regulated stage where the text author's intent reigned supreme as the ideal of civic education. Gottsched, Lessing, Goethe, and Schiller dismissed such extemporizing or improvisational theaters as inferior to theaters offering plays with "fixed texts." Yet the Hanswurst character and his descendants persisted under multiple names in Vienna to engage audiences in discussions about new class positions, particularly those of city dwellers or of the emergent bourgeoisie, groups seeking self-images as classes at pains to define their rights and privileges over and against the traditional aristocracy. To many scholars' eyes today, however, such critique seems less than revolutionary, since we are accustomed to defining social-critical positions in more radically Hegelian-revolutionary terms, as an antithesis emerges to counter the thesis of hegemonies needing reform.

From this perspective, the average *Volkstheater* play appears to German critics as part of a quiescent Viennese *Vormärz*, the "Pre-March" era leading up to Europe's bourgeois revolutions of 1848, or of Austria's pre-revolutionary *Standesstaat*, the Empire's corporate state. This era is delimited by the political repression of Prince Metternich, his censorship of the public media, and growing public discontent in that nervous political window between the 1789 and 1830 revolutions in France and the European Revolutions of 1848. Traditional critics stress how little open political discussion seems to be present in this theater. In their eyes, the average Viennese comedy will affirm true love over money, "the way things are done" over innovation, and staying within one's own class rather than pretending to be what one is not. At best, this theater explores limits to bourgeois commercialism and to abuses of power associated with money or position.

Such literary critics ignore the fact that, in the original context, Hanswurst and his theater performed dramas of public life with clear claims to being political. The improvising "Italian Comedians" who are his precursors had been banished from Europe's theaters long before the German theater had done so. In 1697, for instance, they had been ejected by Louis XIV from the French court because the King suspected them of lampooning his morganatic wife, Madame de Maintenon—a very public gesture, immortalized in a (now lost) painting by Watteau. Such comedy *engagée* often took up such public issues in nuanced ways, appealing through humor to its audience's critical intelligence, common sense, and fairness. In other words, from the first this theater tradition spanned classes and challenged class-bound interests, without recourse to open revolution.

After introducing the European traditions from which the *Volkstheater* springs, the present discussion will turn to one of the first Austrian masters of the genre, Adolf Bäuerle (1768–1859), whose 1817 play *Die Bürger in Wien* (*Citizens in Vienna*) exemplified social critique in the era of the Congress of Vienna. The genre finds a kind of apotheosis in mid-century in two extraordinary plays, two comedies of marriage and social-climbing: Franz Grillparzer's only comedy (*Lustspiel*), the 1838 *Weh dem, der lügt (Woe to Liars)*, and Johann Nestroy's 1840 *Der Talisman*. Each adapts source material from beyond the borders of the Habsburg Empire to critique the *mores* and social structures of the Vienna they know. Based on a French farce, *Talisman* tells the story of the red-haired Titus Feuerfuchs, who can make a career only when he gets a wig to cover up that socially objectionable hair; he renounces the chance at a marriage in a higher class when he tires of the deception. *Woe to Liars* expanded an anecdote from Gregory of Tours' *History of the Franks* to follow how Leon, a scullery lad, rescues s bishop's nephew from captivity, with the help of a heathen countess whom he is ultimately to marry, after crossing class lines. These three plays will stand for a longer tradition of European comedy used for public critique of the ruling classes. Despite the assertions of German critics, these plays offer visions of what a changed social hierarchy might mean if a change in society were brought about, preferably through evolutionary changes in consciousness rather than through political revolution *per se*.

Grillparzer's *Burgtheater* play in this genre, a Shakespearean comedy in iambic verse, has gone down in theatrical history as the flop that caused him to withdraw from the stage when his upper-class audience felt compelled to hiss it off "their" stage. In contrast, Nestroy's play is remembered as his greatest success, with its musical interludes calculated to appeal to the taste of the less elite audiences of the suburban *Volkstheater* beyond the Vienna city walls. In consequence, *Talisman* has not been considered serious playwriting, given its first performance venue in the suburban theaters that offered vaudevilles instead of tragedies.[4]

Such plays amplify what was at stake in the theater space described by Sonnenfels and Grillparzer, as previous chapters have argued. From a European perspective, both plays emerge as lineal descendants of famous works such as Beaumarchais's *Barber of Seville*, plays in which clever servants show up the weaknesses of their nominal betters, and their dramaturgy can be trace back as far as the Roman comedy. These drama genres framed effective political and social critiques in the hands of playwrights who understood how they could be used to respond to or even circumvent censorship.[5] This theater, far from representing the

---

4   James Van Horn Melton argues that there is a dialectic between the upper- and lower-class public spheres in these theater texts; see "Von Versinnlichung zur Verinnerlichung."

5   Here I am trying to recoup a sense of the concerns shared by the audiences of Vienna, no matter what class. While lively scholarship on the Viennese

aristocratic legitimacy of the Baroque theater or reflecting Biedermeier passivity, not only used humor and double entendres to circumvent censorship, but also taught its audience a revolutionary view of society: it did not redraw class boundaries, but rather saw in them a system of checks and balances against abuses in official power structures. The goal of the present discussion, then, is to show what kinds of politics could be accomplished in the public space of the Viennese theater, what resources the *Volkstheater* provided to playwrights and audiences, and what kinds of critique it may have fostered.

An eighteenth-century comedy tradition

The *commedia dell'arte* is the European comic theater form most familiar today, not the least because its stock characters are memorialized in the innovative and familiar porcelain masterpieces by artists like Johann Joachim Kändler (1706–73) for Meissen, a reflection of its popularity in seventeenth- and eighteenth-century Europe.[6] The *commedia dell'arte* was first and foremost a performing tradition in which actor-singer-dancers embodied stock characters including Pantalone, Harlequin, Columbine, Punchinello, and others in a repertoire of scenarios that were to be adapted into local contexts by improvisation.

By the 1750s, however, that performing tradition came under pressure from public censors, requiring the performers to turn into playwrights, or to find suitable text materials elsewhere. The Italian

folk theater of the *Vormärz* has appeared since the Second World War under the leadership of early scholars like Rommel and later experts like W. E. Yates, the folk theater is often still dismissed as serious literature, since it descends from older, less aesthetically credible dramatic genres (especially the *Zauberposse* [magical farce] or the spectacle-driven Baroque theater, the most famous late example of which is Mozart's/Schickenader's *Magic Flute*). Yet, at the time, the dramatists of this theater defined themselves as playwrights who used a different voice than did their colleagues at the *Burgtheater*. For a succinct introduction to the history of the *Volkstheater*, see Hilde Haider-Pregler, "Entwicklungen im Wiener Theater zur Zeit Maria Theresias," and Herbert Zeman, "Die alt-Wiener Volkskömodie des 18. und frühen 19. Jahrhunderts."

Outside the German literary canon, Viennese folk theater has found lasting resonance: plays by Johann Nestroy, arguably the most eminent of Viennese folk theater authors, have been adapted by Thornton Wilder (*The Matchmaker*, readapted as *Hello, Dolly!*) and Tom Stoppard (*On the Razzle*); the dramaturgy of this theater prefigures that of Brecht in *Threepenny Opera* (parallels noted, but little pursued, despite Brecht's early experience in Bavaria).

6   For an overview of the *commedia dell'arte*, see Allardyce Nicoll, *The World of Harlequin* (1963). Bauer, in "'Volkstheater' et 'Nationaltheater'," sets the *Volkstheater* next to Gozzi, other Italians, and French comedians, noting, for example, Lessing's comparison of the Neuberin plays with those of Marivaux (p. 21 n. 7). For a comprehensive discussion of the porcelain *commedia dell'arte* figures, see Meredith Chilton, *Harlequin Unmasked* (2001).

incarnation of these plays, written by masters like Carlo Goldoni (1707–93), was often played on street-scene sets resembling local public spaces; they were peopled by Hanswursts who appeared under local names (sometimes derived from the actors who played them). Their French and English relatives were often encountered as court- or society-associated settings, in the hands of playwrights like Marivaux, Beaumarchais (*Figaro*), or Sheridan. The sets on which these pieces were played were designed to help evoke the "natural" milieus of the players—in Italy, a street scene; for Marivaux and Sheridan, the unnamed room in a great house. In France, he was *Punchinello*; in England, his original stage brother, Punch, took center stage first as an everyman and later as a puppet: "he makes his entries not in one set role or position but in dozens. His commonest business is that of a servant, but he is also at times a peasant, a baker, a slave-merchant, an innkeeper, a painter, even the head of a household and a lover" (Nicoll, 87). In all variants, these stages told stories of clever servants besting abusive "betters" in order to enforce social justice. These were theaters of quick wit and quicker feet and voices, actors' collusion with the audience, and "happy endings" achieved with clear rebukes to those who would let *mores* and fashion triumph over true sentiment and social justice.

This seventeenth- and eighteenth-century comic theater was intentionally a vehicle for pointed social criticism of the public community. As Goldoni himself wrote in the preface to the first collection of his comedies (1750), very much in the tradition of Calderón:

> The two books on which I pondered most, and of which I shall never repent having put to my use, were the World and the Theatre. The first offers to my view more and ever more human characters, paints them for me so naturally that they seem to be put there to provide me with endless themes for pleasing and instructive plays; it represents for me the outward signs, the power, the effects of all the human passions; it gives me strange episodes; it informs me about current habits; it instructs me concerning the vices and errors most common in our age and country—vices which deserve the disapproval or derision of wise men; and at the same time it points out for me in virtuous persons the means by which Virtue resists such corruptions. ... The second book, the book of the Theatre, as I practise it, tells me how I must present on the state the characters, the passions, the events which I have read about in the book of the World—how to shade their tones so as to give them greater relief, how to choose those tints which may render them pleasing to the tender eyes of the spectators. Above all, I learn from the Theatre to distinguish

what is more apt to make an impression on the sentiments, to arouse wonder or laughter or some such pleasing delight in the human heart, a delight which arises chiefly from discovering in the play errors and follies naturalistically depicted and put elegantly before the audience. (Cited in Nicoll, 205–6)

Goldoni draws here on the Baroque convention of the *theatrum mundi* to justify comedy as a vehicle for edification in a pre-revolutionary world. His version of the world-theater reflects contemporaneous assumptions about social estates and stations, representing how individuals understood themselves in fixed roles contributing to the whole. His characters are most often members of guilds, families, or powerful households rather than of social classes in the modern sense. Goldoni seeks to put on the stage parables of those "vices which deserve the disapproval or derision of wise men," to exercise a very specific social-moralizing function within the world of his spectators.

Virtually every European capital in the eighteenth century knew such theaters—so-called "Italian Theaters" (i.e., theaters for comedy, and music theaters). By the latter part of the eighteenth century, the tradition was evolving locally such as English pantomime and Punch and Judy puppet shows, the French comic opera, or even the story-ballets.[7] Goldoni gained his reputation by transforming the *commedia dell'arte* into a more realistic theater, first discarding the masks still worn by many actors (probably deriving from Carnival plays) and minimizing improvisation, and then writing down his texts. These changes naturally also signaled a shift in the genre's conventions, opposed by the likes of Count Carlo Gozzi (1720–1806, author of *Turandot* and *Love for Three Oranges*), who warned against Goldoni's realism. Such opposition may have reflected a natural resistance to growing urban incursions into a favored court form.

At its best, that theater's practice in the eighteenth century was anything but the coarse burlesque for which it was lampooned by Gottsched and other early germanophone advocates of state theaters. That such comedic actors improvised by no means meant that they were undisciplined or inferior. Each character stereotype that they brought to life on stage had its own costume style (or mask[8]),

---

7   The story ballet evolved under early masters like Jean-Georges Noverre (1727–1820) and Gaetano Vestris (1729–1806) in Paris, or as late as Auguste Bournonville (1805–79) in Denmark. Sonnenfels discussed Noverre in his *Letters* as part of Vienna's theater scene.

8   A series of paintings held at the Ringling Museum in Sarasota, Florida, documents these masks: "The Disguises of Harlequin," by Giovanni Domenico Ferretti (1692–1768).

movement patterns, and conventions for gesture and speech. Such
set pieces needed intensive rehearsal and talent in acting, dance, and
voice modulation. The result was a thoroughly stylized approach to
performance, in which improvisation was integrated into plots of
mathematical precision by actors well versed in rhetoric and able to
interact with their audiences and with the concerns of the day.

    When an author like Goldoni emphasized "realism," therefore, he
was not so much interested in producing replicas of a specific time and
place as he was in representing social stratification and the religious
or legal rights and duties that pertain to them. He represented not
abstract generalities, but the people one *might* meet on the typical street
corner and how their good and evil behaviors impact the whole of the
known world. As Nicoll summarized: "Goldoni was concerned with
bringing character, social criticism and moral purpose to the stage"
(205). This improvisational stage, transformed into an urban social–
political theater, became the Viennese folk comedy that came into
its own around 1800 in a newly emerging world city. Today's world
audiences know it best from opera plots, particularly from Mozart's
comedies featuring amorous swains, avaricious uncles, and debauched
counts who are ultimately brought to rights. The hero of the typical
Volkstheater play was named *Kasperl* or *Staberl*, or *Thaddädl*, an everyman
figure embodied by a particular actor for the length of his career.[9] He
is recorded in playbooks submitted to the censors of Metternich-era

9   For history of the Viennese *Volkstheater* in context, see W. E. Yates, *Theater in
    Vienna* (1996), Herbart Zeman, "Die alt-Wiener Volkskömodie" (1985), and the
    afterword in Johann Sonnleitner, ed., *J. A. Stranitzky* (1996); for the actors, see
    Reinhard Urbach, *Die Wiener Kömodie und ihr Publikum* (1973); for the context
    of the theater establishment, see W. E. Yates, Allyson Fiddler and John Warren,
    eds, *From Perinet to Jelinek* (2001), especially the "Introduction" (9–22), which
    acknowledges this theater's political content, expressed particularly in its use
    of dialect (10).

    Johann Hüttner, "Volkstheater als Geschäft" (1986), shows the limits of extant
    research, including a conspicuous gap in research on British theater (128–9).
    In a parallel vein, Peter Branscombe, "The Beginnings of Parody in Viennese
    Popular Theatre" (2001), focuses on terminological problems in describing
    genres and their growing appeal to urban audiences, especially in "an absence
    of barriers between the social classes, so that even poorer inhabitants are not
    automatically denied access to knowledge of the activities of the 'smarter'
    theatres" (23).

    Jürgen Hein, "Nestroy's 'Epic' Theater" (1998), argues that many different
    layers of the plays—especially songs, interpolated stories, gestures, and the
    like—still require study (91). For information on the theater repertoire, see
    Brigit Pargner, "Charlotte Birch-Pfeiffer und das kommerzielle Theater im Wien
    des 19. Jahrhunderts" (2001), and Johann Hüttner, "Der ernste Nestroy" (1998),
    on the *Theater an der Wien*. Hüttner also traces *Theater als Geschäft* in his 1982
    Viennese *Habilitationsschrift*.

Vienna by actors like Josef Felix Kurz-Bernadon, one of Vienna's most famous early *Kasperls* (the actor Kurz took the name of his character into his own), who entered into literary history as comic playwrights.

The internal history of the *Volkstheater* often points to Adolf Bäuerle (1768–1859) and his play *Die Bürger in Wien: Locale Posse in drey Acten* (*Citizens in Vienna: Local Farce in Three Acts*) as the first great example of the modern *Volkstheater*.[10] It premiered in the *Theater in der Leopoldstadt* on October 23, 1813, and was revived for the *Theater an der Wien* on July 15, 1817, starring Vienna's revivified Hanswurst: *Staberl*.[11] His life is colored by the Vienna of the era, noted for a new luxury trade spurred on by the assemblage of European *glitterati* who came with the Congress of Vienna. Staberl plays out the drama of social standing and money as it would have appeared as a particular problem for a new, aspiring, urban bourgeoisie, living off and with these outsiders, but in many ways struggling to redefine an identity alongside that of the traditional powers as their own finances and opportunities were improving after a European war.

Bäuerle revealed himself as a canny marketer as well as playwright. When he published the text, he asserted his role as author of a fixed text, describing how he had to rework for printing material that had evolved under very specific performance conditions.[12] His foreword to

---

10 *Die Bürger* is cited here from the Fürst edition; it has been reprinted in Sonnleitner, ed. (1996).

11 For the most complete account of the figure, see Hansjörg Schenker, *Theaterdirektor Carl und die Staberl-Figur* (1986), which includes two plays, an overview of the theaters involved, and a review of the literature on the actor most closely associated with the role, Karl Carl. His bias is clear: "Staberl war der letzte wirkliche Hanswurst, den das Wiener Volkstheater hervorbrachte" (35). Noteworthy too is his account of how the censors were stalemated (101ff.), and the relation of Carl's theater to the "Vaudeville-Jahr" of 1843 (122). His take on the character is significant: "Was Staberl spricht tritt hinter die Frage wie, wo und an wen der spricht" (141). He also points out that other Staberls existed: Ignaz Schuster, for example, played the role twenty-five times in 1813 and eighteen times in 1814, and a few times a year thereafter (143). He also includes a list of "Staberliaden" (160), which are not unlike the list of *Lazzi* (skits, see Mel Gordon [1983]) associated with the *commedia dell'arte*.

Aust, Haida, and Hein's *Volksstück* (1989) offers a fine brief overview of Bauerle's *Die Bürger in Wien* (130–4), summarizing: "Staberl ist kein Charakter, sondern eine Funktion, er ist auch keine 'Offenbarung des Volksgeistes' (Rommel, 1952, S. 680), sondern komisches Zerrbild der Haltungen und Handlungen der patriotische gesinnten Bürger, die sich selbstbewußt und selbstgerecht gegenüber allem Fremden und Unbürgerlichen behaupten ... eine kritische Relativierung des Selbstbewußtseins und des teilweise penetranten Patriotismus der Bürger" (132).

12 Most prominent was the censorship that existed in Vienna even after Maria Theresia declared freedom for theaters "Spektakelfreiheit" in Vienna after 1776.

the published text also claims his version of Hanswurst, Staberl, as a
man of the new generation. Clearly echoing Goldoni, he adds that he
was at some pains to rework familiar stock characters and situations
into a play for a specific time and place:

> *Citizens in Vienna* was originally an occasional piece. After Staberl's
> character had made its good fortune everywhere, even in north
> Germany, I was intent on drawing out analogous relationships on
> the plays, and to subordinate the whole of the play to its lively
> hero. Through that choice, the plot quite naturally lost a lot, but I
> was not allowed to add a better one in place of the other because
> Staberl was already popular. (3)[13]

In "subordinating the plot to the hero," Bäuerle has transformed
his character from a stock character into the hero of a written play
directed specifically at Vienna's audiences and politics. The result,
set in Leopoldstadt, is the story of Joseph Redlich, "Bürgerlicher
Bindermeister" (master cooper, barrel maker, whose name means
"honorable"), and his children, as they try to reconcile the demands of
love, their futures, and their position in the city (as employees, owners,
and members of the *Bürgerwehr*, the civil guard who defend the city
against unnamed sources of unrest).

The play's central conflict was a plot familiar in variants to audiences
for at least a century, adapted to reflect "real" citizens in the era of the
Congress of Vienna. The family's daughter, Käthchen, is in love with
a "young poet," Carl Berg, whom she cannot marry because he has no
prospects; her mother is trying to marry her off to the older and richer
merchant Muller. The poet Carl will not succumb to the Romanticism
and despair of a Werther because he has managed to find a patronage
job: "I have just come from Count Pfahl, he was quite taken by me, his
secretary has died, I will get his position and 1,000 fl. remuneration"
(6).[14] Despite his newly rekindled hopes of a better reaction from her
mother, his beloved warns him in stock language about the values of
the working bourgeoisie: "that is still not enough. My mother thinks
too much of hard cash and riches for her to prefer a mediocre salary

---

13 "Die Bürger in Wien waren anfänglich ein Gelegenheitsstück. Nachdem der
    Charakter des Staberl überall und selbst im nördlichen Deutschland Glück
    machte, war ich bedacht, die analogen Beziehungen aus dem Stücke heraus
    zu nehmen, und das Ganze dem muntern Helden des Stückes unterzuordnen.
    Dadurch hat natürlich die Handlung sehr viel verloren, und eine bessere für
    die letzte anzubringen, ließen die bereits gerne gesehenen und durch Staberl
    erhobenen Situationen nicht zu."

14 "So eben komme ich vom Grafen Pfahl, er ist ganz für mich eingenommen, sein
    Sekretär ist gestorben, ich erhalte diesen Platz und 1000 fl. Besoldung."

and your talents" (6).[15] Joseph Redlich, her father, is easier to convince that respectable employment, not money itself, is quite sufficient for this poet to take a bride. Redlich lives up to his name, insisting that a suitor's character matters most:

> I am not one of those fathers who simply want their children to marry right, I am a citizen and proud if my daughter pleases a clever man, because clever men are more to me than rich ones, and whoever is learned is ahead of all those others who, even rolling in gold, cannot write their names. However, clever people should also consider how one is supposed to live from science, I like to see clever people use their pounds well and bank their talents for interest—therefore, my dear Poet, consider your advancement and knock once more—someone will be found who will say "come in." (9)[16]

Honest citizen Redlich understands in the abstract the values of German *Bildung* (cultivation, education) but also points at the need to fulfill practical responsibilities. He approves of his daughter's suitor because he has taken the responsibility of a job and thus has prospects, not because he has talent.

The stock Hanswurst character Staberl is brought into this mix as a clever servant who tests these resolves. He himself is always looking for advancement (*Fortkommen*) and direct profit, repeating as his tag line, "if I'd only made something off of it" (*wenn ich nur was davon hätt'*). The audience sees him very much in the tradition of Mozart's Figaro, as a jack-of-all-trades who seeks to make his way without advantages of birth. He is, in turn, a servant, a tradesman, and an umbrella-maker (*Parapluiemacher*), aware of his environment but not subject to it:

> At your service, Mr. Redlich, at your service! Now, what's new, since I'm just passing by?—One hears nothing about war these

---

15 "das ist noch zu wenig. Meine Mutter hält zu viel auf bares Vermögen und Reichthümer, als daß sie eine maßige Besoldung und deine Talente vorziehen sollte."

16 "Ich bin keiner von den Vätern, die ihre Kinder bloß *reich* verheirathen wollen, ich bin ein *Bürger*, und stolz, wenn meine Tochter einem *gescheidten* Menschen, gefällt, denn g'scheidte Leut' sind bey mir mehr als *reiche* Leut', und wer was gelernt hat, geht jedem voraus, der wenn er auch in Gold steckt, seinem Nahmen nicht schreiben kann—allein gescheidte Leut' sollen auch darauf denken, wie man von der Wissenschaft leben kann, von g'scheidten Leuten seh' ich es gern, wenn sie ihr Pfund gut anwenden, und ihre Talente auf Interesse legen—daher mein lieber Dichter, denken Sie auf ihr Fortkommen, und *klopfen* Sie einmahl wieder an, wird sich schon wer finden, der herein sagt—"

days; time passes much too slowly for me because of all that peace. I hear we will march against the Kalmuks—that would be alright with me, if I could only make something off of it . [...] Oh, I'm no fool, oh no, I'm clever, everyone talks about clever Staberl, everywhere, from far and wide I am sought out to hold forth on my political opinions. The meat roaster over there says I should have gone to college and become a speaker in the English Parliament; on account of my beautiful diction and the fluidity of my speech, I could have protected people with my thoughts. My father, however, did not see eye to eye with this and raised me instead to deal with the fluidity of the heavens, where I also protect people, but only with my umbrellas. (10)[17]

He is part of the luxury goods trade that came to Vienna with the Congress: out of poor workshops, in utter poverty, glove-makers, embroiderers, lingerie-makers, and umbrella-makers, they came to serve the new urban market that brought Europe to their shops and carts.

Staberl's talents are applied as Redlich would have wished, as a commodity that, with luck, can guide an individual successfully through life. Significantly, Staberl also plays into society's expectations: he can, for example, switch effortlessly between dialect and *Hochdeutsch*, to perform whatever roles might be expected of him as he exercises his various talents, and to fit into various corners of the urban bourgeoisie:

Yes, I've drawn ahead by a century; I see everything, know everything, understand everything, comprehend everything, judge everything—if I only could only make something off of it. (*In High German, and with direct address to the audience.*) Other people are fifty years behind me—or didn't I predict everything that happened in the last twenty years? The whole triumphal

---

17 "Gehorsamer Diener, Herr Redlich, g'horsamer Diener! Nu, was gibt's Neues, weil ich g'rad so vorbey spring'.—Hört man nichts von einem Krieg; mir ist die Zeit völlig lang vor lauter Frieden. Ich höre, wir werden den Kalmukesen marschieren—mir wär's recht; wenn ich nur was davon hätt'. ... Ey! Ich bin kein Narr, o nein, ich bin g'scheidt, überall red't man von dem g'scheidten Staberl, weit und breit werd' ich gesucht, um meine politischen Meinungen von mir zu geben. Der Bratelbrater da drüben sagt, ich hätte studieren sollen, und ein Redner im englischen Parlament werden, wegen meinem schönem Vortrag und der Flüssigkeit meiner Sprache, ich hätte durch meine Gedanken die Menschheit beschirmen können. Mein Vater hat aber dieß nicht eingesehen, und hat mich zur *Flüssigkeit* des Himmels auferzogen, da *beschirm'* ich denn auch die Menschheit, aber bloß mit meinen Parapluies!"

procession from Kulm to Paris, the liberation of Leipzig, the leaders of all the victories that we have had? Don't I know that London lies across the ocean, and that Stockholm and Stockerau are two different things? ... It is high time that my achievements were rewarded—that there would for once be a war in which one could protect oneself by using my umbrellas against the rain of bullets—*that* war I would welcome. Why? Because I would make something off of it!—But the way it has always gone instead is that best customers come back to me without hands; if it continues this way, I will be a well-disposed beggar. Well, yes, if a person doesn't have any hands, what should he hold an umbrella with? (11)[18]

He portrays himself as the new man of Vienna, a member of a new urbane class who knows that "Stockholm is not Stockerau" (a small town outside of Vienna). No matter his talents, Staberl would not try to jump classes; he wants only class justice in a new century dependent on commerce, the military–industrial complex, and on Europe's political situation under negotiation in Vienna. War brings trade to the few, misery to the many, and opportunities for profiteering. As Therese Redlich, the mercenary mother, summarizes: "no hour passes here without the fortune of Europe being discussed: are you longing for war again, or do you all perhaps have secret information?" (13).[19]

The war has affected Staberl's Vienna socially and politically, as well as commercially. The play's eponymous *Bürger* are all "political brothers" who, like Staberl, are eager to profit from circumstance. These *Bürger* are a kind of comic Greek chorus, toasting the people and the soldiers they will be forced to become, rather than battles or

---

18 "Ja um ein Jahrhundert bin ich *voraus* gerückt; ich kenn' alles, weiß alles, versteh' alles, begreif' alles, beurtheil' alles, wenn ich nur was davon hätte. (*Hochdeutsch und mit Beziehung.*) Andere Leute sind um fünfzig Jahre hinter mir—oder hab' ich nicht alles vorausgesagt, was wir seit zwanzig Jahren erlebt haben? Den ganzen Siegesgang von Kulm bis Paris, den Leipziger Befreyungstag, den Majoratherrn von allen Siegen, die wir gehabt haben? Weiß ich nicht, daß London über'm Meer liegt, und daß Stockholm und Stockerau zweierley sind? ... es wäre einmahl die höchste Zeit, daß meine Verdienste vergolten würden—daß es einmahl einen Krieg gäbe, wo man sich mit meinen Parapluies vor dem Kugelregen schützen könnte—den wollt' ich loben, warum? Weil ich was davon hätte!—Aber so, wie es jetzt immer war, sind mir die besten Kundschaften ohne Händ' zurückgekommen; wenn das fortging', würd' ich ein aufgelegter Bettler; nun ja, wenn ein Mensch keine Hand mehr hat, mit was soll er denn ein Parapluie halten?"

19 "[E]y, da vergeht ja keine Stunde, wo hier nicht das Glück von Europa berath-schlagt wird: sehnt ihr euch etwa schon wider nach einem Krieg, oder habt's vielleicht gar schon geheime Nachrichten!"

military leaders (29); ever merciful, they will take up a collection for those disadvantaged by the war (30). Politics, however, retains a local flavor and has local value. For instance, Staberl can use politics to get himself invited to dinner, where he orders "dumplings in old German style" as evidence of his patriotism (*altdeutsche Knödel*, 16). The *Bürger* follow him as a mass of hungry friends who lustily show their own patriotism in song, no matter how little they are actually interested in affairs of state.

Still, this community has its own politics, a sense of mutuality. These citizens see themselves as members of a *Gemeinschaft* rather than a *Gesellschaft* (a community, rather than a society, to use Ferdinand Tönnies' 1887 terminology). That sense of local responsibility (not money or state politics) turns out to be the determining factor in resolving the play. The rich suitor, Müller, is not part of that Viennese community, despite his impoverished origins and subsequent upward mobility; he remains a stranger with origins "over the border," where he learned to define himself in class-bound social-climbing terms through which he can justify his right to a bride who does not love him: "I deserve her, too, I am in my best years; and joys shall not be lacking for my wife and you [her mother]. You will have coaches, valuable clothes, jewelry!—Mother and daughter are masters of my money chest!"(18).[20]

What Müller lacks in tact he also lacks in moral fiber: he gives his bride a necklace, which her mother identifies as worth 1,000 *Gulden*. However, he has taken the jewelry from a neighbor to settle part of a debt (19). The girl is incensed that he values money most of all: "Do you believe that I am so miserable that I could sell my honorable intentions for a piece of jewelry?" (20).[21] Staberl will summarize it less charitably: "He stole from widows and orphans" (62).[22] A true citizen of his world will value hard work over success, love and honesty over status, community over the individual, morality over money.

Such didactic messages run throughout the text, emphasizing the differences between the Viennese bourgeois and outsiders (under-scored by long jokes about "wine of vintages 97 and 64," historical references to the Directory of the French Revolution and the Seven Years War, respectively [48–9]). At the end of the play, bourgeois

---

20 "Ich verdiene sie auch, ich bin in meinen schönsten Jahren; und an Freuden soll es meiner Frau und Ihnen [Frau Therese Redlich] nicht fehlen. Sie werden Equipage haben, kostbare Kleider, Schmuck!—Mutter und Tochter sind Herren meiner Casse!"

21 "Glauben Sie, ich sey so elend, daß ich um einen Schmuck meine ehrlichen Gesinnungen verkaufen könnte?"

22 "Witwen und Waisen hat er bestohlen!"

communitarian values triumph over foreign guile, individual success, and money. Müller proves himself a cad when he grabs the girl, who wrests herself free and throws herself into the Danube. Poet Carl proves his real worth when he saves her, thereby winning his bride from the hands of her grateful father. Müller lives down to his own moral character as he tries to bribe Staberl so he won't be charged with assaulting Käthchen: "I don't want to escape from the court, but just from how things look" (74)[23]—he has already served a jail term for fraud, "wegen Betriegereyen" (77). Underscoring this point as a chorus stressing solidarity and mutual care, the *Bürgerwache* stands guard over the city with the support of their women, helping everything to come out right.

As in the theaters of Sheridan and Marivaux, as in Mozart's operas, *Citizens in Vienna* revolves around recurring questions of love, money, and status. But the clever servants and companions from the *commedia dell'arte* have been turned into clever independent working citizens with loyalty to their community and faith in a future prosperity born out of solidarity. Bäuerle's characters are capable of holding jobs and are not beholden to courts, no matter that they ultimately survive or fall in the wake of international politics. They are self-policing, self-aware independents; and their nominal fool, Hanswurst or Staberl, is actually an *Adabei*, a man about town looking for opportunity in the citizens' world and values. Through his humor and double entendres, he teaches that society can be good, if all concerned do their jobs properly within the whole. Just as importantly for the realism of Bäuerle's play, these characters recognize that individual circumstances can be changed by political winds, and that official power structures must be subject to the checks and balances of good bourgeois sense.

Later Viennese Staberls will be cut from the same distinctive cloth, defining class identity in terms of morality rather than fiscal status or family. They claim the city as a new environment, a newly self-conscious chorus of mutual support that keeps them free, in contrast to the world of Beaumarchais's Figaro, who remained essentially trapped within a world not of his making. The Viennese playwrights of subsequent generations would share Bäuerle's concern with the position of individuals within the group, as part of a new urban bourgeoisie. With Bäuerle's Staberl, the traditional comedy themes of love, marriage, and money are inserted decisively into Vienna as part of current affairs and the contemporary sociopolitical world. And today's scholars of Nestroy and his contemporaries do show how, between the Congress of Vienna and the 1860s, the *Volkstheater* proliferated its messages, comprising a range of genres, including the *Lebensbild*, the *Lokalposse*

---

23 "[I]ch will ja nicht dem Gerichte, sondern nur dem Aussehen entgehen."

(a distinctly dialect play), and various other types of comedic morality plays (Yates 1996, 8).

This Staberl-as-urban-critic remains central to the Viennese theater of the nineteenth century, long after his German cousin Hanswurst was banished from German state theaters. Officially, under the pressure of censorship, Staberl no longer extemporizes, but there is evidence that the actors playing him would play cat-and-mouse games with the censors,[24] especially in their musical turns—in their topical ditties (*Couplets*) or quod-libets (parody medleys).[25] The preservation of these texts is, paradoxically, due to the state's decision that the improvisatory style had to be restrained by censorship, an imperative that became more urgent after the 1830 revolutions in France. By the 1840s, at least fifty years of such written plays are documented for the Viennese suburban theaters—or rather, approximately fifty years of texts were recorded by the Austrian censors. As the *Volkstheater* becomes nominally better-regulated as a theatrical institution, however, the comparatively mild politics of authors like Bäuerle will evolve into more radical critiques of the urban middle classes under pressure from values not their own.

Not surprisingly, given Grillparzer's thorough familiarity with European theater, including not only forms of tragedy but also French vaudevilles and English comedies, the dramatist tried his hand at this hallmark genre of the Vienna state. Yet he wrote only a single, purportedly anomalous *Volksstück* that was an abysmal failure on the Viennese stage at its 1838 premiere: *Weh dem, der lügt* (*Woe to Liars*). That narrative from literary history, however, ignores what the genre offered Grillparzer.

Grillparzer: Changing the body politic

Grillparzer completed *Weh dem, der lügt* after an extended trip to England and France, where, as was his wont, he visited and read much theater, including popular and comedic theaters. The material

---

24 Extemporizing was nominally illegal since it was forbidden by Maria Theresa in 1752, but it happened repeatedly. See Fred Walla, "Johann Nestroy im Urteil und Vorurteil der Kritik," which surveys common critical errors, especially those surrounding performance practice. For example, the real threat in publishing a play was financial: a published play could be pirated, instead of securing royalties per performance (244); later in the century, Nestroy's supposed extemporized passages were documented in prompt-script variants (252), and in sanitized versions in the censor book (252).

25 On the couplets/refrains, see W. E. Yates, "'Ich will hiemit gar nicht gesagt haben, daß Herr N. entlehnt …'," which also includes a discussion of sources. For an overview of the music in these plays, see Jürgen Hein, "Zur Funktion der 'musikalischen Einlagen' in den Stücken des Wiener Volkstheaters."

had occupied him since 1820, but only the political situation of the late 1830s made it seem urgent to finish and stage, referring as it does to appropriate political roles for kings and underlings alike. It is definitely a play with a political moral, closer to the fairytale plays of Ferdinand Raimund (such as the 1828 *Der Alpenkönig und der Menschenfeind / The Alp-King and the Misanthrope*) than to Bäuerle.[26] Some do acknowledge that it is "closely related to the Viennese popular traditions" (Krispyn, 202); because it rests on the two-world problem of the Baroque (Seidler), it cannot be described as only a comedy, despite its comic elements—the reason why some critics believe it failed for a public expecting something broader.

Yet *Woe to Liars* was not necessarily fatally flawed. In an 1878 revival, it succeeded for an audience in a decidedly different political climate.[27] Grillparzer felt the play to be solid and attributed its failure first to bad casting and then to the long-standing animus of the Habsburgs against him. As he notes cryptically around the time of the premiere: "The vultures in Schönbrunn are purportedly very unsatisfied with their keeper, because they were given fresh meat where their favorite dish is carrion. They say, and correctly, to be sure, that he should have arranged things according to their taste" (Tgb. 3343).[28]

In the worst estimation of some critics today, "[i]t is not a play critical of the times, with crypto-revolutionary tendencies" (Scheibelreiter,

---

26 In the criticism of the 1830s and 1840s, a debate about the *Volksstück* arose as the gentler, more romantic and moralistic comedies of older generations (especially Ferdinand Raimund's *Zauberpossen*) gave way to the harder-hitting, more naturalistic satire of Johann Nestroy, framed as "idealistic Raimund versus critical Nestroy" (Yates 1994, 6). I am eliding Raimund here—a significant error in terms of the history of the *Volkstheater* in Vienna—but interesting parallels exist between his "idealism" and the social-criticism that emerged in the contemporaneous ballet libretti, derived from Romanticism.

27 Krispyn traces the play's reception history, before and after 1878/9, the season of its breakthrough when its audience was purportedly less in need of "comforting superiority" over barbarians (Krispyn, 208). Critics today disagree about why the play originally failed. Scheichl takes it as a play that violated cultural boundaries (Christian versus Barbarian) as well as class decorum: "die Adelssatire konnte am Hoftheater nicht unbedingt mit enthusiastischem Beifall rechnen" (Scheichl 1988, 143). Yet others counter that the 1820 draft had a considerably worse barbarian whom Grillparzer later again transformed into a figure more parallel to the Christians (Krispyn, 208).The play can seem weak (Scheichl, "Atalus" [1991]), or lacking tragedy (Angress). However, Roe brings it into line with Weimar Classicism; Jones describes the play as being about *Menschlichkeit*.

28 "Die Geier in Schönbrunn sollen mit ihrem Wärter sehr unzufrieden sein, weil er ihnen frisches Fleisch gegeben hat, indes doch Aas ihre Lieblingsspeise ist. Sie sagen, und zwar mit Recht, er hätte sich nach ihrem Geschmacke richten sollen."

66).[29] Yet to the contemporaneous audience, Grillparzer's play had clear political overtones: the heavily aristocratic audience purportedly whistled at the line asserting that a person's face is their coat of arms (Bandet, 145). Soon after its performance, August Sauer acknowledged that it implicitly threatened revolution: "The fear of revolution ascended the throne of Austria with Emperor Franz, and the fear of revolution ruled Austria until revolution itself drove out the ghostly hallucinations of its own being" (quoted in Krispyn, 207).[30] For the suburban audience that had seen plays like Bäuerle's and operas like *The Magic Flute*, however, Grillparzer's comedy may have seemed considerably more familiar and less shocking than it had to the aristocrats of the *Burgtheater*. Or perhaps Grillparzer had gone just a little too far by taking a play attacking class position into its temple of the arts, the *Burgtheater*, where it was all too legible to an audience that wanted to assert its class privileges in the way that Bäuerle had shown.

Woe to Liars begins in the historical mode of the *Volkstheater* tradition, as an adaptation from history brought to the audience as a tale of a heroic man from humble roots. It is based on politically-charged material from the end of an empire: an anecdote out of Book III of Gregory of Tours' *History of the Franks* (c. 590), a history written by and about the Gallo-Roman landed gentry whose ancestors had been Roman senators. The original fable is brief. The two sons of Clovis declared a truce, and took hostages as guarantees. One of these was Atalus, nephew of Bishop Gregory of Langres (an ancestor of Gregory of Tours). All hostages were turned into virtual slaves as state labor under their Frankish masters; they were "set to groom horses" (175). Atalus' uncle tried to ransom him, but could not meet the price demanded. To resolve the hostage situation another way, Leo, a cook's assistant attached to Gregory's household, volunteered to have himself sold to the enemy as a cook. Working faithfully for a year, he got the trust of his new masters. Eventually, he managed to sneak the hostage out, with help from a priest. Leo's reward was to be made a freedman and given a landholding of his own (179). It may well be significant for Grillparzer's take on the material that his source also contains Gregory's reflections about true believers in the Holy Ghost, contrasted with unbelievers: Leo's is a story of faith and dedication rewarded.

Grillparzer's expansions to his source material uniformly aim at critiques of state rulers, as evaluated from the side of the upper classes. His principal addition to that material was a frame narrative that sets

29 "[E]s ist kein zeitkritisches Stück mit kryptorevolutionärer Tendenz."
30 "Die Furcht vor der Revolution bestieg mit Kaiser Franz den Thron Oesterreichs und die Furcht vor der Revoluton beherrschte Oesterreich so lange, bis dies selbst die gespentischen Wahnbilder ihres Wesens bertrieb."

the play's tone and which is carefully resolved as the final curtain drops.[31] This frame introduces Leon, the historical Leo transformed, and tricks the audience into believing that he has a revolutionary agenda. The curtain rises on a Leon brandishing his kitchen knives in front of the castle manager, the *Hausverwalter*, demanding to see the Bishop, his employer. The manager panics, and calls for help, to which Leon responds: "'Tis just my joke" ("'s ist mein Scherz ja nur" [I, l. 6]). Then he is sent back to the kitchen (I, l. 11). Grillparzer's harmless joke catches the audience expecting a story of the downtrodden revolting against oppression. What the audience actually gets is a Leon with class-consciousness who believes the structure of his society is being eroded, as he expresses in a speech very much in the tradition of the *Volkstheater*:

If a kitchen is the place where one cooks,
Then you will seek for one in vain in the whole castle.
Where no one cooks, there is no kitchen, Sir,
Where no kitchen, there is no cook ... .
But as I began to show my art,
It's all been called much too expensive, much too much so.
     (I, ll. 13–23)[32]

Woe to Liars thus begins with a confrontation between a higher and a lower servant, about Leon the cook being used improperly, a situation that almost drives him to enlist in the military (I, ll. 34–60). The Bishop had been Leon's model for a proper master of a house, but that is no longer the case because the master has reduced the household and neglected what remains:

He was to me a picture of all greatness,
And I now see such a dirty patch,
His avarice, such a malicious nasty blot
On the white robe of his purity,
And that I have to see it. (I, ll. 66–70)[33]

---

31 Even Dagmar C. G. Lorenz, while making "Grillparzer, Dichter des sozialen Konflikts," overlooks the frame in her discussion (87–95).

32 "Wenn eine Küch der Ort ist, wo man kocht,
So sucht ihr sie im ganzen Schloß vergebens.
Wo man nicht kocht, ist keine Küche, Herr,
Wo keine Küche, ist kein Koch. ...
Doch als ich anfing, meine Kunst zu zeigen,
Ist alles viel zu teuer, viel zu viel."

33 "Daß er ein Bild mir alles Großen war,
Und daß ich jetzt so einen schmutzgen Flecken,

Leon has been shaken by seeing the Bishop involved in a scene of penny-pinching worthy of Ebenezer Scrooge:

> Recently he had me called
> And he gave me money from a great chest
> —the kitchen money, namely, for a week—
> but before he gave it over, he took a silver piece,
> and looked at it ten times, and kissed it finally,
> and stuck it in a little sack that stood large
> and stuffed full in a corner of the chest.
> Now I ask you: a virtuous man
> And he kisses money. A man who suffers hunger
> And who heaps up savings in a sack stuffed full. (I, ll. 88–97)[34]

The *Hausverwalter* tries to excuse the Bishop because he is sad to the depths of his soul ("betrübt im Innern seiner Seele" [I, l. 102]), because his nephew has been taken hostage.

The audience may well give credence to Leon's doubts when they first see Gregor. The Bishop is distracted, lost in thought about his own lies, which he describes oddly:

> If I had been truthful, when the king
> Recently asked me if I needed anything.
> And had I asked for freedom for my child,
> Would he not be free and my heart quiet?
> But because I was angry, to be sure for a good reason,
> I answered: Lord, I don't need your property;
> Give it to the flatterers who otherwise rob your land.
> Then he turned away from me fiercely,
> And Atalus still languishes in chains. (I, ll. 161–9)[35]

---

34   Als Geiz ist, so'nen hämische gartgen Klecks,
Auf seiner Reinheit weißen Kleide seh
Und sehen muß, ..."
"Er ließ mich neulich rufen
Und gab mir Geld aus einer großen Truhe
—Die Küchenrechnung nämlich für die Woche—
Doch ehe ers gab, nahm er 'nen Silberling.
Und sah ihn zehnmal an und küßt' ihn endlich,
Und steckt' ihn in ein Säckel, das gar groß
Und straff gefüllt im Winkel stand der Truhe.
Nun frag ich euch: ein frommer Mann
Und küßt das Geld. Ein Mann, der Hunger leidet
Und Spargut häuft im Säckel, straff gefüllt.
35   "Denn wär ich wahr gewesen, als der König
Mich jüngst gefragt, ob etwas ich bedürfe,

Leon's heart melts, like the audience's is supposed to, as he overhears this, and he is moved at Gregor's grief. Yet Leon is moved not to forgiveness, but rather to confrontation: the Bishop is not taking proper care of himself, not eating properly, and thus breaking faith with those who rely on him. The bonds of social structure, Leon implies, have been violated, and the audience sees that has been done in the name of a false piety.

Gregor defends himself by underscoring human failure: Leon had just gotten angry when he threw his knife and apron onto the ground. Gregor is, significantly, also interested in where people belong in society, even while he neglects the duties of his own station. Thus he demands that Leon puts his apron back on: "I like to see in people signs of their activities. As you stood in front of me earlier, bare and without money, you could just as well have been a petty thief" (I, ll. 196–7).[36] Leon picks up the hint about needing to have a station in society and turns it back on Gregor: "But as a cook, not as Leon, but as your cook, your servant, Lord, I accuse you all of hate" (I, ll. 209–11).[37] Failing to take what is your due is also a violation of the normal order—a master cannot skimp on food and hurt the household.

Leon admits that he bought meat for the Bishop out of his own pocket but came to hate the situation when he saw the Bishop penny-pinching and kissing money. Only this admission brings out the play's key lie: Bishop Gregor admits that he's saving money to try to pay his nephew's ransom out of his own funds, not out of congregation money (I, ll. 299–301). Just as he did in front of the king, Gregor tried to fix the situation by himself, neither asking for nor receiving help of any sort, even from those whose role is to give it. Yet he has only collected 10 of the 100 pounds ransom necessary. Leon's first thought is a reaction based on the warriors only the king could provide: take ten men and free Atalus by force. But this is unacceptable. Since hostages and truces are involved, that act would upset a very complicated political balance.

Und hätt ich Lösung mir erbeten für mein Kind,
Er wär nun frei und ruhig wär mein Herz.
Doch weil ich zürnte, freilich guten Grunds,
Versetzt ich: Herr, nicht ich bedarf dein Gut;
Den Schmeichlern gibs, die sonst dein Land bestehlen.
Da wandt er sich im Grimme von mir ab
Und fort in Ketten schmachtet Atalus."

36 "Ich mag am Menschen gern ein Zeichen seines Tuns./ Wie du vor mir standst vorher, blank und bar,/ Du konntest auch so gut ein Tagdieb sein."

37 "Allein nicht als Leon, ich klag als Koch,/ Als euer Koch, als euer Diener, Herr: / Daß ihr euch selber haßt."

Finally, Gregor leaves it to God to sort it out: "To You, Father of all, into Your hands I commend my son" (I, ll. 334–5).[38]

The real help arrives in the form of a mental bolt of lightning: Leon claims to have been suddenly inspired by a "little plan" to infiltrate the enemy camp as a cook and then free the hostage. Leon is given permission to try, as long as he does not lie about what he is doing (I, ll. 381, 384).[39] After all, Gregor notes, a hostage taken illegally may be freed, and so admitting his role keeps him safe. Leon circumvents further discussion about lying by playing into Gregor's belief that the cook has been appointed by God to this task. Leon thus gets his wish without undercutting the Bishop personally, and without confronting him for his lack of faith in society's organization. The plan is put into action as Leon sells himself to a poor pilgrim to be sold into slavery. Leon will rely on his wits to uphold his promise not to lie. Of course, convenient visions from God are never lies.

Grillparzer has expanded his source material considerably, adding motivations for Leon's story and interpolating the psyche of a good but flawed man at the core of the Bishop. The frame narrative does indeed introduce the questions of lying and truth-telling which so many critics stress, because truth only works situationally in this world: one person's lie is another's truth. Yet the frame also stresses how various stations in society depend on each other: faith in fellow humans is crucial to the group's survival, not just an abstract difference between truth and lies. Once Leon understands Gregor's problem, for example, he is more than willing to help solve it, at the pain of his own body. Yet Gregor sees this help as God's gift, not as Leon's. Gregor is, in this sense, still lying to himself. To be sure, Leon carefully arranges things so he himself does not lie or contradict the Bishop. Yet what Leon has to combat is abuse of power, not lies *per se*. When, for instance, Leon sells himself into bondage as a cook, that contract is illegal (or at least immoral) and so does not need to be upheld.

Grillparzer's second great expansion of his source material is his repopulation of the barbarian court, a change that does not simply contrast barbarian and Christian, but also brings into play a contrasting household order. To mirror Gregor's household, Grillparzer shows the audience a second *ménage*, that of Count Kattwald, a vain nobleman who hopes for an even vainer one (Galomir) as his son-in-law. Leon gains access to the Count through his ability to be an "artist" of the kitchen who will impress all at the daughter's (Edrita's) wedding (*Künstler* [II, l. 512]). In this household, Leon falls almost entirely into the role of the clever servant who bluffs and skirts the truth while

---

38   "Du Vater aller,/ In deine Hand befehl ich meinen Sohn!"
39   "Im Innern hat des Guten Geist geleuchtet, … Und sei dir selber treu und Gott."

doing God's will, while never overtly lying. Yet the bride, Edrita, is different from her father. She is being compelled to marry "dumb Galomir" ("Den dummen Galomir" [II, l. 705]), but she is actually in love with the hostage Atalus. She also gets on well with Leon, showing her openness to people across stations—she is quite willing to search out herbs and help in the kitchen.

The question posed by this household in the play revolves around class duty and class prerogative. Edrita's antipathy to Galomir is extreme. Because of her reaction, many critics read Galomir as stupid because he is often inarticulate. But Grillparzer did not mean him that way. He meant him as a healthy, well-bred thoroughbred animal (British slang of the era would have called him a "blood"): "animal but not stupid" ("tierisch, aber nicht blödsinnig" [II, l. 1252]). Significantly, Atalus does not behave any better, despite his superficially better manners. He still insists on his station and rights when he refuses to help in the kitchen:

Finally, I tend the horses, because I must,
And because it is a noble, knightly animal.
But tend the kitchen? I would rather, right here on this spot,
Leave my life, limbs cut into pieces. (II, ll. 828–31)[40]

Kattwald eventually forces Atalus into the demeaning job—he threatens underlings, while fawning over Galomir.

The escape is planned, but it is ultimately through Edrita that Leon manages to snag the key from a Kattwald sleeping in a drunken stupor. When they escape, Atalus whines about hunger, while Leon, echoing his master Gregor, says to trust in God. God brings them Edrita, although Leon initially does not trust her, despite her willingness to be converted to the "holy teachings" ("fromme Lehren" [II, l. 1316]). When Galomir pursues them, she acts as decoy; several others in Kattwald's employ aid in their escape. Finally, they get to Metz, still in enemy territory, they believe. They are saved because the fort has been taken by the Christians. Gregor has come to save them and send the barbarians home. Edrita again proves her nobility by being humble, begging to be made a Christian; Gregor confirms that she is no barbarian, but rather "dear and well-made" ("hold und wohlgetan" [V, l. 1755]). Nobility will out, not because it is Christian or has the right bloodlines, but because it does the right thing to preserve the social order.

---

40   "Die Pferde hüt ich endlich, weil ich muß
Und weils ein edles, ritterliches Tier.
Doch in der Küche? Eher hier am Platz
Laß ich mein Leben, gliederweis zerstückt."

Grillparzer, at this point, modifies the original ending of his story. The historical Leo gets as his reward his freedom and some land on which to raise his family. The play, however, forces a class confrontation. At first, Leon declares his intent to go away to the army, now that Atalus is free and has declared his intent to marry Edrita. Atalus tries to claim her as noble, but Gregor points out that he is lying in a different way:

Atalus: She also descends from the counts in Rheingau.
Gregor: And so, you believe, also of equal birth to you?
The human's face is his coat of arms.
I had no other intent with you,
But if it is God's will … (V, ll. 1766–7; 1772–4)[41]

Gregor realizes that Atalus' desire is simply a social lie, and so he forces Leon to admit his own love for the girl. Atalus has erred in insisting on his nobility as an entitlement to his own will.[42] Gregor thus acts to affirm Leon's nobility of deed, instead of a nobility of birth. This may well be the speech, and presumably the decision, that the more aristocratic patrons of Vienna's *Burgtheater* found objectionable.

Gregor's great closing speech casts the whole question of falsehood into a new light. There is no such thing as a truthful person, but only one who can make good come of bad situations:

Gregor: Who will interpret for me the colorful, confused world?
They all speak the truth, are proud of it,
And she lies to herself and to him, he to me,
And then to her again: he lies because someone lied to him—
And they all speak the truth, all, all.
I note that no one has torn out the weeds yet.
With luck, wheat may still grow over them. (V, ll. 1800–6)[43]

---

41   "Atalus: Auch stammt sie von den Grafen her im Rheingau.
        Gregor: Und also, meinst du? auch dir ebenbürtig? …
        Des Menschen Antlitz ist sein Wappenschild.
        Ich hatte andre Absicht wohl mit dir,
        Doch wenn es Gottes Willen nun—"
42   Scheichl underscores that Edrita calls Atalus a *Junker,* a Prussian nobleman (139).
43   "Gregor: Wer deutet mir die buntverworne Welt?
        Sie reden alle Wahrheit, sind darauf stolz,
        Und sie belügt sich selbst und ihn, er mich
        Und wieder sie: Der lügt, weil man ihm log—
        Und reden alle Wahrheit, alle. Alle.
        Das Unkraut, merk ich, rottet man nicht aus.
        Glück auf, wächst nur der Weizen etwa drüber."

Gregor thus forces Atalus to do the right thing: "to grant the girl to the one who saved me, oh, and whom she loves" (V, ll. 1808–9).[44] Gregor's solution thus does more than state that truth and lies are relative, but rather affirms a nobility of deed and disposition beyond birth. To make this conviction socially acceptable, Gregor adopts Leon as a second son.

This gesture, more significantly, also closes the frame of the play: Gregor will ask the King to validate this adoption and give Leon not only his freedom, but also "rank and standing and reputation" ("Rang und Stand und Ansehn" [V, l. 1811]). Gregor will thus ask the King for the kind of favor he did not ask for Atalus, who has also learned to see merit in new places. The closing speech of the play, aimed at Atalus, seems at first to be cryptic. Yet it is the speech of a Bishop speaking to a vain nobleman who has finally done a generous act, but who in so doing has also lost the girl he believed he loved:

> You are sad. Just raise your eyes from the ground,
> You were deceived in the land of deception, son!
> I know a land that is the throne of all truth;
> Where lies are recognized as just colorful set of clothes
> That the Maker has designated transitory,
> And then he wrapped them around the dynasty of sin,
> So that their eyes would not be blinded by the light's rays.
> If you wish, then follow, as was earlier ordained,
> There one finds a treasure that cannot be robbed from you by
>   deception,
> One that rises and grows until the last days.
> And as for these two here. May they suit each other.
>   (V, ll. 1815–25)[45]

Gregor here overtly forgives Atalus' earlier offense of trying to take Edrita, which will not be held against him since he was in the land

---

44 "[D]as Mädchen dem zu gönnen,/ Der mich gerettet, ach, und den sie liebt."
45   "Du bist betrübt. Heb nur dein Aug vom Boden,
         Du wardst betäuschet im Land der Täuschung, Sohn!
         Ich weiß ein Land, das aller Wahrheit Thron;
         Wo selbst die Lüge nur ein buntes Kleid,
         Das schaffend Er genannt: Vergänglichkeit,
         Und das er umhing dem Geschlecht der Sünden,
         Daß ihre Augen nicht um Strahl erblinden.
         Willst du, so folg, wie früher war bestimmt.
         Dort ist ein Glück, das keine Täuschung nimmt,
         Das steigt und wächst bis zu den spätsten Tagen.
         Und diese da. Sie mögen sich vertragen."

of lies when it happened and so forgot the path of proper behavior. Gregor is by no means saying that Edrita would be a bad wife for him; her pedigree was never in question. Instead, Atalus had committed the error of acting unilaterally. If he had married her, he would be living another kind of lie in ignoring her wishes. One alternative ending that Grillparzer discarded underscored Atalus' failing in not being in control of himself, that only Leon was "master of himself" ("des *einen* völlig Meister, seiner selbst" [l. 1252]).

Many critics take this ending as an affirmation of Christian over barbarian, or as the affirmation of a morality play that makes Leon's fate dependent on his betters (e.g. Krispyn, 209). But the frame narrative points to the importance of Gregor's change of heart and sensibility. In the act of truth-telling that disenfranchised Atalus, Gregor proved himself the good father that Leon thought he had lost. Gregor and Atalus have not overcome lies, but rather their sins of pride and willfulness. Gregor's new world needs a new order, where underlings are not driven to lies and where superiors do not abuse their power by ceasing to listen and lying to themselves.

Why did this message not succeed in Grillparzer's time? Here, the question of performance necessarily intrudes on the play's reception. In his letters, Grillparzer indicated that none of the aristocrats were meant to be played as satire. His critique of the first cast was that they took the easy way out, playing Galomir as stupid, and Atalus as an effete oaf. Indeed, the structure of the play, hinging on the frame narrative, would argue for playing them straight. All the aristocrats, Gregor and Kattwald included, suffer from the illusion that they alone know the truth, and that no one under them might know the truth better than they. Yet that false truth had caused the initial loss of Atalus; it is ultimately why Atalus cannot win Edrita's heart, as a man who prefers to be with the "knightly horses" rather than in the kitchen that sustains the house. These aristocrats remain convinced of their own stations, but they are at worst short-sighted, not overtly foolish.

Thus Grillparzer's play would overtly threaten any audience complacent about its own status. In this tale of truth-telling, the common people can be right, conspire against their betters, and, in their goodness, triumph over those who would enslave them. This is very much the kind of warning about public and private uses of reason that Immanuel Kant would offer in "Was ist Aufklärung?" (and Grillparzer had studied Kant [Scheibelreiter, 69]). Leon may or may not have actually had a vision from God about what he was supposed to do, but the situation was resolved through the Bishop's faith in him and through his own abilities and confidence in his role in society. When individuals are true to themselves they will succeed; if they deny their feelings and submit to what is "supposed" to happen, they will deny themselves and foreclose the new future that Gregor has given Leon and still foretells for Atalus.

The play is thus considerably less about abstract definitions of truth or lies than many of today's critics assume, and much more about society as a framework forcing many to lie. No matter their pedigrees and how well they match on paper, it would be a lie for Atalus and Edrita to marry. They are different, not because he is Christian and she a barbarian (she is clearly a devout convert-to-be), but because she loves the cook with the heart of a lion, who is as brave as she is in admitting the right thing to do. The bishop has learned this truth that there are many ways to lie, in deed and in heart, not just in the letter of the law. Unless such lies are acknowledged as failures of the social structure, not individual moral failures, there will be no future for this land.

Grillparzer has crafted a play in the tradition where a clever servant is rewarded for saving his betters, yet redefined its moral in modern terms. In one sense, *Woe to Liars* resolves its conflict much in the same way Shakespeare's *Tempest* does, where a well-meaning leader must be shown the people's truth and decide to change. Yet Grillparzer defines the changes necessary in his Vienna: transformations of consciousness about the nature of truth, lies, privilege, and entitlement. Should this not happen, revolutionary change will surely supersede the much preferable evolutionary change. Kitchen boys may, in fact, become the agents of that change, if the upper classes do not choose to lead. Change comes from the kitchens, the farmyards, and the women, where society's real power rests, and not from throne rooms. Grillparzer's couple has broken the social hierarchy by espousing moral codes very recognizable to Bäuerle's Viennese burghers, but not necessarily in ways acceptable to an entrenched upper class.

Despite its reputation, then, *Woe to Liars* is an exemplary Grillparzer play, structured to raise questions. The audience sees a bishop, a cook, and sundry aristocrats on the stage, each learning how to question their own expectations and how their lives are structured. The play leads its characters to solutions, but the real questions are left to the audience. Grillparzer merely asserts the need for change, adaptation, and modernization within an essentially stable social system. The contrast between *Woe to Liars'* happy end and the expectations of the typical mid-nineteenth-century audience, however, must necessarily warn against the inevitability of a revolution in a state where class privilege is asserted to the detriment of humanity, dedication, and love. If the play has a happy end, it only appears so to those who share a vision of the state as guaranteeing the well-being of its citizens— as a nation rather than simply a political entity existing to uphold damaging, reified images of class and prerogative.

Nestroy: The legitimacy of class structures

Within a very few years of Grillparzer's *Burgtheater* "failure," Vienna's most famous actor-playwright, Johann Nestroy, will again stage the politics of class relations, but in the popular theaters in the suburbs, not at the *Burgtheater*. Despite the parallels between his social politics and Grillparzer's, however, his plays more closely resemble Bäuerle's. Nestroy's most famous Hanswurst variant, Titus Feuerfuchs from *Der Talisman* (1843),[46] is a close cousin of Bäuerle's Staberl as a critic of any middle class that can be alienated from its roots by money. Yet Nestroy will engage in a much more aggressive social politics than his predecessors.

As a performer, Nestroy was noted for his bravura satiric acting and singing (he had started as an operatic bass), and for his "aggressive caricature," his topical humor (often believed to be obscene), and the grimaces, gestures, and suggestive poses that he used to circumvent the censor (Yates 1994, 3–4). Yet contemporaneous Viennese critics saw nothing amiss in comparing Nestroy with Dickens, the Roman satire, or Shakespeare. Fürst Schwarzenburg called him "ein wirklich Shakespear'scher Geist" (Nestroy, 138). As part of the European traditions that include the *commedia dell'arte* and the *comédie-vaudeville* of Paris, Nestroy's plays were received locally as topical, engaged theater pieces in a tradition combining song, text, and other theatrical gestures.

Der Talisman was a hit in 1840, with Nestroy playing Titus Feuerfuchs, but not only because of his legendary comedic acting. The recent historical–critical edition of the Nestroy plays confirms how carefully crafted this work actually was as a public investigation of social moral problems. There are, at a minimum, three versions of the story that reveal Nestroy's very political reworkings of his material: the source French material, the censor book (the version that had to be submitted to the police authorities before performance was permitted), and the unexpurgated text that presumably represents a version closer to what Nestroy played on the stage. These various versions allow us to recapture at least part of what today remains a hidden debate about the politics of this popular theater, a debate that is echoed in the contemporaneous press in a more "coded" language that calls its critique bawdy

---

46 On *Der Talisman* particularly, see Peter K. Jansen, "Johann Nepomuk Nestroys skeptische Utopie," which analyzes text language and genre conventions, and Hauke Stroszeck, *Heilsthematik in der Posse*. Walla notes that *Talisman* disappeared after Nestroy's death, yet became popular again after World War II (261). W. E. Yates, *Nestroy and the Critics*, especially chapter 5, is useful in understanding the recent Nestroy edition, especially with respect to adaptation.

rather than biting. The three versions, however, make it very clear what was at stake in the play for the audience and the censor alike.[47]

As was Nestroy's wont, he stole a very recent hit from abroad to rework as his own theater property: *Bonaventure, Comédie-vaudeville en trois actes et quatre tableaux*, by M. M. Dupeuty and F. de Courcy, which had played in Paris in 1840.[48] Documents show how carefully Nestroy broke down the original and translated sections as a preparation to a very thorough rewriting, far beyond what is conventionally termed an adaptation. For instance, the third act is almost completely Nestroy's own, while the satirical song digests from current popular tunes, the *quod-libets*, differ diametrically from those in the original. In *Bonaventure*, songs are used as they would have been in opera, to establish characters' moods and states of mind and show off the actors; some are settings of classical poems, not even written as part of the play text *per se*. In *Talisman*, in contrast, the songs comment on the dilemmas in which the characters find themselves; they break the frame of the proscenium and allow the actor to break character and address the audience directly with topical commentary.[49]

The two plays share a single core fable: the eponymous out-of-work hero cannot be employed because of his red hair and social prejudices. When he saves a wigmaker from a carriage accident, he is given a wig that is the "Talisman" through which he can make his fortune. The plot eventually involves three wigs: the black (or brown) wig which endears him to the widow of a head gardener whose job he inherits, and ultimately to a chambermaid, the widow of a huntsman or *Jäger* (who puts him in livery as an upper house servant); a blond wig, which helps him become the secretary of the rich widow who employs them all; and a gray wig, which helps him become the seemingly stable heir of his rich cousin, a brewer. Ultimately, however, the clever servant will eschew this artificial rise through society on the basis of his looks, and will marry the goose- (or turkey-)girl who shares his red hair. In

---

47 For the original French text and a German translation, see Herles, as well as the appendices of the critical edition. Mautner, one of the major scholars of the Viennese folk theater, provides a good discussion of the piece's setting of the piece; despite his reliance on older, more expurgated editions, his analysis remains valid.

48 "Es ist freilich richtig, daß Nestroy bei der Konstruktion der Handlung zu Vorlagen griff oder traditionelee Schemata der Kömodie anwandte. Doch seine eigentlich Kunst bestand darin, die Vorlagen und Schemata den sozialen Konflikten seiner Zeit und seines Ortes auszuliefern, und auf solche Weise die harmonisierende Dramaturgie nach allen Regeln der Kunst zu verscheißen" (Scheit, 96–7).

49 This dramaturgy is commonplace in the *Volklstheater*, and is the presumed origin of Brecht's *Verfremdungseffekt*, estrangement effect.

both versions, the hero is the son of a schoolmaster, and thus verbally dexterous, smart, and able to exploit the situation (and in Nestroy's version, to repent of this exploitation).

On closer examination, however, the treatments of this common fable diverge seriously. The French version is a comedy of manners about who marries whom, very much in the vein of the lighter moments of *Twelfth Night* or *Midsummer Night's Dream*, without darker moments. Nestroy's version, in contrast, makes it clear from the outset that the play is about social distinction, the politics of money and class structure, and boundary testing across classes. Women also play expanded roles in this mid-century Viennese stage community, since Nestroy's hero and heroine, Titus and Salome, share the limelight and critiques of their community. Into his source material, Nestroy also interpolates a new first scene very much in the spirit of Bäuerle, turning people at a bucolic dance into a Greek chorus commenting on the play.[50] In this addition, even the lower orders are themselves implicated of prejudice against the heroine, the red-haired goose girl, Salome Pockerl, with "double string bass colored" hair ("Mit die Baßgeig'nfarben Haar" [Nestroy 1993, 7]).

When only the ugliest fellow in town will dance with her, Salome has the first monologue: red is a nice color, the color of roses, and so she'll go back to her geese, who don't laugh at her, as everyone in society does. This scene is echoed in Titus' entrance song, also an interpolation into the French version:

It's the dumbest thing when people split hairs …
Because one has to follow the hairs,
And in so doing one scores a perfect hit. (Nestroy, 11)[51]

The full song text does, to be sure, slander females: women are only safe once their hair goes gray—at which point they go and dye it! Yet Nestroy's moral is clear: "The world judges heads without using its heads, and even if one puts on one's head, it doesn't help because prejudice is a wall against which all the heads that have butted against it will return bloodied" (Nestroy, 11–12).[52] None the less, Nestroy has

---

50 The second scene in Nestroy's play is the first in the French version: the gardener's widow is ignoring the advances of a gardener who wants to marry her and become the chief gardener. In Nestroy's version, he has a distinctly Shakespearean name: Plutzerkern—pumpkinseed, in Austrian dialect.

51   "'sist dümste, wann d' Leut' nach die Haar urtheil'n woll'n, …
Drum auf d'Haar muß man geh'n,
Nacher trifft man's schon schön."

52 "So kopflos urtheilt die Welt über die Köpf', und wenn man sich auch den Kopf aufsetzt, es nutzt nix, das Vorurtheil ist eine Mauer, von der sich noch alle Köpf die gegen sie ang'rennt sind, mit blutige K[ö]pf zurück gezogen haben."

transfigured the French Bonaventure, a wily servant like Figaro, into Titus who challenges society's behavioral norms.

The names of the changed characters are significant additional proofs for the drift of the adaptation toward overt politics. The French hero and heroine are Bonaventure ("good fortune," the name of a saint known for his learning, the friend of St. Thomas Aquinas, whose feast day is July 14—Bastille Day) and Jeanne ("burned at the stake" with her red hair, like Joan of Arc). But Nestroy chooses for his hero the name Titus, perhaps as a nod to Shakespeare's Roman general from *Titus Andronicus*, an old man with a sense of honor, but with a temper that can turn his good will bad (as it did for *Lear*).[53] And Salome is the princess, the daughter of Herod, who gets the head of John the Baptist on a platter—John the Baptist who was, after all, the herald of Jesus' arrival promising that things will be better for the common man.

Such changes help to document Nestroy's critiques of social prejudice rather than gender or upper class snobbism. Where Bonaventure complains about being called a "carrot," not about lacking a job, Titus complains about being jobless and hungry. Nestroy thus represents prejudice as a structural concern of society: "No, humanity, you shouldn't lose me, appetite is the tender band that joins me to you, which reminds me three or four times a day, that I cannot rip myself out of society" (Nestroy, 13).[54]

Many such small changes confirm Nestroy's thorough attention to the effects of artificial social hierarchy. In both plays, the hero's father was a schoolmaster (Nestroy, 14; Nestroy, 242 in French). Yet Bonaventure wants to go to England as a servant, while his girlfriend, the turkey maid Jeanne, tries to get him a job as a farmer (Nestroy, 242). Titus never mentions emigration, he simply wants a job; the goose girl, Salome, tries to get him a job as a baker. The two worlds are thus structured differently: Bonaventure lives in a world of great houses and peasants, while Titus and Salome realize that urban jobs exist as well, jobs in the city that are independent of patronage.

In both plays, the hero's rise begins when he rescues a man from a coach accident, a man assumed to be noble, but who is actually a

---

53 The classical reference is intentional. See Ulrike Längle, "Die Haupt des Titus Jochanaan Feuerfuchs: Die biblische Salome-Geschichte im *Talisman*." After a review of other interpretations, Längle points out that Salome is quite literally after Titus' head; she also traces other story analogues that appear in the text (*Titus Andronicus*; Mozart's *La clemenza di Tito*), but ultimately decides that the play focuses on prejudices against Jews (89), thus becoming not the story of John the Baptist (*Johnanes der Täufer*), but of a Christian, *der getaufte* (91).

54 "Nein Menschheit du sollst mich nicht verlieren, Apetit ist das zarte Band welches mich mit Dir verkettet welches mich alle Tag 3–4 mahl mahnt, daß ich mich der Gesellschaft nicht entreissen darf."

hairdresser with an unfortunate name from the revolutionary point of view: Leduc, or Marquis. The hero's reward is the eponymous wig that will temporarily pull the hero and the goose girl apart, and set him on a new career path. In the French version, the two sing a love duet: "she's the girl for me." Salome's song is quite different in tone, outlining how men have an easier time in love than women do because of social role-playing: "Ja, die Männer hab'ns gut, hab'ns gut, hab'ns gut"—men have it good, good, good (Nestroy, 22). Men can run after women, hang around in bars, and never lose their reputations. Today, we easily see this as a very feminist interpolation, underscoring the play's themes of prejudice and reputation, even though Salome has no hopes of social advancement. The first act of both versions ends with Titus/Bonaventure acquiring a new job as a gardener thanks to the wig, and deciding to do as little work as possible. Bonaventure caps his achievement with a song emphasizing that he'll spend his days in comparative ease. Significantly, Nestroy moves a very different version of this song to the opening of Act II, where he makes it a group drinking song—Titus is never as eager to be lazy as Bonaventure is.

Both are scarcely in their new jobs (and into the clothes of the deceased gardener, his brown/black wigs, and maybe the bed of the widow employing them), when the chambermaid (Justine, or Nestroy's Constantia) tells them of an opportunity to find a "better situation" ("eine bessere Condition" [Nestroy, 37]): they can don livery (the clothes of the chambermaid's dead husband), and convince the lady of the house to promote them to *Jäger*. When Salome and Constantia argue about Titus taking such a patronage job from the nobility, Salome marks the chambermaid as somehow already acting above her station, in a world outside of the city: "It's a shame—such city nerves for a farm girl" (Nestroy, 41).[55]

The plot thickens when it becomes clear that the chambermaid is actually involved with the hairdresser Marquis/Leduc, who may ruin everything. Titus/Bonaventure has been asleep, but then is awakened to be introduced to the lady of the house; he grabs a blond wig from the room where he nodded off. Mme de Château-Gaillard, yet another widow seeking a handsome employee, falls in love with the blond Bonaventure, and reads Voltaire to him; Nestroy's Frau von Cypressenburg wants to make Titus her secretary and consultant for her literary pursuits. The hero gets his third set of clothes with his second wig, as the widow shows him off to her noble friends (he has "Tournure" in the German—he's a great looking blond footman).

Titus and Bonaventure begin their changes of fortune when they are ordered to fire the people who'd gotten them this far. "Time changes

---

55   "'s is a Schand solche Stadtnerven für a Bauerndirn'."

much," "Ja, die Zeit ändert viel," Nestroy lets Titus sing, outlining how relations between men and women change (Nestroy, 56–7). No sooner does Titus throw his clothes out the window in his escape from the widow (Salome catches them), than his hair is revealed, and his social rise is terminated (Nestroy, 61). Nestroy starts his third act with Titus' monologue about money, underscoring that he lost more than the chance at a dalliance: "The proud edifice of my hopes has burned down without insurance, the stocks of my fortune have fallen 100 percent, and thus my active balance stands at the roundest balance that there can be—namely, zero" (Nestroy, 62).[56] His most pressing question remains: "Where do I turn to find quarters for the night, without a *Kreutzer* of money?" (Nestroy, 67).[57]

The end of the French play has a *deus ex machina*: Bonaventure flees while being sought for deception and crimes, but he is found at the moment when he receives a legacy, which makes everything all right and enables him to marry Jeanne, two redheads together founding a dynasty critical of traditional orders.

Titus' route to his beloved is longer and more contorted. The hairdresser confiscates the black and blond wigs. Titus retorts, in a song refrain, that he's had enough, that if it doesn't rain, it pours: "Da hab'i schon g'nur" (Nestroy, 77). But a wig changes his fortune again, a worn gray one that had been the gardener's, but which now surprises his uncle with false *gravitas* when Titus notes that the gray hair came from worry (*Kummer*) (Nestroy, 79). This so cheers the uncle about Titus' good character that he agrees to buy Titus a barber shop. Significantly, the lady of the estate, Frau von Cypressenburg, had interceded to enable this result, acknowledging: "I have bothered myself with the man for a half hour, but his leathern, waterproof soul is impermeable to the dew of eloquence" (Nestroy, 75).[58] When Titus' gray wig is knocked off, everything begins to falls apart, until Cypressenburg again intercedes. She and Constantia had brought a notary to make the uncle's legacy legal. They force the situation, asserting that the uncle really still means to make Titus the sole heir (*Universalerbe* [Nestroy, 82]). A little matter like hair, and the little joke they all planned with the wig, could not, they assert, have fooled such an astute gentleman, and so he could not possibly be mean-spirited.

---

56 "Das stolze Gebäude meiner Hoffnung is assecuranzlos abbrennt, meine Glücks-actien sind um 100 Prozent g'fallen—, und somit beläuft sich mein Activ-Stand wider auf die rundeste Summe, die's giebt, nehmlich auf Null."

57 "[W]ohin sich jetzt wenden, daß man ohne Kreutzer Geld ein Nachtquartier find't?"

58 "Ich habe mich eine halbe Stunde abgequält mit dem Manne, aber seine lederne wasserdichte Seele ist undurchdringlich für den Thau der Beredsamkeit. Er will ihn etablieren, weiter nichts, auf Erbschaft hat er keine Hoffnung."

Crucial to note is that Titus only wants a business: "I don't need an inheritance" (Nestroy, 85).[59] His French exemplar, Bonaventure, decided to marry his equal, Jeanne, and then got a kind of divine reward for following class structure: his inheritance. In contrast, Titus rejects the suits of both the chambermaid and the gardener's widow, both interested in his money, and marries the goose girl *despite* his chances of moving up: "That I cannot marry anyone who speculates on me as a rich man, that is completely understandable, and that I will only marry the one who loves me without interest, that again is completely understandable" (Nestroy, 85).[60] Titus will marry Salome and have a pack of red-haired children so that society will get used to the sight. His children, he knows now, will inherit everything. He thus decisively opts for simple justice and hard work as the true measure of a man or woman.

Nestroy's adaptation thus addresses social issues to the very end: money as key to class affiliation, hard work, prejudice, the war of the sexes, and what makes a true man. In the process of his odyssey, Titus experiences two worlds of work, one questionable and one more legitimate. Real professions, those requiring honest labor, are barber, baker, goose girl, teacher, and brewer. More questionable professions are those associated with the wearing of livery, and hence more with looks and patronage than necessarily with productivity: huntsman, head gardener, and private secretary—positions where looks and glibness, not ability, can be the keys to advancement. The play ends with a gesture familiar from Richard Strauss and Hugo von Hofmannsthal's great opera, *Der Rosenkavalier*. The Frau von Cypressenburg proves her nobility, ultimately, by making the uncle do the right thing, just as the opera's Marschallin has to arrange the right marriage for her young and poor cousin and affirm young love, circumventing the greedy relatives and Baron Ochs' repugnant assertion of privilege. In Nestroy's play, however, the play's message is more explicitly aimed at social climbers rather than at the upper classes. When Titus decides to do the right thing and marry Salome, the chambermaid and the gardener's widow both go off in a huff; they don't see that his choice was right, and that their motives for falling in love were either superficial or mercenary (or both).

This critique of individuals seeking to move up in the world in all the wrong ways pervades Nestroy's play. Only Nestroy requires his

---

59   "Erbschaft brauch ich keine."
60   "Daß ich nun keine von denen heurathen kann, die bey mir bloß auf den wohlhabenden Mann speculiert, das versteht sich von selbst, und daß ich nur die heurathen werde, die mich ohne alles Interesse liebt, das versteht sich wieder von selbst …"

hero to confirm that his education at the hands of his schoolmaster father has brought him little but the ability to seem well-spoken and bright:

FvC: And which literary education has he received?
Titus: A kind of *millefleurs*-education: a hint of philosophy, a touch of jurisprudence, a shade of surgery, and a taste of medicine. (Nestroy, 50).[61]

These achievements make him acceptable as a secretary, but they will not guarantee his happiness or self-determination. In a parallel critique of the worst a city can provide, Salome noticed that the chambermaid had fairly dramatic "city nerves." And the song texts clearly point to evils associated with people who use social ties to make money. You marry the girl, says Titus, and you end up supporting all their relatives ("Da hab'i schon g'nur"/"Enough of that" [Nestroy, 7]).

The shifts between Bonaventure and Titus thus clearly point to a critique of the purportedly educated middle classes, including their prejudices about art. Titus can refer to "Ottokars Glück und Ende" (a play by Grillparzer), to Othello, and to Händel and Mozart. When Titus nods off in Cypressenburg's house, his snore is a nice in-joke: "O-zartes – Ha-Handerl" (Nestroy, 47).[62] Titus, therefore, is prepared in a superficial sense to negotiate a class boundary (as Bonaventure ultimately did not seek to do), but he ends up questioning the boundary between the working classes, as traditionally defined, and a new rising class of urban labor.[63] He is not simply contrasting city and country manners, but drawing a line between honest work and a society based on externals. Bonaventure's escape from misplaced love thus in the adaptation turns into Titus' repentance for having put on airs. Titus is Figaro, claiming his own away from illicit incursions by other classes; Bonaventure was just a fool saved from himself by chance.

The result is a play that is very much revolutionary in content: it anticipates the image from Grillparzer's *The Poor Fiddler* (*Der arme Spielmann*), when the city-dwellers emerge into a tidal wave of workers at a festival outside the city walls, and are subject to the power of these

---

61 Frau v. Cypressenburg: Und welche litterarische Bildung hat er Ihm gegeben? Titus: Eine Art Millefleurs-Bildung; ich besitze einen Anflug von Geographi[,] einen Schimmer von Geschichte[,] eine Ahnung von Philosophie, einen Schein von Jurisprudenz, einen Anstrich von Chirurgie, und einen Vorgeschmack von Medizin.

62 Such cross-class addresses were part of the Volkstheater tradition, from the time of Prehauser and Kurz-Bernadon on. The actors crossed over between comedy and serious drama and were not limited as sexual comics (Scheit, 53, 57).

63 Again, critics have long noted cross-class gestures in the plays (cf. Scheit, 67).

children of labor and service ("Kinder der Arbeit und Dienstbarkeit") as the flood of their bodies can sweep carriages away. Nestroy has thus wedded broad comedy to a very astute critique of would-be rising classes and their false fronts, poor education, and pretense, as well as their prejudices. At the same time, no class is immune to the seductions of such possibilities: from goose girl on up, everyone in the play must come to their senses and do their job, or risk making fools of themselves—or worse.

How carefully Nestroy adapted his source materials is key to his sense of audience and to his social-critical messages. Names, details, and songs are all aimed very tightly at an audience rich enough to attend the suburban theater: wage earners above the subsistence level, plus occasional richer patrons. At the same time, many in that new urban audience are living lives outside traditional society; they, like Titus, have been out of jobs and have taken what comes along, many times falling into new situations, new values, or new dilemmas. They are in danger of losing their souls to these changes, Titus' fate suggests, if they put on airs like the hairdresser rather than do the right thing, as Titus will. Money doesn't make the man, but honest labor and following traditions honestly will.

From the point of view of modern politics, this message may not seem very political, but it is pointed, if one sees the play aimed at Vienna's suburban audiences. It is an old truism that people living in palaces are not necessarily right, or rich. Nestroy adds that this doesn't mean that peasants are no better, especially if they work to increase their own advantage at the cost of others. This is not the familiar class-based critique of capitalism that warns of the alienation of classes from one another, but rather the challenge for all classes in society.

Nestroy represents his world on the recognition that money, status, and a station in life are easily detachable from each other, and that they concern all classes of society, not just the rich. The real world can have poor aristocrats, rich peasants, and do-gooders who actually work for their own benefit rather than for others. If there is a revolution implicit in this play, it is not directed at capital or class structure; instead, it is a moral call for all members of society to reject false values so that they stop betraying themselves and their community. This revolution is in the tradition of Sancho Panza, who proved himself a very good governor (after being appointed as the butt of a joke), but then who lays the job down because it is too much responsibility for those who have not been prepared for it. In *Don Quixote*, the threat is clear: a Duke and Duchess who make sport of their charges are likely to be replaced from the unlikeliest of places. In *The Talisman*, Nestroy's Titus is indeed a firebrand who carries the proverbial torch of honest labor and honest love into the world—and the eventual *Universalerbe* who will soon possess economic power, as well.

Nestroy's theater may be the best remembered nineteenth-century appeal to a public available in germanophone cultures, but, as we have seen, he was by no means the first author to take his audience seriously as a political force in the era of Europe's uprising politically fraught era. Nestroy, like Bäuerle and Grillparzer, document the increasingly brittle social climate of a Vienna that will see the upheavals of 1848, with the rest of Europe. Those revolutions will depose Emperor Ferdinand I in favor of his nephew, who would become the iconic Franz Joseph I—and they will find their resonance in Nestroy's work, as the next chapter will address. Yet *Talisman* already points to the source of political discontent in breaks between the nobility and their inside servants and the newer commercial classes—a world edging toward a certain break. After all, its hero's name echoes Shakespeare's *Titus Andronicus*—a fiction of revenge for a defiled daughter, leading to a change of regimes.

Public change, historical continuity

Three plays from Vienna of the *Vormärz* share very consistent visions of what is necessary for ensuring their society's domestic tranquility. Each offers a paradigm for political stability in a society under pressure, couched in humor and romance and embodied in individual heroes of great charm and empathy. In the societies staged, each profession has its place, but it should not necessarily be confined to a fixed station— as times change, so do their duties, rights, and obligations. None the less, an individual's rise above the station he is born into is never an answer in itself (Nestroy, Bäuerle); nor is a fall from a station or the upholding of any idea of an immutable social status (Grillparzer). In these plays, the eighteenth-century *Standesstaat* that the playwrights inherited needed reform, rather than to be abolished. Each shows that even members of a single class are not all equal in gifts and disposition, and that classes should all be considered equal before the Lord, able to contribute centrally to the general well-being.[64] Staberl, Leon, and Titus explore the limits of their class positions and reject only those who use their positions poorly, to damage rather than help.

What these playwrights recognize is something very like Kant's differentiation between public and private uses of reason. Individual

---

64 For the hereditary view of the *Standesstaat* and the stresses on it, see Hannes Stekl, "Unterschichten und Obrigkeit im Wien des ausgehenden 18. Jahrhunderts," and Günter Düriegl, "Wien: Eine Residenzstadt im Übergang von der adeligen Metropole zur bürgerlichen Urbanitat." Gerhard H. Weiss has a less sanguine interpretation of Nestroy's view of 1848 in his "The Revolution on the Stage."

jobs must get done, and well, for everyone to survive: it would not have been a crime or shame for Atalus to work in the kitchen, as Edrita realized—this is a private, moral decision about what is right rather than an assertion of public status. Yet at the same time, the parameters and rewards for all such jobs must be subject to public discussion, and even to revision. Grillparzer's *Hausverwalter* makes a bad decision when he sends the cook Leon back to the kitchen, guaranteeing the castle's food, but not using the man for his capabilities; Nestroy's chambermaid makes an equally bad one when she assumes that a suit of livery creates something better out of an outside servant, Titus. Bäuerle's Staberl shows his quality when he underscores how marrying for money is not enough; Titus, in turn, shows his quality when he looks to inherit a livelihood, not a free ride; Leon marries a noble barbarian from a class above him—a nominally "improper" but correct decision ratified by the Bishop in adopting the cook into his noble family. What counts in all these plays is doing society's work in good faith and being receptive to change, yet not change initiated by arbitrary and absolutist prescriptions of equality or revolts against them. Equality, after all, can be as evil a myth as any status hierarchy is, if it fossilizes and substitutes titles for deeds. A bishop using his own money will be poor; a barber with a smattering of education can act like a secretary, but will do more damage than good; marrying out of your station for money removes you from the protection of that group. In all three plays, therefore, the fable of the action espouses an interlocked vision of society.

If such plays are considered representatives of Biedermeier complacency, as German critics are wont to assume, then they have seriously underrated the political challenges offered to an urban audience confronting a changing economic and social landscape—an audience able to engage in debate about its communal future. Overall, they offer strikingly parallel analyses of the rise of a new class that need not be alienated from the base of society through money alone, a class that will gladly serve, if their rewards are commensurate with their risks and their service. In a more legalistic sense, this is the image of a society not ruled by privilege and by money, but rather by duty and achievement, no matter on how small a scale, based on skills freely offered and openly acknowledged, an alternative vision to that of the Protestant work ethic that would come to fruition in the German Empire, and a decisive move away from the stereotype of enlightened absolutism.[65] This is the revolution from the prompter's box that would fulfill

---

65   For a discussion of the hereditary situation of absolutism in the Habsburg state, see Karl Otmar Freiherr von Aretin, "Das Josephinismus und das Problem des katholischen aufgeklärten Absolutismus."

Schiller's sense of the stage as educational, a revolution that needs no barricades or weapon except the rapier wit of a political comedy. This is the "stage as a moral force"[66] used in the name of social transformation and public discussions of what changes must bring, presented in forms drawn from Europe's culture, by writers engaged with their worlds rather than geniuses hoping to lead it, starting discussions within a public comprising many classes and interests, both inside and outside of Vienna's city walls, in an increasingly diverse public space.

---

66 This again refers to Schiller's "The Stage Considered as a Moral Institution" ("Die Schaubühne als eine moralische Anstalt betrachtet," 1784).

Four   Eclipses, Floods, and
         Biedermeier Catastrophes:
         Public Spaces *in extremis*

The genre painting of the Viennese literary Biedermeier sought and
found reality in its own way: it captured typical situations from
Viennese life with all their uniqueness, it showed the Viennese
access to the world and passed it to the next generation in many
ways: humorous, satirical, idyllic, sad, sentimental, with straightforward wisdom or in a coarse, noisy way, in standard language
and in dialect. It decisively determined the forms of writing, as
well as the images that the Viennese had of themselves and their
world. (Zeman, "'Niederländische Gemäldewahrheit,'" 80)[1]

The theater introduced in the previous chapters sought to engage its
audiences and to question the master narratives of society on the basis
of its own experience. Just as critically, those audiences were not simply
the elite or the educated middle classes. It is no accident that all three
plays revolve around ordinary working Viennese and their milieu,
including the great houses and businesses in which they worked in the
Vormärz, the era before the 1848 revolutions.

Art historians and musicologists prefer to refer to this era as
the Biedermeier, a term that originally was the name of a fictitious,
humorous bourgeois gentleman created in 1848 for a Munich periodical,
Fliegende Blätter. The term was transferred into the history of art and

---

1   "Das Genrebild des Wiener literarischen Biedermeier hat die Wirklichkeit auf
    seine Art gesucht und gefunden: Es hat typische Situationen des WIener Lebens
    mit allen Eigenarten festgehalten, es hat den Zugang des Wieners zur Welt gezeigt
    und humoristische, satirisch, idyllisch, traurig, sentimental, in schlichter Weisheit
    oder auf derb polternde Art, in Hochsprache und Mundart der Nachwelt erhalten.
    Es hat die Erscheinungsweise der Dichtung, es hat das Bild, das die Wiener von
    Wien, von sich selbst und von der Welt machten, entscheidend mitgeprägt."

decorations around 1900, to refer to the lifestyle and furnishings typical of the bourgeoisie in Central Europe. As Herbert Zeman defines it above, the arts and crafts movements bearing that name, especially its genre painting (focused on everyday life), has much in common with literary Biedermeier seen in the *Volkstheater* plays of Bäuerle, Nestroy, and Grillparzer. Both the era's stage works and paintings celebrate the people of Vienna: the scholar in his garret, the child, the peasant, the ideal landscape illuminated by divine light, and the nuclear family— fixtures in the paintings of Ferdinand Georg Waldmüller (1793–1865) and Peter Fendi[2] (1976–1842), just as they were in the dramas of the *Volkstheater*.[3] That Vienna, as we have seen, seems to be a culture of growing luxury and privilege, social-climbing, and censorship that was threatening to lose its moral compass—what Heinz Politzer called the "unfathomable Biedermeier" (*das abgründige Biedermeier*, the subtitle of his book on Grillparzer).

Zeman's analogy also brings up the compelling visual dimension of Biedermeier literature, especially its genre pictures or tableaux of disasters, natural or otherwise. Both the paintings and the literature are replete with representations of floods (the final scenes of Grillparzer's *Der arme Spielmann* [*The Poor Fiddler*],[4] closely paralleled by Peter Fendi's *Szene aus der Überschwemmung von 1830* [*Scene from the 1830 Flood*][5]), eclipses (Adalbert Stifter's "Die Sonnenfinsternis am 8. Juli 1842" ["The Eclipse of 8 July 1842"]), and other natural disasters (the lightning strike in Stifter's *Abdias*; the blizzard in *Bergkristall*). What binds them even closer to the drama material explored in the last chapter, however, is not their explicit tie of "natural" disaster, but their implications for individual humans who must choose what is right and

---

2   See the exemplary "The Poor Widow of an Officer" ("Die arme Offizierswitwe," 1836), reproduced at http://commons.wikimedia.org/wiki/Peter_Fendi# mediaviewer/File:Peter_Fendi_-_Die_arme_Offizierswitwe.jpeg   (accessed August 8, 2011).

3   This chapter has been heavily reworked from an earlier published essay: "Eclipses, Floods, and Other Biedermeier Catastrophes" (2002).

4   One of only two prose works produced by a writer known principally as a playwright, it was begun in 1831, completed in 1842, but not published until 1847, in an almanac in Pest dated 1848 (Bahr, 301–2): *Iris: Deutsche Almanach für 1848*, published by Gustav Heckenast, Stifter's publisher. Appearing out of the way and basically swept from public view by the political situation of 1848, it received practically no notice until it was reprinted in 1871 in the *Deutscher Novellenschatz* by Paul Heyse (Cowen, 9). See Katherine Arens, "Grillparzer's *Fiddler*: The Space of Class Consciousness," for an extended version of the argument made here.

5   Also represented in Eduard Gurk's "Roßau, Schmidgasse am 2. März 1830." Reproduced   at   http://commons.wikimedia.org/wiki/File:Eduard_Gurk-_ Roßau,_Schmidgasse_am_2_März_1830.jpg#file (accessed August 8, 2011).

moral to do when their worlds are disrupted—just as the heroes of the plays had to do.

The present chapter will argue that these purportedly "Biedermeier" paintings and visual reference in the era's literature have much in common: they are based not only on their creators' belief in the rationality of the audience, but also on how that audience was educated. Evidence from the school curricula and the texts themselves will argue that they follow a very consistent rhetorical strategy to engage their audiences. Like the plays of Bäuerle, Grillparzer, and Nestroy introduced earlier, the era's visual representations also present images that are legible to their audiences because they rest on the era's master narratives and on common references from Europe's cultural history. Yet, like the plays, these visual representations undercut the seemingly natural or realistic logic of these narratives and ask their viewers to ask deeper questions about the public spaces and everyday scenes they show.

This discussion will thus begin by introducing the stories that art historians have recovered as typical critiques of everyday life communicated in paintings that initially seem to be awash in sentiment or bathos, but then, slowly, emerge as public questioning of the day's issues, as well. The visual art of the Biedermeier reveals itself as needing to be read, in ways that the citizens were taught to do in school. After that, it will turn to a selection of literary genre pictures, to show their use of visual representations to create a critical optic on class and legitimacy—that is, to show that they share a particular strategy of representation designed to heighten their audience's consciousness about the political situation. Like the texts encountered earlier in this volume, they do not necessarily advocate any particular revolutionary politics, but they find new links between public morality and the purported truth of history, in the context of their own experiences. This visual rhetoric, in addition, was available to both conservatives and liberals—to potentially revolutionary voices like Nestroy's, as well as in religious contexts that recognized it as related to strategies for reading that the church supported for centuries.

As subsequent parts turn back to literature, Adalbert Stifter (1805–68), along with Nestroy and Grillparzer, the third great author of the Austrian canon, is brought as evidence for the wide adoption of this rhetoric.[6] Even though he is more commonly associated with German

---

6   Stifter is most often discussed as a regional realist, and so is generally represented next to Gottfried Keller and Theodor Storm, yet with little detailed reference to his situation in Austria; for a recent example, see Albrecht Koschorke, "Erziehung zum Freitod: Adalbert Stifters pädagogischer Realismus" (2008). The norm in that twentieth-century scholarship was to treat Stifter's work thematically, under concepts like "resignation" or "humanism." As anglophone scholars

Realism and the second half of the nineteenth century, he none the less has access to the same pedagogical-critical imperatives, albeit in prose forms, under discussion here. And Stifter was also a landscape painter, very attuned to the visual in his prose.[7]

One of Stifter's newspaper essays, the introduction to a famous collection of his novellas, and the only play by Nestroy that does not rest on European sources, all use this specific rhetoric to demonstrate how, when catastrophes set in, traditional optics fail.

Genre painting and critical reading

In a volume on the *Wiener Biedermeier*, Klaus Albrecht Schröder argues that the era's focus on domesticity is "a private present, a collective act of compensation for political disempowerment" ("Epocheneuphorie," 7).[8] None the less, he goes on to recover the era's genre painting as creating a very specific kind of public dialogue, familiar from centuries of European painting.

Genre painting refers to everyday life (realistic, imagined, or romanticized), a tradition that extends back to painting of the Dutch Golden Age. These paintings, Schröder notes, "tell stories" in realistic ways, without intending to be real: "The sum of the genre paintings does not yield a kaleidoscope of reality" (Schröder, "Kunst," 9).[9] However, they are often difficult for outsiders to read because they are extraordinarily tied to the local. Schröder even believes they are "not autonomous," because the stories serve other ideals, even as they try to create a "dialogue between picture and viewer" that comments on a shared life (*gemeinsamen Lebenszusammenhang* [Schröder, "Kunst," 11]).

---

of the late nineteenth century have turned more toward issues of nationalism and gender, rather than representation, Stifter has fallen from view outside of germanophone scholarship. The bicentennial of his birth saw the publication of a collection that reviews the state of the art on his work: Jattie Enklaar, Hans Ester, and Evelyne Tax, eds, *Geborgenheit und Gefährdung in der epischen und malerischen Welt Adalbert Stifters* (2006), which includes work on his use of visual images (see Thomas Montfort) and the "Gentle Law" (Alfred Doppler). A special issue of *Informationen zur Deutschdidaktik: Zeitschrift für den Deutschunterricht in Wissenschaft und Schule* 1 (2005), edited by Herwig Gottwald, Christian Schacherreiter, and Werner Wintersteiner, provides a kind of "introduction to teaching Stifter," including a timeline (Gottwald), discussions of the social background (Ulrich Dittmann), and examples of his narrative art (Gottwald). The classic discussion of the Biedermeier as an era of culture is Friedrich Sengle's *Biedermeierzeit* (3 vols, 1971–80), in which Stifter figures prominently.

7   For a typical discussion of Stifter's attention to the visual, see Tove Holmes, "'… was ich in diesem Hause geworden bin'" (2010).
8   "eine [private] Gegenwelt, … kollektive Kompensationshandlung für politische Entmündung."
9   "Die Summe der Genrebilder ergibt kein Kaleidoskop der Wirklichkeit."

Genre paintings appeal to their audiences by representing affects and experiences. Yet what distinguishes the Viennese pictures from their precursors is that they operate in clearly marked historical spaces, not just the kinds of abstracts associated with parables. Wolfgang Häusler stresses that the pictures refer particularly to the historical situations of their audiences, to the "self-knowledge and world view of the bourgeoisie" (Häusler, "'Biedermeier' oder 'Vormärz'?," 43). Artists like Josef Danhauser deal with the contrasts between rich and poor, for instance (Schröder, "Kunst," 16). Others are consistent about physiognomy and "reading faces" that bear clear local marks.

At base, then, these paintings are activist. In general, they try to use affect to teach morals (*ihre moral-pädagogische Wirkung* [Schröder, "Kunst," 14]), albeit often with a degree of idealization in their style of representation. Yet they also consistently contrast an ideal situation with a real one, using rhetorical tactics:

> On the one hand, normative rules—topics, the system of figures of speech, the lessons of mode and decorum (thus the dicta of the three "genera dicendi")—refer back to the immutable essence of the humans themselves. On the other, claims to an immutable validity are bound up with a strong affinity to affects and their expression: a moment that points directly to the mutable subject. (Schröder, "Kunst," 29)[10]

In Schröder's view, the paintings rest on a rhetorical tension between two frames of understanding encompassed in one scene—two narratives occupying a single historical space, each tied up with conventional representation and with questions of validity (cf. Frodl and Frodl, 44). Even under conditions of more extreme censorship after 1830, the painting genre did not re-treat eighteenth-century forms, based more on myth and ideals rather than realities,[11] as they retained claims to raising issues about social justice.

The contemporaneous view of genre painting, however, is less reticent than these current scholars are. In tracing the persistence of genre pictures, Herbert Zeman cites Ignaz Jeitteles' *Aesthetisches Lexikon* (1835). Jeitteles' definition of genre is explicitly about the rhetorical purpose of these pictures:

---

10 "Zum einen sollen die normativen Regeln—die Topik, das System der Redefiguren, die Modus- und Decorumslehre (also die Lehre von den drei 'genera dicendi')—zurückgehen auf das unveränderliche Wesen des Menschen selbst. Zum anderen verbindet sich der Anspruch auf die unwandelbare Gültigkeit mit einer starken Affinität zu den Affekten und deren Ausdruck: Ein Moment, das unmittelbar auf das veränderliche Subjekt verweist."

11 "Der Refeudalisierung waren Grenzen gesetzt" (Häusler, 35).

The characteristic of genre painting is the representation of the real in contrast to the ideal, and it is distinguished from history-painting, just as the small, gay story is from the great history of the world—without any higher aim, than to be true and witty; it can move in either the serious or comic spheres, even if the element of the comic is the real terrain of genre-painting. (Zeman, "'Niederländische Gemäldewahrheit,'" 73)[12]

Even though scholars today agree that genre painting becomes more historicist-naturalist in the course of the century, this quotation none the less underscores what is less explored today: the specific historical references that could link moral imperatives to political ones as a kind of history from below.

Indirectly, Zeman makes this connection in linking genre painting and the plays of Kotzebue, Iffland, and Raimund, as well as the *Volkstheater:*

The Viennese authors of the Biedermeier era [...] knew the aesthetic projects of visual art and transposed it—as the example of Grillparzer demonstrates—onto the characteristic forms of their own production. Their nearness to the presentation of genre paintings came about almost without notice. (Zeman, "'Niederländische Gemäldewahrheit,'" 74)[13]

Thus the overtly political dramas of the era also used the visual logics of fine art in the era. Note, too, that Jeitteles' description is echoed in Stifter's famous *Gentle Law* (*Sanftes Gesetz*), where the author—also a painter—draws attention to the small and cheerful as revealing of history as are its great events.

It is none the less still easy to undervalue such oblique appeals to public morals as socially or politically revolutionary. Yet such attention to moral uplift was indeed part of an active tradition in education in several Catholic nations of Europe. From the mid-eighteenth century on, Austrian politicians debated the relation of education and the state.

---

12 "Der Charakter der Genremalerei ist Darstellung des Wirklichen im Gegensatze des Idealen, und unterscheidet sich von der Historienmalerei, wie die kleine heitere Erzählung von der großartigen Weltgeschichte, ohne höhere Strebung, als wahr und geistreich zu seyn, sie möge sich in ernster oder komischer Sphäre bewegen, wiewohl das Element des Komischen das eigentliche Gebiet der Genremalerei ist."

13 "Die Wiener Autoren der Biedermeierzeit ... kannten die ästhetischen Anliegen der bildenden Kunst und übertrugen sie—wie das Beispiel Grillparzers zeigt— auf die Geartetheit ihrer eigenen Produktionen. Die Nähe zur Gestaltung von Genrebildern stellte sich beinahe unversehens ein."

An earlier version of these debates had come to fruition in seventeenth-century France, in debates about Jansenism and the Port-Royal reforms, which were aimed at dealing with problems of divine grace, divine-right rule, and the absolute corruption of individuals due to original sin. The Jesuits had argued for a rational grace morality that allowed individuals to disobey laws that they felt were immoral, and that would allow the pope to topple princes (Seibert, 10–11), making them the agents who suppressed Jansenism in France.

The European story is more complicated. Reformed forms of Catholicism had arisen to combat crypto-Protestantism, as Enlightenment ideals forced absolutist states to entertain visions of an enlightened Christianity—in Austria, particularly as a response to the comparative conservative Baroque Christianity associated with Austria's post-Napoleonic reactionism. Yet such movements, like Jansenism itself, soon became aligned with the ruling house: what had started as a political and religious response to the Protestant Reformation began to reinforce the dynasty. Not surprisingly, Maria Theresa and Franz Stephan, together with other influential families, were believed to be Jansenists in educational reform ("ebenfalls war in der Beamtenschaft eine jansenistische Einstellung verbreitet" [Seibert 1987, 13]). Morality and politics remained closely linked in discussions about implementing these Jansenist models for individual Enlightenment in the education system.

Adolf Ficker notes that the educational system of eighteenth-century Austrian *Gymnasia* was essentially Jesuit, albeit moving toward a more liberal evaluation of individual abilities (Ficker, 113). Originally, the first-year curriculum presented the rudiments of grammar and syntax, the second, "poetics, rhetoric and logic, physics, metaphysics." By the eighteenth century, this curriculum was sometimes considered too narrow for practical life, and so the Piarists were given control over the schools in the Bohemian crown lands, then in Austria itself (Ficker, 114). They added Greek and German, history and geography, and math and physics to the curriculum, and each region in the Empire was allowed to make its own changes to tailor the curriculum to local circumstances. Other orders took over various other educational instructions, such as the Benedictine *Schottenstiften* in eighteenth-century Vienna, which were characterized as a "philosophical institute of education" ("philosophische Lehranstalt" [Ficker, 114]). After the Jesuits were suspended in 1773, science became an even more important part of the curriculum, when Baron van Swieten again reorganized the curriculum. Ernst Seibert traces how, by the second half of the eighteenth century, these conflicts were also being played out in children's literature and in translation politics.

In the narrow sphere of school governance, these eighteenth-century battles for reform receded by the nineteenth century, but they had lasting effects on the school systems, leaving Austrian education framed as moral education, particularly in the service of the state. Literacy projects in the classroom were straightforwardly engaged as relevant to politics as well as to everyday life. The description of that curriculum mirrors what Grillparzer assumed about historical narratives:

> The *study of philosophy* is the mediating ring that unites elementary education with education for the professions.
>
> After the youth has learned to express his thoughts in correct language, in elementary school, then he learns to specify concepts, compare, draw conclusions. And this is the achievement of *logic* and *metaphysics*. *Natural theology* and *moral philosophy* show him the correspondence of religion and healthy reason.
>
> *History*, which earlier had been taught to students in terms of its important moments, is now exposed as the source of experience, as the mirror of morals and customs, the mistress of bourgeois transformation (*vitae civilis magistra*), as a doctrine of cause and effect, as a true psychology of the human race. (Wolf, 44–5)[14]

Civic-moral education was thus consciously implemented into the curriculum. For the present purposes it is also significant that learners were taught how to negotiate their relation to the world through a doubled optic, historical/literal and then also moral.

School readers, for example, offered retellings of bible stories that were drawn into explicit parallels with figures of the *Herrscherhaus* by calling stories in parallel names.[15] Seibert documents wider impacts

---

14 "Das *philosophische Studium* ist der mittlern Ring, der die Elementar- mit der Berufslehre vereinigt.

Nachdem der Jüngling in der Elementarlehgre gelernt hat, seine Gedanken sprachrichtig auszudrücken, lernt er nun Begriffe bestimmen, vergleichen, schließen. U. dieses leistet die *Logik* und *Metaphysik*. *Die natürliche Theologie* und *Moralphilosophie* zeigt ihm die Uebereinstimmung der Religion mit der gesunden Vernunft.

Die *Geschichte*, welche früher in ihren wichtigen Momenten den Schüler gelehrt wurde, wird nun als die Quelle der Erfahrung, als der Spiegel der Sitten, die Meisterin des bürgerlichen Wandels (vitae civilis magistra) als eine Lehre von Ursache und Folge, als eine wahre Psychologie des menschlichen Geschlechtes vorgetragen."

15 This practice continued well into the nineteenth century. Joseph Roth's Trotta tried to get a fictional account of how he saved Franz Joseph at the battle of Solferino removed from the history books, which the Emperor remembered until the end of his life (cf. *Radetzkymarsch*, chapters 15 and 18). One particularly interesting story, "Ohne Bewilligung" by Leopold Kompert, tells how a Jewish

of these battles, but for the present purposes it suffices to note that students using these books would be accustomed to drawing parallels between morality fables and the legitimacy of the monarchy. What would reinforce such equations across class lines, in addition, is that writers of such morality fables drew on another eighteenth-century movement: Sentimentalism, *Empfindsamkeit*, which throughout Europe was a literature of the hegemonic classes, but one with exceptional critical potential.

> It is remarkable that this reception of the Enlightenment and Sentimentalism found its continuation in the youth literature of the subsequent era (after about 1775, and not only out of the hands of ex-Jesuits). This is revealed in the reception of poets like Gellert, Geßner, Gleim, and Klopstock in collections or newspapers that were expressly meant for children and youth. (Seibert, 33)[16]

Sentimental authors were included in the textbooks of the Habsburg state because their works were deemed appropriate to moral education. These choices document a kind of public literacy that artists in all media could straightforwardly rely on: their publics understood that rhetorics needed to be read politically-morally, and in more than one voice, beyond the literal. In this framework, it would be legitimate to consider this rhetorical and reading tradition in essence a very specific mass media literacy whose critical potential has been underrated.[17]

Facts about literacy and school attendance support such conjecture about what the Austrian public could be counted on to know. In December 1774, the first general school ordinance (*Reichsvolksschulgesetz*) required attendance at school between the ages of six and twelve. Statistics for Bohemia and Moravia are likely to be indicative for the monarchy as a whole, as shown in Table 1.

---

peasant was heard by the Emperor who "gave him a family," that is, permission to marry and establish a legal household in an age that restricted the number of Jewish families in specific regions.

16   "[Es] ist doch bemerkenswert, daß diese Rezeption von Aufklärung und Empfindsamkeit in mehreren jugendliterarischen Publikationen der Folgezeit [nach za. 1775] (nicht nur aus der Hand von Exjesuiten) eine Fortsetzung findet. Dies zeigt sich bei der Aufnahme von Dichtern wie Gellert, Geßner, Gleim und Klopstock in Sammlungen bzw. Zeitschriften, die ausdrücklich für Kinder und Jugendliche gedacht waren."

17   The case for Sentimentalism as a political rhetoric is made by John R. J. Eyck in *The Tragedy of Sentimentalism and Politics in Enlightenment Europe* (1999).

Table 1

	1775	1785	1791
Böhmen	14.000 Schüler	117.000 Schüler (2.200 Schulen)	–
Mähren	1.000 Schüler	67.876 Schüler	224.471 Schüler

Source: Seibert 1987, 210

This growth in literacy occurred in an era when state politics went from potentially liberal to definitely conservative, as a reaction to the French Revolution.

No matter the state's politics, however, moral education remained the watchword of the Habsburg school systems, albeit with differing emphases. The curriculum itself was later pruned back, after complaints about school stress, to become more minimalist. None the less, the early phases of this expansion fell under the umbrellas of enlightened Christianity. In the decade of Josephinian rule, as noted, the curriculum was expanded to more topics, under a kind of "encyclo-pedist" influence, with a more practical bent. Yet complaints about "school stress" made themselves heard and the curriculum retreated to its religious-practical framing in the 1805 School Order (Seibert 1987: 211). Overall, the cause of literacy stagnated on the state side, leaving adult readers to find new domains of public literature and culture—but it left public education in place as I described it. Whatever the politics of the authorities, readers were conditioned into "moral-patriotic" education, which could straightforwardly be used to comment not only on morals, but on the *patria*, as well, especially when saints' lives in school books were paired with stories of the emperor.

Such "official" literacy can lead us back to genre paintings with a new appreciation for claims of their political relevance. Their familiar moral content would be read as implicating politics, not only society, as they "told stories" that helped their viewers understand their worlds—almost exactly as Grillparzer described it. Such stories could be constructed to require audiences to exert their critical faculties— politicized readings did not require overt political content. Whether in narrative forms, in theatrical tableaux, or in genre paintings, scenes encoded for the morality of everyday life in that era are thus neces-sarily also encoded politically, official or otherwise. For the present purposes it is critical to underscore that such moral-political encoding could be used for either conservative or liberal causes—even to focus attention on the officially repressed darker side of life in the Austrian state in the mid-nineteenth century, including overcrowding, hunger, overwork, social alienation, and censorship.

In this sense, more liberal readers tutored in the finer points of public morality may well have been able to read these images straightforwardly as critique, directed at the great social lies of Restoration Austria under Metternich. By using social-rhetorical figures familiar from both everyday life and the state hegemony, artists could turn language and images censored by the state to their own purposes. As Stifter would argue in the 1853 "Preface" to his story collection *Colored Stones* (*Bunte Steine*) and exemplify in *Witiko* (1865–7), the course of the world need not be found only in its great events, but also in the everyday, repeated actions that habituate each of us into a view of the "normal" world.[18] Disasters (natural or manmade) can interrupt that world at any moment, changing the audience's vision of the world and their own place in it.

It is no accident, therefore, that Peter Fendi's great painting of the 1830 Vienna flood[19] has two famous associated images: Eduard Gurk's 1830 images of Emperor Franz II/I and Erzherzog Ferdinand and Erzherzog Franz Carl visiting flood victims,[20] and Johann Matthias Ranftl's 1840 "Dog Tragedy"/"Hundetragödie" from the 1838 Budapest flood.[21] Fendi's patriotic image initially looks like a cross between Théodore Géricault's *The Raft of the Medusa* (1818–19) and a plague column, as people caught in the flood try to rescue themselves by climbing into building windows on upper floors. However, on closer inspection one cannot overlook the fact that those who are saved by the climbing into the windows of the upper floors of the local courthouse (*Ortsgericht*) seem to be upper class. In a similar critical approach, Ranftl (1804–54), dubbed the "Hunde-Raffael," depicts a flood in Budapest by showing a mother dog chained to a doghouse being washed away, with

---

18 Wolfgang Wiesmüller's "Die Europa-Diskussion im 19. Jahrhundert und der historische Roman" (2007) explains *Witiko* as a comment on current history.

19 Reproduced at http://www.reproarte.com/Kunstwerke/Peter_Fendi/Szene+aus+der+%C3%9Cberschwemmung+von+1830/12776.html (accessed August 8, 2011). Fendi's painting is also in Frodl and Schröder, eds, *Wiener Biedermeier*, plate 110.

20 Reproduced at http://english.habsburger.net/module-en/neu-im-programm-wohnungen-mit-wasseranschluss-zu-viel-und-zu-wenig-wasser-in-wien/neu-im-programm/MB%20ST_W5%20MOD5%2001.jpg/?size=preview&plus=1 (accessed August 8, 2011). The Gurk watercolors are also reproduced in Koschatzky, *Biedermeier und Vormärz*, 74–5.

21 Reproduced at http://www.reproarte.com/picture/Johann+Matthias_Ranftl/Scene+from+the+inundation+1838+in+Budapest/15038.html (accessed August 8, 2011). Ranftl's painting is also in Frodl and Schröder, eds, *Wiener Biedermeier*, plate 179. My thanks are due to Michaela Laichmann of Vienna for the Gurk reference, and to Thomas K. Wolber of Ohio Wesleyan University for help in locating the Fendi painting.

her puppies sliding off its roof. They are drowning because the people who chained them are not there to save them.[22]

These pictures were purportedly all well known at the time because they were publicly exhibited and reviewed. Taken together, they can easily be read as telling the kind of satirical stories about society familiar from Hogarth and Fragonard, yet with even more overt political edges. The parallels to news images of New Orleans after Hurricane Katrina are unavoidable: images of human suffering that were almost universally read as images pointing to government neglect.

Even though critics today are less willing to accept as art such post-Enlightenment representations of public sphere morality, it is not difficult to recover such images as both moral and political. Yet it is also instructive to see how such tableaux are built up, to see how their audiences are brought to draw analogies between public morals and the state.

The eclipse and the butterflies: *Dies irae*?

There are things that one knows for 50 years, and then, in the 51st, one is astounded about the momentousness and fearfulness of their contents. This is what happened to me in the total eclipse that we in Vienna experienced on the July 8, 1842 in the earliest morning hours, under the most favorable heavens. (Stifter, "Sonnenfinsternis," 102)[23]

The paradigm for such activist literacy might well be Adalbert Stifter (1805–68), who is remembered on the quiescent side of the moral-political divide pursued here.[24] The playwright Friedrich Hebbel called

---

22 The painting is reproduced at https://reproarte.com/de/component/virtuemart/szene-aus-der-ueberschwemmung-1838-in-budapest-detail (accessed January 20, 2015).

23 "Es gibt Dinge, die man fünfzig Jahre weiß, und im einundfünfzigsten erstaunt man über die Schwere und Furchtbarkeit ihres Inhaltes. So ist es mir mit der totalen Sonnenfinsternis ergangen, welche wir in Wien am 8. Juli 1842 in den frühesten Morgenstunden bei dem günstigen Himmel erlebten."

24 Stifter is well-documented in the secondary literature as both a brilliant writer of prose (central to Austrian writers into the twentieth century) and a political. For an overview of the secondary literature, see Eisenmeier (1964), Seidler (1972a, 1972b, 1981), and Lachinger (1990). His image as a Biedermeier conservative pervades his early modern reception in *Germanistik*, in the texts that set up the standard terms of his reputation: in English, Gump (1974) and Swales and Swales (1984); in German, Staiger (1952), Irmscher (1971), and Sengle (3 vols, 1971, 1972, 1980). A more recent set of reevaluations is found in a number of volumes that bring more realistic historical and scientific concerns into focus; see the following edited collections: Enklaar et al. (which includes John's essay describing the new

him "the comma in a tailcoat,"[25] and he is remembered philosophically[26] and historically[27] as the author of the "Gentle Law" (*Sanftes
Gesetz*). Yet Stifter can straightforwardly be recovered as a "painter in
words" who used the strategies of the genre-painting in which he was
trained in his stories and essays, to educate his readers.

The passage quoted at the start of this chapter is the opening of
perhaps the best known of Adalbert Stifter's newspaper essays, "The
Eclipse of July 8, 1842" ("Die Sonnenfinsternis am 8. Juli 1842").[28]
This essay is a masterpiece of pictorial description. His eclipse pours
heretofore-unseen colors over a landscape, as celestial effects transform
human vision. His text correlates that visual evidence with current
ideas of fate or the divine (as a product of favorable heavens [*günstiger
Himmel*]) and questions the limits of human understanding at moments
when the universe suddenly seems alien. "The Eclipse" is thus as much
about a solar phenomenon as it is about human (especially scientific)
knowledge—about physics and metaphysics as competing forms of
human understanding.

Stifter starts by offering a more personal perspective, commenting
on the event as part of his own experience. He had, he states, known
the theories of eclipses for years:

> But when the eclipse then actually did begin, where I stood on a
> lookout high above the whole city and saw the appearance with my
> own eyes, then to be sure quite different things transpired than I had
> ever thought of, either awake or in dreams, and about which one
> who had not seen the marvel would not think of.—Never and never
> in my whole life was I so shaken, so shaken by fear and the sublime,
> as in these two minutes—it was nothing less than as if God had
> suddenly spoken a clear word, and I had understood it. (103–4)[29]

historical-critical edition [2006]), Hettche, John, and Steinsdorff (2000), Lachinger
et al. (1985), Laufhütte and Möseneder (1996), and Roli (2001).

25 See Lothar Schneider, "Das Komma im Frack: Adalbert Stifter, von Hebbels
Kritik aus betrachtet" (1996) for details on this review.

26 See Domandl (1972, 1976), Schäublin (1975), Helmetag (1986), Zeman (2004–6),
or Koschorke (2008) for discussions of Stifter's philosophy.

27 For discussions of Stifter's ideas of history, many of which stress his conservatism, see, for instance: Borchmeyer (1980), Neugebauer (1982), Wiesmüller
(1985, 2007, 2008), Häusler (1992), Bulang (2000), Maurer (2005), Ritzer (2010),
or Gordon (2012).

28 This essay receives little comment from scholars. Recent exceptions are Barbara
Potthast, "'Ein lastend unheimliches Entfremden unserer Natur'" (2008), who
presents it in relation to modernism, and Alexander Stillmark's short introduction, "Adalbert Stifter: The Eclipse of the Sun" (1997).

29 "Aber da sie [die Sonnenfinsternis] nun wirklich eintraf, da ich auf einer Warte
hoch über der ganzen Stadt stand und die Erscheinung mit eigenen Augen

Here, Stifter uses the subjunctive to talk about his experience of God, underscoring that he is speaking of a narrative about God, not direct revelation.[30] His first reaction was to descend from his vantage point "like Moses descending from the burning mountain," with new images of the world. Why does his world change so decisively? His answer is couched in two rhetorics, one from science, and the other from the Bible.

The event is most straightforwardly argued in biblical terms. God simply had ordained the event for individuals, as part of his creation:

A thousand times a thousand years ago, God arranged this for today, at this second; he laid the fibers in our hearts for us to experience it. Through the writing of his stars he promised that it would come, after thousands and thousands of years; our fathers have learned to decipher this script and predicted the second at which it must occur. We, late descendants, raise our eyes and our telescopes toward the sun at the indicated second, and see, it comes—understanding is already triumphing that it was able to calculate the magnificence and the arrangement of the heavens and learn from it—and, indeed, this triumph is one of the most just for humanity—it is coming, quietly it grows—but see, God also gave this something for the heart, something that we had not known about in advance and which is a million times more valuable than what the understanding comprehended and could calculate in advance. He gives him the word: "I am." (Stifter, XIV, 104–5)[31]

---

anblickte, da geschahen freilich ganz andere Dinge, an die ich weder wachend noch träumend gedacht hatte und an die keiner denkt, der das Wunder nicht gesehen.—Nie und nie in meinem ganzen Leben war ich so erschüttert, von Schauer und Erhabenheit so erschüttert, wie in diesen zwei Minuten—es war nicht anders, als hätte Gott auf einmal ein deutliches Wort gesprochen, und ich hätte es verstanden."

30 This case is made in Arens, "An Alternate Stifter: Psychologist," which argues for Stifter as an educational psychologist who was interested in a much more active engagement with his readers than most readers today believe.

31 "Vor tausendmal tausend Jahren hat Gott es so gemacht, daß es heute zu dieser Sekunde sein wird; in unsere Herzen aber hat er die Fibern gelegt, es zu empfinden. Durch die Schrift seiner Sterne hat er versprochen, daß es kommen werde nach tausend und tausend Jahren, unsere Väter haben diese Schrift entziffern gelernt und die Sekunde angesagt, in der es eintreffen müsse; wir, die späten Enkel, richten unsere Augen und Sehröhre zu gedachter Sekunde gegen die Sonne, und siehe, es kommt—der Verstand triumphiert schon, daß er ihm die Pracht und Einrichtung seiner Himmel nachgerechnet und abgelernt hat—und in der Tat, der Triumph ist einer der gerechtesten des Menschen—es kommt, stille wächst es weiter—aber siehe, Gott gab ihm auch für das Herz etwas mit, was wir nicht voraus gewußt und was millionenmal mehr wert ist,

This is a curious passage, in one reading very theistic in tone, stressing how divine truth *feels*. In another reading, it is also Kantian: our knowledge of the phenomenon is produced by the understanding as a narrative combining facts empirically noted and rationally considered. Still, that rational narrative converges with an unexpected, sublime experience, proof for the heart of a kind of divine plan beyond humanly knowable. Stifter here casts faith and reason as symmetrical, or syncretic, in this event. The "facts" of the event are not at issue; what needs to be understood is the rest of the event, to show its impact on individuals—"die Empfindung nach zu malen" (XIV, 105). Here, faith meets reason at the limits where both ultimately fail.

To capture the knowledge about the eclipse held by the human heart, mind, and soul alike, Stifter narrates the event from both perspectives and then adds a third, using the vocabulary of art. Stifter's vantage point is on the roof of a house, his "Warte," likely the "Hohe Warte," one of the highest points in the city of Vienna, the site of an observatory. But in his account, it is just a roof to which he climbs at 5.00 a.m. When the sun comes up, he can see the Danube and, in the far distance, the "Hungarian mountains," together with fog over the horizon and "billows of clouds" (*Wolkenballen*). To speak about Vienna means to survey the city center and its symbol, "St. Stephen's Church, which rises up toward us out of the city, properly graspable and nearby, like a dark, quiet mountain range emerging from the rubble" (XIV, 105).[32] Onto this familiar scene will break the end of the world, and the Lord will appear, *dies irae*. A new and frightening view of the world rises out of the mist over the city, observed by people with telescopes—the text enacts a transition from science to the realm of religious experience.

The people around Stifter are suddenly transfixed by a catastrophic change in perspective. All suddenly focus on one point, joined in experience, looking toward the Tower of St. Stephen's (XIV, 106).[33] The physical event brings with it a group change of heart:

> Finally, at the minute predicted—just as if it [the sun] had received the soft kiss of death from an invisible angel—a fine strip of light drew back from this kiss, the other edge surged forth subtly and golden in the glass of the telescope—"it is coming," now they also said, even those only with smoked glass but otherwise with

---

als was der Verstand begriff und vorausrechnen konnte: das Wort gab er ihm mit: 'Ich bin' […]."

32 "die Stefanskirche, die ordentlich greifbar nahe an uns aus der Stadt wie ein dunkles, ruhiges Gebirge aus Gerölle emporstand"

33 "alle nach derselben Stelle des Himmels blickend, selbst auf der äußersten Spitze des Stephanturmes … das Ziel von Millionen Augen" (XIV, 106).

their bare eyes looked up—"it is coming"—and with excitement everyone looked on its continuation. The first strange, alien sentiments rippled now through their hearts ... (XIV, 106)[34]

The optical effect happened at the "minute predicted," but its affect is unforeseen. Stifter shows us how the situation represents not science, but the sublime, "the marvelous magic of the beautiful" (XIV, 106): "There dwells already in the monstrous space of the heavenly the sublime that overcomes our souls, and yet this space is, in mathematics, nothing but large" (XIV, 107).[35]

As the sun begins to disappear, birds and people are still in motion. The moon finally "ate away" the sun (*wegfraß* [107]). And a new world appears:

Finally, the effects also became visible on earth, and ever more so, as the sickle glowing in the heavens became ever smaller; the river no longer shimmered but became a ribbon of grey taffeta, dull shadows lay around us, the swallows became agitated, the beautiful soft glow of the heavens was extinguished, as if it had been filmed over with death, a light cool breeze raised itself and blew against us, over the meadows stared an indescribably unusual light, but as heavy as lead, over the woods all motion vanished with the play of lights, and there was peace upon them, but not the peace of slumber, but that of insensibility—… faces became ashen gray—this gradual dying was shattering, in the midst of the morning freshness that had reigned up until a few minutes earlier. (XIV, 108)[36]

---

34 "Endlich, zur vorausgesagten Minute—gleichsam wie von einem unsichtbaren Engel empfing sie den sanften Todeskuß – ein feiner Streifen ihres Lichtes wich vor dem Hauche dieses Kusses zurück, der andere Rand wallte in dem Glase des Sternenrohres zart und golden fort—"es kommt", riefen nun auch die, welche bloß mit dämpfenden Gläsern, aber sonst mit freien Augen hinaufschauten—"es kommt"—und mit Spannung blickte nun alles auf den Fortgang. Die erste seltsame, fremde Empfindung rieselte nun durch die Herzen ..."
35 "schon in dem ungeheuern Raum des Himmlischen wohne das Erhabene, das unsere Seele überwältigt, und doch ist dieser Raum in der Mathematik sonst nichts als groß."
36 "Endlich wurden auch auf Erden die Wirkungen sichtbar und immer mehr, je schmäler die am Himmel glühende Sichel wurde; der Fluß schimmerte nicht mehr, sondern war ein taftgraues Band, matte Schatten lagen umher, die Schwalben wurden unruhig, der schöne sanfte Glanz des Himmels erlosch, als liefe er von einem Hauche matt an, ein kühles Lüftchen hob sich und stieß gegen uns, über den Auen starrte ein unbeschreiblich seltsames, aber bleischweres Licht, über den Wäldern war mit dem Lichterspiele die Beweglichkeit verschwunden, und Ruhe lag auf ihnen, aber nicht die des Schlummers, sondern die der Ohnmacht— ... die

This image, described in a page-long run-on sentence signaling how intense the experience was, shows the death of the normal world, a graying out of the landscape, transforming it into the color scheme familiar from Hieronymus Bosch's apocalyptic paintings. The city, the purportedly greatest achievement of humankind, becomes a "play of shadows without substance" (*ein wesenloses Schattenspiel* [XIV, 108]).

Significantly, the scene is a "sad sight" that causes the public to gasp collectively and then lapse into the silence of the grave: "a properly sad sight—one disk stood covering the other … an 'ah' came out of every mouth in one voice, and then, the stillness of death, it was the moment when God spoke and men listened" (XIV, 109).[37] The clouds mount like special effects, against the deadened landscape and mute people:

> the clouds at the horizon that we had feared earlier now really augmented the phenomenon; they now stood up there like giants, from the tops of their heads, a fearful red ran down, and in deep, cold, heavy blue they arched under into themselves and pressed up against the horizon— … colors never before seen by an eye were seen, streaking through the heavens—the moon stood in the middle of the sun, but no longer as a black disk, but half transparent, and at the same time as if it were washed with a light shimmer of steel … (XIV, 109)[38]

Completing the baroque visual allusions to conversion and salvation, a ray of sunlight, a *Lichtpyramid*, falls on the Marchfeld, and a flood of light the color of sulfur onto another location. The city and people have become shades, phantoms of a world of scientific cause and effect that has given way to a world of light and feeling:

> the phantom of St. Stephen's Church hung in the air, the rest of the city was a shadow, all rumbling had stopped, there was no more movement on the bridge; because every wagon and

---

Gesichter wurden aschgrau—erschütternd war diese allmählige Sterben mitten in der noch vor wenigen Minuten herrschenden Frische des Morgens."

37 "ein ordentlich trauriger Anblick—deckend stand nun Scheibe auf Scheibe … ein einstimmiger 'Ah' aus aller Munde und dann Totenstille, es war der Moment, da Gott redete und die Menschen horchten."

38 "die Horizontwolken, die wir früher gefürchtet, halfen das Phänomen erst recht bauen, sie standen nun wie Riesen auf, von ihrem Scheitel rann ein fürchterliches Rot, und in tiefem kalten, schweren Blau wölbten sie sich unter und drückten den Horizont— … Farben, die nie ein Auge gesehen, schweiften durch den Himmel—der Mond stand mitten in der Sonne, aber nicht mehr als schwarze Scheibe, sondern gleichsam halb transparent wie mit einem leichten Stahlschimmer überlaufen …"

rider stood still, and every eye looked heavenwards—never, never will I forget those two minutes—it was the swoon of a giant body, our earth.—How holy, how incomprehensible and how frightful is that thing that surrounds us constantly … the light, when it withdraws from us even for so short an instant. (XIV, 110)[39]

This painterly description specifically recalls images of the end of the world. Stifter cites Lord Byron's poem "Darkness" (1816), in which people set their homes on fire to make light when the sun disappears— a Romantic poet is added to Stifter's world of religion, science, and visual art. When total darkness falls over Vienna, people cry and faint—women as well as "a serious, solid man" (*ein ernster, fester Mann* [XIV, 111]). Bringing his description full circle, Stifter cites the Bible on how graves split open when Christ died, and how the curtain of the temple was rent asunder.

But over the course of the passage, Stifter does not ultimately argue theistically: "Such majesty, I'd even say the nearness of God, appeared in these two minutes, so that the heart felt it had to stop beating" (XIV, 110).[40] Again, Stifter adheres to the subjunctive to frame God's existence, marking his passage with *as if* to stress it is a narrative rather than a truth of revelation. He will revert to biblical language to resolve the *dies irae* moment, the moment when the Lord has come with his righteous wrath ("But just as everything in creation has its just measure, so too did this event" [XIV, 111]),[41] and when the terrifying experience is over: "the world of masks had disappeared, and ours was here again" (XIV, 112).[42] Yet even in this moment of supreme affect, Stifter reminds us that what we see is not a reality, but simply our understanding of a field of data. The passage resolves in an almost cinematic fade-in, as color and animal sounds return to the scene, and then the essay closes, having worked though narratives to "explain" this event as science, art, and religion would have done. Each of these perspectives fails to

---

39 "[D]as Phantom der Stephanskirche hing in der Luft, die andere Stadt war ein Schatten, alles Rasseln hatte aufgehört, über der Brücke war keine Bewegung mehr; denn jeder Wagen und Reiter stand, und jedes Auge schaute zum Himmel—nie, nie werde ich jene zwei Minuten vergessen—es war die Ohnmacht eines riesenhaften Körpers, unserer Erde.—Wie heilig, wie unbegreiflich und wie furchtbar ist jenes Ding, das uns stets umflutet … das *Licht*, wenn es sich nur so kurz entzieht."

40 "aber auch eine solche Erhabenheit, ich möchte sagen, Gottesnähe war in der Erscheinung dieser zwei Minuten, daß es dem Herzen nicht anders war, als müsse er irgendwo stehen."

41 "Aber wie alles in der Schöpfung sein rechtes Maß hat, so auch diese Erscheinung."

42 "[D]ie Larvenwelt [war] verschwunden und die unsere wieder da."

exhaust the phenomenon; even formal laws of nature elide the various possible understandings of a natural event, including the *Dies Irae*. The phenomenon remains greater than its parts.

Stifter's essay moves easily among these frames of reference, including the religious vocabulary of the baroque or Counter-Reformation, as well as that of artistic representation and scientific explanation. Each frame's narrative carries with it its own element of truth and a posited morality, and so his comparison stresses the limits of human understanding, the point where reason reaches its limits. Similarly, when the sublime breaks into everyday experience, that experience is expressible only as an affective understanding, through biblical diction or art, or in words anchored in group tradition, personal-psychological motivation, and historical contingency. What participants in such an event *see* happen may not be what has *really* happened, if that vision is not directed by both the head and the heart. Stifter's vantage point on the "Hohe Warte," a modern scientific landmark, is juxtaposed with St. Stephen's Church, to suggest that the event spans concerns of heaven and earth, history and individual experience, and the narratives that encompass the eclipse redefine human knowledge as a set of domains, each with its own point of view and strategy of interpretation. Many of Stifter's journalistic essays highlight how very political such juxtapositions can be,[43] in revealing limits on human understanding; his essays often express Enlightenment optimism about human learning, as well as defining the limits of human understanding in any of its modes:

Thus human learns from human, group from group, century from centuries, and the ideal of humanity gets ever richer and moves towards its boundary of perfection; we, the living, cannot even guess at how infinite it is, because, if we were to understand it, we would already have to possess it. ("Wirkungen der Schule" [1849]; *Vermischte Schriften* [ed. Steffen], 258)[44]

The living can never reach an ideal state of knowing, since learning is a process and a direction, not a goal that is achievable in historic space.

---

43 This discussion here ignores that many of Stifter's essays have explicitly political topics, such as the "Rückkehr nach der Revolution" of 1849. Remember that Stifter taught in the household of Pauline von Metternich, and so could not have been oblivious to contemporary politics.

44 "So lernt Mensch vom Menschen, Geschlecht vom Geschlechte, Jahrhundert von Jahrhunderten, und der Inbegriff der Menschheit wird immer reicher und geht einer Grenze der Vervollkommnung entgegen, von welcher wir Lebenden gar nicht einmal ahnen können, wie unendlich sie sei, weil wir, um sie zu begreifen, dieselbe schon innehaben müßten."

There is always the chance of an eclipse, distorting our sense of the world, disrupting our knowledge, and opening other narratives.

Stifter understands pious morality, the power of the images of baroque Catholicism, and science alike; he uses here with great power a rhetoric of analogy that poses questions in the space between the stories told by each of these domains.[45] Understanding through the mind and the human heart are not necessarily compatible; neither sentimentalism nor rationality itself can overcome eruptions of terror, awe, and wonder that shake all human understanding, rational or otherwise.

Given Stifter's use of analogical rhetoric in staging his description of an eclipse, it is worth revisiting his most famous essay, the 1852 foreword to his *Bunte Steine*, "Das sanfte Gesetz" or "Gentle Law," which is conventionally read as a confession of theism or pantheism, or as a Biedermeier aesthetics of withdrawal from politics and society. Stifter begins by speaking very personally: "The charge was once raised against me that I only represent the small things, and that my characters are always ordinary people" (9).[46] Yet as a companion piece to the "Sonnenfinsternis," this essay emerges as a considerably more sophisticated exploration of nature, history, and human understanding, not just as Stifter's personal testament to an aesthetics of the insignificant in life, as so many critics assert in different says.

The "gentle law" actually begins with an analysis of writing as an act of interpretation. When an author writes, he reveals as much about himself as he does about his subject: "If something noble and good is in me, it will in and of itself permeate my writings" ("Vorrede," Stifter 1981, 9).[47] When the author writes, he reveals his moral understanding, as a "speck of good to contribute to the construction of the eternal" (9–10). The most infamous line of the essay contains a list of *naturalia* and natural phenomena that Stifter considers "great": "The breezes of the air, the gurgling of water, the growth of grain, the waves of the ocean, the greening of the earth, the shining of the heavens, the shimmering of stars—I consider these things great" (Stifter 1981, 10).[48]

---

45 The vast majority of older Stifter scholarship discusses individual stories, providing authoritative close readings, often in connection with his work as a visual artist; see, for example, von Wiese (1962), Stiehm (1968), Mahlendorf (1981), Sjörgren (1986), or Schiffermüller (1993), but the approach persists (Jakubów [2006], Martyn [2013], Holmes [2010], and Japp [2008]). A newer generation takes up his connections to science (e.g., Hertling [1985], Häusler [2009], Ireton [2010, 2012], or Keleman [2013]).

46 "Es ist einmal gegen mich bemerkt worden, daß ich nur das Kleine bilde, und daß meine Menschen stets gewöhnliche Menschen seien."

47 "Wenn etwas Edles und Gutes in mir ist, so wird es von selber in meinen Schriften liegen ..."

48 "Das Wehen der Luft das Rieseln des Wassers das Wachsen der Getreide

Such ordinary phenomena of human experience often escape scrutiny, and they are less easy to explain than more catastrophic natural phenomena like lightning.

Critics generally take this passage as evidence of Stifter's devotion to a God-centered universe. Yet they overlook the sentence's verb construction: Stifter *considers* these items great (*halten für*). Through his consistent use of such circumlocutions, Stifter avoids assertions about God's existence and instead focuses on the mechanisms of individual understanding—on how natural phenomena can be *considered* great. Belief and empiricism have little to do with each other: when people consult a compass at many times and places, they "learn" that its needle points north—and they have transformed experiences into a principle, a "law" (Stifter 1981, 11). In this way, the "speck after speck" of data that science uncovers—bits taken from the "mass of appearances" and the "field of the given"—are assembled into laws ("Vorrede," Stifter 1981, 11). Not even the scientific method, therefore, can be isolated from other kinds of understanding. Once such laws are evolved, they may even serve to move individuals to fear and pity by natural phenomena, as a kind of reactive catharsis (Stifter 1981, 12). The "field of givens," a field of phenomenal evidence evaluated scientifically, can also be understood morally and affectively.

Stifter's "gentle law" thus does not point at understanding God through his creations, it is instead a call to see that any understanding is a narrative that can have many forms—scientific, moral, or affective—as a separate rationality that can impact the group to which it is imparted (Stifter 1981, 13). If this dictum is respected, not just knowledge, but also an intellectual community is created, with higher human accountability:

> [T]hus we feel raised in our humanity, we feel ourselves rendered general in our humanity, we feel the sublime as it sinks everywhere into our souls, through which immeasurably great energies in time or space are wrought together into a form-filled whole commensurate with reason. (Stifter 1981, 13–14)[49]

This vocabulary is sentimentalist as much as it is theistic, and here, as in the "Eclipse," Stifter quietly compares the understanding of science

---

das Wogen des Meeres das Grünen der Erde das Glänzen des Himmels das Schimmern der Gestirne halte ich für groß."

49 "so fühlen wir uns in der ganzen Menschheit erhoben, wir fühlen us menschlich verallgemeinert, wir empfinden das Erhabene, wie es sich überall in die Seele senkt, wodurch unmeßbar große Kräfte in der Zeit oder im Raume auf ein gestaltvolles vernunftgemäßes Ganzes zusammen gewirkt wird."

with that of the human soul: he constantly asserts "we *feel*," or "we *understand as*," rather than "we learn" or "we know." Stifter consistently restricts his question to exclude ontological and theological questions about God and revelation and to focus on human understanding. All knowledge passed on through tradition, history, or experience is simply a narrative, a story composed according to a moral rule, to define a particular moment in historical justice (Stifter 1981: 14). Even general laws of nature are historical, just as moral laws are (14). Stifter's "gentle law" is thus not an ontological admonition, it is an epistemological one, pointing at a communal space of observation and discussion: "Just as, in natural history, opinions about what is great have continually altered, so, too, has it been in the moral history of humanity" (Stifter 1981, 15).[50] A culture that ignores the historicity of its judgments is subject to error. Decadent cultures will stress the content of experience; religious cultures can rely too much on empty form (15).

Taking these two essays in parallel opens up his Biedermeier in new ways, tying his representations tightly into the epistemology at play in the era's genre paintings, as well. Many of Stifter's prose works frame natural disasters as moments calling human understanding and interpretation into question, most notably the bolts of lightning in *Abdias*, or the blizzard on the mountain pass in *Bergkristall*. Such chance occurrences become tragic because human understanding fails, often willfully, in an extreme situation. Such tales do use sentimental rhetoric—the rhetoric that they themselves would use in experiencing the incidents—to appeal to his audience and help them find an emotional catharsis, but also to uncover new moral understandings of situations. His tragedies are often set at the moments when individuals step outside the group and violate moderation (*Maß*, as in the "Vorrede"). It is likely that individuals will remember such tragedies emotionally, or rationally, instead of acknowledging their own roles from a more empirical point of view. It is especially significant that Stifter's novellas usually locate the narration of an event within a frame presenting a long historical perspective (most famously, in "Der Hochwald") to show that short-term interpretations of an event are often very different from long-term effects (see Neugebauer). Through strategic juxtapositions of historical memory with current situations, sentiments, and facts, Stifter implicitly trains his audience how to question received wisdoms of the heart or of the mind, even while recognizing their past validity.

In this reading, the "Preface to the Colored Stones" participates in the moral pedagogy attributed to genre painting. Moreover, while Stifter does not explicitly tie such narrative understandings to politics in

---

50   "Wie in der Geschichte der Natur die Ansichten über das Große sich stets geändert haben, so ist es auch in der sittlichen Geschichte der Menschen gewesen."

these short essays, he does in his longer fictional works, such as *Witiko* (1865–7) and *Indian Summer* (*Der Nachsommer*, 1857). The Freiherr von Risach has retired from the government and withdrawn, which created a beautiful world, but one without its own male children, no direct line of descent. There, as in these essays, Stifter paints a tapestry of folk wisdom and scientific truth, faith, and art, all the while valorizing the past but also laying out the necessity of changing for the future. Risach explicitly forbids his heirs to leave his house unchanged, no matter how attractive it seems to them. In *Witiko*, as in *Der Hochwald*, the world and its politics impinges on the small houses of locals, often catastrophically: even the smallest, most remotely situated individuals cannot pretend that they are engaged with powers beyond their ken. In all cases, Stifter gently, lovingly, cautions his readers against too-simple interpretations, be they religious or secular, artistic or scientific. Since interpretations are made by humans, they can be—must be—remade.

Not just eclipses, but also Stifter's "small things" of nature function within narratives that help individuals orient themselves in the world. As Stifter's narrator in "Eclipse" insists: the things you know for fifty years are called into question in the fifty-first, as things break into your cozy everyday world. Catastrophes test the scope and quality of social-political narratives about human hearts and understandings, just as acts of God like eclipses call us to question human understanding of the world. Stifter's "genre prose," to coin a term, thus functions much as do Biedermeier paintings: they tell stories whose resolutions require a change of consciousness, an acknowledgment that there are multiple stories to be told about any set of facts, and that individuals who do not pursue these multiples are sacrificing parts of their futures and their humanity.

Scholars of Stifter interpret such texts as evidence of his increasing conservatism, once he leaves Vienna for Linz and for a position as inspector of local primary schools. Yet if they are set into the context of the present argument, Stifter's "gentle law" is much less a recommendation than a warning. His Alpine valleys, mountain passes, and city observatories remain connected to the world outside their borders, which may at any time erupt into their experience. At those moments, new public discussions and new narratives are required—and the kinds of education that teaches that understanding is narrative, not a product of revolution. This is undeniably a kind of liberalism that believes in the power of education over tradition—the kind of liberal politics that did indeed reflect Vienna in the mid-nineteenth century, with revolution coming from within individuals rather than from politicians.[51]

---

51 See Pieter M. Judson, *Exclusive Revolutionaries* (1996), for the definitive treatment of Austrian liberal politics in the era.

Revolution in Vienna

That revolutions are cognitive and local rather than world historical is not Stifter's point alone, as the *Volkstheater* examples from the last chapter amply document. A unique play by Nestroy, *Freiheit in Krähwinkel* (loosely, *Freedom in Podunk*, 1848), argues the problem of revolution in parallel terms for an urban theater audience. *Freiheit in Krähwinkel* is Nestroy's only play lacking a source text, and critics point to it as questioning Nestroy's commitment to liberal politics in the era of revolution.[52] *Freiheit in Krähwinkel* was a product of the 1848 revolutions in Vienna, appearing quickly after censorship was lifted in March of that year, with Nestroy appearing in the role of Ultra, the journalist. It was a hit after its July 1 premiere.

Contemporary critics could (or would) not use it to decide what Nestroy's politics were (Nestroy 1995: 2). None the less, the play is constructed to emphasize a rethinking of the immediate past, in a field-and-ground reverse between two tableaux, each offering one narrative about the historical moment. The first section of the play, in two acts, represents the revolution; the second (the third act) is reserved for the "Reaction."

In the tradition of Bäuerle's *Citizens of Vienna*, *Freiheit* opens with a tableau, a visually threatening mob populating the stage. They are the inhabitants of *Krähwinkel*, the fictional town whose name was coined by Jean Paul (Nestroy, 86) and made famous in Kotzebue's play *Die deutschen Kleinstädter* (*German Small Towners*, 1801). Nestroy here questions what is actually meant by revolution in such a small town, when various classes, from aristocrats, through civil servants, and finally to the ordinary working people, experience what may be nothing more than a dream.[53]

The *Krähwinkler* are eager for the revolution because, in the dark time of their present, they feel oppressed by their leadership ("die Zeiten der Finsterniß"; Nestroy 1995, 10: 17).[54] They have heard about the revolution and so want to assert their place in it, to throw off the shackles of political and spiritual darkness that have restricted them:

---

52 John R. P. McKenzie, in "Nestroy's Political Plays" (1998), for instance, says that *Freiheit*'s German setting allows the audience to avoid some of its political implications (128), and that the people won't live up to the political challenge (135).

53 Gerhard Scheit underscores how the dramatic tradition of the Hanswurst retained a very political gesture. Other literature on the *Volksstück* is voluminous.

54 Nestroy is cited by page and line numbers, where available.

The head of our city does with	Der Chef uns'rer Stadt thut mit
us what he wants ...	uns, was er will! ...
The people of Krähwinkel,	Die Krähwinkler,
dammit all,	Mordsapprament,
Are also Germans.	Sind eb'nfalls ein deutsch's
	Element. (Nestroy 1995, 9: 8–13)

Oppression in Krähwinkel comes from the middle management, which controls all aspects of city life. Chief among them is Klaus, the bailiff (*Rathsdiener*), who is referred to as an informant (*Spitzel*) by an ordinary worker, a Night Watchman (*Nachtwächter*), who has been denounced for reading about the revolution in foreign papers.[55] His "crime" is a public defense of revolutionary opinions. From the perspective of the powers that be, that Night Watchman has committed the worst crime thinkable: "At night they think about what they have read during the day, which the government of Podunk does not love" (Nestroy 1995: 11, 15–17).[56] Ever the loyal civil servant, Klaus justifies the town's current "oppression" using the party line familiar from every conservative putsch: that the government is censoring the news media to keep order and provide bread for the people. The civil servants isolate the so-called "revolutionaries" from the rest of the townspeople to "protect" the land. As part of this policy of containment, the Night Watchman's daughter—Walpurga, clearly the target of a "witch hunt," in Nestroy's telling naming—has been identified as a revolutionary and thus is not deemed a proper companion for Klaus' daughter (Nestroy 1995: 13, 1–2).

The Night Watchman, however, knows what is really at stake: the self-interest of those in power. For instance, Klaus' informants manufacture "crimes" to foment revolution—so that they will not be put out of their jobs defending the town. The reporter Ultra's opening song confirms the political mood. In his outside observer's version of what is actually going on, this little town is dealing with the death throes of absolutism:

---

55 "auswärtige Blätter ... sogar östreichische" (Nestroy 1995: 11, 4–5).
56 "Sie denken bey der Nacht über das nach, was Sie beym Tag gelesen haben; das liebt die Krähwinkler Regierung nicht."

They reigned without limits,	Unumschränkt habn s' regiert,
No one moved a muscle,	Kein Mensch hat sich g'rührt,
Because if someone had dared	Denn hätt's einer g'wagt
and said a free word,	Und a freyes Wort g'sagt,
he would have been rewarded	Den hätt' d'Festung belohnt.
with jail.	Ausspioniert habs s' All's
They spied on us all equally,	glei,Für das war d'Polizey;
That's what the police were for;	Der G'scheidte is verstummt,
The smart guy is mum,	Kurz 's war Alles verdummt.
In short, everything was dumbed	Diese Zeit war bequem
down.	Für das Zopfensystem.
This age was comfortable	(Nestroy 1995: 15–16)
For the periwig-system.	

Times changed and reversed this dumbing-down of the public. As a journalist, Ultra has followed this revolution through Europe, watching liberty flood Europe: "Then the oppressed underlings began to think" (Nestroy 1995: 16, 20–1).[57] Paris revolted, dethroning Louis Philippe. The Germans followed suit, and then even the Austrians did. Now, however, Ultra has ended up in this hole in the wall, where only Night Watchmen read about such goings on: "Out of an Austria gloriously radiating freedom, my dark fate leads me here to Podunk" (Nestroy 1995: 17, 31–2).[58]

At this point, however, Ultra's purportedly liberal, anti-monarchist point of view becomes considerably more radical. He denounces Europe's revolutions because they accomplished much less than they had promised. Other countries' revolutionaries, for instance, were granted many freedoms, such as freedom of thought—as long as they didn't tell anyone about them (Nestroy 1995: 18). When the hitherto unthinkable happened, and censorship was lifted, the poets in these other states were allowed to speak out. More precisely, according to Ultra, they were left with no further excuses for their not having taken a public position yet: "the poets have sacrificed their most favorite excuse" for not having taken positions yet (Nestroy 1995: 19, 10–11):[59]

In the first eight days of freedom, Vienna's journalists have achieved the fabulous distinction of having Austria's newspapers banned abroad; and if you would page back four months in these

57 "Da fieng z'dencken an/Der gedrückte Unterthan ..."
58 "Aus dem glorreichen freiheitstrahlenden Oesterreich führt mich mein finsteres Schicksal nach Krähwinkel her."
59 "[D]ie Dichter haben ihre beliebteste Ausred eingebüßt."

Austrian newspapers, you won't find anything but a little bit of polemic about the theater ... (Nestroy 1995: 20, 5–10)[60]

Ultra's own paper, supporting the revolution, has only thirty-six subscribers (Nestroy, 21, 14–15). Krähwinkel's Night Watchman is thus not representative of Europe's citizenry, which seems not to be particularly interested in new freedoms.

To underscore the contrast between the ideals of the revolution and their reality, Nestroy has set up competing tableaux. Like their comrades in other cities, the citizens of Krähwinkel do initially try to join the revolution and throw out their oppressive government. They plan a demonstration. As any good journalist would, Ultra adds his color commentary about the public mood: "I am freedom, through and through: my blood is red freedom, my brain is white freedom, my glance is black freedom, my breath is glowing freedom" (Nestroy 1995: 24).[61] "Red white black" freedom does not, however, get much official response from the *Staatskanzley*, represented in the play by the career civil servants Siegmund and Reakzerl—according to their names, a legendary German hero (a nationalist) and a conservative. The Night Watchman had it right, after all: these lower officials are simply worried about their careers, not about the legitimacy of rule or the mayor's regime. Inside city government, business is as usual: corrupt. A widow (Frau von Frankenfrey) is trying to get the mayor to change her husband's will, to swindle a convent out of a promised legacy. All parties discuss graft with aplomb. If Krähwinkel is typical of its "reformed" cities of the revolution, then revolutionary Europe has actually meant very little for individual towns.

This point is underscored in another way when Ultra is drawn into the "official" reactionary movements, into official attempts to keep the public mood "stable." As a journalist celebrating new revolutionary liberty, Ultra is understandably reluctant to accept the job of local censor that he is offered:

A censor is a pencil-made-man, or a man turned into a pencil, a slash-made-flesh marking out all products of spirit, a crocodile waiting on the banks of the stream of ideas to bite the heads off

---

60   "Wiens Journalisten haben in den ersten Acht Tagen der Freyheit die fabelhafte Auszeichnung errungen, daß die Östreichishcen Blätter in Ausland verboten worden sind; und blättern Sie Vier Monath zurück in diese östreichischen Blätter, so werden Sie Außer ein Bisserl Theaterpolemik nichts finden ..."

61   "[I]ch bin Freyheit durch und durch; mein Blut is rothe Freyheit, mein Hirn is weiße Freyheit, mein Blick is schwarze Freyheit, mein Hauch is glühende Freyheit." Note that these colors are *not* those of the 1848 revolutions.

the poets swimming in it ... the censor is the living confession of the great, that they can only rule over dumbed-down slaves, but not over free peoples. (Nestroy 1995: 26–7)[62]

He decides that the job runs counter to the public good. Klaus, as a seasoned bureaucrat, takes the situation more straightforwardly: revolutionary sentiment is spreading like cholera, which will ultimately cause a loss of influence for his classes (*Verlust des Einflusses* [Nestroy 1995: 31]). Significantly, his daughter fears only for her father's position: "Hopefully, nothing will happen to the bureaucrats" (Nestroy 1995: 34).[63] To spy on Klaus at home, Ultra ends up disguising himself as "Pater Fidelus," a Ligourist (part of the Redemptorist order, which was founded in Naples to work for the poor, but which was thrown out of Austria in 1848). By the end of the first act, a widow warns Ultra that the Mayor is dreaming of calling out the soldiers—staged as a dream-tableau straight out of the 1848 Revolutions, with many topical allusions.[64]

Not surprisingly, as the threatened revolution nears, the Mayor gets drunk in the company of a group of aristocrats who use poetry to avoid revolutionary rhetoric (Nestroy 1995: 42). Ultra infiltrates this group, this time by pretending to be a Russian (and by speaking Pig Latin). Out on the streets, the situation heats up as the women of the town get involved: "Where are you going?—I wanna go see a bit of revolution" (Nestroy 1995: 48).[65] Significantly, it is the women who declare "Freiheit in Krähwinkel" by the end of the second act (Nestroy 1995: 52). "Die Reaktion" of the third act also starts with females, but this time in aristocratic salons. Like their husbands, aristocratic females like poetry (bad, overly sentimental poetry), but not the uproar: "For one thing, freedom is what ruins men" (Nestroy 1995: 54).[66] Ultra brings them the news of the ongoing revolution, to try to get them to keep their men at home.

Ultra's supposed metamorphosis into reactionary happens when the Krähwinkler are applauding the removal of oppression, and, not surprisingly, he plays both sides of the situation. Dressed as a

---

62 "Ein Censor is ein Mensch-gewordener Bleystiften oder ein Bleistiftgewordener Mensch, ein Fleischgewordener Strich über die Erzeugnisse des Geistes, ein Krokodil was an den Ufern des Ideenstromes lagert, und den darin schwimmenden Dichtern die Köpf' abbeißt. ... die Censur is das lebendige Geständniß der Großen, daß sie nur verdummte Sclaven treten, aber keine freyen Völker regieren können."
63 "Wenn nur den Beamten nichts g'schieht."
64 See the scene notes in the McKenzie edition of the play.
65 "[W]o wollens denn hin?—A Bisserl Revolution anschau'n."
66 "Die Freyheit is einmahl das, was die Männer ruiniert."

Metternich-era diplomat, Ultra intercedes with the upper classes, then recostumes himself as a worker to negotiate with the other side. His diction always matches his clothes. When he looks like an aristocrat, he speaks poetically, if nonsensically: "The night was always the element sponsoring my acts. The great forces of the earth are stars; in consequence they can only shine when it is dark. In the sun of freedom, the star shine disappeared, thus one may not allow them to shine too long" (Nestroy 1995: 65).[67] In a more plebeian mode, he sings a long *quod-libet* about revolution happening everywhere but in Austria, in "Neapel, England, Rußland, Frankreich":

Freedom unites us,	Eine Freyheit vereint uns,
just like the sun shines on us …	So wie a Sonn' nur bescheint
We come to clarity.	uns, …
Healthy sense will find the truth	Wir kommen zur Klarheit,
And, despite arguments,	G'sunder Sinn find't schon
Austria will shine brightly	d'Wahrheit;
through the centuries	Und trotz die Diff'renzen
praised, admired—	Wird Östreich hoch glänzen
We stand here, quite boldly,	Fortan durch Jahrhundert
We fear no thrusts,	Gepriesen bewundert—
Even if the ferment is great,	Wir steh'n da, ganz famos,
Nothing more will happen here.	Wir fürchten kein'n Stoß,
	Is die Gährung auch groß,
	Bey uns geht nix mehr los.
	(Nestroy 1995: 75)

In Austria, notably, the revolution has already been rolled back—the "Kamarilla" has arranged things differently (an unmistakable reference to the Austrian court and to the negotiated Habsburg abdication of 1848 which brought Franz Joseph to the throne).

The play ends on the street, on a barricade, under a full moon—in a tableau of darkness illuminated. The "revolution" has not happened among the bureaucrats, or even among the intelligentsia: only the women of the town revolt. To increase the pressure on official Krähwinkel, some dress as students (there are none among workers). Some noblewomen take on military roles, dressing as officers. The change of regime in Krähwinkel is effected bloodlessly, and through blind chance, not conviction. While the locals know that there are no

---

67 "Die Nacht war immer das Element meines Wirckens. Die Großen der Erde sind Sterne, folglich können sie nur dann leuchten, wenn's finster ist. In der Sonne der Freyheit verlischt das Sterngeflimmer, drum darf man sie nicht zu lange leuchten lassen."

students in this revolution, the mayor fears the fake ones enough to run off to London. The oppressor has been banished: "The reaction is over" (Nestroy 1995: 76). Ultra has the final commentary on the reactionary forces: "Thus as it was in the grand scheme of things, so we have seen it in miniature: reactionary forces are ghosts, but we know that ghosts only exist for the timid; thus if we don't fear them, there is no reaction" (Nestroy 1995: 77).[68]

Ultra's final pronouncement echoes Marx's "spectre haunting Europe." But the specter is not revolution itself. Logically, the revolution may be necessary to eliminate graft and manipulation in government. But people do not necessarily join either the revolution or reaction for logical reasons. That revolution itself may be an illusion: the mayor has left because of a mob of angry women in student drag, but the system continues essentially intact. "Reaction is a specter" challenges an audience which may itself be under the illusion that the revolution has triumphed. In Krähwinkel, as in Habsburg Austria, the aristocracy and other bureaucrats remain in place.

Ultra's final pronouncement may be less against revolution *per se* than against the complacency of a people which believes it has won a revolution just because the mayor has left town (or, by extension, because Metternich has left Vienna). Actually, the only one of the old order who *has* left is that mayor—the rest of the Krähwinkler are left posturing in the dark (lunatics under a full moon?), or making bad poetry. The men posture to retain their positions in the old bureaucracy; the women cross-dress as male students to claim revolutionary power. The press is willing to go underground and negotiate, but it ultimately remains outside the situation. All in all, little will be changed unless those people take the initiative. Emotion and the excitement of revolution will not bring a political triumph; they occasionally need a guide, a public voice of reason, like Ultra might be. As a cross-dresser himself (a spy in disguise), Ultra can play on all the sides of the revolution, if he merely changes his clothes—he does not fall prey to revolutionary or reactionary sentiments alone.

Still, the play is undeniably political: Nestroy writes at the moment that Austria's revolution turns into reaction "for the public good," and the play forces the audience to inevitable questions: where did the revolution come from? Who is deceiving whom? What has really changed? Nestroy's answer is very like Stifter's: maybe nothing has really changed, except our perspective on what is necessary and natural. And that knowledge is, ultimately, a moral question: why do

---

68   "Also wie's im Großen war, so haben wir's hir im Kleinen geseh'n, die Reaction ist ein Gespenst, aber Gespenster giebt es bekanntlich nur für den Furchtsamen; drum, sich nicht fürchten davor, dann giebt's gar keine Reaction."

we believe, for example, that revolution is a threat, when there hasn't even been one?

The Night Watchmen of Nestroy's society may still read papers critically, but new ideas will not necessarily change society. Ultra demonstrates that neither reason nor poetry, faith in revolutionary truths or the state's rationalizations are enough in themselves. Ultimately, a revolution can mean nothing more than a human catastrophe under a moonlit night—a lunacy, dream, or night-terror, perhaps a collective delusion that leaves the world essentially unchanged, despite the great need for change. Nestroy shapes the logical and emotional "truths" of the revolutionary age into tableaux, to show that they are constructions, like the various social truths that need to be rethought in times of trouble. Krähwinkler freedom is ultimately an illusion, a fancy-dress ball run by fear instead of a true desire for reform, from the top levels of society all the way through to the lowest.[69]

Freiheit in Krähwinkel thus asks public questions about debates that need public airing, without providing too-simple answers. It shows again how European play traditions still provided ample space for original political speech, as Nestroy expressed clear dismay about revolutions that were actually not happening. The split-screen effect of the two tableaux doubles the overall ambivalence of a concept like "revolution," with the purportedly happy ending feeling very much less so to the audience—a dramatic ploy resembling the ambivalence of the end to Grillparzer's *Woe to Liars*, as well.

Speaking politically in an era of fragmentation

The purportedly complacent Biedermeier works discussed here may seem in one sense to valorize order, the divine, and civic duty. Yet all contain revolutionary threats that are by no means thinly veiled for an audience used to a certain kind of moral-political rhetoric, and trained to compare narratives. The pieces all work in logical juxtapositions that undercut narrative certainty, reinforced with the experiential force of visual representations without words.

Stifter's essays teach his audiences the limits of conventional explanations (be they scientific, religious, or moral), as comfortable, familiar human perspectives are eclipsed and nights of the soul emerge at moments of tragedy. Nestroy's play offers his audience a guide to why neither the revolutionary nor the anti-revolutionary parties of 1848 have been telling the truth about political and social change in his *Krähwinkel*, where revolution has simply caused emotional reactions on both sides, and little, if any, reasoned change. No matter how in

---

69   Gerhard H. Weiss, "Johann Nestroy: The Revolution on the Stage," argues for a more middle-class moral for *Freiheit*.

control this new national class might think it is, all argue for fates lying in forces that come from outside the nation.

In a real sense, then, critics have been right in calling these authors of the Biedermeier anti-revolutionary—they do not want the sudden, violent ends of the worlds they know, or to have human history blown away through radical change. Yet at the same time, all three believe in the education they have received, which allows for the assumption that their readers or audiences may know more than any "official" point of view, be that view social, religious, scientific, or simply inherited as tradition or history. These authors take their teaching missions very seriously, opening up public spaces slyly, balancing evidence so that no one side comes off as either the heroes or villains. The rhetorics and images are often sentimental, but they are never harmless in pointing careful readers and viewers toward their extraordinarily revolutionary implications. The authors are *not* trying to impose their own revolutionary agendas on the readers or viewers, but each text explores the gap between what can be seen by anyone with a clear pair of eyes, and what is said. None of these texts resolve those gaps into clear political agendas. Instead, they show *and* tell, using rhetorical gambits familiar to all of Europe for a millennium to get their audiences to overcome their limits and engage anew with the needs of the present. They are not trying for Hegelian reversals in consciousness: they simply realize that the middle classes may ultimately prove to be as limited in vision as the aristocrats of the earlier revolution were, if they do not use their abilities to rescript the worlds and worldviews they have inherited. Science can be just as mind-numbing a prejudice as the religion of the upper classes ever was.

Art historians believe that, over the course of the nineteenth century, genre painting converges almost imperceptibly with the explicit social imperatives of naturalism. Stifter's essays make the case for an equivalent development in the rhetorics of prose representation, and Nestroy's play structures its argument in contrasts of rhetoric and visual sites. The "restored" Austria of the Metternich era had a public that many artists have presumed capable of engaging in discussion. Their genre pictures in painting, words, or stagings teach their audiences the limits of official scripts about faith and reason in a world that has legislated both, to the detriment of both the human mind and soul. Morality and ideals, after all, conform to historical imperatives with clear political limits, no matter how harmless, traditional, and timeless they seem. And the literacy that allows individuals to decipher these limits will transform not only a single nation, but also all those enmeshed in it.

As genre pictures, these texts are resolutely local, and hence do not have the overt appeals to the greater framing of Europe that the texts in earlier parts of this discussion had. But they all still work in clear juxtapositions of the local and larger, outside powers in clear acknowledgment of European traditions for artistic communication, not just germanophone ones—they believe in the Hanswurst that Weimar exiled from the stage. More importantly, they sometimes portray the nation as an extended community "like us," but the nation-state does not figure prominently in their calculations—they build communities, not states, and the various "powers that be" are either absent or just like the rest of the town.

Their approach to public discussion and public education is none the less strikingly modern, because they question their own society's master narratives, the stories they tell about history, religion, and science particularly, as instruments of self-delusion that can ruin individuals and communities alike. They are very aware that their society has reorganized over the first half of the nineteenth century; they also see a crushing need to foster public discussion about changes, if futures are still to be made.

Part Two
At the Margins of Europe, In the Heart of Europe

The Austria-Hungary of the Habsburgs that sponsored the bloom of urban culture represented in the works of Sonnenfels, Grillparzer, Nestroy, and Stifter ceased to exist at the end of the First World War. This culture in the heart of Europe—not just a germanophone culture, but also one that transmitted impulses across many languages—extended through the Balkans and North Italy, as well, connected by many multilingual networks that allowed for quick translations and dissemination of texts, and for endless provincial tours for actors. These networks persisted in hidden forms throughout the twentieth century, and many of them reemerged after the fall of the Eastern Bloc, just as Austria's reference points in Europe became more relevant in the purportedly post-national European Union. Yet in 1918, every official discourse unwittingly aimed at erasing the memories of the kinds of public discussion and public spaces that existed there.

Woodrow Wilson's famous Fourteen Points had called for national self-determination and autonomy in the world. On October 14, 1918, Austria-Hungary's last emperor, Karl I, had proposed a federation of German, Czech, South Slav, and Ukrainian regions of the one-time empire. That solution arrived as a dead letter, since a Czechoslovak Provisional Government had already been formed, and since US Secretary of State Robert Lansing had issued a note on October 18, supporting it. Czech independence was declared on October 28, and the Slovenes, Croats, and Serbs followed on the 29th. Hungary ended its personal union with Austria-Hungary on the 31st. On November 11, Karl renounced his right to speak for Austrian affairs; he did so for Hungary, his second crown, on November 13. There was no letter or declaration of abdication, supposedly leaving room for his recall. The Treaty of Saint-Germaine-en-Laye (September 10, 1919) established

Austrian borders as we know them today and forbade its union with Germany without Allied permission. (Hungary lost two-thirds of its territory in the equivalent Treaty of Trianon, signed on June 4, 1920,)

Rump Austria was known by local wags as the *Wasserkopf* (the hydrocephalic head, referring both to its shape and to its concentration of intellectuals rather than artisans and laborers) once German-speakers from all regions of the ex-empire congregated on it and bilinguals went to their new nation-states. Its heritage was propagated into the Habsburg successor states as its intellectuals and civil servants took roles in other governments (most notably, Tomáš Masaryk and Edvard Beneš in Czechoslovakia, its first two presidents, but including Béla Kun and György [Georg] Lukács in Hungary and many others). This broad forced intellectual diaspora was to benefit Europe and the United States throughout the twentieth century, especially in the arts, social sciences, and humanities.

Austrian intellectuals of the twentieth century, after the dissolution of Austria-Hungary in 1918, were clearly at a loss. No matter how often Austria-Hungary had been declared in decline in the course of the nineteenth century, a nation and its culture had evolved within a progressively less functional state structure. After 1918, Austria without its other territories entered a cycle of inflation and recession, even before the 1929 world downturns. Its artists and writers looked to Berlin as the new market for their wares; actors and musicians played both markets, especially to replace networks of German theaters lost to national fragmentation in Central Europe. Hollywood also absorbed a mass of talent remembered today as supposedly emigrating from "Germany" and "Russia," the vast majority of whom were actually from Austria-Hungary and from Galicia, the region of the lost Empire that was and is part of the Ukraine; many of these talents had grown up speaking German, Hungarian, Yiddish, Polish, or another of Central Europe's Slavic languages, rather than Russian. The "shtetl" child-hoods of the studio moguls, mythologized to emphasize that they were self-made men, were often spent not in rural villages, but in the small towns of the Habsburg Empire that had newspapers, small theaters, and connections to state educational institutions.

Fortune was not good to the states emerging from Austria, which ceased to exist a mere twenty years after their forced origins and chaotic first years (including the assassination of Austrian Chancellor Engelbert Dollfuß in 1934). On March 12, 1938, the German army marched into Austria to stave off a vote for independence scheduled by Chancellor Kurt Schuschnigg (over Hitler's opposition) for March 13, a vote that promised to bring the Austrian Nazi party into power. Schuschnigg was replaced by Arthur Seyss-Inquart. Hitler was greeted in Vienna on April 2 by 200,000 Austrians. That plebiscite was eventually held on April 10, at which time 99.73 percent of the Austrian vote went for unification with Germany—in an election that was not directly manipulated, but which was by no means a secret ballot. Austria became the *Ostmark* and assumed new culpability as a partner in the Third Reich.

After the war, in an attempt to recover independence, and to banish memories of the Nazi era, the *Anschluß* was declared null and void by the Provisional Austrian Government on April 27, 1945, with support of the Allied powers. That declaration was made in light of the 1943 Moscow Declaration, signed by the US, the United Kingdom, and the Soviet Union, which declared Austria the first official victim of "Hitlerite aggression." Yet the country existed in a quadripartite occupation until the formal State Treaty was signed on May 15, 1955, and the country was declared permanently neutral, outside the NATO West and the Eastern Bloc alike, but a member of the United Nations. It joined the European Union in 1995, after the fall of the Eastern Bloc made reconsideration of its neutrality feasible. Other notable moments in that recent history will be discussed in more detail below.

The discussions in this part focus on how twentieth-century Austrian intellectuals dealt with the loss of their cultural heritage to two World Wars and a subsequent Cold War and with their own sense that that heritage still could speak to a public that was not blinded by nationalism. They retained the sense of public space and of a nation as a collection of many groups, all with not only the right but also the need to engage with each other, with the master narratives used by the state and other authorities to maintain their own power, and the morality of those narratives. Just as important, these twentieth-century intellectuals retained a sense of Europe's history and art traditions— they defined their nation not in terms of a state, but in terms of that history and its reference to their present. They remembered the "sun over Austria" and how many different maps had charted courses for various Austrian futures; they could still rely on audiences who could deal with ambiguity rather than happy ends.

After World War I, Hugo von Hofmannsthal and Arthur Schnitzler not only became the most prominent germanophones of the interwar period, they both preserved a vision of a distinct and continuing Austrian contribution to their Europe, no matter how far their nation-state had receded from international visibility and significance in its reduced political shape. Each in his own way, both updated Europe's nineteenth-century artistic traditions in the twentieth century as part of their attempts to re-institute a European culture, with Austria central to it. That new European Austria was to help mend a continent by reinvigorating its shared cultural heritage, no matter growing threats to community and ethics through modernization and capital. They and the other writers represented in this part's chapters all attempted to reclaim that European heritage (or at least Austria's place in it) as representing a new space—a nation of many languages and cultural traditions; they wrote from Vienna (but never exclusively), and about something beyond the state.

After World War II, Austria had managed to survive politically (not divided for a generation as Berlin was, for example, although occupied by the Four Powers until 1955); its anomalous neutrality forced its politics into various roles between NATO and Eastern Bloc politics. Starting immediately after Austrian independence, Austrian voices quickly took up an international role—protesting NATO, the demonizing of Eastern Bloc countries, and, finally, Austria's own heritage of denial. None the less, marketing a new international image, one tailored to outside expectations, Austria has achieved both notoriety and visibility in the European Union of the millennium.

To show how Austria's intellectuals coped with these political catastrophes and the repeated necessity of finding spaces for public critique and discussions, the case studies in this section again take up writers identified with the Austrian canon—Hugo von Hofmannsthal (1874–1929), Arthur Schnitzler (1862–1931), Peter Handke (b. 1942), and the *Wiener Gruppe* (h. c. artmann [1921–2000], Friedrich Achleitner [b. 1930], Konrad Bayer [1932–64], Gerhard Rühm [b. 1930], and Oswald Wiener [b. 1935]); Otto von Habsburg will return as a representative of Austrian history as it narrates itself in the latter twentieth century.

These cases document how references to Europe and its culture remain viable for these authors to stage their critiques of the European nation-states, and how they still hope to foster public discussions about issues that appeal to their readers' moral and cognitive judgments rather than to state rationalities.

Five Hofmannsthal's European
Revolution: Recapturing a Space
for Common Culture

The world of Bäuerle, Grillparzer, Nestroy, and Stifter became the object
of nostalgia by the start of the twentieth century, often under the rubric
Wien anno dazumal (the Biedermeier "good old days"). In the 1980s,
Vienna's image was given its decisive contemporary form in a series
of museum exhibitions in Europe and the United States dedicated to a
Vienna in 1900 as a *fin de siècle* and end of a world, defined as the last
flowering of a dying, decadent culture, just waiting to be disassembled
by the Western allies as part of the settlements after World War I.

Among the greatest of Austria's twentieth-century writers by any
assessment, Hugo von Hofmannsthal (1874–1929) survived through
most of the era's cultural and political traumas, making the transition
between the aesthetic culture of the turn of the century, when he had
started his writing career as a young, gifted lyric poet, and the interwar
era when he sought his place in a European culture that was itself soon
to be doomed.[1] Yet Hofmannsthal remains tagged as an aesthete, like
his most famous dramatic character, Hans Karl Bühl in *The Difficult
Man* (*Der Schwierige*, 1921), a man who after World War I fell out of
touch with modernity and became unsupportive of innovation. The
worst reading of Hofmannsthal's career, based in no small part on
his interwar participation in the Salzburg Festival as the author of
Everyman (*Jedermann*, 1922), casts him as falling prey to the kind of
nationalist thinking that fostered the rise of Nazism.[2]

---

1   Hofmannstahl is one of the most heavily researched authors of the germano-
    phone canon, but mostly in an aesthetic/poetics vein. For an overview of
    the author's works and varied reputations, see Thomas A. Kovach, ed.,
    A Companion to the Works of Hugo von Hofmannsthal (2002).
2   For more extensive overviews of the scholarship on Hofmannsthal, see
    Matthias Mayer, *Hugo von Hofmannsthal* (1993), Hans-Albrecht Koch, *Hugo*

Such generalizations ignore Hofmannsthal's actual career. Well before the turn of the century, he argued that cultural change was inevitable and necessary, but that it should never be engaged in a precipitous manner, since change must be based on the European heritage as lived and experienced by all, not by the arbitrary assumption of nationalism. After World War I, Hofmannsthal sought out innovators like Max Reinhardt, the *Ballets Russes,* and other icons of avant-garde culture as exemplars of that change and as possible collaborators. None the less, he was not trying to *replace* Europe's culture with a revolutionary new one, as a modernist would. Instead, Hofmannsthal wanted culture to facilitate a revolution from within rather than a wholesale clean-sweep of older forms—a revolution based on the kind of European ideal that his Austria would have recognized before its demise.

Instead of projecting a new ideal *eu-topia* available nowhere on earth, Hofmannsthal sought remedies for the war's disruptions of the common European culture under threat of loss, where he hoped to create a space for pluralistic discussion that could transcend class and the boundaries of modern nation-states. That new space would foster not the kind of cultural nationalism that would soon ground the rise of fascism, but rather a cure for Europe's disruptions, a way to heal the damage of World War I and to modernize the continent with respect to its history.

In his account, Europe could only be restored by the actions of a community that engaged its present through *eine mittlere Sprache,* a language "in the middle" that could mediate among all parts of society in specifying common needs for the new epoch. This common cultural space of communication would also be faithful to the historical experience of the group, building a bridge between past and future, one much like that which Hofmannsthal attempted in his work with theater director Max Reinhardt in staging *Jedermann* for the Salzburg Festival in 1922. He did not sense in his insistence on community the danger in the vision of the *Volk* that others were gathering around him. A common space did not imply to him a determinist cultural ideal, but rather a state of heteroglossia, where parties might discuss. Nor did it equate that healing with the restoration of an arbitrary lost utopia; the people were a present community, not a *Volk* of the past, and they need to change with time. Hofmannsthal, in other words, understood the

von Hofmannsthal (1989), and Wolfram Mauser, *Hugo von Hofmannsthal: Konfliktbewältigung und Werkstruktur* (1977), the latter of which devotes an illuminating chapter on the *Rosenkavalier:* "Identitätsbildung und Spielkonstellation: *Der Rosenkavalier*" (127–37), arguing for its use of typological characters drawn from antique comedy and tragedy, arranged in "constellations" "Zueinander und Gegeneinander" (137).

public spaces of his new Austria in much the same way that Nestroy and Grillparzer had—as spaces fostering the community.

This choice also tips Hofmannsthal's readers to the fate of inherited community structures in his modern world. Despite critics' attempts to cast *fin de siècle* Vienna as decadent, this poet-playwright does *not* argue for the aesthetic cultivation of an elite, but rather for texts that help public discourse to evolve. As he sees it, countries with a better-developed sense of public discourse, like France, have a better-developed popular literature, and a language that can mediate among (and hence bond) all sectors of society, a language that comprises a heteroglossia (to use Bakhtin's term).[3] Hofmannsthal, like his predecessors, finds that public space of mediation in the theater, and the language to profit from that space in the rich traditions of the European stage.

The documentation for that assertion is broadly present in Hofmannsthal's work, if it is read as part of an Austrian or Austro-Hungarian tradition rather than as a precursor to Nazism. Not just his most famous texts, like the "Lord Chandos Letter," or the libretto from the *Rosenkavalier*, but also his late essays "Writing as the Spiritual Space of the Nation" / "Der Schrifttum als geistiger Raum der Nation" and "Value and Dignity of the German Language" / "Wert und Ehre deutscher Sprache" (both 1927) stem from and document his belief in the cultural legacy of an Austria which was part of Europe. They argue for the persistence of a germanophone cultural space that was different from the state configurations that emerged after World War I and, as he saw it, threatened to remove germanophone culture from European history.

In these various texts, as this chapter will pursue, Hofmannsthal is by no means simply looking backwards to seek a lost *eu-topia*, a lost, *pleasant* Europe that would "never be the same" as it had been (as critics like Michael Steinberg argue he did). Instead, his work reveals that he has continued the long-term project begun at the start of his career: the renovation of Western European traditions for a new generation. Resisting not modernization, but modernism (with its insistence on a birth *ex nihilo*), these essays document Hofmannsthal's hopes for a cosmopolitan art that was neither elitist nor nationalist—an art that mediates rather than excludes because it grows from the historical experience of the group, not just from an elite. Hofmannsthal, in other words, maintains a belief in the ability of a community

---

3   "Die Blüte dieser Tendenz ist die Sprachnorm, welche die Nation zusammenhält und innerhalb ihrer dem Spiel widerstreitender Tendenzen—der aristokratischen wie der nivellierenden, der revolutionären wie der conservative—Raum gewahrt" ("Wert und Ehre deutscher Sprache," [*RAIII*, 25]).

enlightening itself through an engagement with its present and its past. He believes, moreover, that Austria's past and future are European and germanophone, not German-nationalist. From this perspective, the essays remain keys to his vain hopes after World War I for recreating a common European culture that would not fall prey to the leveling and elitist assumptions of cosmopolitanism, but which would valorize the national voice of a germanophone culture that had not yet existed in its full form.

Lord Chandos and Bacon

By any measure, critics do still assess Hofmannsthal as espousing European culture rather than nationalism; he is cast as later advocating public political discussion facilitated through literature. His reputation as an aesthete, however, rests on a popular but narrow reading of perhaps his most famous essay, his 1902 "Ein Brief" (the "Lord Chandos Letter"), presented as an "Invented Conversation." Familiarly, that letter's fictional setting is the Elizabethan England of 1600, and its fictional addressee is Francis Bacon.[4]

The "Chandos Letter" concludes with one of the most famous sign-offs in German literature: "this foreseeably final letter, that I write to Francis Bacon"[5] ("Brief," 55). But grammatically, this statement works two ways in German: it is either "the last letter" that Chandos ever would write, as critics generally read this passage, or it can be "the last letter that he would write *to Bacon*." That reading of the sentence is a key to one of the most contested careers in Austrian literature, and it speaks especially to the question of Hofmannsthal's linguistic skepticism around 1900 and his subsequent turn to what seems to be an ethnic-nationalism in the interwar era. Critics like the symmetry of assuming that the later Hofmannsthal is a powerful poetic voice who falls silent like his fictional Chandos. Taking the opposite tack and tracing how only Chandos really fell silent, not his author, opens up a Hofmannsthal whose commitment to Europe and his community led him not to reject poetry, but rather to reframe it, exploring its role as part of Europe's theater heritage.

The basic lines of the "Lord Chandos Letter" are familiar: its fictitious writer expresses his experiences about language, classical scholarship, and the reliability of language as referring to a real world. These doubts purportedly drive Chandos out of society to seek a refuge in nature, to recapture a source of knowledge and individual experience. Yet if Chandos is actually behaving as a withdrawn aristocrat who

---

4   A more completely argued version of this section can be found in chapter 4 of Arens, *Empire in Decline*.
5   "[D]iese[r] voraussichtlich letzt[e] Brief, den ich an Francis Bacon schreibe."

does not want to embrace Bacon's critique of language used by the group (as idols), then the biographical author has moved in precisely the other direction: Hofmannsthal (metaphorically) has not "stopped writing letters" to his public, but actually just started writing them, when he uses the public space of drama rather than the more private and personal sphere of lyric poetry. That the "Lord Chandos Letter" had originally been planned for the Berlin paper *Tag* as the first of a planned series of "Invented Conversations and Letters" that never came to fruition also stages it as a possible *critique* of aristocracy rather than an affirmation of aestheticism ("Ein Brief" [Ritter ed.], 277).[6] Both Hofmannsthal and his contemporary, Arthur Schnitzler, carefully distinguished which of their plays worked for Vienna and which for Berlin, as they needed to be careful of finances after World War I.

The references to Elizabethan history in the piece also bring the relationship of aristocratic experience and the public to the fore. The "Chandos Letter" is a communication written by a fictitious member of a real family on the occasion of his withdrawal from public life in general and his planned return to his family estate in the country. The historically attested Chandos family is remembered as holding an important portrait of Shakespeare, now in the National Portrait Gallery (London). One member of the family, Grey Brydges (the eventual 5th Baron [1579/80–1621]), was responsible for a 1601 conspiracy with the Earl of Essex against Queen Elizabeth I that landed him in prison. Released after Elizabeth's 1603 death and bearing the family title, that Baron Chandos was known for the lavish hospitality of his estate, Sudeley House. A very public politician turned private person.

That real Francis Bacon makes this political dimension to Hofmannsthal's essay more overt (cf. Schultz). Born 1561 as one of two sons of the Lord Keeper of the great seal (with little financial security), Bacon's career began as a barrister and queen's/king's counsel; he then rose to solicitor general and attorney general. He, too, was a friend of the conspiratorial Earl of Essex, although he presided over Essex's informal trial. After Elizabeth's 1603 death, Bacon continued in the service of James I in various capacities, including the position of Lord Chancellor. Having again fallen out of official favor in 1621, Bacon was imprisoned, dying in 1626 from a case of bronchitis contracted

---

6   H. Stefan Schultz' "Hofmannsthal and Bacon: The Sources of the Chandos Letter" is still definitive for its discussion of the internal borrowings of the letter. I have argued that Hofmannsthal's letter borrows from the Prague-born and -raised philosopher Fritz Mauthner (1849–1923). See the notes to the *Erfundene Gespräche und Briefe* (*Sämtliche Werke XXXI*), where the editor Ellen Ritter agrees there were in fact borrowings from Mauthner in Hofmannsthal's work (281); see also the entire "Erläuterungen" to the text, included on pp. 277–300. Gerhard Fuchs, in contrast, is doubtful about Mauthner influencing Hofmannsthal (2).

in an experiment. His philosophical masterpiece, the *Novum Organum* (1620), is regarded as a starting point for modern natural science and empiricism, since it discusses the limits of deduction for producing knowledge from experience of nature.

For the present purposes, it is most notable that Bacon also discusses the ways in which language can cause human error. He outlines various "idols," false images in the mind, including idols of the tribe (*idola tribus*—preconceived notions that regularize and flatten experience), idols of the cave (*idola specus*—individual preconceptions due to personalities), idols of the marketplace (*idola fori*—words taken by specialized groups and removed from their common meanings), and idols of the theater (*idola theatric*—words frozen in academic usage, no longer applicable to the world). If Chandos rejects Bacon, then, it may be due to his rejection of Bacon's analysis of language, one that denigrates strictly personal uses of language as damaging. After all, the poetic Chandos espouses such idols of the cave.[7] Hofmannsthal's Chandos began in precisely the kind of mystic state that Bacon felt was dangerous: "In a kind of persistent drunkenness, all existence appeared to me at that time as a grand unity" (47).[8] Perhaps inspired by Bacon's critique, Chandos feels that he must discard language completely before he can reconstitute his relation to and understanding of the world—where he had earlier hoped to gain wisdom by "deciphering" the wisdom of the ancients, in a kind of language mysticism.

Chandos may have actually taken Bacon's logic to heart. First, Chandos loses his ability to use abstract nouns to make judgments and thus his faith in deductive logic: "abstract words, which the tongue must naturally use to bring any judgment whatsoever to light, dissolved in my mouth like moldy mushrooms" (48–9).[9] Abstract words for concepts are learned by rote, as social overgeneralizations that relate more closely to a society's values rather than to representations of reality. As Chandos' disintegration proceeds, he next realizes that words refer only to conventional ideas, not to anything "real"

---

7   Jacques Le Rider, in *Hugo von Hofmannsthal: Historismus und Moderne in der Literatur der Jahrhundertwende*, pursues another line of critique: he identifies Bacon with Stefan George (125), thus equating Chandos with Hofmannsthal—the complete reverse of what I am arguing here. Michèle Pauget believes, in contrast, that Bacon and Chandos are a doppelgänger in the essay (105), but one who regrets a lost world, not lost words.

8   "Mir erschien damals in einer Art von andauernder Trunkenheit das ganze Dasein als eine große Einheit: geistige und körperliche Welt schien mir keinen Gegensatz zu bilden ..."

9   "die abstrakten Worte, deren sich doch die Zunge naturgemäß bedienen muß, um irgendwelches Urteil an den Tag zu geben, zerfielen mir im Munde wie modrige Pilze."

beyond them: ("nothing more could be encompassed within a concept. The individual words swam around me ... through which one emerged into nothingness" [49]).[10] But at this point, Chandos' critique becomes debilitating. He can no longer write, he thinks, because he has lost his access to individuality: "the deepest, the personal aspect of my thinking, remained excluded from the round dance [of words]" (50).[11] He thus retreats to speechlessness, and to mute nature, outside the language of the real world, rather than following Bacon through to his own conclusions (54). From this perspective, the "Chandos Letter" begins to look like some other famous narratives of personal disintegration from German literature—the letters documenting Heinrich von Kleist's "Kant crisis" or Daniel Paul Schreber's 1903 "Memoirs of My Nervous Illness" (Georg Büchner's fictional *Lenz*). Chandos, like his historical namesake, pulls out of the fray and withdraws to his country house—a beautiful aesthetic gesture, perhaps, but in Hofmannsthal's world, not an ethical decision.

The readers of this essay will know that, where Chandos fell into speechlessness, Hofmannsthal has embraced the public in new ways, speaking through the theater. If Chandos found language to be wanting, his experience was caused by his unwillingness to use language as part of a community; he finds himself unable to use the "simplifying eye of convention" (49), and thus he loses his conventional orientation. In this reading, Chandos is perhaps less confused than repulsed by the realization that ordinary language's concepts are conventional, with their meaning grounded within the community of users. An individual who rejects that community also rejects the worldview in it—and hence language.

Philip Lord Chandos' problem may thus be an affective response rather than a cognitive one: he is having an emotional crisis because of Bacon, who is telling him his most cherished ideals of language being "his" are false.[12] He feels that language has been revealed as "unnatural," far removed from the structure of the universe, rather than simply as "conventional." In other words, Chandos has demonized the base principles of language that Bacon interrogates. Thus it is fitting that he withdraws to the country, and to the purportedly more secure order of nature—or rather, out of society's conventions, out

---

10 "[N]ichts mehr ließ sich mit einem Begriff umspannen. Die einzelnen Worte schwammen um mich ... durch die hindurch man ins Leere kommt."

11 "das Tiefste, das Persönliche meines Denkens, blieb von ihrem Reigen ausgeschlossen."

12 In this sense, it may be Chandos who is meant to be a follower of Stefan George, in Hofmannsthal's world, with Hofmannsthal being Bacon, who remains in public service until his death.

of the world of observations and counter-observations that would ultimately make critique an effective part of public dialogue. Clearly, Hofmannsthal seems more in line with Bacon himself: seeing restrictions, but moving forward toward valuing collective experience rather than individual expression.

Remember, too, that the "Lord Chandos Letter" is a fictional utterance in a tradition that includes not only famous would-be encounters, but also parodies. And thus its fictional writer may be the butt of a joke, one all the more effective because he is so recognizable: Chandos is overly subjective, inward directed, individualistic, and unwilling to consider induction and work with others as an option. In consequence, when Lord Chandos rejects language in favor of individual experience, he also rejects the real power inherent in language: convention—its interface with a community. Chandos' historical namesake gave up politics for throwing parties, no longer contributing to the mainstream of Jacobean England, while Bacon kept up his engagement. Hofmannsthal's Chandos is an egocentric lyric poet who has become aesthete and self-performer, withdrawn from his ability to witness Europe's traditions, a kind of Elizabethan Oscar Wilde without Wilde's ability to perform public critique of conventional mores. As a "Fictitious Encounter," then, the "Lord Chandos Letter" may be a very different invented conversation than critics have realized, the story of an objectionable aesthete who indulges his own sensibilities. Rejecting Bacon means rejecting the historicized knowledge of the group in a very particular way.

This point can be substantiated in another way by referring to further of Hofmannsthal's essays, a genre he used for public cultural advocacy: some were speeches to specific audiences or to commemorate deaths, anniversaries, or official functions; many were reviews of books, artists, and theater (mainly, actors); a few offer overt political commentary (mostly from World War I); and others were taken from forewords and other publicity on books, especially when, in his late career, Hofmannsthal began to use editing and publishing as a way to advocate for his own vision of what the literary heritage needs to be. They were, in addition, originally scattered widely across journals and newspapers.[13] Yet they echo the reading of the "Lord Chandos Letter"

---

13 Some of the "essays" in the published editions, moreover, are actually drafts that may not have been intended for publication. The difficulties in dealing with these texts are exacerbated further by the current edition status. The ten-volume Fischer edition breaks the essays down into three volumes (8: 1891–1913; 9: 1914–24; and 10: 1925–9), with the third volume also containing "Aufzeichnungen"; an added fourth volume includes some famous "essays" of different sort under the title of "Erfundene Gespräche," including the "Brief des Lord Chandos." Those "Erfundene Gespräche" are included in vol. 31 of the

pursued here and show Hofmannsthal's commitment not only to the public, but also to European culture as a whole.

Hofmannsthal's essays often espouse the idea of Europe, especially in the interwar context recovering from the wreck of World War I. He would, I believe, like the current notion of an "Enlightenment project" to describe the critical imperatives of this moment. He seeks a Europe which can modernize without becoming a machine, and which represents communities rather than just rationalities.

The cosmopolitanism of the lost nation

Hofmannsthal's essays take up a wide range of cultural topics in germanophone literature, and he seems at pains to prevent the Austrian canon from being submerged into a ruinous German one. He advocates for authors of the Viennese *Volkstheater* (a form he will draw on himself in *Ariadne auf Naxos* and *Rosenkavalier*), including Eduard von Bauernfeld and Raimund, and for virtually all germanophone literature since Classicism and Romanticism. Yet he also tries to reconnect his readers with canonical European literature, especially Modernism—figures from Decadence and Naturalism (D'Annunzio and Pater through Wilde and Ibsen) back to classics like Balzac, Shakespeare, and Marlowe, but also representatives of contemporaneous literature (as recent as Hans Carossa)—an elite literature that, however, he never uses as an elitist tool to exclude readers. In so doing, he is reminding his readers that there is a common *European* literature behind the literatures of various nations.[14]

Critical for the present discussion is also the fact that a culture needs to be considered as a community that shares a ground in history, geography, tradition, and experience, not just ethnicity or a single language. Thus when Hofmannsthal announces a new book series, he explicitly argues for an Austria composed of many ethnic groups and notes that the series will include a volume of Slovenian folksongs (albeit in German translation), and one of political speeches ("Ankündigung

---

new *Sämtliche Werke*, although the three or four volumes that will be dedicated to the essays have not yet appeared. As a final complication, the Fischer edition has the texts divided into thematic groups (theater reviews or art review are distinguished from book reviews and author appreciations, for example). Bernd Schoeller, with Rudolf Hirsch (vols 8 and 9) and (for vol. 10) Ingeborg Beyer-Ahlert, have done a commendable job of documenting and annotating the essays; the *Sämtliche Werke* in progress will have variants and will have the advantage of a chronological arrangement, rather than one by topics, as Schoeller et al. have done. When they appear, they should be the editions of record.

14 A different, considerably extended version of this material is presented in Katherine Arens, "Hofmannsthal's Essays: Conservation as Revolution" (2002).

A. E. I. O. V. Bücher aus Österreich"/ "Announcement of the AEIOU Books from Austria" [*Reden und Aufsätze* II.428; henceforth RA plus volume and page).

Today's scholars of Hofmannsthal consider his interest in the *Volkstheater* and other European dramatic forms to be antiquarian. Yet in the essays devoted to the topics over his whole career, he stresses how these forms need to be recovered as vital to the community. Hofmannsthal's 1893 essay on the dramatic legacy of a major playwright of the *Volkstheater*, "Eduard von Bauernfelds dramatischer Nachlass," for instance, notes that it is an error to play period works in contemporary clothes, because each era needs to be understood in its particularity— women and servants of his own day differ from those of the Biedermeier (*RA* I.187–8). Such plays can show audiences their own history, because the writers who created them are marked by their historical moments: "Writers usually, for their whole lives, work through the experiences of a certain epoch of their development, when their feeling was intense and so, in contrast, most later ones seem pale repetitions" (*RA* I.186).[15] Texts thus are rooted in a *place*; they do not speak from eternity.

Hofmannsthal considers it critical to preserve such texts, not in acts of piety but rather to keep a record of a set of lives and experiences, preserved in particular, historical forms of language: "thus a breath of home wafts out of language, something beyond all words. In it, so many faces move like dark passing shadows, so much landscape is in it, so much youth, so much inexpressible" ("Französische Redensarten" [1897] *RA* I.237).[16] He uses the word *Heimat*, but this needs to be divorced from later concepts of the folkloric and museum. In calling language a *homeland*, Hofmannsthal sees language as alive, as the vehicle through which a group recognizes itself and sets its stamp on its members (his term is *Prägung*, which also recalls the minting of coins) ("Der Dichter und diese Zeit" [1906] *RA* I.58). Hofmannsthal thus defines the "great books" in the spirit of national masterpieces, as they were defined in Romanticism: as texts expressing and reinforcing the best in the community, working against the injurious effects of bad writing. The important writer acts as his age's eyes and ears, recording the culture's experience and *Bildung* in language (*RA* I.77).

For this reason, Hofmannsthal does indeed believe that the modern era (starting in his estimation between 1790 and 1820) is an age of

---

15   "Die Dichter verarbeiten meist ihr Leben lang die Erlebnisse einer gewissen Epoche ihrer Entwicklung, wo ihr Fühlen intensiv war und dagegen das meiste Spätere als eine matte Wiederholung erscheint."

16   "so weht aus der Sprache ein Hauch der Heimat, der jenseits aller Worte ist. In ihr bewegen sich wie dunkle verfließende Schatten so viele Gesichter, soviel Landschaft ist in ihr, soviel Jugend, soviel Unsägliches."

cultural decline. Moreover, the terms that he uses precisely reflect Horkheimer's and Adorno's critiques of the Enlightenment as enforcing rationalization under the rising capitalist nation-states. Those decades were a time "in which the German forms himself into a comrade of a higher epoch of culture, without the spirit of trade, speculation, or politics" ("Vom dichterischen Dasein" [1907] *RA* I.84).[17] Such statements sound utopian and backwards-looking today, but Hofmannsthal is simply speaking of effort: in this era, German literature and music were brought to a flowering in Austria (significantly, he does not take a position on Weimar classicism). Mozart is one representative of that moment in Austria,[18] but the *Volkstheater* also brought its tradition to fruition then, in a succession of writers extending (in his account) from Grillparzer, Raimund, and Nestroy, and up to Rosegger.

In talking about such traditions, however, Hofmannsthal needs to negotiate between current political realities and history. The *Volkstheater* is part of a great cultural tradition that was *Austrian*, *germanophone*, and *European*, and not *German* or *Prussian*, resting on several hundred years of history and shared cultural experience that the Germany of Hofmannsthal's own era did not possess. He tries to remind his contemporaries that the Weimar Republic (unnamed) is a political entity that does *not* derive from the mainstream of germanophone cultural history or from a historical state other than Prussia. In consequence, the "Germany" that exists after World War I uses a version of the German language that has no historical roots—one that is actually North German in its historical inspiration, and which has undergone several rounds of eliminating "foreign" words from its dictionary.

Colloquial Austrian German, in contrast, was grounded in a different history. It was, Hofmannsthal claims, the most mixed (*gemengteste*) and culturally rich language of the world, encompassing popular and elite registers, including a language of the military and one for diplomacy: "But we have and had, next to the bourgeois one, an aristocratic language, and aside from the language of the inner city, one of the suburbs, and this again is not like the language of the towns around Vienna, not to mention of the flatlands" ("Unsere Fremdwörter" [1914] *RA* II.363).[19] This is the image of a

---

17 "in denen ohne Handelsgeist, Spekulationsgeist, politischen Geist 'sich der Deutsche mit allem Fleiß zum Genossen einer höheren Epoche der Kultur bildet'."

18 "Österreich ist zuerst Geist geworden in seiner Musik und in dieser Form hat es die Welt erobert" ("Österreich im Spiegel seiner Dichtung" [1916] *RA* II.13).

19 "Aber wir haben und hatten auch neben der bürgerlichen eine aristokratische Sprache und neben der Sprache der Innern Stadt eine Vorstadtsprache; und diese wieder ist nicht gleich der Sprache der Ortschaften rings um Wien, ganz

fully articulated linguistic community, with dominants and dialects, sociolects and specialized forms of expression—the living heritage of a germanophone nation, conceived as a full historical culture. But the political legacy of World War I has lost this legacy from its sight and attention. Germany ignores Austria's existence: "One might say, even in the very serious context of today, that Austria is, to Germans, one of the least familiar or poorest known lands of the earth" ("Wir Österreicher und Deutschland" [1915] *RA* II.390).[20] Hofmannsthal thus draws careful distinctions between political entities and cultural ones.

Hofmannsthal's Austria was a particularly rich cultural space that had been broken apart by the treaty of Versailles, and whose legacies were being scattered and squandered. Moreover, his Austria is a cultural entity specifically marked as European since, historically, it was defined by Europe, as the continent's defense against the Ottoman Empire. Hofmannsthal admits that there is a relationship between Germany and Austria: Germany has "clan relations with one of the great components of Austria" ("Wir Österreicher und Deutschland," [1915] *RA* II.391).[21] But *Reichsdeutsche* (Germans of the Empire) do not understand the historical entity that is Austria, one that is an "incomplete project," not something that exists in a permanent form (*RA* II.393–4).[22]

In this context of "Germans and Austrians," Hofmannsthal begins to take on a political tone that is surprisingly ethnic-nationalist:

Because Austria needs an unending influx of German spirit: Germany is Europe to it. […] What we Austrians must constantly demand is the purest of its spiritual power. That purest power, however, can only be passed from state to state as it is from individual to individual, only with the highest tension. When Germany gives us less than its highest and purest, it becomes our poison. The best in German life, given and taken under high tension, is also the life of lives for our Slavs, whether they have the final say or not in these confusing and dark times. And

zu schweigen vom flachen Lande." Translation mine; see David S. Luft, *Hugo von Hofmannsthal and the Austrian Idea* (2011) for translations of this essay (61–6) and others making the case for Hofmannsthal's "Austrian Idea," his idea of a cultured nation without a nation-state.

20 "Es darf, auch in dem heutigen sehr ernsten Zusammenhang, ausgesprochen werden, daß Österreich unter den Ländern der Erde eines der von Deutschen ungekanntesten oder schlechtest gekannten ist."

21 "Stammesverwandtschaft mit dem einen der großen Volkselemente Österreichs."

22 "kein schlechthin Bestehendes, sondern eine ungelöste Aufgabe."

we owe it to them to give it to them. ("Wir Österreicher und Deutschland. [1915] *RA* II.394)[23]

This potentially alarming statement points to a historical paradox that recurs throughout Hofmannsthal's essays: Germany (especially as realized in cherished figures like Goethe) is in one sense a source of germanophone culture, in the form of shared cultural traditions that Austrians receive repeatedly.[24] Yet historically, Austria has taken the best of those shared traditions and made them into something else, something that the Germany of postwar Europe has not been able to appreciate.

While Hofmannsthal's use of terminology like *Volksgut*—the traditional property of "the people"—is disturbing in retrospect, he leaves no doubt that he was speaking of European history and tradition rather than genetics (or eugenics). His Europe is a cultural heritage that can turn the *masses* back into the *people*:

> The mission of Austria, in which I believe and for which a monstrous blood offering is being given by our people in these months, united with the Hungarian people, is a European mission: how could we bear conceiving of that Europe as something that no longer exists, spiritually or morally, that Europe from which we have received our thousand-year-old mission and that must be continuously renewed for us, or else we should congeal and die out? Austria needs Europe more than all others—it is, after all, itself a Europe in miniature. ("Krieg und Kultur" [1915] *RA* II.417)[25]

---

23 "Denn Österreich bedarf ohne Unterlaß des Einströmens deutschen Geistes: Deutschland ist ihm Europa. ... Was wir Österreicher von Deutschland beständig verlangen müssen, ist das Reinste seiner geisten Kraft. Ein Reinstes aber kann von Staat zu Staat, wie von Individuum zu Individuum, nur unter einer hohen Spannung gegeben werden. Wo uns Deutschland ein Minderes gibt, als sein Höchstes und Reinstes, wird es uns zu Gift. Das Höchste deutschen Lebens, unter einer hohen Spannung gegeben und genommen, ist auch für unsere Slawen, ob sie es in verworrenen und getrübten Zeiten Wort haben oder nicht, Leben des Lebens. Und dies an sie zu geben sind wir ihnen schuldig."

24 "Wir empfingen von den Deutschen wieder und wieder einströmendes Volksgut" ("Wir Österreicher und Deutschland" [1915] *RA* II.394)

25 "Die Mission Österreichs, an die ich glaube und für die ein ungeheueres Blutopfer in diesen Monaten von unsern Völkern vereint mit dem ungarischen Volk gebracht wird, ist eine europäische: wie könnten wir es ertragen, jenes Europa, von dem wir unsere tausendjährige Mission empfangen haben und das sie uns beständig erneuern muß, woanders wir nicht erstarren und absterben sollen, als ein im geistigen und sittlichen Sinne nicht mehr existierendes zu denken? Österreich bedarf mehr als alle andern eines Europa—es ist ja doch selber ein Europa im Kleinen."

No nation can exist without other nations, in a state of productive tension. Hofmannsthal's European Austria came to its cultural maturity around 1800 in such relations of productive tension, and he feels that it is endangered a century later by two dominant trends: provincialism and overdone particularism ("Österreich im Spiegel seiner Dichtung" [1916] *RA* II.21), both of which tend to insulate Germany's legacy from Austria.

Hofmannsthal's Austrian culture thus needs to correlate with real, lived experience and traditions, not simply with a set of political borders:

> Culture is not something dead and closed off for us, but something alive, the enmeshing of spheres and powers of life, of the political and the military, the connection of the material with the moral. (*RA* II.24)[26]

Hofmannsthal is, however, not arguing for a cultural unification of Austria and an improved Germany, but rather a commitment to Europe and a kind of "spiritual universalism" (*RA* II.25). This Austria descends from the legacy of the *Heiliges Römisches Reich* and the Catholic Church, within which Austria functioned as a border colony (*Grenzkolonie* ["Die österreichische Idee" (1917) *RA* II.455, 456]).[27] That is, Austria emerged *out of Europe*, not from a mythic German space, and it is still defined in relation to it.

The author's approach to Austrian culture and its future in Europe remains consistent: Europe needs germanphone legacies, but as represented in Austria, not in Prussia:

> This Europe that wants to reestablish itself needs Austria: a construct of unaffected elasticity, but a construct, a true organism, pervaded by an inner religion of itself, without which ties among living powers are not possible; Europe needs it, in order to grasp the polymorphous East. ("Die österreichische Idee" [1917] *RA* II.457)[28]

---

26 "Kultur ist uns kein Totes und Abgeschlossenes, sondern ein Lebendiges, das Ineinandergreifen der Lebenskreise und Lebenskräfte, des Politischen und des Militärischen, die Verbindung des Materiellen mit dem Sittlichen."

27 See also Luft, *Hugo von Hofmannsthal*, 99–102, for a fine, complete translation of this essay.

28 "Dies Europa, das sich neu formen will, bedarf eines Österreich: eines Gebildes von ungekünstelter Elastizität, aber eines Gebildes, eines wahren Organismus, durchströmt von der inneren Religion zu sich selbst, ohne welche keine Bindungen lebender Gewalten möglich sind; es bedarf seiner, um den polymorphen Osten zu fassen."

Hofmannsthal's Austria has a moral authority as part of Europe, as he will again underscore in a set of notes on "Prussians and Austrians" that are reprinted as part of the essays ("Preusse und Österreicher" [1917]).[29] His historical prejudices emerge clearly: "Prussia: made up, an artificial construction, by nature a poor land, [...] most disciplinable masses, boundless authority ... Austria: grown, a historical tapestry, by nature a rich land" (*RA* II.459).[30] Even the art of the two German nations differs, with Berlin's theater focusing on the "pathological and bizarre," or on decorativeness, while Austria's theater, in the tradition of Mozart's opera, develops "out of the aristocratic and, at the same time, popular culture of old Austria" ("Proposition" [1917] *RA* II.231, echoed in "Das Reinhardtsche Theater" [1918]).[31]

Hofmannsthal takes up the topic of Austria's cultural identity repeatedly after the end of World War I. In one set of essays, he addresses the widespread trope (promulgated most visibly by Hermann Bahr) that the Baroque is Austria's natural inheritance. Its emphasis on pageantry is part of the South's heritage, he announces in a discussion of the Salzburg Festival: "The idea of the Festival is the actual idea art form of the Bavarian-Austrian clan" ("Deutsche Festspiele zu Salzburg" [1919] *RA* II.255).[32] Because two German states share this legacy, the *Festspiel* belongs on the border, to unite various strands of culture, wedding Mozart to Goethe and Schiller: "Thus Weimar approaches Salzburg: the dividing line of the Main River is at the same time emphasized and suspended. The distinctive characteristics of the southern German clans emerge sharply, and their cohesive elements appears to the soul" (*RA* II.255).[33] Poets like "Ferdinand Raimund" (1920) embody this inheritance of the pageant, as well, when they show characters who emerge simultaneously as "an individual and at the same time a world. The boundaries between him and all others belonging to that world are quite fluid. He belongs to a community: Vienna, and he shares with this community everything that he has" (*RA* II.118).[34] Such public stagings of the language and the culture

---

29 See Luft, *Hugo von Hofmannsthal*, 103–6, for a complete translation.
30 "Preussen: Geschaffen, ein künstlicher Bau, von Natur armes Land, ... Disziplinierbarste Masse, grenzlose Autorität ... Österreich: Gewachsen, geschichtliches Gewebe, von Natur reiches Land ..."
31 "aus der aristokratischen und zugleich volkstümlichen Kultur des alten Österreich."
32 "Das Festspielgedanke ist der eigentliche Kunstgedanke des bayrisch-österreichischen Stammes."
33 "So tritt Weimar zu Salzburg: Die Mainlinie wird betont und zugleich aufgehoben. Süddeutsche Stammeseigentümlichkeit tritt scharf hervor und zugleich tritt das Zusammenhaltende vor die Seele."
34 "ein Individuum und ... auch zugleich eine Welt. Die Grenzen zwischen ihm und

create a community and propagate the heritage through the present into the future.

In Hofmannsthal's estimation, however, the World War threatened this legacy and at the same time showed where it needed modernization, if it were to be viable for the new century. For example, Austria lacked the kind of political language that the European powers had ("Adam Müllers Zwölf Reden über die Beredsamkeit" [1920] *RA* II.123). Two countries existing as politically separate but sharing a common language is a possibility, judging by the examples of Belgium and France, two countries that remain distinct despite their many commonalities. For Hofmannsthal, the issue is the heritage of the community, not fleeting political boundaries:

> The connection of Austria with the totality of Germanness, and on the other hand the freedom and partial foreignness with which Austria stands *vis-à-vis* the Germanness of the newly united Reich, is far more than merely a connection of language. It rests on the fact that Austria was a part of the old Reich, the Holy Roman Empire as well as the German Union, and that sixty years ago, while Switzerland perhaps had liberated itself, in fact and formally, from the old German Reich more than four hundred years ago. ("Bemerkungen" [1921] *RA* II.473)[35]

Germanness is not identical with Germany. Passages like this argue the cultural priority of Austria over Germany, despite the latter's current political dominance. The optimal Austria that Hofmannsthal seeks to recover from Europe's historical wreckage is universal, blended, and humane in a way that the German Empire is not: "the present German Reich does not show the entire face of the German character in Europe, that this face cannot be recognized without those traits of an older and higher Germanness that are preserved in Austria" (*RA* II.476).[36]

---

und allem andern, was zu dieser Welt gehört, sind ganz fließend. Er gehört einer Gemeinschaft an: Wien, und er teilt mit dieser Gemeinschaft alles, was er hat."

35 "Der Zusammenhang Österreichs mit der Gesamtheit des Deutschtums, andererseits die Freiheit und teilweise Fremdheit, mit der Österreich dem im neuen Reich vereinigten Deutschtum gegenüber steht, ist weit mehr als bloßer Sprachzusammenhang. Er ruht darauf, daß Österreich ein Teil des alten Reichs, sowohl des Heiligen Romischen Reiches als dann des Deutschen Bundes war, und dies bis vor sechsig Jahren, während etwa die Schweiz sich schon vor mehr als vierhundert Jahren faktisch und formal vom alten deutschen Reich abgelöst hat."

36 "daß das gegenwärtige Deutsche Reich nicht das ganze Gesicht des deutschen Wesens in Europa zeige, daß dieses Gesicht nicht ohne die in Österreich erhaltenen Züge eines älteren und höheren Deutschtums erkannt werden könne."

This might simply be taken as local patriotism and prejudice, but Hofmannsthal's commitment to a nation whose culture is European rather than the property of a single political space is undeniable. For him, a culture is based on a language, history, and traditions that anchor a nation's identity and give it the power to survive because it is rooted in experience, not just in transitory and abstract master narratives of history:

> For the world around us, which we are accustomed to call reality, is a war (and a balance) of powers that are fictions; to add or to subordinate them to a new fiction, however, rests on the authority of a spiritual power. A group that undertakes to force a new reality onto a dying one must at the very least consider itself an elite, in order that, if their work is not to be undertaken in vain, they be taken as one by the next epoch to arise. ("*Europäische Revue*: Eine Monatsschrift" [1926] *RA* III.79)[37]

History is made by the persistence of experience, not by proclamation or sudden shifts in the narratives used to turn experiences into tradition.

This definition of Austria as a European culture, however fraught it seems to post-1945 ears, opens out new dimensions to two of the greatest of Hofmannsthal's late essays. The first originated in a speech: "Das Schrifttum als geistiger Raum der Nation: Rede, gehalten im Auditorium Maximum der Universität München am 10. January 1927" [1926] ("Writing as the Spiritual Space of the Nation" [*RA* III.24–41]);[38] the second is the introduction to a collection of maxims about the German language: "Wert und Ehre deutscher Sprache" (1927) ("Value and Honor of the German Language" [*RA* III.128–33]).[39] "Writing" is, notably, dedicated to Karl Voßler, noted philologist and Rector of the university, thus making both essays into debates about language as a space of culture.

Here, Hofmannsthal's definitions of the nation receive clearer contour. First and foremost, a nation must have a community at the heart. Young nations like America and Germany do not have that:

---

37 "Denn die Welt um uns, die wir die Wirklichkeit zu nennen gewohnt sind, ist ein Kampf (und ein Ausgleich) von Mächten, die Fiktionen sind; ihnen aber eine neue Fiktion zu gesellen oder überzuordnen, ist die Befugnis der geistigen Potenz. Eine Gruppe, die es unternimmt, einer absterbenden Wirklichkeit neue Wirklichkeit aufzudrängen, muß zumindest sich selbst als eine Elite empfinden, um dann, wenn ihr Werk nicht vergeblich war, von der nächst heraufkommenden Epoche als eine solche empfunden zu werden."

38 See Luft, *Hugo von Hofmannsthal*, 157–70.

39 See Luft, *Hugo von Hofmannsthal*, 171–5.

Not because we live on home soil, not because of our physical contact in trade and exchange, but principally because we are bound to a community in a spiritual dependence. [...] In language we find our way to each other, a language which is something completely different than just a natural means for mutual understanding, because in language the past speaks to us, powers have their effects on us and become directly formidable for those who can neither be given space nor have boundaries set by political institutions—a singular connection effective between the generations, we divine something in power behind it, something that we dare to call the spirit of the nation. ("Das Schrifttum," *RA* III.24)[40]

That nation has an identity mediated in writing, as a *Schrifttum*, a body of writing of all sorts, including anecdotes, political speeches, and newspaper articles. Thus he is also countering elitist assumptions about art to redefine "national literature" as writings that remain part of the community. He wishes to avoid divisions in class enforced through such writing ("the unfortunate rift in our people between the educated and the uneducated" [*RA* III.24]).[41] For Hofmannsthal, class difference is not a condition of literacy so much as a question of access, and the stage allows the heteroglossia of society to play itself out in productive critique, perhaps even to evolve. When these various sectors of the public each exert their "particular tendencies" in using language and remain in productive rivalry, then there is a nation.[42] Thus "writing," *Schrifttum*, *écriture*, in all its forms, including popular literature, defines the real space of the nation, creating the space between audience and writer, binding all into a whole that is not *zerrissen* (fractured).

Hofmannsthal is clearly utopian in his hopes, but perhaps more crucial is his warning that an elite culture cannot be elitist—that the

---

40 "Nicht durch unser Wohnen auf dem Heimatboden, nicht durch unsere leibliche Berührung in Handel und Wandel, sondern durch ein geistiges Anhängen vor allem sind wir zur Gemeinschaft verbunden. ... In einer Sprache finden wir uns zueinander, die völlig etwas anderes ist als das bloße natürliche Verständigungsmittel; denn in ihr redet Vergangenes zu uns, Kräfte wirken auf uns ein und werden unmittelbar gewaltig, denen die politischen Einrichtungen weder Raum zu geben, noch Schranken zu setzen mächtig sind, ein eigentümlicher Zusammenhang wirksam zwischen den Geschlechtern, wir ahnen dahinter ein Etwas waltend, das wir den Geist der Nation zu nennen uns getrauen."

41 "der unglückliche Riß in unserem Volk zwischen Gebildeten und Ungebildeten."

42 "Die Blüte dieser Tendenz ist die Sprachnorm, welche die Nation zusammenhält und innerhalb ihrer dem Spiel widerstreitender Tendenzen—der aristokratischen wie der nivellierenden, der revolutionären wie der conservative—Raum gewahrt" (*RA* III.25)

self-declared upper classes cannot isolate themselves from the public face of the nation, which he describes very much in the way that Benedict Anderson would later call an *imagined community*:

> The nation, held together by an indestructible tapestry of the linguistic-spiritual becomes a belief community which encompasses the whole of natural and cultural life; a nation-state of this sort appears like an inner universe ... The concept of space that emanates out of this spiritual whole is identical with the realm of spirits that the nation occupies in its own consciousness and in that of the world. (*RA* III.27)[43]

This "inner universe" defines the power, role, rights, and duties within a nation defined as a community. Yet Hofmannsthal refuses to equate that nation with the Germany of his era, which does not have the necessary preconditions (cultural traditions) to become a community. His accusation that Germany operates in the "realm of spirits" echoes the charge that it has the "disease of abstraction," familiar from both Marx's *Theses on Feuerbach* and Benjamin's *Theses on the Philosophy of History*. His era's Germany has the *idea* of a community or nation, rather than the reality, since there is nothing natural, traditional, about it.

Significantly, he also explicitly tries to circumvent the image of the poet-genius that has been cherished by the *Bildungsbürgertum* in the wake of German Classicism—a vision in the ascendant in Germany, albeit ruinous for cultural evolution. He asserts that the poet can neither create nor lead the nation, but only articulate what the nation already is on the basis of its history and experience. Thus the nation, not the poet, is the true agent of national formation or change:

> The poet at times fights for language—not in order to cooperate in the creation of language norms in which the nation binds itself in a true unity, but as the magic power that it is—he wants to make it serviceable, his spiritual passion is so great, in the highest moments he will really feel something passionately observed vibrate in sympathy with the rhythm of his life, and then he will truly be a poet. (*RA* III.33)[44]

---

43 "Die Nation, durch ein unzerreißbares Gewebe des Sprachlich-Geistigen zusammengehalten, wird Glaubensgemeinschaft, in der das Ganze des natür-lichen und kultürlichen Lebens einbeschlossen ist; ein Nationsstaat dieser Art erscheint als das innere Universum ... Der Raumbegriff, der aus diesem geistigen Ganzen emaniert, ist identisch mit dem Geisterraum, den die Nation in ihrem eigenene Bewußtsein und in dem der Welt einnimmt."

44 "Um die Sprache ringt [der Dichter] zuzeiten wirklich—aber nicht mitzuwirken an der Schöpfung der Sprachnorm, in der die Nation zur wahren Einheit sich

That is, the poet stands in service of the nation's language, lending form to its ineffability and making its currents visible.

Thus Hofmannsthal's familiar call for a "conservative revolution" takes on a new face as he moves into a historical consideration to define his goals. The germanophone culture of which he speaks is not only a product of Europe, but one of the Renaissance and Reformation, which promised to bring Europe out of the middle ages: "The process of which I speak is nothing but a conservative revolution of a dimension not known in European history. Its goal is form, a new German reality in which the entire nation could participate (*RA* III.41).[45] Scholars often adduce this quotation as attesting Hofmannsthal's acceptance of a proto-Nazi nationalism, but such a reading reflects hindsight. His late essays stress groundedness in history and community as the basis for a critical group consciousness that can overcome the limitations of the past. Such a reading may point to Hofmannsthal's possible naïveté about the ability of a group to resist co-optation by a self-declared elite like the Nazis, but it also expresses his belief in community and its discussions in public space.

Hofmannsthal echoes that point in his other great cultural history essay, "Value and Honor of the German Language" ("Wert und Ehre deutscher Sprache" [1927]). Here, he outlines how the German language needs to function as a mediator, so that the community may join into a commonality of understanding missing in the politics of his era, so that "that which is understood along with each word" ("das in jedem Wort Mitverstandene") will join each hearer in ongoing discussion, with

> the social element within which both, the speaker and the spoken to, know themselves as affiliates; about the individual who stands across from another, not as much that individual's acts of self-differentiation, not the individual's claim that leads too easily to denial, but the intertwined network in terms of which each of us comes to stand in groupings within the totality, in typical relationships with institutions and projects. It is not so much what individuals are for themselves that should be expressed in their language, but rather that what they imagine. In acts of speaking, the totality represents itself. In such everyday speech, something

---

bindet, sondern als die magische Gewalt, die sie ist, will er sich sie dienstbar machen, seine geistige Leidenschaft ist so groß, in den höchsten Momenten wird er wirklich ein leidenschaftlich Erschautes bis in den Rhythmus seines Leibes in sich nachzittern fühlen und dann wahrhaft Dichter sein."

45 "Der Prozeß, von dem ich rede, ist nichts anderes als eine konservative Revolution von einem Umfange, wie die europäische Geschichte ihn nicht kennt. Ihr Ziel ist Form, eine neue deutsche Wirklichkeit, an der die ganze Nation teilnehmen könne."

is predominant in the relations between the words, where they build families among themselves, even as they all the same refuse to express their deepest potentials. (*RA* III.128–9)[46]

In his diagnosis, the community of German-speakers in his world has only a language of utility, a series of individual languages without a center and hence without an associated nation. But in a recourse to history, that nation may be rediscovered: "Language is a large realm of the dead, deep beyond plumbing; thus we receive out of it the highest things of life. Our timeless fate exists in it, and the dominant force of the community over everything particular. Through it we stride into the people, that is what we feel" (*RA* III.132).[47] And among the works which contain those "highest things of life" will be plays that he will hope to include in the Salzburg Festival: *Faust*, his own *Ariadne*, mystery plays like his own *Jedermann*, and the Johann Strauß, Jr., operetta *Die Fledermaus*.

The Nazi affiliation with the Salzburg Festival would later help to stamp Hofmannsthal as a conservative nationalist. But he saw the restaging of such works as a way to reinstitute the center of the traditional "south German (Bavarian-Austrian) theater spirit" and the language culture he sought to set against Prussian-Germany ("Das Salzburger Program" [*RA* III.178]). He is, on the one hand, asserting the necessity of a national theater in the sense familiar since Schiller, yet one stressing social partnership rather than aesthetic leadership as the way to achieving that nation. This is, explicitly, not the modernist theater of cities like Berlin, whose modernist theater portrays principally the crass and evil of the city, not speaking to the rest of the nation ("Das Publikum der Salzburger Festspiele" [*RA* III.184–5]).

Hofmannsthal speaks decidedly out of space and time in these essays, but his attempts to recover a community and a culture out of

---

46 "das gesellige Element, worin sich beide, der Redende und der Angeredete, zusammen wissen; von dem Einzelnen, der ihm gegenübersteht, nicht zu sehr dessen Sich-Unterscheiden, nicht der individuelle Anspruch, der ja leicht zu Ablehnung herausfordert, sondern die Verflochtenheit, gemäß der ein jeder zu den Gruppierungen innerhalb der Gesamtheit, den Einrichtungen, den Unternehmungen in gewissen typischen Verhältnissen steht. Nicht so sehr das, was er für sich ist, soll in seiner Sprache sich ausprägen, als das, was er vorstellt. In seinem Sprechen repräsentiert sich die Gesamtheit. Es herrscht in einer solchen Umgangsrede zwischen den Worten ein Etwas, daß sie untereinander gleichsam Familie bilden, wobei sie alle gleichmäßig verzichten, ihr Tiefstes auszusagen."

47 "Die Sprache ist ein großes Totenreich, unauslotbar tief; darum empfangen wir aus ihr das höchste Leben. Es ist unser zeitloses Schicksal in ihr, und die Übergewalt der Volksgemeinschaft über alles Einzelne.
    Unmittelbar schreiten wir durch sie in das Volk hinein, das fühlen wir."

the political debris of Europe are consistent. His goal is to reclaim the value of elite literacy, yet not the elitism characteristic of the "new" German nation, and to foster the space for political discussion that germanophone Europe has lacked. To do so, he must conserve traditions and archive past experience for his fellow Austrians, but never to encourage them to look backwards. Instead, he demands that abstractions give way to communication in public spaces—that all culture appears as popular culture, yet with a claim to being a reservoir of what the nation knows, much more than just amusement.

As he had in the "Chandos Letter," Hofmannsthal in his essays confirms the modern era as originating in the Renaissance rather than the Enlightenment, a move shared by the philosopher Ernst Cassirer but specifically decried by the Frankfurt School, especially by Habermas' *Structural Transformation of the Public Sphere*. Hofmannsthal here draws a line between the modern era and modernism because he rejects the idea of the Enlightenment as an era that is complete and against which his present has been forced to react (as the Frankfurt School would have it, positing it as a dialectic). Instead, it is an ongoing project for a nation that hopes to grow and live, aware of its past and its models, but aiming at a new future.

After World War I, any such commitment to public Enlightenment might indeed have appeared a lost cause. Hofmannsthal clearly overestimates the power of public culture to improve itself, but he cannot be seen as arguing for any sort of German or German-Austrian restoration—the nation he seeks still needs to be formed in the context of the new era. Naïvely, Hofmannsthal assumes (as do many others of his era) that even Slavs can become German, when "German" means a specific form of European culture deriving from Renaissance-humanist values. Moreover, from the vantage point of a post-national Europe, it is critical to see how he balances the global and the local in preserving traditions, but insisting that they, like the *Volkstheater*, must speak from and for the community. From his position in the interwar era, after the dissolution of Austria-Hungary into modern nation-states driven by politics and capital rather than culture, Hofmannsthal is also pleading for the recovery of a "German" culture that could be divorced both from Germany and from compulsory monolingualism—and for this culture remaining part of Europe.

Toward a revolutionary conservatism: The modern European
The readings offered here are supported by existing evidence for Austrian cultural traditions that define public spaces and public discussion as moral and political, far away from the instrumentalized public sphere that Adorno and Horkheimer critique. They require a revision of Hofmannsthal's image to make him a servant of European

culture and its legacy in the era of total destruction after World War I—to align at least part of his project with that of Chandos' Francis Bacon rather than with Chandos himself. He seeks not a restoration of Europe, but a recovery of its ground and its ability to move forward that were endangered and on the brink of extinction, given current political trends. This act of recovery is a moral duty for the artist, and the basis for a community's ability to speak to the issues of its own present—to engage in discussions and raise their own consciousness.

Hofmannsthal used his essays and his editing projects of the interwar period to make that possible, but he also used the theater as the true mass medium of the day (and there is evidence he was interested in film for the same reason). What he achieved is not necessarily appreciated by scholars today, because so much of his dramatic work came in the form of libretti for operas, especially for Richard Strauss. The earliest important one was his 1910 libretto for Richard Strauss' great opera, *Der Rosenkavalier* (premiered 1911), which derives quite overtly from the tradition of the *Volkstheater*.[48] Like Nestroy's Frau von Cypressenburg from *Talisman*, Hofmannsthal's opera's Marschallin has to prove herself a proper member of the upper classes by taking care of those subject to her influence. Through acts of coercion (if not outright blackmail), both will arrange for inheritances to fall where they find them necessary, not especially where an inflexible social order might demand them go. Yet where Cypressenburg simply wants Titus to be rich enough to be self-determining (and hence essentially inert, because he will not have to work), the Marschallin is actively conspiring to

---

48 On the women in the opera, see Lilian R. Furst, "No Bed of Roses: The Women in the *Rosenkavalier*," who offers a feminist reading, showing that the the women are idealized while the men are ironized. Most discussions of *Rosenkavalier* place it in the idea of Habsburg nostalgia (e.g. Swales, who explains *Der Schwierige* in a similar way: "The play manifestly is a valedictory tribute to the 'Vielvölkerstaat' of Old Austria, and contributes powerfully to that 'Habsburg myth', which invests the paralysis and decline of the last century or so of the Danube monarchy with a rhetoric of meta-national nobility" (182). Robert Vilain, "'Stop all the Clocks,'" speaks of *Rosenkavalier* and *Arabella* in parallel terms: "In both operas the characters' various attitudes to the passing of time are anchored in clearly depicted historical settings, the specificity of which was extremely important to Hofmannsthal" (193), while acknowledging that "the characters of comedy are figures whose action is half-way between the infinite potential of real human beings and the rigidly delimited scope of puppets" (196). He believes, however, that Hofmannsthal is not in control of the dramatic statements made: "The Strauss-Hofmannsthal correspondence largely confirms the superiority of Strauss' feel for drama" (196), and that "the characters of comedy are figures whose action is half-way between the infinite potential of real human beings and the rigidly delimited scope of puppets" (196). I disagree with both latter statements.

subvert class-bound customs and to join an old title to new money under the banner of love, not social status.

This is a canny reuse of the tradition of the Viennese Hanswurst. From its opening scene, *Rosenkavalier* cites this theater in its heyday, at the close of the eighteenth century; even more explicitly, *Ariadne auf Naxos* puts actual *commedia dell'arte* performers on the stage. What Hofmannsthal adds, however, is the fact that "everyman" is an every-woman: his Staberls are female.

What Hofmannsthal achieved in these libretti is underappreciated, since the performance traditions follow the music rather than the texts to find their coherence. For instance, the conventional staging of *Rosenkavalier*, stressing the would-be aristocratic manners of unaccep-table new-money glitterati, tends to obscure its more socially aware comment on love, marriage, and social status. The music follows the upper-class image of love: when Octavian, the Cavalier of the Rose, meets the heiress Sophie and falls instantly in love, Strauss' score evokes the wonderment of the moment. Yet the libretto tells a different tale: the purportedly love-struck Sophie is anything but naïve. To be sure, she is immediately enthralled by Octavian, but he only secures his place in her heart when she remembers that he is listed in the "Mirror of the Nobility," the peerage—an ideal candidate for a social-climbing heiress and her father. She is one of those citizens in the luxury trade that Staberl and Titus criticized, unable or unwilling to acknowledge humanity outside of status and money. While Strauss set their fondest dreams to music in this opera, Hofmannsthal will follow his prede-cessors in seeing the peerage as an institution of the past.

Hofmannsthal's text reveals itself as distinctly harsher than Richard Strauss' music, when he forces his aristocrats into the more compre-hensive world of the *commedia dell'arte*. The Marschallin's imperial morning *levée*, for instance, includes two Italians as part of the crowd seeking her favors, money, and patronage. Valzacchi and Annina, two modernized versions of traditional trickster characters, will under-score the themes of respect and public sanction, as well as questioning too-simple notions of class virtue.

First, Valzacchi proves himself corrupt as he tries to sell the Marschallin the equivalent of *The National Enquirer*, the "Die swarze Zeitung." She rebuffs him, which leads him to ask, in broken German, to "be of service" to the libertine Baron Ochs. Yet Valzacchi is neither Staberl nor Figaro, but a man caught in a search for money and status: "Yer Grace is looking fer something. I see, your Grace 'as a need. / I can serve. I can take care of it" (*Rosenkavalier*, 25).[49] Entering into Ochs'

---

49   "Ihre Gnade sukt etwas. Ik seh,/Ihre Gnade at eine Bedürfnis./ Ik dan dienen, ik kann besorgen."

employ, Valzacchi and Annina play "niece and uncle" in order to spy on Sophie and guard her chastity: "Your Grace has jealousy; each step the lady takes, we are there!" (*Rosenkavalier*, 25).[50] Simultaneously, the Baron plans to seduce his next victim, the fake maid Mariandl (Octavian in drag). He is a predator, convinced of his own value (he notes with no irony that "no night is too long" for a woman in his arms).

Act II sees the false servants spying on Sophie, but after Octavian engages in a duel for his beloved and wounds the Baron, the balance of gender roles shifts. Annina proves herself more entrepreneurial than her male counterpart. Working more as an independent agent than as Valzacchi's confederate, Annina reports the situation to Sophie's father, Faninal, in the hopes of some reward:

The young cavalier	Der junge Kavalier
And his Miss Bride, your graces,	und die Fräulein Braut,
Were already wed,	Gnaden,
Secretly, your graces.	waren im Geheimen
(*Rosenkavalier*, 35)	schon recht vertraut, Gnaden!

Yet Annina will give up her work for Ochs and Faninal when she realizes she will be only ill-rewarded, bringing the question of station and gender to the fore. She does not question her role as a servant, but she does help to invalidate Ochs' wishes, when she decides he has swindled her out of a second tip. As her revenge, she begins to work to set up Ochs' Act III downfall, leading her confederate back to a more socially responsible, and hence more moral, position as well.

The Marschallin's revenge comes straight out of sentimental drama or eighteenth-century court comedy: Octavian dresses up as a putative widow with a pack of children, all purportedly Ochs'. Police are called to the scene of his/her "domestic dispute," and s/he testifies that Ochs is the "husband" who had abandoned her: "That's him. He's my husband. That's him, that's him./ He wants to marry a second time, the scoundrel,/ a second innocent girl, just as I was" (*Rosenkavalier*, 38).[51] Ochs' public reputation is at stake when the servants call the innkeeper ("der Wirt") and three waiters as public witnesses, given from the point of view of small businessmen whose inn and reputation could be ruined by the Baron's tryst. As the innkeeper notes: "The

---

50 "Ihre Gnade ist in Eifersukt ... Jede Sritt die Dame sie tut, ... wir sind da!"

51 "Er ist es! Es ist mein Mann! Er ist's! Er ist's! /Er will ein zweites Mal heiraten, der Infame,/ ein zweites unschuldiges Mädchen, so wie ich es war!"

reputation of my house! Why does my house have to live through this!" (*Rosenkavalier*, 39).[52]

The police listen to Annina's tall tale, while Valzacchi summons Sophie's father—servants form an avenging community to destroy an inadequate aristocrat. The police commissioner is forced to investigate this scandal for "all of Vienna" ("Die ganze Wienerstadt" [*Rosenkavalier*, 41]), as "a Viennese masquerade" ("eine wienerische Maskerad" [*Rosenkavalier*, 43]). Ochs is sent off with Annina's scorn, as she quotes his hubris back to him: "I just have the luck of the Lerchenaus again" (*Rosenkavalier*, 44).[53] He will go off without his rich bride, footing the bill for damages due to his dalliance and general lack of sense, as Sophie and Octavian go off to join old blood with new money. The Marschallin and the clever servants have let love triumph, bringing the sense of the heart to the situation.

Like Nestroy, Grillparzer, and Stifter, Hofmannsthal does not advocate open or formulaic revolution against the existing orders: the Marschallin proves that at least some titled nobility may have a place in society, if they remember their responsibility to the collective. Thus the Marschallin has simply enacted justice through a reputation-ruining ruse about illegitimate children, as Cypressenburg had done with Titus' uncle. Yet these two aristocratic and powerful women show an interesting asymmetry in class manipulation that may help to confirm Hofmannsthal's commitment to a more integrated community: Cypressenburg attempts to meddle with middle-class fortunes, while the Marschallin entraps one of her own class, Baron Ochs. Even more significantly, the Marschallin cannot correct the situation by herself: she needs clever servants to conspire with her against the worst impulses of the Baron and the *nouveaux riches* in the Faninal family. The ethics of her personal *hommage* to love and beauty are definitely not those of the bourgeoisie—she remains truer to the eighteenth century than to the nineteenth. At the same time, however, she finds her leverage in public reputation, not in money, beauty, or status alone; her own class's values alone cannot right the situation.

Hofmannsthal's world is thus in many ways a continuation of those familiar from Nestroy and Bäuerle, all sharing a world of types: servants and masters, social climbers and would-be couples. Yet in Hoffmannsthal's treatment, the world of the ethical servant/hard-working businessman is a female one. Hofmannsthal's Annina shares with her forebears a clear acknowledgment that society is stratified, and that there are ways in which the strata ought to interact, when not perverted by social-climbing and money. What differentiates her from

---

52   "Mein renommiertes Haus! Das muss mein Haus erleben!"
53   "Ich hab' halt schon einmal ein Lerchenauisch' Glück!"

her male predecessors, however, is her willingness to help a "good aristocrat" to bring love into the world, transcending class boundaries without crossing them. She is, in consequence, only an instrument in the story, and not its focus.

To be sure, Annina stays in the *commedia dell'arte* and *Volkstheater* tradition by bringing fate and love out of the private rooms of the upper classes and back out onto the streets, under the scrutiny of the ordinary working people, if justice is to be done. Ultimately, however, Annina and Valzacchi will disappear, leaving the innkeeper and the policeman to keep civic order. As servants, they have only gossip at their disposal—serving the upper classes does not necessarily guarantee a future, in neither Hofmannsthal's nor Nestroy's view.

More disturbing about the ending of *Rosenkavalier* is the fact that Octavian and Sophie do not know about any of the forces that brought them together, nor do they realize how dependent their union is on the public. Unlike the Marschallin, they will not likely remember that they owe their happiness to the lower classes and to acts of revenge on evil aristocrats. By the terms of the nineteenth century's *Volkstheater*, the social contract in *Rosenkavalier* is seriously in tatters, when the servants actually agree to work for aristocrats rather than for the middle classes. Faninal, a member of the upper bourgeoisie, has sold himself and his daughter out to an outmoded world of decadent aristocrats (however beautiful they are when they are young) and to a system of dependency without ethics, a culture of gossip and superficial reputation rather than a community.

The Marschallin can arrange that that sale is at least superficially brilliant, but what will happen to this young pair when the light of day replaces the candle snuffed out by the blackamoor as the curtain drops? Strauss is not in doubt: whatever comes will be beautiful; Hofmannsthal's libretto, however, can find little sense, daylight, or open space in what ultimately is a closed space of bedrooms, *chambres separées*, and drawing rooms. In the last assessment, Annina is not Staberl because she has not found her own honest labor, although she will side with honest tradesmen rather than corrupt aristocrats. As the Marschallin notes, women don't have that kind of choice.

Hofmannsthal, then, is no naïve social critic, even before World War I. He sees the problem in the terms familiar from the *Volkstheater*—that no class is living up to its obligations—and thus his commitment to finding a nation in a language takes on new urgency. His solution, a language in the middle (*eine mittlere Sprache*), should allow a community to restore itself, a necessity because it has begun to eat its own young, both inside and between classes. In this sense, Hofmannsthal's *Volkstheater* offers less a class critique than an ethical one, warning that any class can be alienated from its own humanity if station and money are valued more than hard work and honesty. Even Hofmannsthal, who is offering specific, knowing tributes to the eighteenth century in his various libretti, acknowledged this threat in the *Rosenkavalier*, when its concluding triumph of love is not tested—it may not survive the scrutiny of everyday life.[54]

Here again, the Viennese theater that had not banned Hanswurst has again allowed him to use the clothes of a contemporary city-dweller rather than a courtier. In his earlier nineteenth-century incarnations, such Hanswurst characters engaged and overcame the threats to their new class position: Hanswurst must not fall back into nostalgia for the countryside, nor aspire to be a member of a class he is not part of. In the twentieth century, in the hands of modern masters like Hofmannsthal, Hanswurst yielded center stage to Zerbinetta and Annina, his female counterparts, who interjected life into court traditions that were showing their wear.

Hofmannsthal's wit is subtle in the voice and gender casting that shows in visual terms how necessary such Hanswursts still might be. In *Rosenkavalier*, the audience accepts the illusion that the beautiful aristocratic couple will procreate—but cannot ultimately forget that they are, after all, two sopranos. In *Ariadne auf Naxos*, when the theater's patron allows its decorum to slip, the cross-dressed composer (another pants role for a female voice) cannot, through art, control the chaos that the lower-class *commedia* has wrought by intervening in his beautiful tragedy.

A century earlier, Mozart had already shown how such comedies may leave their audiences more than slightly unsettled. The end of *Così fan tutte* (1790) is exemplary: two pairs of lovers find each other again, after their game of deception turned unexpectedly serious and is worked through. Yet in reclaiming their original betrotheds, each is left with a doubt about whether they have found the correct mates. Hofmannsthal's stage audience, in turn, must question if, in fact, love can and will conquer all and so must take positions about other romantic illusions, about money, status, and happiness. This comedy tradition, therefore, works to problematize too-simple assumptions of society, acting as a true educational institution rather than a revolutionary one—precisely the kind of public medium that Hofmannsthal described in his essays.

Subsequent twentieth-century Austrian writers often claim the *Volkstheater* as their own (from Ödön von Horváth through Peter Handke and Peter Turrini), which argues for the salience of Hofmannsthal's

---

54 Note, too, that in *Ariadne auf Naxos*, one of Zerbinetta's interpolations into the Ariadne tragedy is a request for her to come out of her cave and talk to the rest of them, so that her sadness be alleviated.

choice: the tradition is by no means exhausted. Hanswurst's nominal banishment is a scholar's fiction, an idol of the academics; he (or she) remains alive and well at that border between high and popular culture that Hofmannsthal wants to preserve. More critically, that theater tradition retains its critical proximity to ideas of community and its necessarily ethical public space that persist from the nineteenth through the twentieth centuries in Austria.

Six Schnitzler and the Space of Public Discourse: The Politics of Decadence in *fin de siècle* Vienna

The *fin de siecle*'s dominant stereotypes became Austria's legacy in the interwar period, as receptions of Hofmannsthal readily documented. Yet Austria's most visible twentieth-century playwright, Arthur Schnitzler, realized early in his career that he was being stereotyped for being a remnant of pre-war Vienna. In a famous letter to Jakob Wassermann (November 3, 1924),[1] Schnitzler complained that he had been relegated to being a "poet of a lost world" (*versunkene Welt* [Wagner, 342]). That lost world was in this case not a national tradition of letters, as it was for Hofmannsthal, but a social phenomenon of *fin de siècle* Vienna: the growing affluence and decadence which Schnitzler purportedly reacted to and mirrored in his plays and novellas, yet without real political acumen.

The historian Robert A. Kann summarizes this prejudice well: "For us, Schnitzler is the classical example of an unpolitical poet, and that even if we ignore the cliché, already done to death, that his themes are just death and love" (Kann, "Die historische Situation," 19).[2] The culture he reflected was decadent, backward, and above all, baroque. Offering a more positive evaluation of that history in 1971, Martin Swales summarized:

---

1 In *Briefe 1913–1931* (1984), 371.
2 "Schnitzler gilt uns als das klassische Beispiel eines unpolitischen Dichters und dies selbst wenn man von der zu Tode gehetzten Klichévorstellung, daß seine Themen nur Tod und Liebe seien, ganz absieht." Or even more suggestively: "in the reception the politically threatening elements are often suppressed in favor of the preferred image of Schnitzler as a chronicler of decadence and eroticism. ... Schnitzler emphasizes the means by which the political suffuses daily life and individual consciousness" (Tweraser, 27).

one should mention the specific cultural tradition of Austria, something that distinguishes so much of its creative literature from that of Germany: the Baroque. Many of the themes from Baroque literature are restated in a way that gives them a particularly modern resonance. The notion of the *theatrum mundi*, of man as a player on the stage of life, the juxtaposition of "Schein" and "Sein," of "dream" and "reality," these and many other legacies from the Baroque assert themselves in one form or another in much of the literature of the "Jahrhundertwende." ... The whole Baroque tension between delight in the multifarious confusion of the world on the one hand and a desperate conviction of the taint and corruption of earthly joys on the other is very much part of the experience of the Austrian "Jahrhundertwende," and, indeed, of the literature of our own time. (Swales [1971], 23–4)

In such judgments, Schnitzler falls prey to a different version of the stereotypes that have pigeonholed Hofmannsthal, as well. Nowadays, it is Hofmannsthal who is usually considered "Baroque," with his explicit references to the European past. None the less, Schnitzler would repeatedly complain about his own reception, as he did in 1926: "This not wanting to see—this glance banned to looking only at erotic problems—this assiduous not wanting to know about the political half."[3] But Schnitzler's world has accreted its own patina of (morbid, sexualized) imagination that covers up his more naturalist view of Austrian society and occludes his attempts to foster precisely the kinds of public discussion in the theater that have been traced here.

Only in the last few years has Schnitzler's complaint been addressed by a few critics, who at least acknowledge that his characters do indeed tie into the social milieu and thus into a kind of politics.[4] Anton Pelinka states baldly: "This image of an unpolitical author ... has its tradition and is false" (Pelinka, 59). He understands that Schnitzler is heritor to Austria's liberal political traditions that were under attack by conservativism by the end of the century, reflecting the decline of the

---

3   "Dies nicht sehen wollen—dieser nur auf das erotische Problem gebannte Blick—diese geflissentliche Nichtahnen von der politischen Hälfte"; said about *Der Gang zum Weiher*, cited in Tweraser, 26.

4   Elizabeth G. Ametsbichler's "Der Reiz des Reigens" is typical in new claims that Schnitzler was less interested in psychological symbolism and perhaps more realistic: "His works provide a social mirror, and in the case of *Reigen* Schnitzler used language that somewhat softened the 'shocking' content of the play. At the same time, however, the language itself is shocking because it ironically emphasizes the superficiality and emptiness of the most intimate of all acts—and of relationships" (295). It still comes down to sex, as it does for the vast majority of today's critics.

influence of the liberal bourgeoisie. The perspective presented in the present discussion, then, encourages us to read the allusions to baroque tradition in another way, as part of the social-critical public space from which the *Volkstheater* originated.

This chapter moves to counter such assumptions, not only by setting Schnitzler next to Hofmannsthal, but also by suggesting that he may in some ways surpass his great contemporary. W. E. Yates' definitive *Schnitzler, Hofmannsthal and the Austrian Theatre* (1992) reiterates the critical commonplace of playing these two off against each other, with Hofmannsthal playing aesthete and Schnitzler voice of decadent individuals. Schnitzler is the particular loser here, as Yates shows his readers "the contrast between the skeptical realist Schnitzler and the myth-making Hofmannsthal" (Yates, 157). Yates here perpetuates a trend that has existed almost from the first, as he shows in comparing the almost simultaneous obituaries of the two playwrights (only two years apart): "It was rare for critical comparisons to be published that came out in Schnitzler's favour" (Yates, 222).[5]

However, such comparisons between Schnitzler and Hofmannsthal are not simply artifacts of critics' labor, they had a basis in history, fueled by the pair's public relationship when they worked on the same stages. Hofmannsthal was often backhandedly complementary about Schnitzler, while Schnitzler acknowledged Hofmannsthal's talent but eventually began to criticize the later works for lacking inner warmth (Yates, 226). Perhaps more importantly, the later, more stylized works by the somewhat younger Hofmannsthal saw him writing more in an internationalist idiom that at times bordered on modernism, while Schnitzler's works persisted in looking more realist or naturalist. As such, the latter's plays and novellas could too easily seem antiquarian, tied to pre-war social structures even when he was addressing the social situations of long-standing that persisted, and even worsened, in interwar Austria:[6] "But inevitably [Schnitzler's] career was often reduced to the long-established stereotype, the chronicler of Viennese eroticism and the *süßes Mädl*" (Yates, 230).[7] To exacerbate this situation

---

5   For a recent overview of Schnitzler scholarship, see Dagmar C. G. Lorenz, ed., *A Companion to the Works of Arthur Schnitzler* (2003).

6   For an introduction to the problematics of this era in Vienna, see Deborah Holmes and Lisa Silverman, eds, *Interwar Vienna: Culture Between Tradition and Modernity* (2009).

7   Even Schnitzler's critical supporters valorize his work by falling back onto these aesthetic stereptypes. For example, G. J. Weinberger, in a chapter on *Die Schwestern oder Casanova in Spa*, compares that play to Hofmannsthal's *Cristinas Heimfahrt*, deciding that there are many similarities between the two, but that Schnitzler's play is better because Hofmannsthal's play is a *Lustspiel* with more formulaic underpinning (see especially 107–8). The argument is solid, but it

whole categories of his work simply do not emerge to critics. With the exception of *Der grüne Kakadu* (1899), for instance, Schnitzler's works based on history receive little systematic analysis.[8] A play about the Napoleonic era like *Der junge Medardus* (1910), made into a major film by Mikhail Kertez (soon to be known in Hollywood as Michael Curtiz, of *Captain Blood* fame, 1923), is seen as anomalous.[9]

---

rests on the premise that both authors deployed traditional forms for similar ends, which I am not asserting.

8   A play like *Der grüne Kakadu* is, to be sure, generally acknowledged as revolutionary—one of the few that are—but even in this case, the politics is seen by critics only as muted. For example, the play-within-the-play is referenced as a simple life/theater reversal of reality frames for the play, not addressing that this particular play is also a *Schmiere*, a burlesque theater with a very specific sociocultural reference. Thus critics like Ernst L. Offermann can ultimately diminish the importance of *Kakadu* as a "Vorform" of the later purportedly more important comedies, rather than a biting, almost Brechtian political satire (12–13), and to assert that Schnitzler's engagement in plays like this (as in his youth) was less than truly political: "Dieses 'Lebensgefühl' ist ganz und gar dasjenige des in Österreich, vornehmlich in Wien, politisch einflußlos gewordenen liberalen Bürgertums und einer Jugend, mit dem Rückzug aus den Narzißmus und die Künste als Wirklichkeitsersatz und einer umfassenden Feuilletonisierung der Realität" (Offermann, 57).

9   Even more sympathetic critics like Ian F. Roe address *Reigen* by noting "Schnitzler's portrayal of human behaviour is perhaps rather less a metaphor of death and despair than the mass ranks of (predominantly male!) literary critics have so frequently claimed" (Roe [1994], 688). He notes similarities of the play to Wilde's or to others' period bedroom farce: "One may certainly detect elements of the *Konversationsstück* beloved of dramatists such as Bauernfeld ..." (Roe [1994], 675). Such evaluations thus again ultimately reduce Schnitzler to a writer of decadence, not to a conscious Naturalist impulse, nor to the kind of modernist experimentation for which Wilde was famous.

This point is underscored by Yvonne M. Ivory, in "The Perils of Post-Holing" (i.e., pigeon-holing), which shows the history of Schnitzler's reception, starting with Ernst L. Offermann (who takes Schnitzler's turn to historical literature as expression of "a more optimistic view on his part of the value of writing" [58]), and ending up with Carl E. Schorske. Schorske plays off Schnitzler's negative social commentary—especially in the late *Der Weg ins Freie*—against what he believes is Hofmannsthal's more optimistic approach—with Schnitzler ending up on the wrong end of the comparison. See also Weinhold, who takes on the plays showing the stereotype of women to argue for their psychosocial determination; Bossinade does a parallel, detailed interpretation of *Reigen* from this viewpoint. To counter such discourse-based readings, Laura Otis, "The Language of Infection," specifically talks about venereal disease being the play's unspoken subtext, not just its stress on emotional and physical and psychological intimacy.

The focus on the psycho-social Schnitzler continues, in dissertations like Nancy Carolyn Michael, *Elektra and Her Sisters: Male Representations of Female Characters in Viennese High Culture, 1900–1905* (Diss., University of Wisconsin,

Schnitzler can none the less be straightforwardly aligned with a more progressive community politics. Several of his lesser-known plays take up their conventions quite consciously, as they stage challenges to his era's liberals and their delusions. I have argued elsewhere that his handling of male and female roles in the novellas reflects an almost Naturalist critique of social roles (Arens, 2003a). The less familiar dramatic works addressed in the present discussion echo those critiques, but also clearly document Schnitzler's continuing commitment to social-political commentary on a failing liberal community that has surrendered its group ideals on the altar of individual privilege. In his memoir, *Youth in Vienna* (*Jugend in Wien*), Schnitzler summarizes his own politics:

I passed my childhood and my first youth not unpunished in an atmosphere determined by the so-called liberalism of the 60s and 70s. The actual basic mistake of this world view appears to me to have consisted in assuming that certain ideal values from the first were fixed and incontrovertible, that in young people the false belief was awakened that they had to strive toward some clearly set goals in a predetermined way, in order to be able, without further consideration, to build their houses and their world on secure ground. One believed then that they knew what the true, the good, and the beautiful were, and one's whole life lay in fantastic simplicity there. (JiW, 325; cited in Scheible [1977], 28)[10]

Madison, 1991) or Julie Doll Allen, *Determining Their Own Destiny: The Portrayal of Women's Emancipation in Lou Andreas-Salome's 'Fenitschka' and Arthur Schnitzler's 'Frau Berta Garlan'* (Diss., University of Washington, 1996).

There have been, to be sure, several recent attempts to place Schnitzler within Western traditions, drawing him closer to Hofmannsthal's reputation. Thus Alfred Pfoser's "Rund um den *Reigen*" points to Schnitzler's possible sources as Choderlos de Laclos's *Liaisons dangereuses*, French farce from Marivaux to Feydeau, episodes out of Voltaire's *Candide*, and especially William Hogarth's "Before and After" etching series (from 1730–1, featuring a nobleman and his conquests, before and after [Pfoser, 14–15]). Pfoser adduces such evidence to refute the poet's image as "Dichter einer verschollenen Welt" (Pfoser, 26).

10 "Nicht ungestraft habe ich meine Kindheit und meine erste Jünglingszeit in einer Atmosphäre verbracht, die durch den sogenannten Liberalismus der 60er und 70er Jahre bestimmt war. Der eigentliche Grundirrtum dieser Weltanschauung scheint mir darin bestanden zu haben, daß gewisse ideelle Werte von vornherein als fix und unbestreitbar angenommen wurden, daß in den jungen Leuten der falsche Glaube erweckt wurde, sie hätten irgendwelchen klar gesetzten Zielen auf einem vorbestimmten Wege zuzustreben, um dann ohne weiteres ihr Haus und ihre Welt auf sicherem Grunde aufbauen zu können. Man glaubte damals zu wissen, was das Wahre, Gute und Schöne war, und das ganze Leben lag in großartiger Einfachheit da."

Still, in this text, Schnitzler calls for a critical reappraisal of these politics and for social modernization through literature, in full consciousness of needing to add a true mass medium to achieve these goals.

Recapturing a Schnitzler more interested in the social politics of the group and the state, not just individuals, requires a certain amount of historical revisionism, yet it is a straightforward project. Against the background of Vienna after the turn of the century, Schnitzler's medical writings set the stage for a reconsideration of his dramas. In this juxtaposition, Schnitzler can be reclaimed as thoroughly participant in the vision of the theater as a political space of checks and balances in the service of politics, as he pleads for a necessary *disillusionment* of a class that was squandering its legacy.

The legacy of liberalism: Life in *fin de siècle* Vienna

Pieter M. Judson's *Exclusive Revolutionaries* (1996) provides the now standard account of how Austria's famed liberal politics of the mid-nineteenth century declined by the end of the century, under pressure from new ethnic-nationalist politics. After the *Ausgleich* (the 1866 *Compromise* that created Austro-Hungary), liberal politics attempted to offer a "liberal, scientific, progressive, and anticlerical critique of traditional society" (Judson, 143). The middle classes developed their political consciousness and identities through "the implicit political character of the cultural, educational, and philanthropic associations," yet without necessarily fostering explicit political engagement (Judson, 144).[11] Carl E. Schorske identifies the institutions that had supported liberalism after 1867 as "the Parliament, the Rathaus, and the University" (Schorske 1981, 114)—politics, science, and aesthetic culture aligned with the elite of the state. As Judson summarizes:

> An efficient and impartial state would enforce civil equality among individuals, while mass education would ensure the eventual integration and participation of all social and ethnic groups in a harmonious community. There would be no need for interest groups to compete for power in a world where individuals had as much freedom to develop their varied potentials as possible. This utter disavowal of politics was one of the most telling and problematic attributes of nineteenth-century liberal rhetoric. It presumed that educated people who disagreed over some aspect of public policy could settle their differences in everyone's best interest without resorting to the naked exercise of power. It presumed that a disinterested balance among interests

---

11 Gary B. Cohen's *Education and Middle-Class Society* documents the rise in pressure for secondary and post-secondary education after 1848.

could be achieved. And it did so because it assumed that everyone worth listening to shared a similar social experience. (Judson, 268)

Ultimately, Judson suggests that this "similar social experience" may have seemed too homogenizing, too centered around the German–Viennese point of view in its vision of humanity, demanding: "Be free, but be like us" (Judson, 268). None the less, "Germanness" was not an ethnicity, but rather "a quality available to all who embraced their progressive political vision" (Judson, 169), an expression of faith in progressive cultural values.

History did not allow such theses to be tested over time. Class progress was brought to a halt by the disastrous collapse (*Krach*) of the Viennese stock market, on May 9, 1873: "Overall production in Austria would not reach 1873 levels again until 1881" (Judson, 167). One-time free market liberals who had earlier profited from access to capital and education now sought bailouts, as the broader public turned against them and cast them as parasites subsisting on public money. Conservatives, in turn, protected their own access to social capital by trying to implement a kind of reverse social engineering, fostering anti-Semitism and discrimination directed at the non-German parts of the Empire.[12] The liberal party finally fell from political power in 1879.

This fiscal history of class evolution had a parallel in cultural history. Enlightenment culture, Schorske feels, had fed liberalism's rise, but Austria's Baroque heritage made the Viennese bourgeoisie cultivate aestheticism, where no other European one did (Schorske 1981, 126). His assessment of the consequences of this adoption for Austrian culture runs in Freudian terms, supporting today's popular images of Viennese decadence: "The artistic culture that was prized by the parents as a badge of status and an intellectual accomplishment often developed in the children a hypertrophied sensibility that made them turn to the arts as a source of meaning when their inherited expectations of a more rational world were undermined by events" (Schorske 1981, 130). Many one-time liberals reacted with frustration against ethnicities, social injustice, and the government, as they espoused aestheticism in a conservative turn of taste. At the same time, an active proletariat culture came to a kind of fruition in "Red Vienna" after World War I: "The Viennese working-class subcultures were complex [... and] also enriched by community standards and norms of behavior created during more than two generations of urban life" (Gruber, 8).

12 John W. Boyer has offered the standard accounts of the political rise of the conservatives in two massive books that concur in large part with those from Carl Schorske's *Fin de siècle Vienna*.

They remained a factor in politics, forcing public housing and rent controls into existence by the 1920s, for example.[13]

Overall, then, these accounts confirm that *fin de siècle* Vienna was actually a study in dynamic political contrasts expressed socially, not just a "gay apocalypse." The city at the end of the century had inherited the core of an educated, socially-aware populace fragmented politically across class, regional, and ethnic lines, but then was forced into the kind of economic turmoil that could not sustain the expansion necessary to capitalize on the hopes held by its unique "imagined community."

And on the streets of the city, by the end of the century, the world as the liberals imagined it—not necessarily how it was—was beginning to come apart. The real living conditions of the mass of Austro-Hungarian citizens were very different than those of the bourgeois liberals whose lifestyle has come to symbolize Vienna (and the Empire) for scholars today. Overall, class divisions became pronounced. For instance, Reinhard Sieder documents the very real class stratification within the purportedly monolithic working class. Families weathered shifting economics by taking in boarders (sometimes multiple boarders, leading to six or eight people living in two rooms), when their wage-earners were ill, or laid off, and at other times, other "working families" emerged as more like "white collar laborers." Engineers, for instance, received premium wages. And even further down the employee food chain were those housed in workers' barracks (Hitler was to live in one of them), a necessity that evolved because there were no rent or lease protections until 1917 (Sieder, 77). The city held all too many blue-collar and service industry employees and manual laborers, many of whom were underpaid, underfed, and underhoused (see Josef Ehmer).

Michael John's article on homelessness, "Obdachlosigkeit," even explains the class hierarchy that existed with the group classified as boarders, stretching from the *Bettgeher* who just rented a shift in a bed when no one else was using it, to the truly homeless *Kanalschläfer* who slept under bridges or in sewers, or who even lived in meadows in the open. Some of this homelessness was due to problems registering domiciles: a third to a half of the turn-of-the-century homeless did not have *Heimatrecht* in Vienna, because it took ten years to attain that citizenship; that legislation changed only in 1910. Between 1900 and 1911, there were about 10,000 *Bettgeher* (John, 173); the city had just over 2 million inhabitants in 1910 (almost a 50 percent increase over its 1890 statistics, making it roughly the same size as the booming Berlin, and a population number which is barely being recouped today, in the early

---

13 For an overview of the planning for social welfare, especially after 1918, see Danto, *Freud's Free Clinics* (2005).

twenty-first century). In 1910 and 1911, a particular housing shortage unleashed demonstrations at the *Rathaus* (John, 189). Liberal Vienna also feared the homelessness associated with such insurrections, incited by the newspapers that dutifully reported on the situations, with illustrations. One temporary solution was the erection of very poor mass shelters, *Notstandsbaracken* (most notably, one in Favoriten, and one in the third district) (John, 175).

No wonder, then, that there were high incidences of family violence, prostitution, and public health problems (especially venereal disease). Sabina Kolleth offers an exemplary situation in "Gewalt in Ehe und Intimpartnerschaft" ("Violence in Marriage and Intimate Partnerships"), which documents family dynamics under stress when their situations were exacerbated by a law code which made women officially subservient to men, especially in financial matters (Kolleth, 146). Because the male head of household was in control, wife beating was rarely severely punished, while female adultery was punished more severely than male (Kolleth, 147). Women of all ages, professions, and estates suffered under such legal sanctions, backed up by a growing wave of pseudoscientific tracts on the "essence of woman" (Kolleth, 148). And social situations also affected what sexual practices were known in such overcrowded, overregulated lives, as Inge Pronay-Strasser documents. Children in these situations played various sex games; pederasty was openly present; flirting was a highly developed art; working women sought divorces (but bourgeois women divorced less often [Pronay-Strasser, 121]); and venereal diseases were rampant.

Not surprisingly, prostitution was legalized in 1873 (Pronay-Strasser, 128). These realities brought the relation of sex and illness into special relief: "In the year 1900 official statistics document 1708 prostitutes under official scrutiny; 319 were added to the tally this year. Of these, 343 were ill with syphilis" (Pronay-Strasser, 128).[14] Prostitution brought with it new status hierarchies: streetwalkers were blamed for impacting property values, while the *Demimondlerinnen* (the equivalent of the French *grandes horizontales*) threatened bourgeois marriages as a class of professional mistresses (Pronay-Strasser, 129). Each of these "classes" had its own clear public image, with the *Dame* as the status to which all aspired (Elisabeth Wiesmayr, 133). Schnitzler's *süßes Mädl* (generally an amateur in the trade, such as a shopgirl who was looking for her rent and/or a husband) had real competition, and locals would have been skeptical from the first about their innocence but not about the finances involved.

---

14 "Im Jahr 1900 weist die Statistik 1708 behördlich unter Kontrolle stehende Prostituierte nach; neu hinzukamen in diesem Jahr 319. Von all diesen waren 343 syphilitisch erkrankt."

Aside from sexually transmitted diseases, lung diseases were prevalent in this overcrowded, undernourished population. The TB mortality rate was 390 cases per 100,000 in 1890, with higher rates in poor districts (Tabor, 222). Perhaps more interestingly, Jan Tabor's "An dieser Blume gehst Du zugrunde" / "You Will Die from this Flower" points out a connection between disease and the era's art. The oddly colored faces familiar from Oskar Kokoshka's, Egon Schiele's, and Anton Romako's paintings may well not represent decadent characters, as so often is assumed. Instead, they show faces with colorations characteristic of particular tubercular or syphilitic infections (225–30)— the faces of victims, not perpetrators, of society's evil. What we see in the tableaux and street scenes of literature like Schnitzler's thus may diverge significantly from what his own era saw. Where they saw the poor, the dangerous, the endangered, and the ill, we see the decadent.

Schnitzler himself was well aware of Vienna's urban crisis and the social health problems that it engendered. From the time of his own *Promotion* in 1885 to his father's death in 1893, Schnitzler was his father's assistant in laryngology at the *Polyklinik*, the major public hospital that Johann Schnitzler had cofounded (Thomé, in Schnitzler 1988, 15). In no small part due to his father's influence, Arthur began early to review for medical periodicals, especially for the *Wiener Medizinische Presse* and its subsequent incarnation, the weekly *Internationale Klinische Rundschau*, where he also was part of the editorial board.

It has become a critical commonplace to assert Arthur's lack of clinical experience and thus to dismiss his medical writings. The editor of the *Medical Writings / Medizinische Schriften*, Horst Thomé, is no exception: "Thus there are many reviews [among Schnitzler's writings], among them many superficial retellings of books and empty short character sketches—lead articles, evocative tableaux, reports from foreign countries, and notes on medicine's fringe regions" (Thomé, in Schnitzler 1988, 16),[15] with pieces including "research on neuroses, especially on hysteria, perversions, and hypnosis, the fashionable sciences of the day, often considered with skepticism by the Viennese medical establishment" (Thomé, in Schnitzler 1988: 16).[16]

Thomé does not consider that *Modewissenschaften* are also signals of issues requiring contemporary commentary. As such, popular

---

15 "So dominieren denn die Rezensionen, darunter auch viele oberflächliche Inhaltsangaben und nichtssagende Kurzcharakteristiken, die Leitartikel, Stimmungsbilder, Auslandsberichte und die Notizen zu medizinischen Randbereichen."

16 "Forschungen zu den Neurosen, vor allem zur Hysterie, zu den Perversionen und zur Hypnose. Das sind die Modewissenschaftern der Zeit, wenn sie auch vom Wiener wissenschaftlichen Establishment mit Skepsis betrachtet werden."

essays like reviews help to locate Schnitzler's own commitment to the ideals of liberalism—to what issues a liberal society had to attend. Despite his reservations, however, Thomé can valorize the important 1889 *Silvesterbetrachtungen* (*New Year's Eve Thoughts*) as precisely such commentary:

> He decries the penetration of illness into the religiously grounded scheme of guilt and atonement [...] In place of unsupported social sanctions, there must be opposed help of physicians [...] Also in the wake of an enlightened understanding of abnormal behavior, the borders of criminal justice can be drawn more narrowly. (Thomé, in Schnitzler 1988: 18)[17]

Thomé also notes that the range of topics in the son's writings clearly parallels the professional interests of the father, bringing the author and the physician much closer together as social commentators interested in

> several groups of problems: the social function of medical institutions, within which knowledge is produced and applied; the formation of scientific theories, which must serve mankind; and finally the professional ethos of the individual physician, who deploys his abstract knowledge in concrete situations that can not be repeated. (Thomé, in Schnitzler 1988: 20)[18]

Historically, however, these issues, like the founding of the *Polyklinik* itself, were critical turning points in the evolution of the city's public health management.[19] Overall, however, Thomé refuses to acknowledge the significance of Schnitzler's medical journalism, calling it "pathetic" (meaning "aimed at pathos" [Thomé, in Schnitzler 1988: 45]), while the

---

17 "Er verwirft die Eindringung der Krankheit in das religiös fundierte Scheme von Schuld und Sühne … An die Stelle der unbegründeten sozialen Sanktion hat die Hilfe des Arztes zu treten. Auch können im Zuge eines aufgeklarten Verständnisses abnormen Verhaltens die Grenzen der Strafjustiz enger gezogen werden."

18 "Dabei ergeben sich mehrere Problemfelder: die soziale Funktion der medizinischen Institutionen, innerhalb derer Wissen erzeugt und angewendet wird; die wissenschaftliche Theoriebildung, de dem Menschen dienen muß; und schließlich das Berufsethos des einzelnen Arztes, der sein abstraktes Wissen in konkreten, nicht mehr wiederholbaren Situationen einsetzt."

19 The *Polyklinik* also probably contributed to anti-Semitism in Vienna. Not only did the new institution challenge the traditional medical practices in the city in a time of economic downturn, but also a very specific medical tragedy placed the large numbers of Jewish doctors under stress. For instance, in Germany, when Friedrich III died of throat cancer, that death was laid at the feet of Jewish doctors.

atmospheric pieces and event reports (*Stimmungsbilder*) are presented as irresponsible "literarizations" of science, evidence of the son's purportedly empty, journalistic subjectivity (Thomé, in Schnitzler 1988: 47). At best, Thomé's Schnitzler is worried about the physician's responsibilities, especially about the possible misuses of medical position and about the complicity of medicine and law (Thomé, in Schnitzler 1988: 49).

Such an evaluation, however, overlooks a key element that Schnitzler thematizes: the author as physician is speaking of, to, and for the public in these pieces. Thomé grounds his evaluations on overgeneralizations about bourgeois-liberal norms (Thomé, in Schnitzler 1988: 53)[20] and as evidence of laments about a deteriorating class position. The texts Thomé has so carefully edited actually can tell another story, if one accepts the idea that reviews and journalism can contribute to public discussions.

In fact, Schnitzler's reviewing and reporting amply document his continuing interest in the social and professional sides of medicine, but they also reveal a rather more complex definition of the role of a physician or an individual in the stressed social space of that Vienna. To be sure, some of Schnitzler's medical writings are journalism in the narrowest sense, such as when he provides travelogues encompassing events surrounding an 1879 conference at which Viennese doctors didn't show up (Thomé, in Schnitzler 1988: 66). Yet he usually writes from the perspective of the community rather than of experts, such as when he reviews textbooks for their usability with as much enthusiasm as he does Freud's legendary 1886 lecture on male hysteria (that is, on Charcot) to the "K.k. Gesellschaft der Ärzte in Wien" (Schnitzler 1988: 74),[21] or Freud's translation of Charcot (1887) (Schnitzler 1988: 90ff.).[22] Significantly, he will also generally review a book's critics, as well as taking care to set it into its appropriate context—he does not simply review the book, he reviews the critical discussions in which it is enmeshed.

What emerges consistently is his attention to social formations in a more differentiated sense. For example, he can review Silas Weir Mitchell's *Fat and Blood* (Schnitzler 1988: 93), the account of the classic rest and food cure that plays in the background of Charlotte Perkins Gilman's 1891/2 short story, "The Yellow Wallpaper," to highlight

---

20 "verallgemeinerungsfähige moralische Normen."
21 For the purposes of the Freud mythology, it is interesting that Schnitzler reports that Meynert offered the resources and case histories from his clinic to prove his theories (Thomé, in Schuster 1988: 79).
22 Schnitzler thinks it's a good translation, but remains somehwat skeptical about non-anatomical diseases.

what might be considered either the weakness in Weir Mitchell's therapeutics or its key element: the fact that the cure works best when the patients are divided from their families, "because as a rule compelling grounds for the duration and intensity of the illness can be found in circumstances in the patient's environment" (Schnitzler 1988: 96).[23]

Schnitzler is also interested in public health and its financing, and so will report on events like the parliamentary debates about the *K. K. Allgemeines Krankenhaus* (Schnitzler 1988, 103ff.), where he advises that nurses need to be treated better, as do the patients (who need, for example, better food), and junior doctors (who board on-premises, with few amenities). In further public writings, he reports on the organization of London hospitals, which are private charities and thus lack teaching physicians on their staffs, a situation which hence restricts the relationships between medical science and practice (Schnitzler 1988: 154ff.). At the other end of the spectrum, he'll report on a physicians' conference in Wiesbaden (Schnitzler 1988: 132) or lambaste physicians who write "pretentious and unbeautiful" prose (Schnitzler 1988: 146).

Schnitzler's most famous medical text is the feuilleton "Silvesterbetrachtungen" (1889, on the occasion of New Year's Eve 1888 [Schnitzler 1988: 173ff.]), an important essay discussing the honor of the medical sciences. We are, he begins, far from the goals of realizing modern scientific thinking—"die in naturwissenschaftlichem Geiste denkenden Menschen"—because of what physicians have not yet managed to do:

> The physician must learn to *see* as no other, slipping most deeply into the secrets of the organic; precisely he must be placed in the front ranks of the unprejudiced, if he has the stuff to conceive of his profession correctly. The massive force of what has been seen, felt, and understood must shake him and convince him.
>
> But the profession of physician is chosen by individuals of quite different natures, unfortunately also by those who are not equipped to think scientifically. They flutter through their science and do not penetrate into its essence. The crass concerns of everyday life do not let them alone for a second, and in the midst of the free atmosphere surrounding them, they hear only the transitory din of the day. While the greatest water source

---

23 "da in der Regel in den Verhaltnissen in der Umgebung der Kranken ein wesentlicher Grund für die Dauer und Intensität der Erkrankung liegt." Note that this is very much at odds with the dominant psychiatric practices in Germany at the time. See Katherine Arens, "Wilhelm Griesinger" (1996).

thunders past them, they drink out of water taps. (Schnitzler 1988: 173–4)[24]

This description in many ways characterizes Schnitzler's own generation of liberals. In one reading, the class rarely lives up to the potential of its own professions and professional identities.

Just as important is his assertion that society is not living up to the task of building a future out of the past, when it exercises judgments out of prejudice (here, about religion):

> We know that these words have been spoken into the wind. We know that we are far from experiencing the end of an era in which a whole class of people will ask first about religion and only then—or even never—about the inner worth of their neighbors. We know that our decade is sick from a grand atavism, and that the mighty work of each friend of humanity threatens to sink into the dust as it tries to clear out the moldering remains of past eras. (Schnitzler 1988: 175)[25]

Science must, in Schnitzler's view, be a tool for progress (Schnitzler 1988: 175), for *Menschenliebe*, for the ethics of the profession, and of our class interests (Schnitzler 1988: 176),[26] a profession that has fallen into undeserved problems at the bedside of Kaiser Friedrich. Note, too, that he uses *Stand*, the word that resonates in Austrian political

---

24 "[daß der Arzt] *sehen* lernen muß wie kein anderer, in das Geheimnis des Organischen sich am tiefsten einschleicht, gerade der müßte, wenn er das Zeug hat, seinen Beruf richtig aufzufassen, in den Reihen der Vorurteilslosen am weitesten vorangeschritten sein. Die mächtige Eindringlichkeit des Geschauten, Empfundenen und Erfaßten müßte ihn erschüttern und überzeugen.

   Aber der Beruf des Arztes wird von gar verschiedenen Naturen erwählt, leider auch von solchen, die nicht die Anlage haben, naturwissenschaftlich zu denken. Sie flattern durch ihre Wissenschaft und dringen nicht in das Wesen derselben ein. Das Krämerleben des Alltags läßt sie keinen Augenblick los, und mitten in der freien Atmosphäre, die sie umgibt, hören sie nur den vergänglichen Lärm des Tages. Während die große Quelle an ihnen vorüberrauscht, schöpfen sie aus Röhrbrunnen."

25 "Wir wissen, daß diese Worte in den Wind gesprochen sind. Wir wissen, daß wir noch lange nicht das Ende einer Zeit erleben werden, in der eine ganze Klasse von Menschen zuerst nach der Konfession und erst dann, oder auch gar nicht, nach dem inneren Wert ihres Nächsten fragen wird. Wir wissen, daß unser Jahrzehnt an einem großartigen Atavismus krankt und daß die mächtige Arbeit jener Menschenfreunde in den Staub zu sinken droht, welche die modernden Reste vergangener Zeiten hinwegzuräumen sich bemühen."

26 "die *ethische* Seite unserer Standesinteressen."

history—an *estate*, and hence a living part of a collective society, not just a profession, a guild, or an economic class.

Expressing this ethic in another way, Schnitzler is very aware that he must review popular science as well as what he considers serious scientific work, because both kinds of texts impact society. Thus he will update his readers on Bernheimer and hypnosis (Schnitzler 1988: 212), a book on sexual hygiene that sounds much like Max Nordau's famous *Degeneration* (*Entartung* [1892]) (Schnitzler 1988: 227), or a set of experiments on the transfer of thought (Schnitzler 1988, 247). He will put such books where they belong, identifying, for instance, "atavistic prejudices that spread a veil of fog over many modern ideas" (Schnitzler 1988: 227),[27] in writers who obscure a debate about modern sexual *mores* rather than learning about it (Schnitzler 1988: 229–30). He would, for instance, much rather see a discussion in what we would call today the Foucauldian vein, relating sexual practices to the legal code by discussing "the contradictions in the laws which impose requirements on nature on the one hand and on society on the other" (Schnitzler 1988: 231).[28] Thus he will note it is no wonder that only women laugh at the performance of a drama in which both husband and wife demand chastity of the other before they marry: "Because women surely know why they smile" (Schnitzler 1988: 232).[29]

Even the famous Cesare Lombroso is not immune to such criticism. In a review of *Genius and Madness* (1891), "a wonderful book … also a sad book" (Schnitzler 1988: 233), Schnitzler debates his basic premise that works of art are documents of madness:

> No. Because for us, genius means what it has achieved. It exists in relation to us only to the degree that it has an effect on us through its products. The sufferings that are imposed on these great ones, the madness that overtakes them, the martyrdom of their entire lives—that they have taken upon themselves. What remains to us of them are magnificent things that edify us. (Schnitzler 1988: 233–4)[30]

---

27 "atavistische Vorurteile, die ihm über manche moderne Ideen einene Nebelschleier breiten."

28 "über den Widerspruch in den Gesetzen, welche einerseits die Natur und andererseits die Gesellschaft fordert, können wir niemals endgiltig schlüssig werden. Individuell empfinden heißt da—diesen Widerspruch nach seiner Weise zu versöhnen suchen."

29 "Denn die [Frauen] wissen sicher, warum sie lächeln."

30 "Nein. Denn für uns hat das Genie die Bedeutung seiner Leistungen. Es existiert in Beziehung auf uns nur insofern, als es auf uns mit seinen Hervorbringungen wirkt. Die Leiden, welche diesen Großen bescheiden waren, der Wahnsinn, der sie überfiel, das Martyrium ihrer ganzen Leben haben sie mit sich genommen. Was uns von ihnen bleibt, ist das Herrliche, daran wir uns erbauen."

As Schnitzler sees it, Lombroso simply revisits ground that Nietzsche had already trodden, and if he really needs to revisit it, then he will need the help of experts beyond his own competence. As he summarizes about a later Lombroso work on political criminals: "here the spring of error gurgles so fulsomely that the solid ground under that system must surely wash out" (Schnitzler 1988: 275).[31] In contrast, Krafft-Ebing's discussion of females and masochism satisfies the requisites that make it science. That text also points to problems with the law rather than simply decrying a state of affairs unclearly diagnosed (Schnitzler 1988, 241; see also a similar review of one of Krafft-Ebing's books on mental illness [Schnitzler 1988: 326]).[32]

No matter that Schnitzler defends scientists against such abuse of science, he will also target the self-declared scientific genius. He shows repeatedly that scientists all too easily fall into self-aggrandizement instead of upholding science, especially at their own conventions: "is it not noteworthy that, where a half dozen otherwise highly educated people come together, a need for empty rhetoric sets in?" (Schnitzler 1988: 251).[33]

At an 1891 science convention, for instance, he decries the lack of substance and the fact that the conventioneers are more interested in food and excursions—and to sharpen his point, he discusses only one speech, an odd piece on the history of gunpowder given by an obscure participant rather than a superstar which lived up to its billing. Most scientists don't realize how foolish they can appear, Schnitzler indicates in inimitable fashion as he reviews a bad book: "I beg of you—one *has* to read that! [...] But no one had to write it" (Schnitzler 1988: 266).[34] Similarly, he will dissect a text by Meynert that he feels is inadequate (a prominent physician should know better), but then be nice to a modest little book by a *Sekundärarzt* that is old fashioned, but which can still teach us something because the writer's engagement with his materials is honest (Schnitzler 1988: 270, 271).[35]

---

31 "[H]ier rieseln die Fehlerquellen so reichlich, daß der feste Grund jedes Systems davon unterwaschen werden mußte."

32 Meynert's work, in comparison, is solid science, but bad writing that needs to be "weniger dunkel" in its explanations (Schnitzler 1988: 242).

33 "Ist es nicht eine merkwürdige Tatsache, daß sich, wo sich nur ein halbes Dutzend sonst höchst Geblideter zusammenfindet, sofort ein Bedürfnis nach Phrasen einstellt?"

34 "Ich bitte, das *muß* man lesen!—Aber schreiben hatte man es nicht müssen."

35 Felix W. Tweraser summarizes how these physicians also turn up in the fiction: "Though many of his physician-protagonists are sympathetic figures, they must negotiate the territory between a social position of power and prestige and their ultimate powerlessness in the face of disease and death" (Tweraser, 107). Supporting my reading, he also comments: "The starting point of Schnitzler's

Such issues recur throughout Schnitzler's medical writings. I have argued elsewhere that, in his short fiction, Schnitzler has taken on an objectivity that sets him apart both from European modernism (whose narrators are considered valuable if not always reliable observers) and from German naturalism (whose authors write about, but rarely for, the lower classes). In that sense, both his medical journalism and his prose tales share story-telling conventions with the *Krankengeschichte*, the patient history, which diagnoses illnesses by looking at the objective circumstances and evidence relating to it. Implicit in that equation is an obligation to do no harm (Vienna's vaunted therapeutic nihilism). The ills that Schnitzler discovers are the products of second-generation Viennese liberalism, the legacy of a liberal optic in the hand of individuals who have profited by it, but who abuse what they have inherited, and who thus will wreak havoc on the innocent from their positions of privilege.[36]

In such opinions, Schnitzler proves that he is considerably more interested in the community and its ills than in individuals' neuroses— he remains firmly committed, not only to individuals, but also to the estates of Austria, to their contemporary society, and to their enlightenment and well-being. And at this point, Schnitzler the physician needs to lead us to Schnitzler the writer. The evidence for this convergence is most straightforwardly recovered from a set of little-known dramatic works that take up his project of social improvement in a different voice. These works modernize genres from the *Volkstheater* traditions to enact clear, biting critiques of his era's bourgeois optic, willfully adopted by those who chose it.

Schnitzler intended that his literature be directly social critical, focused on more than just individual desires enacted or repressed. When, for instance, Schnitzler was working in 1894 on one of his most famous decadent plays, *Liebelei* (a play about a flirtation taken too seriously by one of the partners, in no small measure because of social aspirations), he intended it for Otto Brahm, director for the *Deutsches Theater* in Berlin, early home for the Naturalist movement, and thus for an audience familiar with playwrights like Gerhart Hauptmann. Schnitzler's long-term collaboration with Brahm suggests that he was interested in the theater's political program even more than he was invested in evading in Berlin the censorship of the more

criticism is the individual's relationship to society. It is through the process of socialization that one develops the necessary skills and adopts the rituals that ensure survival within the social fabric" (Tweraser, 6).

36 Thus Schnitzler contradicts Judson by putting at least some of the blame for liberalism's failure on individuals, not forces outside their ranks.

conservative Vienna.[37] None the less, Schnitzler scholars prefer to center his reputation around depictions of sexuality, rather than on the social criticism that he carefully calculated for different audiences.[38] His plays in the *Volkstheater* tradition confirm in their own way a commitment to drama as fostering social critique, just as they open windows on more political readings of his more familiar plays.

Puppets and pantomimes: Beyond the traditions

Schnitzler's *Marionettes / Marionetten* is a series of three one-act plays that were conceived separately and united only on publication in 1906. The first in the series, *The Puppetmaster: Study in one Act* (*Der Puppenspieler: Studie in einem Aufzug*), achieved its final form in 1901, when Schnitzler referred to it as a "character study" (*Characterstudie*) and intended it to be part of the cycle *Lively Hours* (*Lebendige Stunden* [Urbach (1974): 177]); it was also identified as a possible operetta libretto (Wagner, 147). The second play of the three is *Brave Cassian: Puppet Play in One Act* (*Der tapfere Cassian: Puppenspiel in einem Akt*), finished in 1902, and then reworked in 1903 as a libretto in verse for composer Oscar Straus (as *Der tapfere Kassian: Singspiel in einem Aufzug*). It was published in 1904, with the subtitle "burlesque in one act" (*Burleske in einem Akt* [Urbach (1974): 178, 181]). The third in the series was originally intended to have the title *Marionetten*, but ended up as *At the Grand Guignol: Burlesque in one Act* (*Zum großen Wurstel: Burleske in einem Akt*). It was written in 1901 and originally presented in

---

37 The typical analysis of the author's censorship problems is Werner Wilhelm Schnabel, "*Professor Bernhardi* und die Wiener Zensur," which describes the mechanisms of Alexander Bach's censorship laws of 1850 and their effects: "Die Verordnung legte eine Präventivzensur in der Kompetenz der Statthaltereien bzw. der Landesregierungen fest" (Schnabel, 355). Yet that censorship is not necessarily a negative: there was a cartoon in the Munich magazine *Jugend* that had a writer complaining that he can't get his play produced because no one will censor it: "Angesprochen ist die Propagandawirkung, die ein Verbot auf die menschliche Neugier ausübt" (Schnabel, 356). Gerd K. Schneider documents further such details of *Reigen*-reception, as do Alfred Pfoser, Kristina Pfoser-Schewig, and Gerhard Renner.

38 A typical evaluation: "[Brahm] macht aus Schnitzler einen 'Naturalisten,' aber er schadet ihm damit nicht ..." Overall, as Heide Eilert summarizes in her discussion of *Komödie der Verführung* as public commentary: "In der neueren Schnitzler-Forschung setzt sich zunehmend die Einsicht durch, daß Schnitzler in individualpsychologischen Vorgangen kollektive psychische Strukturen aufgedeckt, im Privaten das Öffentliche dargestellt hat ..." (Eilert, 228). See also Klaus Kilian on *Die Komödien Arthur Schnitzlers* as social criticism; Brigitte L. Schneider-Halvorson on Schnitzler's commitment to well-wrought plays; and Werner M. Bauer's discussion of "Ein ungeistlicher Tod," tracing Schnitzler's borrowings from conservative popular novels for women.

Berlin as part of Wolzogen's *Überbrettl* cabaret, before it was reworked in 1904 and staged as a play in 1905 (Urbach [1974]: 178).

A fourth play deserves inclusion here, *The Metamorphoses of Pierrot: Pantomime in a Prelude and Six Tableaux (Die Verwandlungen des Pierrot: Pantomime in einem Vorspiel und sechs Bildern)*; it was published in 1908 (Urbach [1974]: 181). A fifth play that may be included is *The Veil of Pierrette: Pantomime in Three Tableaux (Der Schleier der Pierrette: Pantomime in drei Bildern)*, written for Ernst von Dohnányi with motifs from his earlier story *The Veil of Beatrice (Der Schleier der Beatrice)*,[39] and first published in 1910, after its premiere in Dresden (Urbach [1974]: 185). Both are pantomimes written as scenarios, essentially ballet libretti with dialogue, offering topical critiques of the bourgeoisie: "*The Metamorphoses of Pierrot* builds off a prologue that made visible the conflict between the fantastic and bourgeois order" (Wolgast, 288).[40]

Alexander Girardi, the great player of Nestroy roles, purportedly showed interest in the Pierrot role in *Veil*: "It looks to me like someone wanted to give Schiller a box on his ears" (Wagner, 147).[41] Schnitzler had hoped (in vain) that the famed Max Reinhardt would direct this premiere, or that it might be filmed.[42] "Schnitzler's text for *The Veil of Pierrette* provided his directors with a text that put him in one sense at the cutting edge of the new thinking in dramatic forms that was emerging during the first decade of the twentieth century" (Sullivan 1995: 267).

Max Reinhardt demonstrated repeated interest in these plays. Around 1904, he had already wanted to do a version of the *Marionetten*, especially *Zum großen Wurstl*, but he could not come up with a performance concept to satisfy Schnitzler—Reinhardt wanted a burlesque evening. Schnitzler ended up by playing Brahm and Reinhardt and

---

39 The composer Ernst von Dohnányi was supposed to do the music, but got mad and withdrew because of competition from another one-acter, a setting of *Der tapfere Cassian*, by Oscar Straus (the operetta composer) (Sullivan 1995: 264). Reinhardt did not direct the premiere.

40 "*Die Verwandlungen des Pierrot* bauen auf einem Vorspiel auf, das den Konflikt zwischen Phantastik und bürgerlicher Ordnung veranschaulicht." In a mix of the avant-garde and the old fashioned, Meyerhold put on "Pierrot" in romantic style (Wolgast, 291).

41 "Das kommt mir vor, wie wenn einer dem Schiller eine Watschen herunterhauen tät'."

42 Lawrence Sullivan has traced how *Der Schleier der Pierrette* was pursued into many Russian productions, as parallels to what avant garde theaters and ballets in Russia were doing. The material moved from Schnitzler's prose tale *Der Schleier der Beatrice* (1900), first as a play, then a 1913 prose tale; he transposed it into the Biedermeier era (1815–48), after he started writing it in 1908, for Reinhardt (Sullivan 1995: 264), and possibly with hopes of turning it into film.

their competing dramatic concepts off against each other, despite his preference for working with Reinhardt. In Brahm's handling, the initial performances of evenings of one-acters wedded *Cassian* with *The Green Cockatoo (Der grüne Kakadu)* and *The House Delorme (Das Haus Delorme)*, the latter of which was quickly taken off the bill. After the November 22, 1904 premiere, *Der tapfere Cassian* went on to fail, while *Kakadu* became a hit and a lasting entry in the Schnitzler canon (Wagner, 165).

Zum großen Wurstl, in turn, wandered to the Viennese suburban theater of Josef Jarno, who staged it in the *Wurstlprater*, the amusement park in the great Prater green space:

> The figures appeared as the puppets of a marionette theater, hanging on wires, seemingly the creations of a poet, but at the end, in an irreal closing turn that points toward the theater of the absurd, they end up as subjects of an "unknown man in a blue coat" who cuts the marionette wires. (Wagner, 177)[43]

That performance was a success, with the characters in the frame narrative (an audience composed of actors on the stage) seeming real to the actual audience members. They reacted, for example, to the "Herr im Parkett" as if he were not part of the stage action (Wagner, 178). As Wagner describes it: "Jarno's production of the 'Wurstl' must have been very good, judging by the reviews, after the censor Privy Councilor Habison paid assiduous attention, during rehearsals, that none of the figures would be outfitted, for instance, with masks of people from Viennese society" (Wagner, 178).[44] The famous comic actor Hans Moser played in it, and Jarno himself played the Unknown at the end, dressed like a death's head (Wagner, 178). That the censor feared a topical staging is indicative of the play's potential for current commentary.

That Schnitzler worked with genre conventions from earlier centuries is not in doubt. This series of plays makes several direct allusions to the eighteenth century, the origin of the modern *Volksstück*, but they are not alone in his *œuvre*. The critic Heide Eilert makes further connections in this direction when she discusses Schnitzler's *Comedy of Seduction / Komödie der Verführung*, set in the last days

---

43   "Die Gestalten erscheinen als Puppen eines Marionettentheaters, an Drähten hängend, scheinbar Geschöpfe des Dichters, am Ende aber in einer irrealen Schlußwendung,die ins absurde Theater hinüberweist, als Untertanen eines 'Unbekannten im blauen Mantel' dargestellt, der die Marionettedrähte durchschlägt."

44   "Jarnos Aufführung des 'Wurstl' muß, den Kritiken nach zu schließen, sehr gut gewesen sein, nachdem der Zensor Hofrat Habison bei den Proben eifrig darauf geachtet hat, daß keine der Figuren etwa mit Masken von Personen der Wiener Gesellschaft ausgestattet würde."

before the war, but containing a reference to the 1775 opening of the Wiener Augarten to the public by Joseph II (Eilert, 217), and especially to Casanova, Don Giovanni, and Watteau's *Fêtes galantes* (Eilert, 219). As an aside, Schnitzler apparently also turned up that ball season in Rococo costume when he attended masked balls (Eilert, 218). Schnitzler thus was aware of a direct line from the eighteenth or early nineteenth centuries into the twentieth, the same tradition that Hofmannsthal worked with. Yet in Schnitzler's handling, these forms frame even harsher judgments about the growing self-deception of the bourgeoisie.[45] Schnitzler's characters, even more overtly than Hofmannsthal's, marry for love or money, try for status and prestige, and generally self-delude to the point of self-caricature or even self-annihilation. These plays, in consequence, must be considered as mirrors to his medical diagnoses of the contemporary city scene and the problems with its *mores*.

The details of Schnitzler's plays set them firmly in the tradition of the *commedia dell'arte* and its critiques of the urban bourgeoisie. *Pierrot* alludes from the first to the Viennese bourgeoisie, opening with a prototypical Biedermeier tableau, showing a single-story house and garden of a bourgeois *Hausherr* and his daughter Katharina. They are receiving her suitor, Eduard, "a well-bred and well-dressed young man" (*Pierrot*, 41). Pierrot, "in an elegant summer suit" (*Pierrot*, 41), looks into that garden from among the passers-by on the street outside the garden, copying a famous 1845 painting by Spitzweg that shows a suitor peering over a wall at a young girl under her mother's watchful eye. He throws her a kiss, as we find out that her father and her mother are trying to secure her future as they see it, "referring to the imminent marital fortune of the daughter" (*Pierrot*, 41).[46] Katharina puts Eduard off, as Pierrot flirts over the fence, trying to get her to take a walk in the meadow. No matter how much her mother tries to rein her in, she is seduced, "intoxicated by his words" (*Pierrot*, 43).[47] Eventually, Pierrot will enter through her window with no resistance. The end of the *Vorspiel* turns the fairy-tale into something darker: "PIERROT lets her notice, as if by accident, a handkerchief on which an eleven-pointed crown is visible" (*Pierrot*, 43).[48] This seduction is thus more than allure,

---

45 As Scheible summarizes, the plays stress "die beiden entscheidenden Schwächen des liberalen Bürgertums ... : das partikularistisch auf die eigene Schicht einge-schränkte Selbstverständnis, das alle anderen Bevölkerungsteile ausschloß und so die Spaltung des Bürgertums in besitzende und nicht besitzende Schichten befestigte ..." (40–1).

46 "mit Anspielung auf das bevorstehende Eheglück der Tochter."

47 "[Sie] läßt sich von Pierrots Worten berauschen."

48 "PIERROT laßt, wie zufällig, ein Schnupftuch sehen, auf dem eine elfzackige Krone sichtbar wird."

it promises social advancement in the fake heraldry embroidered on
his property.

The "First Tableau" / "Erstes Bild" reveals Pierrot for what he is:
an actor trying to quit a cabaret/variety show in an inn (*Wirtshaus*),
telling the director and his daughter Anna (who is in love with
him) that he no longer wants to go on stage: "Now I will become a
fine man. Travel in coaches, ride horses, have money and a house"
(*Pierrot*, 46),[49] as he describes his own social aspirations. Still, Pierrot
does go on stage once more to play a *commedia dell'arte* scene with
Columbine; Katharina and Eduard are in the audience. When she
sees Pierrot and presumably is disillusioned by his lack of status, she
agrees to marry Eduard, who is "beyond delighted" ("überglucklich"
[*Pierrot*, 47]). The comedy of marriage has turned into a black comedy
of masks.

The body of the pantomime traces Pierrot's purported pursuit of
Katharina and Eduard, almost a haunting or stalking. First, he changes
clothes with the *Hutschenschleuderer*, a carny in the Prater,[50] and trails
them. When they go into a photographic studio, Pierrot takes the place
of the photographer, which only her mother notices (*Pierrot*, 51). When
they visit a fortuneteller, it's Pierrot in a dress; Katharina flees. When
they go to a shooting gallery (*Schießbude*), she shoots well, until she
tries to take aim at the drummer, who is Pierrot—she flees again. At
night, on the Prater meadow, she meets him, and he denies he's been
following her. But then the basis for the play seems to shift again, as
he notes: "Ah, I begin to understand. You have seen me everywhere—
have thought you saw me everywhere—while you love me" (*Pierrot*,
54).[51] He says he worships her.

Her parents suddenly enter the scene, and to excuse his presence,
Pierrot asserts that he rescued Katharina from a drowning attempt (a
clear reference to a plot element from *Die Bürger in Wien*), for which
they thank him. When Anna runs up, Katharina sees him again in the
costume of the Pierrot from the *Wirtshaus*, and the final twist sets in:
Pierrot and Anna invite the assembled multitude to their wedding, a
proper one within their own class and apart from that of Katharina
and Eduard. The stage directions prescribe a marvelous tableau as a
curtain-dropper:

---

49 "Jetzt werd' ich ein feiner Mann werden. Kutschieren, reiten, viel Geld und ein
Haus haben."

50 This is a job at an amusement park (here, the Wurstlprater): the man who
pushes a large group swing—the same job is held by the hero of Molnár's
Liliom.

51 "Ach, ich beginne zu verstehen. Du hast mich überall gesehen—überall zu
sehen geglaubt—weil du mich liebst."

[B]oth groups turn to depart at the same time. [...] After a few steps, as if involuntarily, both Katharina and Pierrot turn around. Their glances meet for a second, first full of remembering, in tenderness and embitterment—then estranged, for an eternal parting. (*Pierrot*, 56)[52]

On the one hand, this is a typical *commedia dell'arte* outcome, where an unsuitable suitor is rejected and couples united within their proper class identities. But there is a clear additional psychological problem foregrounded in the text: the audience needs to decide which love is real, and which pure calculation as a marriage that is *standesgemäß*—social climbing is put on trial in bourgeois Vienna. After all, Pierrot actually has secured himself a business, even if not a bourgeois heiress.

A paradox of interpretation is built into the play for the audience to resolve according to its assumptions about how class positions work. When Pierrot had refused to go onstage, *the audience* would initially have assumed that he had set his cap for Katharina, across a class line. But to assume that means that one underplays the alternate scenario: Anna, the girl who loves him, also has some money, given that she is an innkeeper's daughter. The final scene reverses the assumed plot: it seems to have been Katharina who was looking beyond her yard, her fixed life, and her assumptions. Or is it her? As an actor, Pierrot was for a moment willing to play along, but it is not clear that he ever was in pursuit of Katharina, or whether he was trying to play odds on a better catch—he may have been correct that *she* sees him out of her own psychological obsession. Do we have a stalker or an obsessed woman?

Here, some clarification can be gained from the traditional Pierrot character in the *commedia dell'arte*. Pierrot is the naïve clown in white, an innocent or fool who is always the victim of others because he trusts people and is an easy target for lies. Sometimes his naïve behavior leads him to be called mad, because all he does is play. Thus Schnitzler's adaptation has a clear second message, if the role is played to type: he may have actually believed the girl was in love with him—he is the innocent seduced by a more compelling girl. Katharina, in contrast, emerges as either calculating or mad. An additional, more speculative layer might lie in the characters' names: St. Anne, after all, is the mother of Mary and grandmother of Jesus, while St. Catherine is either Catherine of Alexandria, last pagan philosopher and virgin

---

52 "[B]eide Gesellschaften wenden sich zugleich zum Gehen. ... Nach ein paar Schritten, wie unwillkürlich, sehen sowohl Katharina als Pierrot sich um. Ihre Blicke begegnen sich auf eine Sekunde, zuerst noch voll Erinnern, in Zärtlichkeit und Erbitterung,—dann fremd, zu ewigem Abschied."

scholar, or Catherine of Siena, another virgin who resisted her father's marriage plans and ultimately helped to resolve the Western Schism (1378).

Revelations of such mixed motivations in sudden field-ground reversals seem to have appealed to Schnitzler, because he uses the same device in *Der Schleier der Pierrette,* albeit with a gender reversal. Here again, the audience sees a story of a "proper marriage," instigated by a father to the emotional and physical ruin of the daughter. In this version, Pierrette is supposed to marry Arlecchino, who is dressed in "a mix of the traditional Pierrot costume and that of old Vienna" (*Schleier,* 112).[53] Here, the conflict is more brutal. In the first tableau, Pierrot is entertaining friends and confesses his love for Pierrette. He leaves and finds in his room Pierrette, dressed in a "bridal gown from old Vienna" (*Schleier,* 116). She has brought poison, which she dissolves in wine as they make a suicide pact. He drinks his but knocks hers out of her hand—she lives, and he dies. The *Zweites Bild* shows her wedding to Arlecchino. Spontaneously, she disappears upstairs, and the ghost of Pierrot appears to her, upon which she discovers she has lost her veil— signaling to the audience that he was her lover. In the third tableau, she enters a room where the dead Pierrot is laid out. Arlecchino is furious and locks her in the room with the body. She goes crazy and dances herself to death; the other couples find her body—a typical ballet scenario, clearly inspired by *Giselle.* That ending signals the lot of the bourgeoisie, opposed to being in love.

Yet reference to the stock characters again complicates the message. Missing from the mix is Arlecchino's (Harlequin's) standard inamorata, Columbine. Traditionally, the pair are two clever servants, with Columbine helping her mistress (rather like Hofmannsthal's Annina from *Rosenkavalier*). Harlequin is often a fool in love and nimble physically (often doing tumbling tricks); he occasionally seems to be malicious, but that is often out of momentary stupidity rather than design. He traditionally wears a black mask as he seems to be doing evil. Schnitzler's variation of the traditional scenarios is thus a reversal. Schnitzler's Arleccchino, however, destroys the room and his improper spouse—the lower class punishing the upper.

If Pierrot and Pierrette traditionally star in plays of deluded love— love as social control rather than affection—then Schnitzler adds another hero, Kassian, to the canon of players that he uses in the next of his plays that games with love across class lines. In 1909, Schnitzler uses this figure to revisit bourgeois marriages a third time, in *Der tapfere Kassian: Singspiel in einem Aufzug,* which had music by Oscar Straus of operetta fame. It was performed and printed in Leipzig, rather than

---

53   "ein Gemisch des traditionellen Pierrot—und des Altwiener Kostüms."

Vienna, and so its historical setting was altered to address the German past, rather than Vienna, as it takes place in a room "in the style of the end of the seventeenth century."

Love and deception again motivate the plot. Sophie loves Martin, her first crush. Kassian, Martin's cousin, arrives to take him on an adventure; Martin admits he loves a dancer (as Sophie had suspected) and will either woo and win her, or commit suicide (*Kassian*, 66). The men gamble, and Martin wins enough from Kassian to finance the trip. Sophie watches as they subsequently argue and duel; Kassian runs Martin through the heart with his rapier.

Sophie's calculation turns more obvious at that point. As Kassian prepares to leave, she tries to seduce him into staying. She jumps out of the window, and Kassian jumps after her. The servant reports about the miracle that happens: "Something highly marvelous has happened— highly marvelous ... The jumping man has caught the jumping girl in mid-air, and both landed below in one piece" (*Kassian*, 75).[54] The play ends with Martin dying as he plays the flute, with his corpse to be picked up at midnight. Kassian ends as the "hero" who saves the girl, but one who actually is out for himself, far away from any emotional attachments except to the world's seductions. None the less, they "take the leap" and "save" each other. Sophie will have her man, no matter the cost.

Schnitzler reworks this story a second time, as the first play in his triptych of puppet plays: *Der tapfere Cassian: Puppenspiel in einem Akt*. In this version, it is clear that Martin leaves Sophie because she suspects his infidelity with the dancer. When this Cassian comes and admires Sophie, they arrange a trade of girls, so that Martin can escape and follow his dancer, "the mistress of the Duke of Oldcastle" (*Cassian*, 110). Martin finances this escape by duping everyone in town at cards, while Cassian flirts with Sophie. Cassian now reveals himself as a cad, as well, planning to seduce the girl Martin will be leaving behind: "Why do I care what happens to the girl, when you are leaving on your trip?" (*Cassian*, 115).[55] Martin is cleaned out at cards, they fight, and Martin is stabbed and dies. The closing tableau again echoes *Giselle*, but with clear infidelity added. Martin gives Cassian a flower to take to the dancer, which he says he'll do the next day. When Sophie hears that, she jumps out the window and turns into "the jumping girl" of the earlier version.

---

54 "Höchst Wundersames hat sich ereignet—höchst Wundersames! ... Der springende Herr hat das springende Fräulein in der Luft aufgefangen und beide sind wohlbehalten unten angelangt."

55 "Was kümmert's dich, was das Fräulein begegnet, da du doch auf Reisen gehst."

The names in this play again point to a subtext, but not from the *commedia dell'arte*. The two men are named after similar saints, very familiar ones within Catholic culture. Kassian is a name borrowed in clear irony from a fifth-century saint who brought monasticism out of Egypt into the West, or from one of several saints and martyrs. In an Austrian context, Martin is indubitably St. Martin of Tours, a Roman soldier who converted and became a monk, living a simple life; he is remembered for splitting his cloak with a beggar to keep him from freezing to death. His November 11 feast day was one of Vienna's quarter days, when rents were due (Martini, Martinmas); it marked the beginning of winter and a carnival day at the beginning of advent. That feast stays in public memory in no small part because of its special culinary moment, as well: the *Martinigans*, a roast goose celebrating the geese who betrayed St. Martin's hiding place when he sought to avoid becoming bishop.

Sophie, named for the goddess of wisdom, dies in both versions of the scenario, which points toward the males' issues as focus for the social critique. Martin and Kassian/Cassian invert the roles and personae suggested by their names—seducers and hedonists instead of hermits, and interested in the wrong kind of women to boot. In the first version, Kassian helps make a miracle in saving Sophie, after fighting a duel—more or less interpretable as noble, within the ranks of lady-killers. In the second, there are no miracles—just two fairly nondescript fellows who want their shot at the duke's mistress, at the cost of another woman's life. The names in the story, therefore, emphasize manipulation of social expectations. Each simply plays out the roles expected of them, as the puppets of the title, with souls that do not match their names or roles.

The second puppet play, *Der Puppenspieler*, stresses to an even greater degree the manipulations of society originating in a set of self-deluding choices. As such, it offers an interesting counterpart to the problems of the cycle's first play, again confronting the audience with questions about who is manipulating whom, and to what end. *Der Puppenspieler* starts when two men, Georg and Eduard, meet each other after 11 years apart. Eduard reveals he is married and that he's been looking for Georg (*Puppenspieler*, 88). The stories they exchange are odd. First, Georg casts himself as a puppetmaster who has the power over individual lives. He establishes himself in this role by telling the story of a man he met in a train: "Suddenly the thought runs through my head: Die! [...] We arrive in Vienna. I get up, get out of the train, the other one does not. The other fellow remains seated without moving. I summon people—he is carried out—he was dead ... dead. The doctors called it a heart attack" (*Puppenspieler*, 90).[56] The police commissar

56 "Plötzlich geht mir der Gedanke durch den Korf: Stirb! ... Wir kommen in
    Wien an. Ich erhebe mich, steige aus, der andere nicht. Der andere bleibt sitzen,

refused to put him in jail for the incident, even while he himself retains some sense of culpability for a murder by intent.

This incident sets up the play's problem: who actually is pulling the strings in the others' lives? It is revealed that Eduard had gone to Boston many years earlier, after the two of them had shared a party with two girls. Ultimately, one of those girls, Anna, followed him and became his wife. Then the situation gets more complicated, as Georg initiates another layer of explanation that calls Eduard's story into question:

> The little one who was so tender with me [Anna] simply did what I wanted. You were the puppets in my hands. I pulled the wires. It was decided that she was supposed to pretend to be in love with you. Because I always felt sorry for you, Eduard. I wanted to awaken in you the illusion of happiness, so that true happiness would find you ready if it ever appeared. And thus I have—as is given to people like me to do—perhaps had even a deeper impact than I wanted to. I have made you into a different person. And if I am permitted to say: it is a more noble pleasure to play with living beings than to let figures made of air swirl around in a poetic dance. (*Puppenspieler*, 93)[57]

Eduard confirms to his wife "that we were his puppets. We danced on his wires" (94).[58] Their son is named George, a tribute to the serious family that came out of a joke (97). "And if one would now just consider that he would not have been born if I hadn't had that idea on that evening ..." (*Puppenspieler*, 101).[59]

Yet then the story gets a second, darker fable grafted onto it: we discover that Georg had traveled all over the world with a woman named Irene. Eduard's Anna had originally been interested in him,

---

regungslos. Ich rufe Leute herbei—man trägt ihn hinaus—er war tot ... tot. Die Ärtze nannten es Herzschlag."

57 "Die Kleine, die so zärtlich mit dir war, tat einfach, was ich wollte. Ihr wart die Puppen in meiner Hand. Ich lenkte die Drähte. Es war abgemacht, daß sie sich in dich verliebt stellen sollte. Denn du hattest mir immer leid getan, Eduard. Ich wollte in dir die Illusion eines Glücks erwecken, damit dich das wahre Glück bereit fände, wenn es einmal erschiene. Und so hab' ich—wie es Leuten meiner Art wohl gegeben sein mag—vielleicht noch tiefer gewirkt, als ich wollte. Ich habe dich zu einem andern Menschen gemacht. Und ich darf wohl sagen: es ist ein edleres Vergnügen, mit Lebendigen zu spielen, als Luftgestalten im poetischen Tanze herumwirbeln zu lassen."

58 "daß wir seine Puppen waren. An seinen Drähten haben wir getanzt."

59 "Und wenn man zugleich bedenkt, daß er nie geboren wäre, wenn ich nicht an jenem Abend den Einfall gehabt hätte ..."

hoping that they might marry, which is why she had played along with the planned joke. Anna played along for her own mercenary reasons: "This comedy was, after all, my last hope, so to speak. You were supposed to become jealous" (*Puppenspieler*, 98).[60] It didn't work: "I naturally had to get used to it" (*Puppenspieler*, 98),[61] which presumably refers to catching Eduard as an alternative. She felt guilty and confessed to Eduard, which brought them together (*Puppenspieler*, 99). She wrote Eduard in America a very pretty letter and came after him—because she loved him, of course (*Puppenspieler*, 100). Then yet another reverse sets in. Georg says he's happy he's not settled like they are:

> If I think that it could have happened to me, that I could have become a settled paterfamilias like you—to sit under a hanging lamp and have a maid in service ... No, let us all be happy that I did not come then. No, I'm not born to dine at a table with white linens. (*Puppenspieler*, 199)[62]

He likes street food and to follow his inclinations. But we find out that this, too, is a fable: he had married Irene, who left him, and they had had a son, who died. His assessment: "Fate would not accept that I would be brought to ground by the cares of everyday life. People like me must be free if they are to live out their appointed span" (*Puppenspieler*, 102).[63] Anna has the last word: "We do not want to take the last thing he has from him" (*Puppenspieler*, 102).[64]

These triple reverses mark how the play interrogates social truths for individuals who function as puppets. Social scripts change when they require different psychological defenses—Schnitzler shows pure social calculation in action and with its inherent conflicts. Yet in all Schnitzler's plays, that social calculation ultimately comes before emotion or choice, with love correlated with pragmatic decisions. If there are any genuine sentiments among these people, they are prescripted by history and station rather than emotion.

---

60 "Diese Komödie war nämlich meine letzte Hoffnung, sozusagen. Du solltest eifersüchtig werden."
61 "Da müßt' ich mich natürlich abfinden."
62 "Wenn ich bedenke, es hätte mir passieren können, ein geordneter Hausvater zu werden, wie du—unter einer Hängelampe zu sitzen und eine Zofe in Diensten zu haben ... Nein, laßt uns alle froh sein, daß ich damals nicht gekommen bin. Nein, ich bin nicht dazu geboren, an einem weißgedeckten Tisch zu speisen."
63 "das Schicksal wünscht nicht, daß ich durch Alltagssorgen an den Boden geschmiedet werde. Menschen meiner Art müssen frei sein, wenn sie sich ausleben sollen."
64 "Wir wollen ihm nicht das Letzte nehmen, was ihm geblieben ist."

Individual interests scripted by social expectations again drive the plot of the third entry in Schnitzler's trilogy: *Zum großen Wurstl: Burleske in einem Akt*. Upstage, the set features a large puppet theater with the banner "Zum großen Wurstl" (*Wurstl*, 121) and a little old-fashioned puppet booth on the left. Stage right, there is a *Gasthausgarten*, with tables and chairs, with open space leading downstage to the prompters' box. The characters who appear burlesque contemporary literature: Graf von Scharlais is the title figure from a play by Richard Beer-Hofmann (1905); "Der Meister" is one from a Hermann Bahr play (1903); "Ein Vetter Brackenburgs" is a cousin of Klärchen's suitor from Goethe's *Egmont*; a *Hutchenschleuderer* ("swing pusher") necessarily evokes the title character from Franz Molnar's *Liliom*, the carny who runs the carousel (and who turns up a half-century later in the Broadway musical of that name). Other book and literary references emerge, such as characters who "whistle beyond good and evil" (*Wurstl*, 178).

Acting like Karl Kraus' later "Optimist" and "Nörgler" (complainer) from *Die letzten Tage der Menschheit* (*The Last Days of Humanity*), two self-declared commentators offer their observations on the situation, serving as on-stage voices like those in Tieck's *Der gestiefelte Kater* (*Puss in Boots* [1797 and 1811]). "The sharp-tongued fellow" (*Der Bissige*) and "the fellow who means well" (*der Wohlwollende*) start by deciding what, if anything, is new about these two competing theaters. Two boys pass out playbills; the director serves as the carny barker, hawking tickets for his show—"speaking Viennese, and now and then a forced high German with false intonation" (*Wurstl*, 121).[65] His theater performance purportedly makes all other theater performances superfluous (*endgültig überflüssig* [*Wurstl*, 122]). Further characters include Herzog von Lavin, his wife, a *Süsses Mädl* (Liesl, a prostitute with a proper heart of gold), her father, another *Hutschenschleuderer*, and a new addition who speaks in weighty verses: "death as Hanswurst, or Hanswurst as death, through whom the nightmarish aspects of this drama can and may be eliminated" (*Wurstl*, 122).[66] Here, Schnitzler has put on the stage a compendium of Vienna's stereotypes; the subsequent action proves his commitment to blowing them up.

In a conceit also used in Hofmannsthal's *Ariadne auf Naxos* libretto, the poet who wrote the play to be performed is upset that the audience is paying less than full attention to his work (in this case, eating). The Director insists that the audience members won't listen if they're hungry (Brecht's famous line comes here to mind: "First food, then

---

65 "wienerisch, zuweilen gezwungenes Hochdeutsch mit falschen Betonungen."
66 "einen Tod als Wurstl oder Wurstl als Tod, wodurch das Schauerliche dieses Drama getilgt werden möchte und dürfte."

moralism").[67] The poet persists: "But that's against our agreement" (*Wurstl*, 123).[68] The curtain goes up, and the characters introduce themselves. One of the *Bürger* in the on-stage audience tries to leave with his daughter, once he hears there is a *Süsses Mädl* on the stage, but he agrees to stay when the girl says she doesn't understand. The scene shows Liesl needing to go to work but being detained by the Hero's embraces. *Der Bissige* from the real audience is bored: "I've had it up to here!" (*Wurstl*, 125). When the Hero, a typical romantic type, claims he wants to go to the country, *Der Wohlwollende* gets nostalgic: "I tend toward moods, not deeds" (*Wurstl*, 126). Schnitzler's play thus shows how unstable the social stereotypes have become.

The interchanges between the play and the audience within the play intensify when an interlocutor, a *Räsoneur* (*Wurstl*, 125), appears as a buffer between them (this again echoes Tieck). The *Räsoneur* aligns himself with the space of the play-within-the-play by speaking in verse, while the stage audience speaks prose. The Hero tries to tell the *Räsoneur* he doesn't belong in the play, to which *der Bissige* in the audience asserts, "it's getting satirical" (*Wurstl*, 125). The *Räsoneur* retorts: "Hanswurst is happy everywhere / the serious man is always moved" (*Wurstl*, 126).[69] The Director quips to the Poet that the Interlocutor character is actually boring, and that he should have been thrown out—an assertion that sends the Poet to cut some verses.

When the play within the play begins, the Hero (*Held*) confesses that he has "seduced girls and broken up marriages." He loves the Duchess von Lawin to no avail (*Wurstl*, 128) but has been accused of an indiscretion and challenged to a duel by the Duke (*Wurstl*, 129). It will not end well, he notes to his seconds: "Well, when we have our breakfasts, you will be long dead" (*Wurstl*, 127).[70] The *Herzogin* comes and notes he should at least know what he's going to get shot for: "So let's get us guilty as quickly as possible" (*Wurstl*, 131).[71] Yet the Hero is "not in the mood" (*Wurstl*, 131). Two members of the stage audience comment: "It's a biting satire on dueling." "It hasn't bitten me yet" (*Wurstl*, 129).[72] When the Duke arrives for the duel, he claims that women kill themselves for him daily (*Wurstl*, 133). The last scenes show the situation deteriorating, as Liesl the prostitute appears and vacillates between the Duke and the Hero (both prior acquaintances). Ultimately,

---

67 "Erst kommt das Fressen, dann kommt die Moral" ("Ballade über die Frage: Wovon lebt der Mensch?," *Die Dreigroschenoper: Der Erstdruck 1928* [Frankfurt/M: Suhrkamp, 2004], 67).

68 "Aber das ist ja gegen unsere Verabredung."

69 "Der Wurstl freut sich allerorten,/Der ernste Mann ist stets gerührt."

70 "Nun, wenn wir frühstücken, bist du längst tot."

71 "So lassen Sie schleunigst uns schuldig werden."

72 "Es ist eine beißende Satire auf das Duell." "Mich beißt's vorläufig nicht."

the Hero tries to get her to die with him. At that moment, Death shows up (and begins to satirize Schnitzler's own *Reigen* [*Wurstl*, 140]), as total chaos descends onto the stage.

The Interlocutor stops the chaos as he breaks the play's frame and sends all home: "Back to everyday life again, to business, into the office, / each returns to the place he came from" (*Wurstl*, 137).[73] The director interjects, almost like Puck from *Midsummer Night's Dream*:

> Thereupon, when the essence of the Enlightenment plays itself out in the background of the century, and art brings forth its fruits, I ask you most humbly to remember that the stage is a copy of what goes on on earth, also called a mirror of the world, that pretends to draw into its purview the sad no less than the happy, [the points] toward which our poets, *poeta vates*, have the pleasure of sailing. (*Wurstl*, 139)[74]

A clearer play on traditional germanophone aesthetics could not be imagined, as the *fin de siècle* bourgeoisie are confronted with the damaging social scripts of their era.

As the play and the on-stage audience break up, characters from other familiar plays enter; marionettes come alive, telling the Duke about the playwright. The Poet threatens the marionettes: "Don't you dare to take control yourselves here in this room" (*Wurstl*, 141),[75] which infuriates them. The puppets' song is peculiar, as they threaten to take over the room:

Hey, now we do what we want to!
Talking, singing, dancing, acting crazy!
The public doesn't matter to us—
Everything goes the way we want it!
If the poet is completely out of his mind,
Let's start our play! (*Wurstl*, 141)

Ei, nun tun wir, was wir wollen!
Reden, singen, tanzen, tollen!
Publikum ist uns egal—
Alles geht nach unsrer Wahl!
Ist der Dichter ganz von Sinnen,
Laßt uns unser Spiel beginnen!

---

73 "Zum Alltag wieder, zum Geschäft, ins Amt, / Ein jeder kehrt zurück, woher er stammt."

74 "Alsdann, wenn sich das Wesen der Aufklärung im Hintergrund des Säkulums abgespielt und die Kunst ihre Früchte trägt, bitte ich ergebenst ins Auge zu fassen, daß die Bühne das Abbild des Erdentreibens, auch Spiegel der Welt genannt, das Traurige nicht minder als das Lustige in ihr Bereich zu ziehen vorgibt, wohin auch unser Dichter, poeta vates, hinauszusegeln die Belustigung hat."

75 "Wagt nicht, selbständig hier im Raum zu walten!"

Finally, "The Unknown" (*Der Unbekannte*) appears with a sword and slices through the puppet strings, so that they fall down: "This sword, though, makes it obvious / who is a puppet, who a human being" (*Wurstl*, 142).[76] The question gets raised: "Am I myself—or only a sign?" (*Wurstl*, 142).[77] He passes the sword over the stage, and all the people fall down. Yet as he leaves, all rise and start over again. Art and life intermingle and undermine each other, and the audience realizes that they, too, might be held upright by strings, as well.

Schnitzler's Punch and Judy plays take up typical themes from the *Volkstheater*, but with specific reference to contemporaneous problems: social expectations, marriage, money, the lack of individual freedom, initiative, and self-determination. The dramatic form carefully marks out field/ground reversals where they do not work in reality—the characters signal clearly where their motivations shift *vis-à-vis* context, opportunism, and traditional expectations. The audience is first seduced into following ordinary assumptions about the innocent and guilty, the hero and the villain, the puppets, the puppet-masters, and the losers in these situations. No matter the superficial answers, the reality behind the situation always involves a fatal reverse of situation—real life resists too-simple scripts.

Traditions as radical modernism

The critics, as noted at the outset of this discussion, prefer to look at the libidinous inner lives of Schnitzler's characters rather than to consider his texts as representing social conditions from Vienna and the *Standesstaat*, the contemporary histories that contemporaneous audiences would have seen.

However, Schnittzler's prose works, both fiction and non-fiction, diagnose the lives of "his" class, the supposedly liberal bourgeoisie who abuse their legacies, or who may have been duped as to the impact and import of those legacies. His characters believe the Dual Monarchy's promise that children could be educated and move into new social roles, yet end up financially ruined, isolated from extended family structures, or ego-centered to the point of self-immolation. By reason of inheritance, connections, or disposition, they will ultimately exist outside the oligarchy, outside traditional power centers of government, military, and economics.

The playwright Schnitzler reveals his characters' lives using different tools than the fiction-writer. Instead of "hearing" the characters' inner monologues of self-justification and self-fashioning, his audiences

---

76 "Dies Schwert hier aber macht es offenbar,/Wer eine Puppe, wer ein Mensch nur war."
77 "Bin ich ich selber—oder nur ein Zeichen!"

watch characters act out their professions, letting behaviors speak instead of inner voices. Significantly, the women in these plays are more shocking than the males, given that they seem to have no independent roles—they follow the limits familiar from *commedia dell'arte*, with few independent choices and almost certain death. In Schnitzler's Vienna, however, losing out in the marriage market might indeed have meant certain ruin, death, turning oneself into "the jumping girl" or the Anna who needs to make someone jealous. In *Wurstl*, when "everyone goes back where they belong," that return to normal is a return to a chaos of unsatisfying identities. Cutting the marionettes' strings neither stops the acting nor frees the characters. Instead, they return to their fables about duels and mistresses.

In the *Kasperl* plays, Schnitzler narrates the lives of the middle classes as burlesques, or as black humor puppet plays, not as liberals under stress—he will neither let his audience empathize with these characters nor forget how absolute social calculation has created this community at odds with itself, eating itself alive from the inside from what should be its emotional center. "Happy families" depend on who pulls the strings of their lives and fortunes; they are puppets of social discourses with virtually no inner lives. Schnitzler's *Puppenspieler* and related plays (*Liebelei*, the *Anatol* cycle) show his contemporaries in the "theater of our lives" (as Hugo von Hofmannsthal described Schnitzler's characters in the prologue he contributed to *Anatol*)—lives that reflect how very ordinary and pre-scripted those lives are as those who live are desperately trying to hold onto their illusions about "how things work."

The social critiques that Schnitzler rehearses here are not original to these plays. As we have seen, Europe has since the early modern era had theater traditions designed to criticize a class self-defined by money and illusions of privilege. Yet what distinguishes these short plays from more familiar works like *Reigen* or *Liebelei* is Schnitzler's emphasis on how very formulaic these lives are—they are black and white sketches of lives, much as Weimar Expressionist art would show them, but legible and perhaps even realistic in a Vienna that understands the *Volkstheater*. Contrary to the assumptions of the bourgeois liberal classes who were in the ascendancy a generation earlier, their children are *not* living lives that are nuanced, unique, and worthy of description; they are not originals but rather the heirs of empty social forms and a liberalism that has forgotten the group. The characters in the plays introduced here profess adherence to a much more restricted ideological catechism: their goal is to save face while they live lives of small spiritual amplitude in Habsburg Europe.

Theater forms enable Schnitzler to reveal the unoriginality and the emptiness of social performances to his audiences—to craft a kind of

meta-commentary based on the audiences' expectation on how the
Volkstheater is supposed to work. These plays, therefore, are evidence
of Schnitzler's commitment to a kind of anti-illusionist theater as
a tool for a novel kind of enlightenment effect—not a Brechtian
Verfremdungseffekt that breaks an illusion by breaking the frame of
its narrative, but a full-fledged challenge to the illusion of stage and
reality, their causes and effects.

The plays discussed here also suggest a reinterpretation of
Schnitzler's craftsmanship. It is the rare critic who ties this humor with
social critique. Egon Schwarz sees at least part of their realism:

> The one-act play *At the Grand Guignol* [...] does more than send
> itself up, although that is clearly present to a great degree. At the
> same time, it allows Schnitzler to make fun of the weaknesses of
> his surroundings and the short-sighted misunderstandings of his
> readers and viewers. (Schwarz, 22)[78]

Yet the majority of critics draw the play into the proximity of the era's
experimental theater, next to Jarry's *Ubu Roi* or like Meyerhold's stagings.
Such theaters also used marionettes in performances, often to comment
on human freedom (Bayerdörfer, 574).[79] Karin Wolgast confirms that
commedia dell'arte pieces were popular throughout Austria and Europe
around 1900, with proponents like Edward Gordon Craig in England
(Wolgast, 285), and Max Reinhardt in Germany, who staged some of
the genre's classic comedies, including Goldoni's *Diener zweier Herren*
and Molière (Wolgast, 286): "Seen in terms of literary history, we are
dealing here with an alternative to the realistic and naturalist currents

---

78   "Der Einakter *Zum großen Wurstl* ... ist mehr als bloße Selbstpersiflage, obgleich
er auch das in hohem Grade ist. Er dient Schnitzler gleichzeitig dazu, sich über
die Schwächen seiner Umwelt und die kurzsichtigen Mißverständnisse seiner
Leser- und Zuschauerschaft lustig zu machen."

79   That connection, however, has not been of particular interest to some of
Schnitler's interpreters:
Zwar ist das Stück [*Der tapfere Cassian*] nicht für Marionetten geschreiben,
aber das Geschehen ist durchaus hölzern. Es stellt das Skelett einer
theatralischen Handlung dar, die aller psychologischen Motivierung und
Nuancierung entkleidet und von aller tieferen Problematik entlastet ist.
Übrig bleiben gängige Handlungsschemata des well-made-play, auf vergrö-
berte Elemantarteile und vereinfachte Verknüfungsgelenke reduziert ...
(Bayerdörfer, 565)
Bayerdörfer here simply ignores Schnitzler's growing commitment to alternative performance techniques (including mime, dance, and even films), and to
newer forms of the anti-illusion theater. *Zum großen Wurstl* is often dismissed
as sketchy for the same reasons, with roles are "Zeichen-Rolle," ciphers, albeit
in the tradition of the Grand Guignol (Bayerdörfer, 570, 567).

of the nineteenth century" (Wolgast, 286),[80] "a dialectical relationship to naturalism" (Wolgast, 286), and a consciously stylized theatrical theater.

Be this theater experimental or naturalist (or both), Schnitzler's works are products of more than decadent imaginations. These plays fall into the context of modernist critiques of the naturalistic stage such as those familiar from Jarry, Giraudoux, and Beckett (*Krapp's Last Tape*); each calls aesthetic illusion into question. Schnitzler's theater has become an "extra-literary theater" ("außerliterarisches Theater").[81] In this sense, Schnitzler uses conventions from Austrian theater history to take up social critique for the broader public. His prose fiction is calculated for the educated middle classes, reminding them to protect the community. These plays, however, confront social fictions more crudely and hence more directly, especially raw self-interest and self-portrayal, and a kind of low cunning that is too often found in the lives of smallholders and business managers, entertainers, and self-employed waiters or waitresses, to say nothing of the shop-girls who will soon be either wives or, if they miss their chances, prostitutes. As Schnitzler attests in his medical writing, these people are threatened physically, as well—by disease, overcrowding, and poverty, because they lack (or eschew) family and group ties.

Naturalism in the hands of playwrights like Gerhard Hauptmann treats victims of society from the outside, allowing his audiences to empathize with their "plights," while remaining divorced from them. Turning them into puppets distances the audience, forcing a more dispassionate evaluation of their situations and motivations and a considerably less affective identification with them. Schnitzler's work

---

80 "Literaturgeschichtlich gesehen handelt es sich um eine Alternitive zu den realistischen und naturalistischen Strömungen des 19. Jahrhunderts."

81 Following up such leads, Michaela L. Perlmann, who singles out *Puppenspieler* as an analytic one-act play (Perlmann, 46–7), while *Cassian* and *Zum großen Wurstl* are seen as especially anti-illusionist (Perlmann, 52), deriving from Baroque world theater (Perlmann, 54–7). Martin Swales makes this tie more explicit:

   In *Zum großen Wurstl* and in *Der grüne Kakadu* he is a remarkably precocious forerunner of the contemporary Theatre of the Absurd, and at the same time a dramatist impregnated with the themes and techniques of Baroque theatrical practice. With *Liebelei* he was acclaimed as a naturalistic revolutionary at the "Burgtheater" and yet he was also close to the tradition of the "bürgerliches Trauerspiel." (Swales [1971], 25–6)

   Swales thus casts *Der Puppenspieler* as a kind of morality play, while, in *Wurstl*, "[Schnitzler] offers the most radical, despairing comment on the world he knows," since it reveals the audience as empty-headed (Swales [1971], 69). He is among the rare voices who considers *Wurstl* a masterpiece (Swales, 266) and takes the piece as Schnitzler's self-caricature in a way that will "belong to the twentieth-century Theatre of the Absurd" (Swales, 278), as in plays like Ionesco's *Bald Soprano* (Swales, 273).

underscores the absurdity in the motivation structure and values that these characters have internalized, not the absurdity of a world waiting for Godot. Schnitzler hopes that his audiences might heal his theater's soul as it intervenes in Vienna's public dialogues about the health of the nation's soul.

Seven   Kasperl and the *Wiener Gruppe*: artmann, Bayer, and Handke

Reenacting its trauma of World War I after World War II, Austria's culture had again to rise from the ashes to seek its place within Europe. Cultural history has again complicated our vision of this restoration because, tacitly or overtly, it still remains largely insensitive to the differences among *German* literature and the several *germanophone* literatures that reemerged in a rebuilt Europe.[1] There is little balance among today's presentations of intellectuals in Austria and two *different* Germanys, as the Cold War's military-industrial complex has made the Frankfurt School's idea of the *public sphere*, mediatized and capitalized, more plausible as a model of public spaces than the older idea of public space that has been the focus here.

Reclaiming such differences is crucial to understanding what it meant to be a public intellectual in that era, especially a public intellectual willing to admit that history and traditions could still be the key to public dialogue. Just as Schnitzler has been pigeon-holed as an author of decadence rather than a social critic, Austrian intellectuals after World War II, especially those who sought the restoration of Austria's culture in Europe, are too often accused of seeking some idealized version of the nation's past. A generation's commitment to social and political critique in Austria's public spaces has been critically undervalued.

Ample material is at hand to correct these assumptions. Taking up a favorite trope of German literature history, for instance, one notable commentator on and contributor to Austria's postwar literary scene, Hans Weigel, pointed out that Austria did not have a *zero hour* (*Stunde Null*) after 1945, as Germany claimed to have had, but rather had a

---

1   For a discussion of this point, see Arens, "The Culture of 'Culture'" (2009). The most complete history of Austrian literature in this era is Herbert Zeman, ed., *Geschichte der Literatur in Österreich*, Bd. 7: *Das 20. Jahrhundert* (1994).

234 Vienna's Dreams of Europe

null point in the imaginary (*Nullpunkt im Imaginären*) (Spiel, 59). Yet that German term "Zero Hour" remains a critical reference point in discussions of Germany's postwar writers, framing today's understanding of Group 47 (including eventual Nobel Prize winners Heinrich Böll and Günter Grass) and their project of reconstructing the German language and its literature through a return to the universals of human experience. The Austrian "null point in the imaginary" that Weigel highlights, in contrast, outlines this nation's search for a more historically grounded cultural imagination and conscious cultural identity.[2]

In fact, such a cultural "null point in the imaginary" rather than a "zero hour" for history guided many Austrian artists to their postwar engagement with their land's cultural and political identities. This framework suggests that Austria's culture needed less to conquer its past—Germany's challenge of *Vergangenheitsbewältigung*—than to relocate (reinterpret, rethink, *reimagine*) that past within public memory. And in this project, once again, the *Volkstheater* emerged as part of Austrian literature's attempts to reclaim both a viable public space for political discussion and a cultural identity distanced from Germany's.

West German literature claims its renascence in the program of *Gruppe 47*; Austria's equivalent was the *Wiener Gruppe* (Vienna Group). Where Group 47 is often remembered today for its prose, the *Wiener Gruppe* found its new public voice in poetry and public performances, especially through h. c. artmann (1921–2000), known more popularly as a dialect poet, and his contemporary Konrad Bayer (1932–64).[3] Among the direct heritors of their legacy was the more internationally famous Peter Handke (b. 1942). A significant but lesser-known part of that legacy was a body of plays using forms from the *Volkstheater*: artmann's 1958 play, *No Pepper for Czermak* (*Kein Pfeffer für Czermak*); Bayer's *kasperl at the electric chair* (*kasperl am elektrischen stuhl*, ca. 1960, but only published in 1985); and Handke's *Kaspar* (1968) and *The Ward Wants to be the Guardian* (*Das Mündel will Vormund sein*, 1969). Only *Kaspar* is more than glancingly familiar to today's critics, because Handke is also associated with Group 47, an affiliation that obscures how his plays express Austrian political resistance to its own history and to the new Europe of NATO.

These plays do not speak only to traditions of Austrian philosophy and a critique of language like Wittgenstein's. Instead, they provide

---

2   Some of the material in this chapter appeared in Katherine Arens, "The Persistence of Kasperl in Memory" (2002); it has been heavily reworked for the present context.

3   Note that artmann in this era wrote his name without capital letters, and that many of the texts from the *Wiener Gruppe* were typeset with lower-case letters and little punctuation, conventions maintained here.

metacommentaries on Austria's own cultural traditions and on cultural processes extending beyond a single nation-state. *Czermak, kasperl*, and *Kaspar* emerge as modern, engaged, black comedies written within the *Volksstück* traditions, aimed at criticizing the Austrian state at the dawn of the Cold War in its public spaces in a voice familiar to its public.

From the *Wiener Gruppe* to *Forum Stadtpark*: The avant-garde in Austria

Austria's intellectual life, like that of the two Germanys, had to be reconstructed after World War II, a process that took off in the 1950s and 1960s, especially after the 1955 *Staatsvertrag* which restored Austria's existence as a state. A number of engaged intellectuals sought to challenge postwar conservatism and willful historical blindness.[4]

The *Wiener Gruppe* became a public aesthetic-political presence in Vienna from about 1951. Like West German intellectuals of the era, they read widely in texts from European and world culture since the 1930s; their particular interest was in Surrealism, Dada, and what would become the French Theater of the Absurd and the Situationist International—the art forms, in other words, that *performed* politics in the public space rather than just turning it into narratives. Where Group 47 went to the book fairs and to radio and television shows, however, the *Wiener Gruppe* went to the streets as an artistic counter-culture, especially through what English speakers would come to call "happenings" (*Veranstaltungen*), such as public funeral processions through city streets, accompanied by manifestos about art and politics.

While Group 47 gradually ritualized its annual performances as an elite writers' group and the voice of Germany's current literary scene, the "members" of the *Wiener Gruppe* denied from the first that they actually were a group. They became such in the public mind only in 1967, when one of their number, Gerhard Rühm, helped to formalize its existence by editing a volume documenting their activity: *Die Wiener Gruppe—Achleitner, Artmann, Bayer, Rühm, Wiener: Texte, Gemeinschaftsarbeiten, Aktionen*. The press was of course eager to have a rubric for this visible but loose collection of intellectuals and artists born in the 1920s and 1930s—a generation with distinct memories of the War, although little direct culpability.

From the first, this group included young artists from all the arts (including architects and actors)[5] who simply sought to share their

---

4   Hilde Spiel, part of that movement, documented the climate early in a volume of the *Kindlers Literaturlexicon*.

5   The *Wiener Gruppe*, artmann said in a 1966 interview, included, for instance, Helmut Qualitinger, Peter Wehle, and Gerhard Bronner, all well-known

interests in modern Western art trends (artmann and Krüger, "Wer es versteht," 16). Rühm met artmann in about 1952, and they shared books and discussions for years. Today, the most familiar among them are perhaps Carl Merz and Helmut Qualtinger, most famous to anglophone audiences from his role in the film of *The Name of the Rose*. However, Qualtinger's most significant contribution to Austria's post-war cultural recovery was likely his 1961 hour-long monologue about *Der Herr Carl*, a shop assistant with a proper "golden Viennese heart" who looked fondly back on the good old days under the Nazis. This monologue exposed the hypocrisy of an Austria that had, even before the end of World War II, been declared the first victim of Hitler's aggression.

As Rühm summarized in the volume's "Vorwort": "it quickly became clear that the majority [of Austrians] had a lot to object to about Nazi war politics, but very little, in principle, against its 'healthy' cultural politics"[6] ("Vorwort," 7). Additionally, postwar cultural politics had not improved: until 1960, for example, Brecht's work was still informally banned from the Viennese stage (Spiel, 84). The public was, in general, worried about its own Nazi past and in normalization; the younger generation was interested in preserving art as a social force in a culture that seemed to resist political interventions. Thus the *Wiener Gruppe* established a public face as part of that younger generation that was appalled at the politics and cultural politics of its elders. The hallmark of that reject was artmann's "eight-point-proclamation of the poetic act," issued in April, 1953, as part of their first great public happening, a funeral cortège through the Viennese streets.[7] In word and deed, the artist-participants proclaimed that art needed to live in the form of spontaneous acts rather than premeditated or calculated artworks; these acts did not need to be confined to words.

The Vienna Group continued in this vein for years, taking on current politics, especially in the European context. h. c. artmann, for instance, reacted to the founding of the new Austrian State (May 15, 1955) with an even more famous manifesto on May 17 of that year. It was signed by twenty-five others protesting various clauses in the treaty: ·

---

actors and cabaret performers onstage and in the electronic media in Vienna (Pabisch, 23).

6   "schnell wurde deutlich, dass die mehrheit wohl vieles gegen die nazistische kriegspolitik, aber im grunde nichts gegen die 'gesunde' kulturpolitik einzuwenden gehabt hatte."

7   "acht-punkte-proklamation des poetischen actes"; for the entire text, see Rühm, "Vorwort," 9–10.

MANIFESTO

we protest with all emphasis
against the macabre punch-and-judy show
which will be played out
with the reintroduction of an army,
no matter how constituted,
onto austrian soil ...

we all have had enough of this
from the last time—
this time, do it without us!

it represents a boundless temerity
a shameless act without compare
spreadinging anti-military propaganda
for ten years
yowling about dirt and degradation while preserving the
appearance of holiness
(the placards are still up ...)
and declaring all of it immoral
and then
in the first breezes of a so-called
final freedom
drafting a youth hardly old enough for school
to handle crap weapons
that is atavism!!!
that is neanderthal!!!
that is preparation
for legalized cannibalism!!![8]

---

8   MANIFEST

       wir protestieren mit allen nachdruck
       gegen das makabre kasperltheater
       welches bei wieder-einführung einer
       wie auch immer gearteten wehrmacht
       auf österreichischem boden
       zur aufführung gelangen würde ...

       wir alls haben genug
       vom letzten mal—
       diesmal sei es ohne uns!

       es ist eine bodenlose frechheit
       eine unverschämtheit sondergleichen

With such texts, they branded Austrian political neutrality as a "punch-and-judy show," a performance of national identity founded on a historical lie. Not surprisingly, these artists became feared public gadflies in Vienna, even when their work remained unpublished. Heimito von Doderer (Austria's most eminent novelist of the elder generation, himself implicated with Nazism, in some accounts) had tried to donate space in his newspaper column to publish their poetry, but an editor overrode the idea. Their manifestos today can straightforwardly be seen as early entries in what scholarship now calls *Nestbeschmutzerliteratur*—literature that fouls its own nest, considered a distinctly Austrian tradition.

Not surprisingly, given his prónounced poetic talent, artmann had the group's first publishing success with his 1958 collection of dialect poetry, *with black ink* (*med ana schwoazzn dintn*)—poems that readers of the time, even those from Vienna, recognized as being in dialect, but not in any actual dialect familiar to them. h. c. artmann was of Bohemian extraction and had access to several different Austrian dialects, which he reputedly could switch between and use to devastating purpose. He claims this collection to be in Breitensee dialect, a dialect from a working class neighborhood. Unfortunately, artmann's success branded them all as dialect poets, to the detriment of their other work. That success also began to loosen artmann from the rest of the Vienna Group; by 1960, artmann would leave Austria because of the intense branding imposed on him.[9] He was particularly disturbed

---

zehn jahre hindurch
antimilitärische propaganda zu betreiben
scheinheiling schmutz und schund zu jaulen
(noch kleben die plakate ...)
als unmoralisch zu deklarieren—
und dann
im ersten luftzug einer sogenannt
endgültigen freiheit
die kaum schulerwachsene jugend
an die dreckflinten zu pressen!!
das ist avatismus!!!!
das ist neanderthal!!!
das ist vorbereitung
zum legalisierten menschenfressertum!!!!" (Rühm, "Vorwort," 18–19)

9   As artmann expressed it: "Ich bin ausgewandert nach Schweden, 1960, nur deshalb, weil es hieß 'Der Mundartdichter Artmann. ... Ich habe vielleicht 0,5 Prozent in Dialekt geschrieben, und jetzt bin ich der Mundartdichter, bei gewissen Leuten" (artmann et al., "Xogt," 21). Rühm claims much greater distance of artmann from the group from the first, and that Bayer's accounts tend to overplay artmann's role (see the comments in his notes to Bayer's *Sämtliche Werke*, II.345–8, note to I.347).

that the horrors from everyday life depicted in his poetry volume (including rape and child abuse) were considered funny, when he had tried to show the cruel underbelly of Viennese life. As artmann summarized: "Vienna is a murderous city. One has to know that. We are no operetta-Kasperls. We are good murderers."[10]

As the 1950s yielded to the 1960s, the *Wiener Gruppe*, like many younger artists, began to feel decisively alienated from the public, as the avant-garde came under scrutiny as somehow alien to Austria: "'avant-gardists' are suspect from the first—they should all go abroad, we don't need 'em in austria."[11] Official culture was at that point aimed at propagating human virtue and nationalistic values by means of literature, citing Josephinian humanism as Austria's cultural legacy. The widespread assumption in the West was that literature was supposed to treat serious questions in dignified forms, leaving politicians to resolve the more mundane questions of everyday existence in peace.[12] Thus Austria's public media, controlled in Vienna, ended up in the hands of the conservative Österreichische Volkspartei (ÖVP).

The younger generation to which the *Wiener Gruppe* belonged was not so easily co-opted or silenced. In 1959, the *Forum Stadtpark* was founded in Graz, holding its first big exhibition in November, 1960. *Forum Stadtpark* and its magazine, *manuskripte*, became the public face of a 1960s artistic revolt in an Austria that would otherwise bypass the West's 1968 political turmoil. When a second postwar generation began writing around 1970, its members shared the *Wiener Gruppe*'s complaints about the *Kulturfunktionäre* in Vienna, the cultural bureaucrats who were threatening to turn Austrian culture into a museum. They also shared the platform of *Forum Stadtpark*. At one point, the *Forum Stadtpark* even wanted to found a second Austrian PEN-Club for authors living outside Vienna and its increasingly conservative artistic climate. They got as far as submitting a petition, which did not arrive

---

10 "Wien ist eine mörderische Stadt. Und das soll man auch wissen. Wir sind keine Operetten-Kasperln. Wir sind gute Mörder" (artmann et al., "Xogt," 35).

11 "rundfunk, fernsehen, verlagswesen beherrscht ein arroganter provizialismus. 'avantgardisten' sind von vornhinein suspekt, die sollen doch gleich ins ausland gehen, in österreich brauch ma des ned" (Rühm, "Vorwort," 33).

12 "In den fünfziger Jahren war die offizielle Kulturpolitik in besonderer Weise darauf aus, mit Hilfe von Literatur menschliche Tugenden und vaterländische Werte zu verbreiten. Literatur als Begleiterin der Restauration sollte letzte Fragen in würdiger Form behandeln, damit die Politiker die vorletzten Fragen des alltäglichen Zusammenlebens in Ruhe lösen können. 'Die Musterschüler von Kalkvater Grillparzer' (Konrad Bayer) waren die sinnstiftenden Autoren …" (Doppler, "Wiener Gruppe," 66). The Bayer quotation comes from a pamphlet about the "situation österreichischer literatur der gegenwart" (*Sämtliche Werke*, I.13–14).

in time to the appropriate meeting of the parent organization and so was never acted on.

Significantly, *Forum Stadtpark* also nurtured Peter Handke (b. 1942), who had moved to Graz and had contact with them since 1961—he read there for the first time in 1964:

> The *Wiener Gruppe* and their considerations about language philosophy cannot have been unfamiliar to [Handke]. As they do, Handke decries realistic writing that would consider literature as a continuation of speech by other means; he prefers a free space, in which experiments with language—language as a test of real existence—should take place. The form of language as its sole content, reality as the formal richness of reality, whose use in new literary experiments has impact on its substance—that is the basis that Handke shares with the *Wiener Gruppe*.[13]

Through *Forum Stadtpark*, two generations of Austrian artists kept up continuous public critiques, carrying forward a political agenda aimed at a domestic audience and at the morality of local political cultures.

Again, however, that Austrian space and its politics could never be considered in isolation. As Rühm put it: "For me, the border between Austria and Germany does not exist. It is a purely political border. I consider it all a German-language region."[14] To assume the existence of such a border between the cultures is nonsense: "That would be provincialism! ... that would be catastrophic."[15] In this sense, that Austrian space for politics that is so central to this generation again occupies a space larger than Austria itself. At the very least, it extends to Germany—and beyond that to Europe.

---

13 "Die 'Wiener Gruppe' und ihre sprachtheoretischen Überlegungen können ihm nicht unbekannt gewesen sein. Handke lehnt wie sie ein realistisches Schreiben, das die Literatur als Fortsetzung des Sprechens mit anderen Mitteln betreibt, zugunsten eines Freiraumes ab, innerhalb dessen das sprachliche Experiment, die Sprache als reale Existenzerprobung stattfinden soll. Die Form der Sprache als einziger Inhalt, die Realität als Formenreichtum der Sprache, deren neuartige Verwendung im literarischen Experiment bis auf die Gegenständliche zurückwirkt—das ist die Basis, die Handke mit der 'Wiener Gruppe' gemeinsam hat" (Böhm, 608).

14 "Für mich existiert die Grenze zwischen Österreich und Deutschland nicht. Es ist eine rein politische Grenze. Ich sehe das als deutschsprachiges Gebiet" (artmann et al., "Xogt," 32).

15 "Das wäre Provinzialismus! ... der katastrophal wäre" (artmann et al., "Xogt," 34).

Kasperl's new politics

Given the political climate that joined the *Wiener Gruppe* to *Forum Stadtpark*, it should come as no surprise that the stage figured prominently in the era's cultural program, and that the *Volkstheater* was called back into the theaters.[16] Moreover, the theater landscape familiar to Hofmannsthal and Schnitzler is also brought into the mix.[17] The Austrian stage authors of this generation repeatedly make the point of confronting traditions, just as the era's avant-garde was claiming to confront history. Just as importantly, those traditions were less nationalist than Austrian *and* European or world in inspiration. These avant-garde Austrians were at particular pains to join traditional cultural forms of expression with contemporary political speech, especially in the medium of literature. Again, Rühm frames this historical imperative succinctly: "I declare my total allegiance to my Viennese Tradition" (artmann et al., "Xogt," 36).[18] That is, he is neither conservative nor modernist, in the conventional sense; he is simply engaged with his present and with what from the past is still relevant and comprehensible, as were the majority of the *Wiener Gruppe* and the younger generation that grew up watching them. Moreover, where the first generation used *Forum Stadtpark* as their platform, the second postwar generation was also sponsored by Residenz Verlag (including, most notably, successful female authors like Barbara Frischmuth),

---

16 Gerhard Scheit refers to but underestimates the power of this comedy as political critique:

Auch das Kabarett der fünfziger Jahre bot im wesentlichen nur jenes Blödeln, an dem das Volks-Bildungs-Bürgertum sich gefahrlos ergötzen konnte. Es erstaunt nicht, daß zur selben Zeit die Wiener Gruppe mit einer Art Über-Kaberett aus solcher Subjektgewißheit des Spießertums auszubrechen und an die von Nationalsozialismus abseschnittenen avantgardistischen Traditionen Europas anzuschließen versuchte (Scheit, 181).

17 "Auf den ersten Blick glaubt man nach 1945 überhaupt nur alte Bekannte zu treffen. Es ist, als hätten eben auch die Topoi und Gestalten des Volkstheaters an der mythischen Gegenwart der Nation teil, als würden sie sich alle versammeln zur endgültigen nationalen Partie: ... in der Publikumsbeschimpfung der Wiener Gruppe sucht der Lustigmacher erneut den direkten Kontake zum Publikum (die Beschimpfung ist freilich nur ästhetischer Schein, in Wahrheit fraternisiert er augenzwinkernd mit seinem avantgardistischen Publikum); H. C. Artmann kopiert in seinen *kaspar*-Stücken mit erstaunlicher Perfektion Kurz-Bernardonsche Burlesken; und im Wiener Aktionismus feiert mit Blut und Kot der alte Wienerische Hanswurst fröhliche Urständ" (Scheit, 184–5).

18 "nur bin ich der Meinung, es gibt zwei Traditionen. Es gibt eine Tradition, die Gustav Mahler so schön als Schlamperei bezeichnet. Es gibt eine andere, die eine progressive Tradition ist. Und ich bekenne mich durchaus zu meiner Wiener Tradition" (artmann et al., "Xogt," 36).

and their politics was aimed at a kind of public education rather than oppositional politics in the narrow sense.[19]

Such progressive traditionalists incorporated modern European art into their own work—especially Dada, Surrealism, Existentialism, and the French Theater of the Absurd, made famous by Beckett and Ionesco (Riha, 157). They would also strive to recover the subversive potential of the traditions in which they worked, often by integrating elements from other dominant world literature—a move that Caribbean theorists of the postwar era would call "cannibalism."[20] Thus the *Wiener Gruppe* used montage and wrote *Lautgedichte*, poems written acoustically rather than according to the sense of words. In addition, artmann was particularly active in referencing contemporary world culture, including popular culture: Hollywood movies and movie stars, the baroque, American literature, and the *Volkstheater* (many of the same moves for which Elfriede Jelinek would become famous a generation later). These writers were developing a literature that did not simply take up exemplars and revivify them for the contemporary situation and audience (as one might perhaps describe Günter Grass' great novel *The Tin Drum* [*Die Blechtrommel*, 1959]), but also add a layer of metacommentary to stress performance and practical politics. Thus artmann's *No Pepper for Czermak* (*Kein Pfeffer für Czermak*, 1958, but published in 1969) references Johann Nestroy as a *Volkstheater* actor (Chotjewitz, 27); Bayer's *kasperl in the electric chair* [*kasperl am elektrischen stuhl*] (1962/3, published only in 1985) refers back to one of the tradition's famous early actors, Stranitzky (Spiel, 90; Böhm, 483).

As Schnitzler had already demonstrated in his puppet plays, the *Volkstheater* was straightforwardly adapted to an avant-garde aesthetics opposing the realistic theater favored by the dominant cultures (conservative or socialist) of post-World War II Europe as political parties moved to subsidize their own legitimate theaters, often to bring "high culture" to the Viennese masses.[21] As a theater that drew the

---

19 "Wer über Tradition spricht, tut gut daran, zwischen Tradition und Tradiitonalismus zu unterscheiden. Traditionalismus greift nach dem Vergangenen, Tradition lebt im Bewußtsein des Vergangenen, nimmt es auf, verbarbeitet und durchdringt es. ... Es handelt sich also nicht bloß um eine radikale Umpolumg, um Destruktion oder Negation herrschender Redeweisen. Es geht vielmehr um das Verhältnis von Anregung und Weiterbildung" (Doppler, 61).

20 This echoes the 1928 *Manifesto Antropófago* (*Cannibal Manifesto*) by the Brazilian poet and polemicist Oswald de Andrade (English translation, Leslie Bary, 1991, available online at http://www.academia.edu/1424345/Cannibalist_Manifesto (accessed May 4, 2015). The term is used to differentiate assimilation from a more active resistant consumption of colonizers' cultures.

21 For a comprehensive overview of this theater politics, see Evelyn

spectator into a common space, Schnitzler demonstrated how it could be brought to share premises with the most politically challenging of modern theaters, of famous contemporary world theaters, with dramaturgy aimed at undercutting dominant audience expectations (Riha, 159).[22] Postwar Austrian theater was particularly interested in public images of social and political morality and in breaking the fourth wall as expressly activist gestures.

The *Wiener Gruppe* was fully engaged in such new projects of activist public drama, aside from its other interventions into public consciousness. h. c. artmann borrowed from many world traditions in the 1950s, as he read extensively in literary history and the world classics. But from early on, his borrowings from the baroque were also evident, down to his habit of using anagrammatic pseudonyms and falsifying his biography, including the picaresque gesture of locating his birth in a mythical village rather than in Vienna's Breitensee—"St. Achatz liegt in Barockanien" (Haslinger, 35). Also within his local literary histories, artmann used Kaspar as his everyman in many contexts, even political ones (as in his 1955 manifesto against state militarism); he also wrote a number of poems and short plays using the figure. The most overtly political of these was *die liebe fee pocahontas, oder kasper als schildwache* [*the dear fairy pocahontas, or kaspar as sentry*], an anti-militarist play. In many of these contexts, artmann's Kaspars are also characterized as cannibals (*Menschenfresser* [Donnenberg, 159]), as they are in the manifesto, images which will recur in his work well into the 1970s.[23]

But the most explicit reference to the *Volkstheater* tradition, a play by artmann that looks very much like a Nestroy play, actually lacked the Kasperl character, even as it launched a direct attack on what had become a cherished stereotype of the Viennese bourgeoisie: *No Pepper for Czermak* (1958), subtitled a "Small Votive Offering for the Golden Viennese Spirit."[24] *Czermak* was presented in the *Theater am*

Deutsch-Schreiner, *Theater im "Wiederaufbau": Zur Kulturpolitik im österreichischen Parteien- und Verbändestaat* (2001).

22 "um ihm den Boden unter den Füßen wegzuziehen."

23 Mechthild Rausch has traced artmann's extensive borrowings of a wide selection of source materials into his *Punch* (1972), including an 1828 British play and a later text from Hamburg. Rausch does so to argue that his "poetic act" has very real historical ties, not just existentialist ones: "Das Kasperltheater war das Ersatztheater der 'kleinen Leute'; in ihm besaßen sie ein Instrument, sich selbst und ihre Probleme darzustellen und letztere, wenigstens im Spiel, lustvoll zu lösen" (Rausch, 173). She does not consider that theater part of a live tradition: "Er versucht nicht, den toten Kasper wiederzubeleben, sondern zitiert ihn und beschwört ihn in einem artistischen Ritual" (Rausch, 177).

24 "Votivsäulchen für das goldene Wiener Gemüt."

Fleischmarkt in Vienna, just before *med ana schwoazzn dintn* (1958) made artmann famous. Czermak takes us into the world of Grillparzer's *The Poor Fiddler* (*Der arme Spielmann*), to a small store revealed as a chamber of horrors instead of an apotheosis of the hard-working *petit bourgeoisie*.

The main figure is a grocer (*Greißler*, or *Kolonialwarenhändler*, a figure customarily named Pantalone in the *commedia dell'arte*) whose store gathers in the whole spectrum of Viennese society. We see him physically abusing his ward, Carolin, when she breaks a window she is cleaning. "Simply imposing just punishment, gentlemen!" he claims when a police detective comes in looking for a suspect (*Pfeffer*, 35).[25] That detective approves of Carolin's punishment, but then interrogates the grocer as to the whereabouts of Czermak, a musician who lives as a boarder (*in Untermiete*) across the street and who is under police surveillance. The grocer swears he would not even sell that man the pepper he wanted, nor help him in any way, shape, or form, and he pleads with the policeman to record that as his formal statement: "I don't want people to go around saying that Gschweidl needs to sell his wares to just anyone, or otherwise his store will have to close."[26] The suspect composer is a "Bohemian good-for-nothing" (*böhmischer Haderlump*, incorporating two senses of "Bohemian" [*Pfeffer*, 37]), ripe for criminal prosecution. These stock characters—grocer, cop, ward, and artist—begin a cycle that takes the audience play through a range of the stereotyped figures adduced in cavalcades of "the golden Viennese heart"—the goodly citizens of the city, doing good in the face of any adversity.

Frau Godl, a poor seamstress aged twenty-nine, owes money to the storekeeper, but she tries none the less to get some butter to entertain her guest, a man who might be her last chance at finding a bridegroom. Gschweidl's response is anything but golden: "Go back up to your fourth floor nicely and keep sewing" (*Pfeffer*, 38).[27] Instead of meekly submitting to his patronizing bullying, she threatens him with ripping open her bodice and yelling that he's up to something. He tells her to go haunt the cemetery—at the very moment when an undertaker (*Pompfüneberer*) comes in demanding beer. After the undertaker and the seamstress, a poor widow, Frau Hunger, enters, begging for a piece of blue paper to make a mustard plaster for her ill son. She can't afford a

---

25   "Nur der gerechten Strafe zuführen, die Herrschaften!"
26   "Ich will net, daß die Leut umeinandergehen und sagen: der Gschweidl hats nötig, seine Sachen zu verkaufen, weil er sonst sein Geschäft zusperren müßt."
27   "gehen S nur wieder schön in Ihnern dritten Stock auffi und nahn S' schön weiter."

doctor, since she is *eine Bettgeherin*, a woman so poor she rents a shift in a bed rather than a room. Naturally, she, too, is thrown out.

At this point, the plays moves from mean into surreal, and the stereotypes are marked as complete grotesques. The audience finds out that Gschweidl has a drawer containing two live but disembodied white hands that he treats like pets, feeding them more than he does his own niece—a visual joke referring to his grasping nature. The cast of types "from old Vienna" familiar from art and journalism then multiply: a water-seller argues about a delivery; an old woman (*eine alte Wiener* like Gschweidl himself) wants to hire—or is it buy?—his niece. The resolution is an act of god: Gschweidl has a stroke while tending his pet hands.

artmann provides two different endings for *Czermak*, each straight out of mythic old Vienna. In both, two angels appear, one good and one bad, speaking *schönbrunnerisch*, Habsburg aristocratic dialect. They watch the grocer have his stroke and then deck out the body as what is known as a *schöne Leich'*, a fine funeral or exquisite corpse; they use the appearance of Resi the flower seller as an opportunity to buy out all her wares at a good price. In the first variant of the ending, a female thief enters the room as the grocer lies there disabled; she steals the hands. The water-seller returns to continue the earlier argument, and Gschweidl asks for water: he is taken out to the well, presumably never to be seen again. In the second variant of the ending, Carolin finds him partially incapacitated, while the two angels comment on her innocence and high color. The stroke has rendered the grocer partially blind, and he begins to berate Carolin for poisoning him in the "best years of his life." The angels arrange for his second stroke and death, to the accompaniment of *Schrammelmusik*.[28] This resolution, with a Catholic-pathetic *deus ex machina*, comes straight out of plays by Ferdinand Raimund, where the gods intervene to set the mortals' situation right. But these angels speak Habsburg German, and they allow vengeance rather than justice *per se*. If this had been Raimund's theater, fate would have intervened to punish the guilty and help him change his mind, rather than murdering him.

Critics have taken this play as one of artmann's poetic acts, with "no clear window onto reality, no mimetic art ... but a metaphoric practice

---

28 Such parodies of "the golden Viennese heart" are not rare in the wake of the *Wiener Gruppe*. A notable entry is a recording of *Heurige und gestrige Lieder* (1979) sung by Helmut Qualtinger and André Heller that includes some original and some nineteenth-century *Wiener Lieder* with precisely such murderous plots. One of their songs has the refrain: "Krüppeln ham so was rührendes, Krüppeln ham was verführerischs. Wenn ich zu den Krüppeln geh, wird mir ums goldene Wiener Herz so warm und weh, o je."

in the medium of a mediated reference to reality." Yet artmann's grocer *is* realistic, if one values traditional discourses, in which stereotypes exert real force in establishing and maintaining understandings of "the Viennese character." The grocer *is* grasping—why else does he feed extra hands?—and he exercises complete control over his ward, including more extreme abuse than Dickens ever thought of. In this world, widows and seamstresses live at the sufferance of their nominal betters; male tradesmen, gainfully employed, become the petty tyrants of their environment and especially of the women associated with them[29] (demanding beer, just to show he can). The powers that be, including the police, run surveillance on anything and anyone who is *other*, different, without punishing real abuse or injustice—a Bohemian with no money and progressive artistic ideas is considered as more dangerous than an abusive domestic tyrant. And only through money or sex can women exert any power at all (as Schnitzler already rendered visible as Vienna's particular truth).

artmann's grocer not only exists in the tradition of the *commedia dell'arte*, he has descendents, as well: by 1961, he finds his parallel in the legendary social-critical consciousness of Merz and Qualtinger's *Herr Karl*, their little grocery clerk who waxes nostalgic about the good old days in the Nazi era. And in the mid-1970s, singer-songwriter Georg Danzer writes and sings about a birthday celebration for "Der alte Wessely" in a neighborhood bar. The song has a disturbing refrain: "Mr. Wessely, nobody can do the Hitler salute as well as you do."[30]

Where the critics claim *Czermak* as aesthetic, the play more clearly shows the nightmare underbelly of current Vienna, a world closer to the twilight spaces and morality of *The Third Man* than to "the good old days": prejudiced, power- and money-hungry, hiding behind façades of respectability, justice, and religion. But where Nestroy would have allowed a clever servant to triumph and bring the social order back into balance (or where Grillparzer allowed his *Poor Fiddler* to be mourned by a good woman), artmann finds only domestic violence, closed spaces, vengeance, and small-mindedness. The "golden Viennese heart" (and soul) has only hands, no mind or heart, and a bloodthirsty streak that does indeed allow the city to eat people alive, consume their hearts and live under the façade of quaint traditionalism. *No Pepper for Czermak* speaks for itself as a parody of the petit bourgeois mindset of a conservative postwar era. Yet it is also a play written with the stock characters

---

29   This becomes a theme for women writers of the 1970s and 1980s in Austria, under the rubric of critiques of *Alltagsfaschismus*. See, for example, Brigitte Schwaiger, *Wie kommt das Salz ins Meer?* (1977).

30   "Herr Wessely, kana kann den Hitlergruaß so guat wia Sie!" Available on the album *Traurig aber wahr* (2011).

of the Viennese folk theater in a city that still knew the tradition, the plays by Raimund and Nestroy that cycle onto the playbills of the *Burgtheater* and the *Theater in der Josefstadt*, along with those of Ödön von Horváth, who, in plays like *Geschichten aus dem Wienerwald* (*Tales from the Vienna Woods*, 1931), offers the most famous contemporary dramatic version of this critique.

artmann's play therefore also underscores the kind of cultural critique that the culture bureaucrats of postwar Vienna were trying to bury under the legend of and advertising for the "golden Viennese heart." Their vision of Vienna was Biedermeier, quiescent, and picturesque, centered around the *Ringstrasse* as a gay apocalypse. artmann's Vienna is indeed a continuation of the baroque and the Biedermeier— thus the Habsburg avenging angels who appear in it, but that city is also murderous, vicious, and unkind, a place where a façade of forced quiescence covers over domestic and political violence of all sorts. That will include the legacies of the Nazi era and the patriarchal bourgeoisie alike that are associated with the term *Alltagsfaschismus* (every-day fascism). Not surprisingly, then, artmann was not the only one of the *Wiener Gruppe* to take up Kaspar and his theater to lambaste Vienna's murderous character in the purportedly quiescent Austrian 1960s.

Electric Kasperl: Self-immolating literature succumbs to the public

Konrad Bayer modernized the Kasperl problematic most decisively in his *kasperl am elektrischen stuhl*, which was published by Gerhard Rühm from a typescript found in Bayer's papers after his 1964 death. The text's use of dialect may have been random, but it agrees with artmann about the murderous conditions of Vienna's everyday life and how it can be presented onstage. Rühm notes, for example, that this *kasperl* had characters named after current critics: "some personal names were twisted versions of those of certain Viennese contemporaries (critics) who bayer felt were particularly unpleasant, for instance schulberg for friedrich torberg, espenlaub fur lieselotte espenhahn, weissenpeter for peter weiser" (Rühm, in Bayer, I.340).[31] But *kasperl am elektrischen stuhl* is also critically embedded in germanophone and European literary traditions, taking over conceits again most familiar to German literary studies from Ludwig Tieck's *Der Puss in Boots*, just as Schnitzler had in his *Zum Großen Wurstl*.

Copying Tieck closely, Bayer's play opens with an audience on the stage, commenting on the action in the auditorium and on the stage

---

31 "einige personennamen [waren] verballhornungen von solchen gewisser wiener zeitgenossen (kritiker), die bayer besonders unangenehm auffielen, z.b. schulberg für friedrich torberg, espenlaub für lieselotte espenhahn, weissenpeter für peter weiser" (notes to the *Sämtliche Werke*, II.340).

alike. They remark on a critic's late arrival, but a female audience member has already usurped his role, disapproving in advance of the play to come, since it does not conform to what the critics favor (a variant of a scene from Tieck): "sir, this beginning does not conform to the requirements of the modern drama and thus it is tasteless" (Bayer, I.261).[32] As more critics enter the scene, the audience turns to typical Viennese *Bühnentratsch*, stage door gossip about who sleeps with whom, which theater people are related to which officials, and the like—all the favorite tabloid fodder for contemporary Vienna. The staged audience, however, actually leaves the hall before the play starts because they claim they have stood too long and need refreshments. Bayer's play, therefore, closely mimics the actual behaviors and attitudes associated with the day's Viennese audiences.

Bayer's inner play follows Tieck's *Puss in Boots*, as well: it is an animal fable, with an evil twist. An announcer (*sprecher*) declaims a prologue on the theater, then the audience hears a lion introducing himself as the ruler of the world, the scourge of the West:

> you miserable people, you mortal owners of the earth, the sea depths, and the vault of the heavens, it is i: the lion of everywhere, ruler over the seven seas of the earth and just as much earth, descendent of maldoror [the count of Lautreamont's hero], son of melmoth, son of hugo schenk [a serial killer], bastard of his majesty the kaiser maximilian of austria and tyrol, son of heliogabal [a decadent roman emperor], son of astaroth [a demon], son of haiphaistos and a hippopotamus, subscriber to daily papers and reading groups, i am evil, the omnipotent prince of the globe, i am the false shadow in a dark house gate, i am the cold hand in the clothes-closet, number ninety-nine in the little lotto, the blood spatter on the autobahn, chief of police in 27 developed states. riches and power, lust and honor I distribute according to my will to my devoted servants. (Bayer, I.264)[33]

---

32 "mein herr, dieser anfang entspricht nicht den anforderungen des modernen dramas und ist abgeschmackt."

33 "ihr armseligen menschen, ihr sterblichen besitzer des erdbodens, der tiefsee und des himmelszeltes, ich bin es: der löwe von überall, herrscher über sieben weltmeere und ebensoviel erde, nachkomme des maldoror, sohn des melmoth, sohn des hugo schenk, bastard seiner majestät des kaisers maximilian von österreich und tirol, sohn des heliogabal, sohn des astaroth, sohn des haiphaistos mit einem nilpferd, abonnent von tageszeitungen und lesezirkeln, ich bin das übel, der omnipotente fürst des erdballs, ich bin der falsche schatten im finsteren haustor, ich bin die kalte hand im kleiderkasten, nummer neunundneunzig im kleinen lotto, der blutfleck auf der autobahn, chef der polizei in 27 kulturstaaten. reichtum und macht, wollust und ehre teile ich aus nach meinem belieben unter meine ergebenen diener."

Confronting this fearsome beast—a spawn of decadent literature and decadent politics alike—is Apollo, who appears dressed as a policeman brandishing a bloody club ("in the service for 30 years, party member," the announcer notes [Bayer, I.265]).[34] Just as the lion represents the night terrors of everyday life, Apollo identifies himself explicitly as one of artmann's everyday murderers: "it is balm to my eyes, when I can graze them on human blood" (Bayer, I.264).[35]

Mythology continues to converge with topical references. Apollo, who traditionally should be able to charm the animals through music, falls into a faint, losing his ability to speak but refusing to be institutionalized. The lion prompts Apollo to speak, trying first to egg him on in dialect, then in the stereotyped forms of standard speech, and even through physical coercion:

> i will only say:
> > object of a sentence (boxes him on the ear)
> > and
> > proposition of a sentence (boxes him on the ear)
> > main clause (hits him on the nose)
> > and
> > subordinate clause (hits him on the nose)
> i hope that suffices. (Bayer, I.265)[36]

The lion comments that he has gained language, just as Apollo has lost it (Bayer, I.266). Eventually, Apollo reclaims his ability to talk about the past. This reenactment of an individual's loss and reemergence into the social space of speech will recur in Handke's *Kaspar* (also masked behind an announcer, *sprecher*, there termed *einsager*).

Again like Tieck, Bayer builds a figure from the folk comedy into the play, a third level of allusion incorporated into the text. The scene is interrupted as Kasperl comes up to report: "'scuse me, i killed my wife" (Bayer, I.267).[37] When he receives no response, he switches to standard German to report very officially (*melden*) that he has thrown

---

34 "seit 30 jahren im dienst, mitgleid der partei."
35 "das ist mir augensalbe, wenn ich im menschenblut kann meine augen weiden."
36 "ich sage nur:
satzgegenstand (gibt ihm eine ohrfeige)
und
satzaussage (gibt ihm eine ohrfeige)
hauptsatz (schlägt ihn auf die nase)
und
nebensatz (schlägt ihn auf die nase)
ich hoffe das genügt."
37 "bidscheen i hob mei frau umbrocht."

his wife out the window. Falling back into his role as policeman and less-than-human being, Apollo simply asks if the corpse is blocking traffic. Dutiful citizen Kasperl responds that the ambulance has already been there, and that the *chefarzt* (head physician) gave him official confirmation (*bestätigung*) of his wife's death—all the paperwork is in place, which is all one ought to care about, after all—perhaps another clear allusion to Grillparzer's *Poor Fiddler*.

This interruption does not please the stage audience, which demands a return to the "real" play about Apollo and the lion. Just as Tieck's poet tries to intercede with the *Puss in Boots* audience, Bayer's *sprecher* apologizes for Kasperl: "sorry, but the guy is an ignoramus" (Bayer, I.267).[38] Two more audience members try to leave, despite their free tickets. Apollo simply wants Kasperl to go away, especially since he lacks the permit requisite for killing a wife (Bayer, I.268). Such permits, you see, would help the police in finding killers afterward. As the situation comes to a head, Kasperl gets fined 50 schillings for this legal problem: "for willful neglect of lawful pre-notification without judicial recourse" (Bayer, I.268).[39] Apollo clubs Kasperl, as the lion comments bloodlessly: "resistance to the power of the court" (Bayer, I.268).[40]

Bayer builds a twist into his borrowing. While Tieck has both a poet and an audience of everyday people in his play, Bayer's Kasperl is himself a playwright, the author of the animal fable, the play's outside turning into its inside: "i like the theater they appear in" (Bayer, I.269).[41] Now a criminal instead of the people's representative, Kasperl is imprisoned in a cage and begins to deliver monologues (*monologisieren*; Bayer, I.269), which is boring, as the *sprecher* and audience members A and B confirm. Now Kasperl begins to talk to the audience about the conditions under which he wrote the play, and about his reasons for playing in it: "first i earn more if i act in it myself" (Bayer, I.270),[42] as Nestroy himself and many other comic actors realized.

Bayer, however, realizes that art doesn't work just this way any more, and so he has a reporter (*giselher*, a royal name from the *Nibelungenlied*) begin a long interview with Kasperl on his work and his approach to language, both characters switching between standard German polite phrases and more germane statements in dialect. Their interview culminates in a long exchange questioning why one ought to

---

38 "tut mir leid aber das ist ein ignorant."
39 "wegen mutwilliger vernachlässigung der voranmeldepflicht ohne möglichkeit von rechtsmitteln."
40 "widersetzlichkeit gegen die amtsgewalt."
41 "i moch theater in den sie vuakomman."
42 "erstens verdien ich mehr, wenn ich selber mitspiel."

talk at all, discussing it as everything from sounds to noise, and noting
that it is dangerous to be taken at one's word:

> reporter: do you speak sometimes?
> kasperl: yes, but never except to amuse myself.
> reporter: do you like to talk?
> kasperl: i only speak to kill time.
> reporter: but it seems to me that speaking is a very dangerous
> amusement?
> kasperl: that's true, but only when someone listens. (Bayer, I.271)[43]

The on-stage audience is beginning to hate the fact that its play has
been hijacked by the author and the media. To quiet them, the *sprecher*
promises that Kasperl will stop soon.

Eventually, Kasperl's frame of reference disintegrates as he tries to
narrate his family's life, mixing its past, present, and future:

> kasperl: believe you me, i want to reveal myself for as long as my
> situation permits. i want to explain everything just as it was, as it
> will be, as it will not be, as it is not, as it never could have been,
> as it was not, as it could be, as it could have been, as it would be
> able to be. (Bayer, I.274)[44]

The result is chaos, with everything, even the number of his children,
still in doubt. His sick wife is revealed as a fiction—he has made her up,
he acknowledges. In frustration, the reporter tries to kill Kasperl with
a dagger, which gives Apollo a chance to reclaim the scene for a proper
curtain-dropper. But the aesthetic damage has been done, as the critic
weissenpeter notes:

> the way the press is presented is unnatural, miserable, one-sided,
> and it applies only to certain elements of the tabloid press whose
> names i do not care to name and whose members have learned

43　"reporter: sprechen sie manchmal?
　　kasperl: ja, aber nie anders, als mich zu unterhalten.
　　reporter: sprechen sie gern?
　　kasperl: ich sprech nur zum zeitvertreib.
　　reporter: aber mich dünkt, das sprechen sei eine sehr gefährliche
　　unterhaltung?
　　kasperl: das ist wahr, doch nur, wenn man zuhört."
44　"kasperl: glauben sie mir, ich will mich offenbaren, bis meine lage es erlaubt. ich
　　will alles sagen, wie es war, wie es ist, wie es sein wird, wie es nicht sein wird,
　　wie es nicht ist, wie es niemals hätte sein können, wie es nicht war, wie es sein
　　könnte, wie es hätte sein können, wie es würde sein können."

their taste, as i know, from serial detective novels of the turn of the century, like "the stone of the offense," "pain in the ass," "hound of the baskervilles" and the like. i don't let myself do that. (Bayer, I.277)[45]

A voice from the crowd approves of his outburst, as if he were a general to be followed into battle: "for god and weissenpeter!" (Bayer, I.278).[46] Theater wars literally break out here, as happened in Vienna under the watchful eyes of the press.

The play culminates with the *sprecher* calling for the electric chair to punish Kasperl (for the disturbance, if not for the putative murder). But a female audience member interrupts, to close the circle on the possible narrative:

halt! This man is mine. before he leaves us he should share my bed, be mine, feel the warmth of a sympathetic female breast, be consoled, … should feel, in its smallest form, the germ yes the family, of what society means. Come to me!! into my arms! kaspar! you! lost soul! (Bayer, I.278)[47]

Kasperl saves himself from this ultimate everyday horror—and probably from the future perfect "I will have killed my wife," as well— by jumping on to the electric chair and having the switch pulled: "go! start!" (Bayer, I.278).[48]

Bayer thus ends his sketch by quite literally executing the author who lost control of the play—or someone else, since Kasperl is *am elektrischen stuhl*, next to it or at the moment when he confronts it, not necessarily on or in it. Someone needs to be executed here, but it is not clear who: the modern public, credulous, gossipy, and mercenary in siding with self-styled critics, has hijacked the play from both the author and his characters. The "everyday murderers" of Bayer's Vienna (the policeman, critics, and the indiscriminate public) will kill the "golden Viennese heart" of this Kasperl, aided and abetted by the

---

45 "die darstellung der presse ist widernatürlich, ekelhaft, einseitig und trifft nur gewisse elemente eines boulevardblättchens, dessen namen ich nicht nennen will und dessen mitglieder ihren geschmack, wie mir bekannt, an kriminalfortsetzungsromanen der jahrhundertwende, wie "der stein des anstosses," "pain in the ass," "hund von baskerville" und ähnlichem bilden. ich verbitte mir das!"

46 "mit gott und weissenpeter!!"

47 halt! dieser mann gehört mir. ehe er von uns geht, soll er mein lager teilen, mein eigen sein, die wärme einer weiblichen mitfühlenden brust verspüren, getröstet sein, … soll kosten in ihrer kleinsten form, keimzelle jawohl familie, was die sozietas bedeutet. zu mir! in meine arme! kaspar! du! ein verlorener!

48 "los! anfangen!"

media and by the various powers that be (too many of whom seem to be thirty-year party members …).

Where Tieck's Hanswurst argued for an art that connected with the people, then, Bayer's may be arguing for the end of the theater itself. Or perhaps of the society that is its audience. After all, his play-within-a-play unfolds outwards into official Vienna, and its author is executed by the media and the public. Bayer's Vienna is thus not only murderous, it is judge, jury, and executioner of individual visions. And his use of the Kasperl figure is anything but the "progressive traditionalism" that critics accuse them of.

The late blooming Kasperl: Handke performs tradition

These avant-garde Kasperl plays were experimental, but they did have the potential to be played in theaters (or at least in cellar theaters): they are funny, pithy, and dark. In other words, they already show the control of public critical space with the kind of social-critical voice that is considered the purview only of a later generation of Austrian authors, especially Peter Handke and Elfriede Jelinek. We have already noted that Handke moved to Graz and learned at least part of his trade from his contacts with *Forum Stadtpark*, but the connections rest in how postwar Austria educated its artistic voices. In 2006, Christine Riccabona, Erika Wimmer, and Milena Meller documented what are called *Die Österreichischen Jugendkulturwochen 1950–1969 in Innsbruck*, a series of intensive summer schools for new art in Austria, where old masters mixed with new talent (Jelinek was one of the main reasons that state funding was withdrawn from that project, because she was already veering toward political pornography, which "good citizens" balked at paying for). Austrian art was there turned into a living legacy there.

Other documentation exists, as well. For instance, Peter Handke early signaled his willingness to link traditional stage forms and new politics. One of his breakthrough absurdist plays was 1968's *Kaspar* (significantly, with a premiere directed by Klaus Peymann, who later would come to bedevil the *Burgtheater* itself). While that title in part refers to the legend of *Kaspar Hauser* (child victim of political violence in the Biedermeier era), the play is also structured as a *Kasperl* play, and as a critique of modern culture, with its depersonalization and regimentation. In general, however, critics have tended to disassociate Handke from the Vienna Group, despite the fact that Handke's debut falls chronologically paired with artmann's various Kasper and *Volkstheater* work and Bayer's *kasperl*. Moreover, his purportedly international inspiration and address is also theirs—both generations were reading and viewing widely.

Handke's own story is told differently in German literary history than it appears in his Austrian context. His most famous "speech play" (*Sprechstück*), *Offending the Audience* (*Publikumsbeschimpfung*), premiered in Frankfurt in 1966. That is also the year he denounced Group 47 at Princeton, in a very public performance announcing the death of traditional literature (and accusing Group 47 of representing that traditionalism)—a critique performed by a writer insisting on a younger voice, sporting long hair and jeans as his personal protest against the German establishment. Immediately thereafter, Handke took up the *Volkstheater* tradition, turning to his own, somewhat more internationalized *Kaspar* in 1968, followed by a play that is another overt nod to the *commedia dell'arte* or *Volkstheater* tradition, his 1969 *The Ward Wants to be the Guardian* (*Der Mündel will Vormund sein*), which also premiered in Frankfurt.

Where artmann's and Bayer's Kaspars are undeniable witnesses attesting to problems in current political situations, however, Handke's *Kaspar* has been almost exclusively associated with the so-called Austrian tradition of the philosophy of language. Critics also see his relation to international Theater of the Absurd, even as they overlook its direct political references. A common evaluation of *Kaspar* sounds like it is a play written by an existentialist: "The meaning of language is heightened to be the basis for human existence ... just as, slightly later, in *Kaspar*, the process of individual growth and the mechanisms for personal awakening are completed through language."[49] This despite Handke's declaration of allegiance to Brecht and hence to a political theater. Note, too, that the French Theater of the Absurd used parodies of French Neoclassicist plays to make its political statements, just as the Vienna Group used its indigenous *Volkstheater*.

Handke also proclaims his allegiance to street theater, in manifestos that parallel the *Wiener Gruppe*'s analyses of an essentially bankrupt theater that needs to be driven beyond its own limits: "Since it is a social institution, the theater seems to me to be unusable for changing social institutions,"[50] he notes in an essay entitled "Street Theater" (*Strassentheater*). Thus Handke is also protesting the growing stagnation of Austrian theater culture (represented in growing state financial allocations to the *Burgtheater* and the *Staatsoper*, to the exclusion of new theater).

Handke's *Kaspar* is an example of his own ability to layer political and aesthetic concerns from several generations. A core line in it is a familiar allusion to Kaspar Hauser, the famous orphan who had been imprisoned in a basement for years, removed from human contact

---

49 "Die Bedeutung der Sprache wird bis zur Grundlage menschlicher Existenz gesteigert ... wie wenig später in *Kaspar*, der Erwachensvorgang und Erweckungsmechanismus durch Sprache vollzogen" (Böhm, 609).

50 Das Theater als gesellschaftliche Einrichtung scheint mir unbrauchbar für eine Änderung gesellschaftlicher Einrichtungen" ("Straßentheater," 305).

(possibly because he was an heir to a throne disputed by Napoleon). Once he escaped, he was considered developmentally delayed, especially in language. Significantly (and unremarked by critics), stage directions indicate that Handke's *Kaspar* is to be dressed like a figure from the *commedia dell'arte*, in the baggy clothes that specifically allude to a Viennese version of the traditional Kasperl figure. Moreover, that multiple Kaspars appear in the latter part of the play signals Handke's detailed awareness of the tradition's dramaturgical conventions, since Kaspar is the only figure in the Italian *commedia* who can be doubled, who is allowed to appear in more than one mask at a time on stage.

Moreover, while the stage space in *Kaspar* appears to preserve the separation between the audience and the stage by allowing the auditorium to remain dark (unlike *Offending the Audience*, which breaks the fourth wall and leaves auditorium lights up), *Kaspar's* space is actually also anti-illusionary, since much of the text also comes from the space beyond the fourth wall. The voiceovers running through the play, piped into the theater auditorium over an intercom system, unite the audience with the stage in a shared third realm—an electronic one. In this sense Kaspar Hauser turned *commedia dell'arte* Kaspar now becomes the Kasperl of the puppet theater that Schnitzler also used, moved by the acts of unseen others. Handke's unseen forces, however, are modern voices: a set of announcers who are overstepping that role and so become *Einsager* (a portmanteau word mixing *Ansager*—announcer, and *einreden*—to convince of or brainwash). This Kasperl is, in another international allusion, also a Frankenstein's monster, something other than human created by the perverted technocratic skills of humanity. (Note that Jelinek will write plays that expand on the Western canon of monsters, as well.)

Handke first marks his stage itself as a non-realistic space, not just an anti-illusion one:

> The play *Kaspar* does not show how it REALLY IS or REALLY WAS with Kaspar Hauser. It shows what IS POSSIBLE with someone. It shows how someone can be made to speak through speaking. The play could also be called *speech torture*. To formalize this torture process it is suggested that a kind of magic eye be constructed above the ramp. This eye, without however diverting the audience's attention from the events on stage, indicates, by blinking, the degree of vehemence with which the PROTAGONIST is addressed. The more vehemently he defends himself, the more vehemently the magic eye blinks. (*Kaspar*, 59)[51]

---

51 "Das Stück *Kaspar* zeigt nicht, wie ES WIRKLICH IST, oder WIRKLICH WAR mit Kaspar Hauser. Es zeigt, was MÖGLICH IST mit jemandem. Es zeigt,

This space implicates the audience and Kaspar in a common speech torture and reactive space, as the magic eye—a Masonic eye, perhaps, as a tribute to Mozart, or from the US dollar bill?—looks down and records the intensity of interaction.

Handke, as noted, also clearly marks his Kaspar as a *commedia dell'arte* figure in his dress and behavior—a modern clown-everyman, destined to wreak havoc in public order in his *commedia dell'arte* persona:

> For example, he has on a round, broad-brimmed hat with a band; a light-colored shirt with a closed collar; a colorful jacket with many (roughly seven) metal buttons; wide pants; clumsy shoes; on one shoe, for instance, the very long laces have become untied. He looks droll. The colors of his outfit clash with the colors on stage. Only on the second or third glance should the audience realize that his face is a mask; it is a pale color; it is life-like; it may have been fashioned to fit the face of the actor. It expresses astonishment and confusion. (*Kaspar*, 63)[52]

Handke's Kaspar, however, does not immediately take up his role as Kasperl, who should be on the street confronting his world. Or does he? In one sense, he confronts what might be the new public space of the 1960s: the anonymous announcers of the electronic media who utter sentences over the loudspeaker, programming Kaspar into the platitudes characteristic of the "ordinary people." Through their actions, he becomes a creature of the electronic media: "My love of order and cleanliness never gives cause for rebuke."[53] At some point,

---

wie jemand durch Sprechen zum Sprechen gebracht werden kann. Das Stück könnte auch "Sprechfolterung" heißen. Zur Formalisierung dieser Folterung wird dem aufführenden Theater vorgeschlagen, für jeden Zuschauer sichtbar, zum Beispiel über die Rampe, eine Art von magischem Auge aufzubauen, das, ohne freilich die Zuschauer von dem Geschehen auf der Bühne abzulenken, durch sein Zusammenzucken jeweils die Sprechstärke anzeigt, mit der auf den HELDEN eingeredet wird" (*Kaspar*, 7). Note that the play has an official English translation, which is used in the present text.

52 "Er trägt etwa einen runden breiten Hut mit einem Band. Erträgt ein heller Hemd mit geschlossenen Kragen. Seine Jacke ist farbenfroh und mit vielen (etwa sieben) Metallknöpfen besetzt. Seine Hose ist weit. Er trägt klobige Schuhe; an einem Schuh ist zum Beispiel das sehr lange Schuband aufgegangen. Er sieht 'pudelnärrisch' aus. Die Farben seiner Kleidung schlagen sich mit den übrigen Farben auf der Bühne. Erst auf den zweiten oder dritten Blick erkennen die Zuschauer, daß sein Gesicht eine Maske ist; ihre Gesichtfarbe ist 'bleich'; sie sieht sehr lebensecht aus; sie ist dem Gesicht vielleicht angepaßt; ihr Ausdruck ist der Ausdruck der Verwunderung und Verwirrung." (*Kaspar*, 10)

53 "Meine Ordnungsliebe und Sauberkeit geben nie zu Tadel Anlaß" (*Kaspar*, 56).

six other Kaspars appear, at least one of whom is crippled, to increase the mayhem. The announcers only stop inculcating platitudes once the other Kaspars are there—when the original has, quite literally, become everyman, a member of a faceless mass that looks like him (Handke indicates they, too, may wear masks).

Loudspeakers also elide the difference between the spaces occupied by Kaspar and the audience. As noted, the performance does not start with the darkening of the theater and opening of a curtain, thus setting the audience apart from the stage space (a convention only of the latter nineteenth century, not the era of the original *Volkstheater*). In this case, a performance space is gradually filled with "conventional wisdom," as the voiceovers offer fragments of social commonplaces, including rules like table manners. Eventually, the Kaspars' masks are altered, to take on expressions of satisfaction, and the central Kaspar's voice comes to resemble that of the announcers. He begins to comment on his own experience of being human, parroting terms they would understand: "I learned to fill / all empty spaces with words (*Kaspar*, 124).[54] This is not positive, as the other Kaspars signal by making odd noises: "no one / may miss the drill" (*Kaspar*, 125).[55] Ultimately, the first Kaspar realizes darkly that he does not know what he is saying: "Every sentence / is for the birds" (*Kaspar*, 132).[56] He begins to look at himself retrospectively, providing a self-interpretation: "All at once I distinguished myself / from the furnishings. / Already with my first sentence I / was trapped" (*Kaspar*, 137).[57] What he has lost is a kind of innocence: "I no longer understand anything literally" (*Kaspar*, 138),[58] and his sense of security with it—"with each new sentence I become nauseous" (*Kaspar*, 139).[59]

His last lines in the play are significant, much more so in the German original than in the standard English translation. Kaspar utters each word disjointedly, and the typography suggests that they have a distinct pause between them: "ich: / bin: / nur: / zufällig: / ich:" (*Kaspar*, 84–5), a line which, inexplicably, is rendered in the translation as a repeated "goats and monkeys" (*Kaspar*, 140) instead of "I am myself only by chance." With this line, Handke comes full circle on a link between social and linguistic critique. That statement is uttered as six other Kaspars create an inarticulate din, just as the main Kaspar realizes he has become a creation of mass culture.

---

54 "Ich lernte alles was leer war / mit Wörtern zu füllen" (*Kaspar*, 69).
55 "keiner darf den Drill / vermissen (*Kaspar*, 70).
56 "Jeder Satz / ist für die Katz" (*Kaspar*, 76).
57 "Auf einmal habe ich mich von der Einrichtung unterschieden. Schon mit meinem ersen Satz bin ich idie Falle gegangen" (*Kaspar*, 82).
58 "Ich nehme nichts mehr wörtlich" (*Kaspar*, 82).
59 "bei jedem neuen Satz wird mir übel" (*Kaspar*, 83).

In this final tableau, Handke alludes to an issue familiar from late 1960s, especially familiar in Anglo-American spheres from the work of Marshall McLuhan ("the medium is the message" is his iconic pronouncement). Handke's critique is also aimed specifically at mass culture, in the form of the electronic announcers' voices that program this Kaspar into his identity as one of a small mob of identical Kasperls. Handke has thus used a traditional Viennese everyman to critique the every-Kaspar in his Europe, modeled as a media-governed space in which we all share (as spectators or in our real lives). This Kaspar emerges into the public under the careful tutelage of what Hans Magnus Enzensberger called "The Consciousness Industry" ("Bewußtseinsindustrie" [1962]). Yet his role is here marked as more than that of a philosophical skeptic of language; he is explicitly made a victim of the mass media. Since the traditional Kaspar is always a "little man" in the middle of working society, the conclusion is inevitable: this Kaspar had been modernized into a member of the great, essentially inarticulate, masses created by the media culture whose voices come over the ubiquitous loudspeakers of society.

Like h. c. artmann or Bayer, then, Handke thus uses a hypertrophied version of the Kasperl-theater to critique the modern West. The theater, handled as both non-illusionist and non-realistic, helps him to recreate the late twentieth century's bourgeoisie, dependent as it is on the mass media—on disembodied, electronic voices which organize public consciousness, interacting only with themselves. The audience and Kaspar both begin to see how that media system works to destroy individuals, just as clearly as artmann's audience must see the violence concealed by the "golden Viennese heart."

A year after *Kaspar,* Handke uses the form of the *Volkstheater* again. His 1969 play, *The Ward Wants to Be the Guardian"* (*Das Mündel will Vormund sein*) uses another stock figure from the *commedia dell'arte,* Pantalone, to stylize and modernize a very old plot: a foolish older uncle who has been appointed guardian for a dependent, usually penniless, ward abuses his position to try to marry either that ward or his ward's intended (a plot familiar from Donizetti's *Don Pasquale,* and varied in Rossini's *Barber of Seville*). Handke presents the characters (again wearing traditional half-masks) in a mute play, a dumb show, but calibrates the outcome of the situation in more modern terms (almost as violent and senseless as the *Funny Games* of Michael Haneke's 1997 Austrian film and its 2008 US remake). Handke's oppressed ward will not simply outwit the guardian and marry the intended, but instead will revolt against him in a senseless, soundless fight to the death.

As the play opens, the audience sees a bucolic scene on a farm, the porch of an old house in front of a cornfield. And the ward seems happy—but that face is a mask: "She presents a face, which represents a considerable amount of joy" (*Mündel*, 158).[60] The two figures, ward and guardian, move into the house, sit down at a table together, and begin to play power games with the objects of everyday life, struggling for custody of their common space as they go about the routines of mundane existence.[61] They mime disputes about who controls the newspaper, the space for leaning their arms on the table, and the like.

Then, finally, chaos erupts onto the scene: the guardian begins to beat on a pan, and then reenacts a ritual from the Feast of the Epiphany (January 6, Twelfth Night). He burns incense and chalks the conventional invocation that one finds on farmhouse lintels over doors in the country: "K+M+B" (*Mündel*, 273), a tribute to the Three Kings' gifts of frankincense and myrrh. This Guardian has thus become a star-singer, the herald of the three kings who seek the Christ Child as the new king of the world. Twelfth Night is also, however, the time of revels and of social reversals, as the play's title signals in more concrete form—he will be at best the herald of the anti-Christ.

What the guardian finds, instead of blessings and revels, is a ward who pelts him with kitchen objects, causing his nose to bleed—an obstreperous baby, who enrages the guardian to the point where he pelts her with dishes and bottles. Eventually, they get outside the house and have a standoff duel with a beet slicer. Then, in almost complete darkness, the audience hears heavy breathing and a death rattle. The final scene reveals the ward, alone, using what had been the guardian's tools. The scene evokes the mayhem of the *commedia dell'arte*, but here the business is serious, literally deadly. The turnabout festivities from Twelfth Night, that might in earlier times have signaled the metaphoric death of the older generation and its power, now bring real death: the real threat of a youth revolt which the older generation will unleash if they, like Pantalone, are the foolish old uncles who stand in their wards' ways.

These two early Handke plays thus drive the conventions of the *commedia dell'arte* into their extreme forms to echo the kind of despair about contemporary society that permeated the work of artmann and Bayer. Yet Handke's world suggests that the bourgeoisie should expect a youthquake or armed rebellion rather than the last gasps of the old order. His theater disrupts the audience's view of "normalcy" on the streets and opens up questions of justice and social justice, as well as identity in language. Moreover, just as the *Wiener Gruppe* had tried

---

60 "Sie stellt ein Gesicht dar, die wiederum ziemlich viel Wonne darstellt …"

61 Note that Austrian authors of that generation confronted the legacy of Nazism by looking not at official politics, but rather at precisely this kind of *Alltagsfaschismus*, the everyday fascism perpetuated within authoritarian family structures. The term was ubiquitous in critical discussions then.

to do with their works, his two plays usher in social chaos which all three playwrights trust their audiences to see as a direct product of tradition unquestioned and still imposed in old forms. In this world, traditions and commonplaces turned into violent forms of abuse of individuals, where the traditional form suggests that evil erupts only when individuals abuse the traditions that heretofore have guaranteed social order. The wards of this society have decisively rewritten the scripts they have inherited, in violent, inchoate acts and words, leaving behind only severed hands and severed heads for audiences to contemplate.

Kasperl in the disorder of Europe

These Kaspar/Kasperl plays, starting with Schnitzler's, modernize the traditional *Volkstheater*, taking it up in full knowledge of its ability to enact social critique and public discussion. Through it, they provoke a too-settled and self-satisfied bourgeoisie audience to deal with aspects of modern life in Austria and Europe. How that everyman fares reveals the social lies and *mores* of purportedly civil society, as he confronts and usually succumbs to the lies and willful misunderstandings imposed by conventional society.

The traditional *Volkstheater* thus has found a new voice in postwar Austria, from the state's refounding, into the Cold War, and finally into the youth revolt of the 1960s. h. c. artmann uses his Kasperl and Caspars in several plays to critique the lies of that nascent state. His grocer, Gschweidl, a linear heir of *commedia dell'arte*'s elder merchant, causes a necessary revolt of the younger generation, which rises to kill him rather than simply triumphing over his petty tyrannies. The contemporary version of this story becomes a fable of totalitarianism and violence, of a father generation killing the souls of its children by not admitting the skeletons in his closet (or in this case, the grasping hands in the cash drawer). The "golden Viennese heart" had become a parody of itself in a country that had ignored its Nazi past and was actively remilitarizing. As the NATO West prepared for a new war in Europe, these writers knew, this generation of evil fathers was quite literally threatening to consume its children again.

Bayer concurred with this diagnosis. In his depiction, those evil fathers were driving their children, like Kasperl, to the electric chair, by their violence, their heartlessness, and their adherence to outmoded social and moral forms. His kasperl becomes not only a victim of everyday violence or the media, but of *state* violence, as would many of the 1968 protesters across Europe (from the Irish Republican Army through student protesters like Benno Ohnesorg, killed by police violence). Bayer himself succumbed to such despair: he committed suicide, leaving his farewell message unfinished.

A member of a younger generation, Handke takes up a very similar generational critique of a Europe eating its own children. His Kaspar is both a stock character and the Kaspar Hauser of history—someone both subject to the public consciousness industry that aims to rob him of his identity and permanently scarred by its expectations. In the generation after the NATO protests featuring the Vienna Group, Handke easily follows their lead to return to Europe's submersion in mass media culture and conformity.

artmann, Bayer, and Handke, members of the respective avant-gardes of their generations, thus straightforwardly follow in the footsteps of Hofmannsthal and Schnitzler, confronting their audiences with revisionist uses of traditional dramaturgy to challenge the lies of bourgeois society. *No Pepper for Czermak, kasperl at the electric chair, Kaspar,* and *The Ward Wants to Be the Guardian* all show that these theater traditions have not lost their critical edge and that the authors who use them have faith in performances closer to popular culture than to the elite.

These examples are not alone in the postwar canon for authors from Austria and southern Germany—any number of Handke's younger contemporaries also take up the form. But artmann and the Vienna Group did not manage to spread their reputations far beyond the local scenes in the way that Handke did, perhaps because they were so specifically political; Handke, in contrast, was and is more easily visible on the European stage, given that he took up a social politics (like media consciousness) that is generally Western rather than specifi-cally Austrian. Where artmann and his colleagues denied the cultural border between Germany and Austria for pragmatic reasons charac-teristic of their own generation, Handke lets his plays appear as European-absurdist rather than Austrian or central European. He (like Thomas Bernhard and Elfriede Jelinek, but much earlier than they did) represents a very savvy adaptive reuse of a theater preserved in modern form in Austria[62]—creating utterly original lessons on society in the form of imports that looked much more familiar in their original contexts.

Such examples document the persistent alignment of *Volkstheater* traditions with social-politics critique and their ability to bridge the elite state-supported theaters of germanophone Europe closer to the relevance of popular culture of protest on the world stage, eliding differences between theater performances and public demonstrations. At the same time, they have preserved a stage that supports an art enacting open critique of social mores, yet one not descending into *Tendenzliteratur,* literature with overly specific didactic or political

---

62   The other modern preservation of this drama tradition is Pirandello, in Italy.

aims. Instead, these works show where problems lie and bring the audience to question public morality rather than official ideology. Just as critically, they work to question the bourgeois condition as part of the West's politics on the world stage (implicating media, NATO, domestic police violence, or the historical legacy of Nazism), not just as Austrian, no matter how local an everyman their Kasperls seem to be. Their society is still very much Schnitzler's *Grand Guignol* and Hofmannsthal's shattered history; their literary and political reference points, Europe.

Eight A New Balkan Challenge: The Reemergence of Austria's Europe

The writers of the twentieth century adduced here have been canonical figures of the literature produced in Austria, but they have acted as writers and political critics on larger stages rather than solely as professional Austrian nationalists. Since Hofmannsthal and Schnitzler, they have been European in their vision and self-authorization, taking as their exemplars concepts from Europe's traditions, not just Austria's. Yet the borders of Europe as sketched from the perspective over a millennium— the definition starting this volume—become a significant issue again after the fall of the Soviet Union and its bloc. Those borders are again being reclaimed, yet differently than they were reclaimed by these voices after the First and Second World Wars traced here. Not surprisingly, "Austrian" voices again play roles in current attempts to recapture a sense of Europe outside and beyond the boundaries of nations and their nationalist imperatives, but this time they come from both right and left.

Most critically, a Europe that after 1989 is reconstituting itself as the European Union retains an ambivalence about its boundaries and margins, as well as its role as progressive and traditional at the same time. Political exigencies have even brought new definitions of that Europe's reach into Slavic regions that have been *not-Europe* since they were seduced (by Pan-Slavist ideologies) or coerced (by Soviet troops) into identifying with a Russian cultural sphere that grades into Asia; Turkey's persistent insistence on its EU candidacy extends that map into the Middle East and (further into) Islam, as well. On the map passed down in one-time Habsburg regions, many of those lands (like Galicia) had long been defined as belonging to or possibly part of Europe. Hofmannsthal's Europe, at least by implication, included these regions; Schnitzler's did not exclude them, and a significant number of his stories play in unnamed cities beyond Vienna, albeit usually in germanophone ones. h. c. artmann, Konrad Bayer, and the *Wiener Gruppe* were resolutely urban and European, but only artmann was actually Austrian. Peter Handke claimed the kind of world literature that Hofmannsthal had, but with a decisive twist toward the Balkans, as we shall see. Just as significantly, these shifting borders of Europe also sponsor a new set of negotiations about the political meaning of Europe, as a conservative nostalgia all too often comes to the fore.

This chapter returns to the question of Europe after the Second World War by returning to the geopolitics of maps rather than to literary landscapes of regions, cities, and neighborhoods—to the "thousand-year-old fabrication" that was Habsburg Austria and its residue in the present. In today's era of political realignment, the Balkans of "Austrian" intellectuals do indeed start in the western districts of Vienna, but those Balkans are again part of Europe, raising older specters of continuity. That traditional European bulwark against the non-civilized was known, in the NATO West, as the mythical other region of *Central Europe*, *Mitteleuropa*, the land between Europe and Russia that (re)emerged after World War II and again after 1989 and the demise of the Eastern Bloc. *Mitteleuropa*, however, is a concept of only recent provenance, given that it had meaning only in juxtaposition with the Soviet Bloc's *Eastern Europe*, as part of a buffer zone that should be considered crucial to the idea of Europe (and which is hotly contested in post-Soviet studies), designated territories which the European Union might consider its own, in what might eventually be a final thrust eastward to the borders of today's Russia.

The European-Austrians of this generation, however, are not only liberal critiques of their societies, as they join a European Union that is gauged to further business and finance rather than culture. In this framework, Otto von Habsburg returns here as a representative of conservative forces behind the European Union (not its only political wing, by far). He was a powerful recreator of Europe myths in the first years after Germany's reunification, creating a set of narratives intended to guide potential Europeans back onto the map of Europe, in a restoration of a united European past that never existed, but should have. His *Return to the Center* (1993; *Zurück zur Mitte* [1991]) will not, however, use *Central Europe*, a favorite term for scholars. Habsburg writes to transcend nationalism and to encourage a consciousness about Europe into existence—in support of then-current politics—but not of the costs for individuals that more liberal politicians would support.

After outlining how Habsburg resolutely attempts to transform NATO's Europe into Austria's, I will turn to two particularly visible authors of "mixed" Austrian heritage, Peter Handke and Milo Dor, who travel through the periphery of this redefined Europe to provide commentary for Austrians about the post-1989 Balkans, again as seen from post-national, purportedly "European" perspectives. Their "travel literature," journalistic essays designed to appeal to the popular imagination, ties the Balkans to Europe in a way unfamiliar to the Cold War powers, who tend to follow the conventions about the Balkans not being part of Europe that has been in place since Rebecca West's 1941 *Black Lamb and Grey Falcon*, and which has recent incarnations in Robert D. Kaplan's *Balkan Ghosts* (1993) for the English-speaking audience and in Austrian politician Erhard Busek's *A European Disturbance* (*Eine europäische Erregung* [2003]) or *Projekt Mitteleuropa* (1986).

Taken together, these texts document the persistence of a map of a Europe with Austria persistently at its center, a map that claims political relevance within Europe for both left and right, just as its cultural equivalent has done. These texts represent any number of Austrian writers and writers of Austro-Hungarian origin who return to the Balkans in the 1990s and beyond, trying specifically to inscribe themselves and their Austria back onto a map of post-Cold-War Europe—some as political, some as more cultural-humanitarian. They specifically work to counter images showing the Balkans are fatally crippled by Europe and to move public consciousness toward acknowledging a Europe that existed before the wars and assassinations of the World War I era, at the start of the region's modern history. The *Austrian* Balkans are cast as the home of Europe's victims, but also its potential partners, a multicultural population that can again take up rightful positions in Europe—their tragedy was ever being considered as *not-Europe* by Westerners who do not look at the longer view. Yet behind this redrawn map of Europe lies a map of culture, ethnicity, and class-bound legitimacy that warrants consideration for its potential dangers, as well—redrawing borders can imply new exclusions, as well.

Habsburg *redux*: Where cultural politics and politics converge

Otto von Habsburg (1912–2011), quite naturally, would always have placed Austria on the map of Europe, given his late twentieth-century roles as politician of the "European idea" and long-time worker for the European Parliament. Yet at times, he strategically calls to witness his position as the eldest son—and hence undisputed heir—to the defunct throne of Emperor Karl. He recast himself as champion of a Europe that must again include the Balkans, moving beyond the too-simple East/West dichotomy that has determined it since World War I.

Habsburg had, for at least twenty years, taken it as his particular mission to resist the map of Europe used by the so-called great powers since the World Wars—and hence to restore Austria to its place. Even before the fall of the Wall in 1989, for instance, the Cold War national designations "East Germany" or the "German Democratic Republic" did not exist in his personal political dictionary. These "East" Germans were, in his version, actually *Mitteldeutsche*, the Germans in the middle between the West Germans and those lost in the historical mists of the East Bloc:[63] "Middle Germany, known as the GDR" (*Zurück*, 9).[64]

Even when Habsburg accepted boundaries on that post-Cold-War-era map of Europe, then, he called attention to alternative frameworks (including germanophone regions lost to Imperial Russia, it seems, which would have been the "Eastern" Germans beyond the "middle" of the GDR). In his somewhat whimsical account, for example, he conjures up alternative histories. As he tells the tale, the wall between the power blocs of Eastern and Western Europe did not fall in November, 1989, when the physical brick-and-mortar barrier between the parts of divided Berlin was chipped away by floodlit crowds near the Brandenburg Gate. Instead, as he noted in a newspaper essay (reprinted in *Zurück zur Mitte*), the Eastern Bloc had actually fallen three months earlier, on the occasion of "das Paneuropa-Picknick":

> The region experienced mass demonstrations, peaceful revolutions, and a reconsideration of European culture and history in the wake of these events, even if, just as was the case before, there was still a dictatorship in the neighborhood. Not only did the Iron Curtain fall many times, but the requirement for visas also did, going with it. Transborder celebrations united people who had to this point lived next to each other, but who could get in touch with each other only with the same degree of difficulty it would take to reach a foreign continent. (*Zurück*, 9)[65]

---

63 "Seit Jahren war es eine wichtige Aufgabe der Paneuropa-Union wie auch eines meiner Arbeitsziele im Europa-Parlament, aus unserem politischen Sprachschatz jede Elemente auszumerzen, die uns durch die gezielte Propaganda der sowjetischen Führung und des Desinformationsapparates des KGB untergejubelt wurden. ... jener, der den politischen und ideologischen Gegner veranlaßt, seine Sprache zu übernehmen, die Schlacht des Geistes bereits zur Hälfte gewonnen hat.

   "Das galt besonders fur die Tatsache, daß der Begriff 'Mitteleuropa' so gut wie gänzlich aus unserem Sprachschatz ausgemerzt worden ist. Man kannte in Europa nur mehr Ost und West. Diese Einteiling war schon darum absurd, weil sie Prag zum Osten und Wien zum Western rechnete, obwohl ein Blick auf die Karte zeigen mußte, daß die Hauptstadt Böhmens weiter westlich als die österreichische Donaumetropole liegt" (*Zurück*, 7–8). At one point, Kohl used "Osteuropa" and the pope corrected him to "Mittleuropa" (*Zurück*, 8)

64 "das 'DDR' genannte Mitteldeutschland."

65 Translations mine. "Massendemonstrationen, friedliche Aufstände und eine Wiederbesinnung auf die europäische Kultur und Geschichte erlebte im Gefolge dieses Ereignisses der ganze Raum, auch wenn es in der Nachbarschaft nach

His world of "Christians and Europeans" (*Zurück*, 11) celebrates the "Paneuropa Picknick" on August 19, 1989—not insignificantly, I believe, in Austria's traditional *Kaiserwetter*, the high summer vacation weather remembered as close to Kaiser Franz Joseph's birthday—just after the third election cycle for the European parliament.

With this event, Habsburg asserts, the Iron Curtain fell at Sopron (Ödenburg), at the Austrian-Hungarian border, rather than in Germany. In his mythic narrative, he shows us the fall of a different Iron Curtain—a curtain of barbed wire:

> When 661 "Central Germans" [GDR citizens] cut through the barbed wire and stormed through the open gate to Austria, it set off the greatest mass flight of Germans out of the GDR since the erection of the wall 28 years earlier. At that point, the "Iron Curtain" was no longer sustainable, not even in world politics ... [after] the wall and the fall of the red tyrants from the Baltic to the Adriatic ... but the picnic proved to be the spark in the dry wood of the Yalta system of injustice. (*Zurück*, 14)[66]

Habsburg here harks back to a European rhetoric much older than himself. He is not simply claiming dynastic privilege (in press interviews, he denied having anything to do with the event—it was a fluke of fate that the event converged with his daughter's birthday plans, even though people making it through received small amounts of Western currency). Instead, he reaches back to the early nineteenth century, before the map of Europe became almost uniformly nationalist.[67] His Europe resisted division according to the East–West compass points that have been the NATO West's line of demarcation since World

---

wie vor Diktaturen gab. Vielfach fiel nicht nur der Eiserne Vorhang, sondern mit ihm auch der Visumzwang. Grenzüberschreitende Feste vereinigten Menschen, die schon bisher nebeneinander gewohnt hatten, aber einander zuvor schlechter erreichen konnten als fremde Kontinente."

66 "Doch als 661 Mitteldeutsche nach Durchschneiden des Stacheldrahtes durch das offene Tor nach Österreich stürmten und so die größte Massenflucht von Deutschen aus der "DDR" seit dem Mauerbau achtundzwanzig Jahre zuvor erfolgte, war der "Eiserne Vorhang" auch weltpolitisch nicht mehr zu halten. ... die Maueröffnung und der Sturz der roten Tyrannen von der Ostsee bis zur Adria. ... Doch das Picknick erwies sich als der Funke im trockenen Holz des Unrechtssystems von Jalta."

67 See Katherine Arens, "Central Europe and the Nationalist Paradigm" (1996), for an overview of how various nationalist frameworks cannot match the situation in Austria-Hungary. For an argument which does not coincide with the perspective offered here, see also Nina Berman, "Hugo von Hofmannsthal's Political Vision" (2002); she does not necessarily construe Austria as having an independent position after WW I.

War II. As was the wont a century ago, he is more inclined to divide Europe north from south according to lifestyles, manipulating not only national visions, but also political ones. Thus it is no surprise that, in August, 1989, Habsburg was accused of luring innocent Germans who were on "vacation" in Hungary across the border. His version is deterministic: he asserts that the event was simply Europe restoring itself: "Pan-Europe is all of Europe" (*Zurück*, 19).[68]

Reinforcing this (dare I say Austrian-political) map of Europe, the individual chapters of *Zurück zur Mitte* rewrite the histories of the states of the one-time East and Central Europe, each in its own national voice. Each of Habsburg's essays uses one of the region's individual histories to draw a line from each that can lead them into an inclusive unified Europe, as central *to* Europe. He begins with his own Austria: threatened with extinction in the World War II occupations, "Vienna seemed as likely as Berlin, with its Wall, to die off" (*Zurück*, 20).[69] It survived then, but now one must ask: "Has Austria a future?" ("Hat Österreich Zukunft?" [*Zurück*, 24]).

Leaving aside Germany for the first, he turns to a pre-Imperial German national formation. His European map asks about "Bavaria as a Province?" ("Bayern als Provinz?" [*Zurück*, 29]), even while he remythologizes it as one of the seats of European Christianity: "The message of Christ came out of Bavaria a thousand years ago and spread into the lands of Central Europe" (*Zurück*, 31).[70] These two Catholic-German states, Bavaria and Austria, point to an almost lost longer historical vision:

In history, Bavaria and Austria were not only bulwarks, but also bridges. In both states, one always thought in terms of the whole region. Thus it is characteristic that the father of the Pan-European Ideal, Richard Count Coudenhove-Kalergi, comes from Ronsperg in the Sudetenland, with its connections to Austria and Bavaria alike. In this concept the eternal mission of Austria and Bavaria finds its most beautiful expressions: the Bohemian lands, Slovenia, Croatia, and Slovakia, but also North Italy all look toward Vienna and Munich ... (*Zurück*, 33)[71]

68 "Paneuropa ist ganz Europa."
69 "Wien schien ebenso zum Absterben verurteilt wie in Deutschland Berlin mit seiner Mauer."
70 "Aus dem heutigen Bayern ging vor über tausend Jahren die Botschfaft Christi in die Länder Mitteleuropas."
71 "Bayern und Österreich waren in der Geschichte nicht nur Bollwerk, sondern auch Brücke. In beiden Staaten hat man stets großräumig gedacht. So ist es bezeichnend, daß der Vater der Paneuropa-Idee, Richard Graf Coudenhove-Kalergi, aus Ronsperg im Sudetenland mit dessen Bindungen an Österreich

Habsburg's Europe is, not surprisingly, also the Europe of *Haus Habsburg*, looking north and east to define its historical mission, part of a Europe that exists up to the national borders of the continent.

Habsburg fears the rhetoric used around reunited Germany, his "fear of Germany." The new Germany, he feels, is looking to redefine itself in the outdated nationalist mode, which is unacceptable to the future of the continent (*Zurück*, 35). That Germany is a historical aberration:

> The future of a Germany that remains true to its European vocation lies in thinking back on these values. Fear of Germany can only be maintained by those who, for ideological reasons, do not acknowledge that collective guilt does not exist. German Reunification was not a setback, but a breakthrough for the European Idea. (*Zurück*, 44)[72]

A better model for post-Wall Europe, in his unsurprising opinion, can be found in the Habsburg past, which had a tradition of freedom and federalism in the European states. So, too, did the Prague of the Habsburg era, "the Bohemian heart" of Europe. There, the Jan Hus monument commemorates a discussion of German federalism opened by František Palacký (*Zurück*, 61): "The Bohemian lands—thus also Moravia and Austria-Silesia—possess rights of primogeniture in Europe. They can insist how they renew themselves in the spirit of Christianity" (*Zurück*, 64–5).[73]

That heritage is shared by the rest of what during the Cold War had been framed as Eastern and Central Europe. Thus Habsburg's Slovakia is the land of Tomáš Masaryk and Edvard Beneš; the Croatians and Slovenians are "coming home" after Tito's demise:

> The Croats have stood for centuries on the outermost walls of Christianity against the Turkish invasion, just as the tradition of the "border people" at the Habsburg military border required.

---

wie an Bayern stammt. In diesem Konzept findet die ewige Mission Österreichs wie Bayerns ihren schönsten Ausdruck: Die böhmischen Lander, Slowenien, Kroatien und die Slowakei, aber auch Norditalien blicken nach Wien wie nach München …"

72 "In der Rückbesinnung auf diese Werte liegt die Zukunft eines Deutschlands, das seiner europäischen Sendung treu bleibt. Angst vor den Deutschen können dann nur noch jene haben, die sich aus ideologischen Gründen weigern, zu erkennen, daß es keine Kollektivschuld gibt. Die deutsche Wiedervereinigung war kein Ruckschlag, sondern ein Druchbruch für die europäische Idee."

73 "Die bohmischen Länder—also auch Mähren und Österreich-Schlesien— besitzen ein Erstgeburtsrecht in Europa. Sie können darauf pochen, wie sie sich im Geist des Christentums erneuern."

They are, through and through, a western civilized people.
(*Zurück*, 74–5)[74]

He tours the rest of the "rebirth of the Balkans" (86) from a similar
perspective, as the rebirth of a European civilization. The passing
of Nicolae Ceauşescu, the region's Jewish heritage, and many other
topics are all parts of a noble European tradition that fell "victim to
the evil spirit of nationalism" (*Zurück*, 97). Note, however, that he
includes Europe up to the Baltic in the future map that would more
accurately reflect Europe's restoration to itself: "Estonians, Lithuanians
and Latvians place their hope in us. Europe would be incomplete
without these people who, more than others, have suffered for their
status as Europeans" (*Zurück*, 102).[75] His vision consciously combats
the legacy of World War II that lived on as late as Reagan's "Evil
Empire" (*Zurück*, 124).

Habsburg's solution is less politically conscious than humanist (and
utopian in the extreme): that the political resolution of that war will
necessarily rest with the politicians and functionaries (*Bonzen*), while
the true politics of the region lies with its civilians, never with their
ex-governments. Here, again, Habsburg's rhetoric overtly implicates
the Nazi period as part of an unacceptable alternative to the future
he prefers: "It is a singularity of modern or purportedly modern
politics that one denounces the guilt of families even while practicing
it repeatedly. That is a fall back into barbarism" (*Zurück*, 152).[76] Even
a country like the GDR has been, in his estimation, a primary victim
of such logic—his steadfast *Mitteldeutschland* and *die Mitteldeutschen*,
"Middle Germany" and the "Middle Germans," lost in the Cold War.

Critical to the present discussion is the distinction between official
and experiential narratives explaining the current map. Habsburg
warns of the psychological consequences of not distinguishing between
what governments enacted through force, and what the people in those
countries actually did themselves. Without this optic, the Eastern Bloc's
successor states will be implicated in a long-term series of disasters, as
victims of post-traumatic stress caused by the optic of Western history:

---

74 "Die Kroaten haben durch Jahrhunderte auf den äußeren Wällen der
   Christenheit gegen die türkische Invasion gestanden, wie es die Tradition der
   "Grenzer" an der habsburgischen Militärgrenze verlangte. Sie sind ein durch
   und durch westlich-zivilisiertes Volk."
75 "Esten, Letten und Litauer hoffen auf uns. Europa wäre ohne jene Völker
   unvollständig, die mehr als andere fur ihr Europäertum gelitten haben."
76 "Es ist eine Eigenheit der modernen oder angeblich modernen Politik, daß man
   wohl theoretisch die Sippenhaftung verurteilt, sie aber ständig weiter prakti-
   ziert. Das ist ein Rückfall in die Barbarei."

They chide themselves for having offered insufficient resistance to the Regime.

Even good people who never compromised themselves by working with the totalitarian holders of power were slowly forced into a feeling of collective guilt, in a development that lies beyond the responsibility of individuals. (*Zurück*, 153)[77]

He thus rejects out of hand the assumption of collective guilt for Bloc inhabitants—a nice parallel to the case of Germany's own collective guilt. In Europe's political future, as he sees it, the West must not blame victims but rather root out the *Bonzen*, the party bosses who exploited them. His Europe is thus a state of mind that must be healed—and can be, now that its map is again not graven in stone.

Habsburg always remains ecumenical, however. Not wanting to offend the self-satisfaction of the traditional Western powers, he still argues for Paris as a cultural center of Europe, a city that is by no means provincial. Yet Habsburg's future Europe will be federated, with many centers, not centralized: "The return of Central Europe—the political home of federalism—into the larger community will, though, give the idea new impetus" (*Zurück*, 164).[78] "National tensions" that accompany centralization will be the downfall of the idea of a continent united. New nation-states will not solve the problems remaining on Europe's map, since Europe can only exist as a macro-region, not as micro-states—*großräumig*, as a larger zone of cooperation (*Zurück*, 167):

Austro-Hungary, and before that the Holy Roman Empire, ruled from Vienna or Prague, had for centuries taken on the role of a shield against the invading hordes from the east. With that, they afforded the West an inestimable service, without which it would not have survived. The destruction of this unity and the Balkanization of the Danube region was without a doubt one of the main causes not only of the First World War, but also for the Soviet Occupation of the region that followed immediately upon it. (*Zurück*, 171)[79]

---

77 "Sie werfen sich vor, nicht genügend gegen das Regime unternommen zu haben.

   Auch anständige Leute, die sich niemals mit den totalitären Machthabern kompromittierten, werden langsam in dieses Gefühl der Kollektivschuld an einer Entwicklung gedrängt, die sachlich jenseits der Verantwortung der einzelnen Menschen gelegen ist."

78 "Die Rückkehr Mitteleuropas—der politischen Heimat des Föderalismus—in die größere Gemeinschaft wird jedoch dem Gedanken neuen Auftrieb geben."

79 "Österreich-Ungarn und vorher das von Wien oder Prag aus regierte Heilige Romische Reich hatte jahrhundertelang die Funktion eines Schutzschildes

He thus persistently advocates for self-determination in the region, as the avenue to a *Gesamteuropa*, total Europe (*Zurück*, 173) that is, moreover, resolutely Christian (*Zurück*, 232–3).

Only near the end of the volume does the historical term "Central Europe" (*Mitteleuropa*) reemerge as a guidepost:

> Herein lies the particular onus for Central Europe. It is no accident that meditations back about the spiritual center of Europe— our Christian heritage and our imperial-federal tradition—fall together with the freeing of our geographical center of our part of the globe. ... The Paneuropean Idea originated on the soil of the old Danube Monarchy. Now, all of Europe must renew itself on the basis of its geographic, historical, and spiritual center. Therein lies our challenge for the years to the millennium. Only then will we do justice to our world-wide responsibility that will determine the start of the next millennium. (*Zurück*, 248)[80]

This is the "paneuropean idea" that Habsburg adopts as the title of a more recent book, where he argues that Europe has to be more than an economic union, it must be a cultural one, as well: the "Paneuropa Picknick" with which Habsburg sought to memorialize the Eastern Bloc's downfall (*Mémoires*, 135).

While the utopianism of such pronouncements remains evident, one should never underestimate the calculation of Habsburg's rhetoric—he is an exemplary historical publicity-agent. In a set of interviews given in French, for example, he spins his model Europe in a framing that more closely reflects Central Europe's imperial past rather than the humanist-democratic ideal represented in *Return to the Center*. An emperor, he notes, can be seen as an exemplary federalist: "L'empereur n'appartenait à aucune de ces nations" (*Mémoires*, 205). And more

---

gegenüber den heranstürmenden Horden aus dem Osten übernommen. Sie leisteten damals dem Abendland einen unschätzbaren Dienst, ohne den es nicht hätte überleben können. Die Zerschlagung dieser Einheit und die Balkanisierung des Donauraumes war ohne Zweifel eine der Hauptursachen nicht nur für den Zweiten Weltkrieg, sondern auch für die anschließende sowjetische Okkupation dieser Gebiete."

80 "Hier liegt die besondere Aufgabe Mitteleuropas. Es ist kein Zufall, da die Rückbesinnung auf die geistige Mitte Europas—unser christliches Erbe und unsere reichisch-föderalistische Tradition—mit der Befreiung der geographischen Mitte unseres Erdteiles zusammenfällt. ... Die Paneuropa-Idee entstand eben auf dem Boden der alten Donaumonarchie. Nun muß sich Gesamteuropa aus seiner geographischen, historischen und geistigen Mitte heraus erneuern. Darin liegt unsere Herausforderung in den Jahren bis zur Jahrtausendwende. Erst dann werden wir unserer weltweiten Verantwortung, die den Beginn des nächsten Millenniums bestimmen wird, gerecht."

importantly, he argues for a trinitarian unity in multiplicity for the political faces he assumes in his political career: "j'étais légitimiste. ... Étant légitimiste, je suis par exemple républicain en Suisse et monarchiste en Angleterre" (*Mémoires*, 267). Such a perspective, reflecting regional historical traditions as well as the coming European federation, would, for example, legitimize both Serbian and Croatian self-determination (*Friedensmacht*, 77), as it would the historical claims of most of the globe's major flashpoints: "Even in the nuclear age and for that which will still come upon us, geography will continue to be decisive" (*Paneuropische Idee*, 234).[81]

Habsburg's political calculation is aimed at underscoring the warm, humanist image of Europe assumed by the *Sonne über Österreich*, a modern international reincarnation of Austria's Josephinian humanism that allowed an empire to free its political serfs. This Europe is the Europe of the eighteenth and the twenty-first century alike, multi-ethnic and able to rethink historical narratives. To be sure, Habsburg greatly overestimates the likelihood that long-term political enemies will actually make common cause to establish this harmonious utopian Europe—he lived long enough to see the Euro, and perhaps the European Union itself, under threat. Yet his European map makes more sense if one remembers that it (and he) were close to the last living representatives of the older, pre-World-War "European idea" that tried to circumvent ethnic nationalism on moral and historical grounds.

No matter Habsburg's (often conspicuously conservative) politics, it is crucial to note that close parallels to his pan-European rhetoric recur throughout Austria's journalism on that new Europe—including a more self-consciously internationalist literary voice whom we have already encountered: Peter Handke.

Handke: Cosmopolitan *flâneur* of Europe

Despite his earlier work among Austrian intellectuals and his Austrian-Slovenian heritage, Peter Handke has taken on a European identity as an author, often living and working in Paris. However, since the fall of the Wall, he has again become a voice for Central Europe, having written a number of controversial newspaper essays about the Balkan Wars of the early 1990s that have turned into slender volumes, each evoking firestorms of reaction.[82]

---

81 "Auch im nuklearen Zeitalter und in dem, was noch auf uns zukommt, ist die Geographie weiter entscheidend."

82 The controversy continues. Some believe that this political position was instrumental in Elfriede Jelinek's Nobel Prize decision, since her body of work is thematically close to his, her range of genres parallel, and her marketing strategies learned in the same places.

One of the earliest of these essays was called "The Dreamer Takes His Leave from the Ninth Land" ("Abschied des Träumers vom Neunten Land"), after a Slovenian legend. It was published in the *Süddeutsche Zeitung* in 1991, on the occasion of the first nationalist battles in the Balkans, fought in various permutations between Slovaks, Croats, and Bosniaks involved in the breakup of Yugoslavia. Cognizant of recent concerns about identity politics, he is careful to assert that he does *not* speak for the Slovenians, although he shares their ancestry. More significant for the present purposes is his clear anti-nationalist rhetoric as he enters this fraught political space: "And I see no reason for the state of Slovenia [to exist]" (*Abschied*, 7).[83] In this, as in most of these essays, Handke steadfastly refuses to support the politics of nation-states and their preferred historical images, preferring to discuss the Balkans as part of the life-world of a current Europe that needs restoration. That non-existent nation-state of Slovenia may nominally be the land of his origin, his *Heimat*, but it cannot and should not be considered a political entity with some sort of enduring right to exist.

For Handke, Slovenia is a homeland only in his dreams and occasionally in his personal experience. At the same time, it has proved to be the only place where things feel substantial to him (*gegenständlich*), a place where he feels he is a "guest of reality" (*Abschied*, 15): "And in spite of all that, I as a stranger have felt nowhere on earth in my life as much at home as I have in the land of Slovenia" (*Abschied*, 11).[84] The actual political border between Italy and Slovenia is thus less a mythical place than it is a real place lying beyond the ken of political history—a geographical unit in a particular karst landscape that creates an *experience* more consistent than any political identity ever imposed on it. That experience remains, no matter what arbitrary political labels are imposed on it.

After all, Handke knows that even the politically amorphous term *Mitteleuropa* is an identity narrative written only late onto this landscape (*Abschied*, 22), one story among many enforcing particular historical points of view, and enacting explicit agendas as master narratives of politics. Such political narratives would have him draw a line counter to his own experience, dividing him from the translator who was his guide to the region, Zarko Radokovic, or they might try to convince Slovenes that they need to "return to Central Europe," a gesture which Handke himself always considered "a passing mood" (*Laune* [*Abschied*, 38]). At best, such politically prejudicial narratives provide evidence for a north-south border separating European stereotypes: after all, no

---

83 "Und ich sehe keinen Grund ... für den Staat Slowenien."
84 "Und trotzdem habe ich mich in meinem Leben nirgends auf der Welt als Fremder so zu Hause gefühlt wie in dem Land Slowenien."

true European, legend has it, wants to be a member of the purportedly lazy south.

Just as he refuses to believe in the persistence of political history, Handke clearly supports the legitimacy of shared experience:

> I ask: is it possible, no, even necessary, for a country and a people nowadays to declare itself immediately to be a state formation (with all the trappings, coats of arms, flags, holidays and border crossing gates), if that state hasn't come to that point by itself, but only as a reaction against something—and in addition, against something from without, and also something that is sometimes annoying or tedious, not actually pressing or crying out for redress. (*Abschied*, 42)[85]
>
> Is that the new modern: forming states out of pure egotism, or purely an act originating in a bad mood (no matter how comprehensible) directed against a brother nation? (*Abschied*, 43)[86]

Politically, the Slovenia that Handke visited in 1991 was simply an accident of history, a group of people talked into being a small state, despite what they shared with the rest of ex-Yugoslavia (*Abschied*, 44). This country was seduced from outside into creating borders that he calls "zones of unreality" (*Unwirklichkeitsstreifen* [*Abschied*, 45]), strange and estranging borders that have not grown naturally out of the region or its history.

In 1996, Handke would again use such *ad hominem* judgments to validate what is "natural" to a region, for another series on the region in the *Süddeutsche Zeitung*, an intervention again ill-received, at best. The culprit this time was a travel narrative eventually published as a book entitled *A Journey to the Rivers: Justice for Serbia* (*Eine winterliche Reise zu den Flüssen Donau, Save, Morawa und Drina, oder Gerechtigkeit für Serbien*). The English edition of this text has a preface telling Handke's version of the political firestorm that this political-personal essay loosed:

> This text, appearing on two weekends at the onset of 1996 in the

---

85 "Ich frage: Ist es möglich, nein, notwendig, für ein Land und ein Volk, heutzutage, unvermittelt, sich zum Staategebilde zu erklären (samt Maschinerie, Wappen, Fahnen, Feiertag, Grenzschranken), wenn es dazu nicht *aus eigenen* gekommen ist, sondern ausschließlich als Reaktion *gegen* etwas, und dazu etwas von *außen*, und dazu noch etwas zwar manchmal Ärgerliches oder Lastiges, nicht tatsächlich Bedrängendes oder gar Himmelschreiendes?"

86 "Ist das die Neumoderne: Staatengründung aus bloßem Egoismus, oder eben aus purer und wenn auch noch so verständlicher schlechter Laune gegenüber dem Bruderland?"

Süddeutsche Zeitung, caused some commotion in the European press.

Immediately after publication of the first part, I was designated a terrorist in the *Corriere della Sera*, and *Libération* revealed that I was, first of all, amused that there were so few victims in the Slovenian war of 1991, and that I was exhibiting, second, "doubtful taste" in discussing the various ways of presenting this or that victim of the Yugoslavian wars in the Western media. In *Le Monde* I was then called a "pro-Serbian advocate," and in the *Journal du Dimanche* there was talk of "pro-Serbian agitation." And so it continued until *El Pais* even read into my text a sanction of the Srebrenica massacre. (*Journey*, vii)

Handke swore that his essay was not intended as a political intervention into the region's devolutionary politics. He simply sought "aesthetic veracity" in expressing his personal experiences of the Balkans (*Winterliche Reise*, viii). He had, he claims, long wanted to visit the Balkans, and he once had been given the chance of appearing at a Belgrade theater festival. Out of that visit, he remembered only the country's rivers. In 1996, he wanted to revisit that land of the rivers, to return to the Balkans and move behind what he had seen in the media: "I felt the need to go behind the mirror" (*Journey*, 2)[87]—behind the screen imposed on the region by news media. The translation ignores the double entendre in this phrase: the *Spiegel* (*Mirror*) is also Germany's major "news" magazine.

The result was his trip, his essay, and a great public outcry: "And whoever is thinking now: Aha, pro-Serbia! or Aha! Yugophile!—the latter a *Spiegel* word—need read no further" (*Journey*, 2–3).[88] The only way he could avoid being a media event, Handke felt, was not to visit the country officially or even as an acknowledged tourist. He hoped to blend in with the aid of his guides: Zarko Radakovic, his translator, the author, and Zlatko B. (a pseudonym for Adrian Brouwer), whom he knew from Salzburg. They set off in October, 1995. Handke's only preparation, he claims, involved seeing a film, Emir Kusturica's *Underground* (1995), which had been panned by many political critics (most notably, Alain Finckelkraut), purportedly even before they had seen it. The trip is narrated in an almost egregiously *faux-naïve* tone: he claims that he will report only what he sees, feels, and thinks about, not the images that he received from the media.

87 "Es drängte mich hinter den Spiegel" (*Winterliche Reise*, 13).
88 "Und wer jetzt meint, 'Hah, proserbische!' oder 'Aha, jugophil!'—das letztere ein *Spiegel*-Wort (Wort?)—, der braucht hier gar nicht erst weiterzulesen" (*Winterliche Reise*, 13).

When he reaches the battlefields of the first Yugoslav war, he thus muses about why the Serbs and the Croats were involved and how he would behave in such a situation: "Thus a part of me could not take sides, much less judge" (*Journey*, 21).[89] The press optic through which he purportedly "knew" the region seems to avoid the facts that he experienced as real: "Who will someday write this history differently, even if only in its nuances—which could do much to liberate the people from their mutual, inflexible stereotypes?" (*Journey*, 26).[90] Significantly, Handke, like Habsburg, ties these narratives into futures. Old, established stereotypes need to be revised, he feels, if the region is to have a future. But the fresh day-to-day experiences which individuals might use to ground new narratives have been suppressed by the media's rehashed images, and so he needs to confront the geographical space anew, to find new images of Serbia grounded in experience.

Handke starts with the local: he interviews people on the Belgrade streets about what they consider their own history, and what they felt Serbs' future would be. Threaded through the answers he receives, he uncovers a base of "normal" experiences that are shared as part of the region's identity narratives, including scenes from everyday life, music, and evidence of a pervasive black market. He does not, however, even try to behave like an impartial interviewer, because he does not hold himself aloof—he is consciously engaging in the space of stories, not histories. Thus he trades stories with his interlocutors, offering his own tale about his Slovenian grandfather in Carinthia (*Winterliche Reise*, 80) who had voted for unification with Yugoslavia in 1920, a vision of oneness, not partisan politics. One interviewee, from the countryside, seeks to engage Handke with his complaints about the national leadership that purportedly caused the people's suffering (*Winterliche Reise*, 85). Yet Handke refuses to engage in political judgments about issues he has not experienced himself, even though the Dayton talks were in progress at the time of his walk through the land of the rivers (*Winterliche Reise*, 85). He demands instead a Yugoslavia outside partisan politics.

The second part of Handke's trip leads him to another river, to the Drina in Bosnia, where he sees groups of soldiers for the first time and realizes what is being done to the lived world experience of the Serbians. He realizes that they are not in a particular state, but that they have assumed a particular state of mind:

---

89 "So konnte ein Teil von mir nicht Partei ergreifen, geschweige denn verurteilen" (*Winterliche Reise*, 43).

90 "Wer wird diese Geschichte einmal anders schreiben, und sei es auch bloß in den Nuancen—die freilich viel dazutun könnten, die Völker aus ihrer gegenseitigen Bilderstarre zu erlösen?" (*Winterliche Reise*, 50).

There remains for me, precisely in the crystal-sharp isolation of almost everyone there, for the first time a sense of something like a *Volk,* otherwise rightly long since declared dead: conceivable because this people so visibly dwells in the diaspora in its own country, each in an intensely personal disjunction ... (*Journey,* 70)[91]

That reference to a *Volk* is somewhat double-edged. To those in Central Europe, the River Drina exists in its own mythic space in the novel *Bridge on the Drina,* which future Nobel Prize winner Ivo Andrić wrote in Belgrade during World War II. The novel traces the people on both sides of the eponymous bridge from the last days of the Habsburg Empire through the latest war—the definition of a *Volk* as a historical creation, based on wars. When one day Handke finally manages to be alone in Serbia, he reports in the "Epilogue," he meditates on how easily reporters miss the essence of this world. Those who should be chronicling the world are only falsifying it, and they have the hubris to assert their grasp of Serbia's truth over any older narratives (*Winterliche Reise,* 122). He again blasts the *Spiegel* magazine and its "Balkan experts" for official reporting that becomes what he calls "word poison" (*Wörtergift* [*Winterliche Reise,* 127]). Significantly, this "official" reporting also naturalizes a German point of view that keeps Yugoslavia from burying its dead (*Winterliche Reise,* 128).

The world of 1995 has accused Serbia of paranoia, but Handke finds a very different world, a nation of orphaned, abandoned children (*Winterliche Reise,* 129), who follow the relit wartime beacon of the *Volk* as a kind of compass pointing the way out of their isolation and distress. This psychological state, Handke knows, will condition individuals' political responses for generations. If the Serbian situation is to be relieved, Europe has to work against this psychological derangement: "To grow up, to do justice to, to embody not only a reaction against the century's night and to aid those which are still so dark; to break out of this night" (*Journey,* 81).[92] This cultural therapy will not be popular, Handke knows, since it does not correspond with the official political

---

91 "Geblieben ist mir, gerade in der eben kristallscharf zu spürenden Vereinzelung fast eines jeden dort, überhaupt erst etwas wie das sonstwo wohl zu Recht längst totgesagte 'Volk" faßbar, indem dieses im eigenen Land so sichtlich in der Diaspora haust, ein jeder in der höchsteigenen Verstreutheit ..." (*Winterliche Reise,* 115).

92 "Erwachsenwerden, Gerechtwerden, keinen bloßen Reflex mehr verkörpern auf die Nacht des Jahrhunderts und die so noch finstern helfen; aufbrechen aus dieser Nacht" (*Winterliche Reise,* 132). I have modified the official translation a bit for correctness.

line of the would-be nation-state. He is proposing a human solution rather than a political one:

> So now it's time for the poetic? Yes, it is, understood as exactly the opposite of the nebulous. Or say, rather than "the poetic," that which binds, that encompasses—the impulse to a common remembering, as the possibility for reconciliation of individuals, for the second, the common childhood. (*Journey*, 82)[93]

At this point, Handke reverts to an image of Europe, reminding his readers about experiences of a shared Western childhood, a key to remembering what Serbia's return to normalcy might feel and look like.

Handke wrote his first set of meditations on Serbia from November 27 to December 11, 1995. Six months later, Handke returned to the former Yugoslavia to update his essays in the *Sommerlicher Nachtrag zu einer winterlichen Reise*. The trip was occasioned by the translation of his earlier essay into Serbian. His new, more official, role does make him nervous, because his *Winterliche Reise* has been misunderstood: "And it was here, for the first time, that I first entertained the idea, after all those reactions to my travel story, that I might have done something wrong, false, yes unjust" (*Nachtrag*, 18–19).[94] He has even been confronted by Serbians about details that he purportedly has gotten wrong. His hotel hosts, for example, hate it that he had reported on a lack of heat in the city—one of a raft of "factual corrections" that are imposed on his experience, his story, as if it had tried to be reporting rather than experience.

At this point, Handke tries to escape his quasi-official role and go out into the landscape again to experience Serbia's geographic reality rather than its people. The result is an odd, depopulated set of images of Yugoslavia's landscapes, which adds to this travel narrative another level of memory and experience about the country. Far out in the country, finally, Handke finds a church, which leads him to meditate about the differences between Islam and Catholicism that fracture the region. And he hears tales told with many tears by country people who "needed him" to listen (*Nachtrag*, 57). Otherwise, he uncovers

---

93 "Kommst du jetzt mit dem Poetischen? Ja, wenn dieses als das gerade Gegenteil verstanden wird vom Nebulösen. Oder sag statt "das Poetische" besser das Verbindende, das Umfassende—den Anstoß zum gemeinsamen Erinnern, als der einzigen Versöhnungsmöglichkeit, für die zweite, die gemeinsame Kindheit" (*Winterliche Reise*, 133).

94 "Und hier war es auch zum ersten Mal, daß ich, nach all den solchen und solchen Reaktionen auf meine Reisegeschichte, es mit dem Gedanken zu schaffen bekam, ich könnte durch mein Niederschreiben etwas Unrichtiges, Falsches, ja Unrechtes getan haben."

only a disoriented land, characterized by "not knowing where to go" (*Nachtrag*, 60).

He does not delude himself that he has made a trip out of history by going to the hinterlands. One may, he believes, none the less still inquire of the Serbs why they committed atrocities and started a new war, in a mindless repetition of the region's history. None the less, to judge the Serbs from that perspective alone would be another kind of foolishness or blindness about how group consciousness comes into being (*Nachtrag*, 81):

> And with "pre-history" I mean not just the memory of the oppression by the Turks centuries ago and the murderous pursuits by the Muslim Nazi-allies decades ago. (Instead of "memory," say perhaps more correctly, "coming to mind," "being in mind"). Doesn't what happened—what was broken (and that *not* by the Serbs)—at the start of the war, before everything else, belong to pre-history? (*Nachtrag*, 82)[95]

The West thinks it knows the brutal history of the region, but it is wrong. The region's memory is not that of the rest of the West. He has found clear traces of another, older stratum of history in the back country, away from the Western media, on his road to Belgrade: "And it was as if we're again entered into another history, into one in which we no longer had anything to say, neither I the foreigner nor even my two Serbian companions" (*Nachtrag*, 87).[96] Notably, this is also the space of Andrić's novel, which conflates the anthropological time of the bridge's villages with historical time.

But to attain any power, the narratives associated with such historical experiences must be integrated with current experience. Handke closes on a note of regret that such histories are actually always written to emphasize official enemies. Again, he demands that a new history of the region be told, not to vindicate the Serbs, but so that the region's state and its state of mind be brought into some kind of correspondence. In this demand, he shares a map of the Balkans with Otto von Habsburg, in that both agree that the region's identity does not

---

95 "Und mit 'Vorgeschichte' meine ich das Gedächtnis nicht allein die Unterdrückung durch die Türken vor Jahrhunderten und die mörderische Verfolgung durch die muslimischen Nazi-Verbündeten vor Jahrzehnten. (Statt 'Gedächtnis' sag vielleicht besser "in den Sinn kommen," "im Sinn sein.") Zählte denn nicht, vor allem, das zu Beginn dieses Krieges Geschehene, nein, Verbrochene—und da einmal *nicht* von den Serben—zu der Vorgeschichte?"

96 "Und es war, als träten wir da noch einmal in eine andere Geschichte ein—eine, in der wir nichts mehr zu sagen hätten, weder ich, der Ausländer, noch aber auch die zwei serbischen Gefährten."

correspond with nationalist images, or with what the Western media tries to make of it. Part of what has been lost in these Balkan narratives is the region's interconnections with "Europe," as they imagine it. Handke does not pursue this demand into his more political meditations, but rather emphasizes the region's need to resolve its experience of itself with its historical narrative and with its present-day course.

In a very real sense, Handke has set himself a quixotic project: to ignore the persistence and predominance of political histories imposed on the regions from without. To believe that it is possible to retreat behind the media, behind the front lines, and find an untouched land is naïve—and, to Handke's credit, his *Sommerlicher Nachtrag* acknowledges precisely those dashed hopes. Yet he continues to assert the value of witnessing everyday life in a way that others do not, even as he does so in the midst of an unresolved political crisis.

Handke persists in denying that his intervention into the images of Serbia was political. In 2006, in consequence, Handke refused to appear as a witness for the defense of Slobodan Milosevic at war-crimes trials, but then he did appear at his funeral to give a eulogy. Reactions were predictably fierce. One of his plays was subsequently withdrawn from the *Comédie-Français*; he was awarded the Heinrich Heine prize by the city of Düsseldorf, which was then revoked. Still, Handke resists what he calls the demonization of the Serbs, while not condoning contemporary crimes—his point seems to be that Serbia is getting the entire fault for a more general regional situation with many acts of villainy involved.

Handke's actual political agenda in this Balkan engagement has not been clarified over time, with most critics settling on his naïveté. For the present discussion, what is important is his unwillingness to consider a nation-state as anything but a fairy tale—an opportunist master narrative that ignores the shared European past of virtually all of the present and future EU territories. He recovers and exemplifies sources for *multiple* narratives of Europe and demonstrates how they jeopardize individuals for the sake of politics defined in the abstract, from above. Overall, then, these essays may not be so much naïve as they are part of his longer-term aesthetic program of trying to recapture the personal and the local out from under the larger narratives that destroy individuality, instrumentalize human relations, and prevent the formation of human community—a message reaching back at least as far as *Kaspar*.

The rejoinder: Milo Dor

Not surprisingly, Handke's meditations about the limits of media coverage of Serbia and its human costs were received less than enthusiastically among intellectuals, not just in the media. Among the most vociferous early reactions was that of Milo Dor (1923–2005), as documented in *Leb Wohl, Jugoslawien* (Good-Bye Yugoslavia), a volume collecting his own essays from 1990–6. The speech Dor gave in accepting the "Prize of the Austrian Booktrade in Support of Tolerance in Thought and Action" in 1990 (*Preis des österreichischen Buchhandels für Tolerenz in Denken und Handeln*) became simply the first in a series of essays responding to the Balkan situation and culminating in a direct response to Handke.

From the start of his volume, Dor's map remains heavily intertwined with Austria's Europe, as shared by Handke; he claims his own heritage as Viennese and European, with a Serbian background.[97] Dor wrote his own responses to the Balkan Wars from the heart of old Vienna, from the Eighth District, Josefstadt, named after the Emperor who freed the serfs, a part of Vienna he calls "our big-city village" (*Leb Wohl*, 7),[98] a twist on the common joke that Vienna is Austria's *Bundeshauptdorf* (capital village). None the less, he grants his district a certain international chic (*Leb Wohl*, 7).[99] His landlord/doorman (*Hausmeister*) is Serbian, his greengrocer (*Greißler*) is Greek; an Italian runs the ice cream store. This is the world of Dor's own heritage. After all, his father was born in the Banat before the turn of the century, and he knew many of the languages of the *k.u.k. Monarchie* (*Leb Wohl*, 10).

From this venue, Dor has watched Serbs and Croats playing out an internationally supported game of nationalism on the basis of stories about imagined historical slights and utopian national destinies, trying "to do justice to the laughable great power allure of the new Croatian or Serbian national leadership" (*Leb Wohl*, 13).[100] The historical substance of the Balkan Wars is, he feels, less than it is made out to be by the political powers of the West: "It is not even a usable one-act play" (*Leb Wohl*, 13).[101] Some arbitrary "national rights" have been made into

---

97 "Meine Vorfahren waren Serben, die vor dreihundert Jahren vor den Türken nach Österreich geflüchtet waren und sich nördlich der Donau, die eine Grenze bildete, und dem fruchtbaren Boden des entschwundenen Pannonischen Meers niedergelassen hatten. Sie bekamen Land, unter der Bedingung, diese Grenzgebiet gegen die Osmanen zu verteidigen. Belgrad war zu dieser Zeit der vorgeschobene Posten des Türkischen Reichs, den die Österreicher zu Anfang des 18. Jahrhunderts eine viel zu kurze Zeit in der Hand hatten, um daraus eine barocke Stadt zu machen. ... So wurde diese "Militarsgrenze" ein getreues Abbild des Vielvölkerstaats" (*Mitteleuropa*, 10–11).

98 "unser großstädtisches Dorf."

99 "das Flair einer echten Großstadt."

100 "um den lächerlichen Großmächtallüren der neuen kroatischen oder serbischen Nationalführer Genüge zu tun."

101 "Er ist nicht einmal ein brauchbarer Einakter."

excuses for national aggression (*Leb Wohl*, 16), in a gesture that runs against the trend of Europe.

Like Handke, Dor moves into a utopian discourse about Europe, but his map retains full view of the links between imagined nation-states, states of mind, and day-to-day politics:

> What, in fact, still remains to us, if we don't simply want to look on helplessly as our vision of a confederation of the free people of Europe, equal before the law, disappears once and for all into the fog of aggressive, self-righteous nationalisms? (*Leb Wohl*, 18)[102]

Dor named his collection after a 1912–13 popular song (*Leb Wohl*, 23), a link he uses to speak of the region as experiencing a time out of joint—"alles aus den Fugen geraten" (*Leb Wohl*, 19)—as the wars of the 1990s weirdly recapitulate the 1912 Balkan War against the Ottoman Empire. On the one hand, one might dream that an ancient destiny is playing itself out in the Balkans; on the other, one might see a tragedy of contemporary nationalism that provides national narratives to replace those of Eastern Bloc socialism—but without any actual change: "The whole seems to be playing itself out according to an ancient scenario" (*Leb Wohl*, 20).[103] And Dor agrees with Handke that the Western press is in a kind of feeding frenzy over the bones of the region, with "an almost unconcealed *Schadenfreude* about the disintegration of Yugoslavia, which one suddenly called a prison, just as had been done in the declining *k.u.k.* Monarchy" (*Leb Wohl*, 22).[104] But all such narratives, no matter what politics they originate in, create mental and political jails, now as in the past.

Dor seeks to reclaim the active historical dimension of these conflicts, especially how the real tragedy of the twentieth century, fascism, is still being played out in Yugoslavia, as it has since the Ustascha supported fascism (*Leb Wohl*, 29):

> A spectre is haunting Europe. It is not the spectre of Communism, with which Marx and Engels tried to scare and terrify the owners of our continent 150 years ago, but rather the spectre of nationalism, of intolerance, of xenophobia, and of the more or less

---

102 "Was bleibt uns tatsächlich noch übrig, wenn wir nicht hilflos zuschauen wollen, wie unsere Vorstellung von einem Bund freier, gleichberechtigter Völker Europas im Nebeldunst der aggressiven, rechthaberischen Nationalismen endgültig verschwindet?"
103 "Das Ganze scheint sich nach einem uralten Szenarium abzuspielen."
104 "eine beinahe unverhohlene Schadenfreude über den Zerfall Jugoslawiens, das man plötzlich als Völkerkerker bezeichnet wie einst die untergegangene k.u.k. Monarchie."

hidden battle for spheres of influence—in a word, the spectre of fascism which, lightly disguised in pseudo-democratic phrases, has begun to spook around again in European regions. (*Leb Wohl*, 26)[105]

Dor points to the 1991 PEN declaration about Croatia as exemplary of the West's inadequate historical knowledge of the region. That declaration states simply that nothing justifies the present aggression in Croatia, or its violation of minority rights (*Leb Wohl*, 31). Such statements, in Dor's view, ignore the most dangerous legacy of the West that was imposed on the region, one that now needs to be accommodated: nationalism. Like Handke and Habsburg, Dor detests this political "solution" which does not fit the region at all (*Leb Wohl*, 35).

Where Dor diverges from Handke is in his willingness to undertake an overt political dissection of the media narratives obscuring the region for Europe's eyes. Like Habsburg, he knows the absurdities of the region's histories in great detail. He explains, for instance, that June 29 is Serbia's national holiday, commemorating a battle lost to the Turks, the start of national oppression in his country. In 1691, his own ancestors trekked (his verb) to Austria in the wake of these invasions (*Leb Wohl*, 41). Yet Dor criticizes more generally how these national myths generate political identities, always enacting the same kinds of scripts, based on the oppositions of victim and victimizer (*Leb Wohl*, 42). Nationalism starts the region on a game of murder with moving targets (*Leb Wohl*, 46-7), as Dor documents with copious historical references (even to German history books). Like Handke, he stresses the psychological fallout of this history in the region, but he outlines more overt political consequences: "The Serbs must, I believe, be freed from the prejudice that everyone except they themselves is guilty of their misfortune" (*Leb Wohl*, 72).[106] National scripts cannot simply be imposed from outside, they have to be enacted from within, and they have taken deep roots in Dor's Balkans, to tragic ends.

With this point, Dor's identity politics take on a new face. Where Handke and Habsburg speak for the region by proxy and lineage, Dor speaks as a resident, owner of a summerhouse in Rovinj, in Istria (*Leb*

---

105 "Ein Gespenst geht in Europa um. Es ist nicht das Gespenst des Kommunismus, mit dem Marx und Engels vor 150 Jahren die Besitzenden unseres Kontinents in Angst und Schrecken versetzen wollten, sondern das Gespenst des Nationalismus, der Intoleranz, des Fremdenhasses und des noch mehr oder weniger versteckten Kampfes um Interessenssphären, mit einem Wort das Gespenst des Faschismus, das, mit pseudodemokratischen Phrasen spärlich verhüllt, wieder einmal in europäischen Gefilden herumzugeistern beginnt."

106 "Die Serben müßten sich, glaube ich, von dem Vorurteil befreien, alle seien an ihrem Unglück schuldig, nur sie selbst nicht."

Wohl, 73). He has experienced the war directly, as he ended up barricaded on an isthmus in the middle of a battle that ruined his family's summer season (*Leb Wohl*, 75). That personal inconvenience is not, however, allowed to take center stage, since Dor has found many more significant casualties of war, such as the Bosnian writer Ivo Andrić, who died in 1972:

> Ivo Andrić is a posthumous victim of the war in Bosnia. The Croatian school authorities have removed his writing from the schoolbooks, the writings of the only Yugoslavian Nobel Prize winner, because, in their view, he did not support "the Croatian cause" sufficiently during his lifetime—whatever that means. (*Leb Wohl*, 88)[107]

This nationalism has thus also withdrawn Croatia from Europe, as it has limited a prize-winning author to being an opponent of their cause rather than a voice for their region internationally.

Dor also reviews the political consequences of such myths. While reviewing the political history of the region since World War II, he points toward a confederation as necessary and declares all parties in the region (including the European allies), not just the Serbs, as culpable (*Leb Wohl*, 92, 96): "Everyone should speak of his own shame, admit his own guilt" (*Leb Wohl*, 118).[108] The region's history is still too palpably linked to World War II, he notes as he visits Tito's palace (*Leb Wohl*, 110). Neither Austria nor Germany behaved well in the region in the twentieth century; neither Serbia nor Croatia is democratic (*Leb Wohl*, 119); war crimes on all sides remain active in memory: "Nationalists always fall into ecstasies when they use the word *Volk* ... the be all and end all of their threadbare ideology" (*Leb Wohl*, 141).[109] Moreover, the West prolongs those threadbare ideologies by acting on nationalistic principles rather than rethinking the region. Serbian army deserters, for instance, will be repatriated out of Vienna, without being able to claim asylum rights (*Leb Wohl*, 144).

The original 1993 version of *Leb wohl* ended with an open letter to Markovic. The later editions include, first, the letters that were

---

107 "Ivo Andric ist ein posthumes Opfer des Kriegs in Bosnien geworden. Die kroatischen Schulbehörden haben seine Beiträge aus den Lesebüchern entfernt, die Beiträge des einzigen jugoslawischen Nobelpreisträgers, weil er ihrer Ansicht nach zeit seines Lebens die 'kroatische Sache'—was immer man darunter versteht—nicht hinreichend vertreten hat" (*Leb Wohl*, 88).

108 "Es sollte jeder von seiner eigenen Schande sprechen, die eigene Schuld eingestehen."

109 "Die Nationalisten geraten immer in Ekstase, wenn sie das Wort Volk aussprechen. ... das Um und Auf ihrer fadenscheinigen Ideologie."

Markovic's response, and then Dor's rejoinder. In the latest edition, Dor adds another essay, "Sarajewo darf nicht sterben"—"Sarajevo Dare Not Die"(*Leb Wohl*, 163), in which he declares the war in Serbia "a war against the civilian population" (*Leb Wohl*, 164). Dor, however, confesses his own burnout, his own inability to stem the tide of nationalist madness in the region, as revenge killings are reported in increasing numbers: "Nationalism in itself is a spiritual malaise that befalls at times the inhabitants of an entire region of a state" (*Leb Wohl*, 167).[110]

It is no wonder that Dor has also added to his collection an essay on Handke, who has, in Dor's account, suddenly taken it into his head to "leave his ivory tower" and engage the Yugoslavia situation: "the late bloomer Handke at the low points of Balkan politics" (*Leb Wohl*, 172).[111] Dor thinks Handke's motives were less than pure and authentic, and that Handke was trying to be an engaged intellectual like the French philosophers, who take it as their right to judge what they do not know. As Dor sees it, Handke takes off, tilting after mass-media windmills and programmatically detesting journalists, even while he is acting more or less as one of them (*Leb Wohl*, 173). Dor suspects Handke's motives, seeing him as a would-be Don Quixote "battling for imaginary justice" (*Leb Wohl*, 173).[112] Dor's Handke picked up, went to Belgrade, and let himself be led around, proving himself "completely without sensibility and tact" (*Leb Wohl*, 174). More centrally, Handke's Yugoslavia seems completely mythical to Dor, since he does not even know the political landscape, such as many important groups in the region working against neofascism, or the "Belgrade Circle" of 100 intellectuals who were trying to do better by the region's history (*Leb Wohl*, 174). Handke, in short, misses what is going on as he purveys into the world a dream of a Balkan region without the reality of the homeless and refugees.

Dor believes that the situation must be rectified by eliminating the nationalist inheritance from World War II and the Cold War. As he quotes Ivo Mazuranic: "One should send war criminals to trial, without respect to their status as folk heroes" (*Leb Wohl*, 176).[113] Where Handke errs fundamentally in assuming that Serbia still exists as a state of mind, then, Dor prefers to cast the region as part of the legacy of the West.[114]

---

110 "Der Nationalismus an sich ist eine geistige Krankheit, die zuweilen die Bewohner eines ganzen Staatsgebiets befällt."

111 "Der Spätzünder Peter Handke in den Niederungen der Balkanpolitik."

112 "dieser töricht naïve Don Quichotte, der auszog, um für eine imaginäre Gerechtigkeit zu kämpfen."

113 "Man soll die Kriegsverbrecher vor Gericht stellen, ohne Rücksicht darauf, ob sie Volkshelden sind oder nicht."

114 In an earlier volume of essays, he outlined the genesis of contemporary nationalist wars as originating in Vienna (*Mitteleuropa*, 14).

Dor's Serbia is, moreover, a part of Europe, just as Habsburg argued it, albeit in a considerably less benevolent, less humanist way. Most critically for the present discussion, however, is that he defines the region as a shared experience, not as a nation-state providing an identity that would rob its citizens of any chance at evolving their own unique ones. As he expressed it in a later essay volume, *Mitteleuropa* (1996):

> If one travels through the space of so-called Central Europe, one notices clearly that a certain feeling of belonging together is not just a myth, but also a tangible reality whose roots reach far back. Disputes with the one-time Austrian colonial power have receded to the background, so that, finally, one can speak freely and without restraint about relations and commonalities, commonalities that make us into an important connecting member in the association of all European peoples. (*Mitteleuropa*, 19)[115]

Dor's *Mitteleuropa* is, not surprisingly, as multiethnic and multicultural as that of the *Sonne über Österreich* authors, because he recognizes its origins as a military defense perimeter. It also extends into Vienna, to his Josefstadt home (Wien VIII). From there, his volume of essays takes us on the grand tour of the centers of the Austro-Hungarian empire: through Istria (influenced by Italy), Venice, the Wojwodina, Dubrovnik, Toskana (Tuscany), the Danube (and the Iron Curtain), Lombardy, Triest, Prague, and his own personal "three cities," Belgrad-Budapest-Wien.

While focusing on a radically different politics, then, Dor's map of Europe ultimately remains more that of Otto von Habsburg than Handke's. Like the map in *Sonne über Österreich*, it is again a conscious fabrication, a *Fälschung*, that lies outside the Europe of nationalism, but it exists as a test case for the new Europe of the EU, under severe pressure by Balkan chaos.

Europe as a state (of mind)

These three Austrian writers of very different political stripes all claim as their political reference points a map of Europe that hosts many different identity narratives rather than simply affirming its nation states. Despite their differences, they share a belief that politics must

---

115 "Wenn man durch den sogenannten mitteleuropäischen Raum reist, merkt man deutlich, daß ein gewisses Gefühl der Zusammengehorigkeit kein Mythos allein ist, sondern eine spürbare Wirklichkeit, deren Wurzeln weit zurückreichen. Die Auseinandersetzungen mit der einstigen österreichischen kontinentalen Kolonialmacht sind in den Hintegrund gerückt, so daß man endlich einmal frei und ungebunden über verwandtschaftliche Gemeinsamkeiten reden kann, Gemeinsamkeiten, die uns zu einem wichtigen Verbindungsglied bei dem Zusammenschluß aller europäischen Völker machen."

be considered on both historical and European scales, and that the ethics of politics requires public discussion, freed from the stereotypes imposed by nationalist narratives and unimpeded by media fictions. Even though they evaluate and use that map differently, they speak out of the conviction that public discussion matters. They even share very similar diagnoses of the historical origins of the Balkan situation.

First: like World War I, World War II and the Cold War that followed it did not draw new maps of the region, but instead they merely formalized centuries-old tensions, especially ethnic-nationalist sentiments. That map failed in all three earlier eras, and so to presume success for them now is merely to prolong the nationalist genocide of the twentieth century in a region that should be defined as part of Europe, but which has been carefully cordoned off as not sufficiently European.

Second: the region is indeed part of Europe, by custom, usage, and mutual orientation, and has been for the millennium (whether that millennium is the international Christian one, Austria's 1996, or the upcoming Hungarian millennium of Christianization). The Balkans are not simply the margin of Europe's traditional power centers (the Austro-Hungarian or Soviet Empires); it is a region whose interests always get spoken for by the European powers. The Greeks would call it a *chora*—the outposts of colonization of Europe, nominally under its regency, but never under its control.

Third: the Balkans are the *chora* of Europe in an additional way, that used by Julia Kristeva in her work since *Revolution in Poetic Language*: that is, it is an order, an organized way of life that is shared and which underlies all the region's overt politics. In particular, one pervasive political narrative has traditionally framed the Balkans as the place where the order of civilization meets chaos or barbarians, yet referring to different barbarians each time it is used. This Balkans defines a conceptual *limes*, a defense perimeter against the inhuman, and a space where Europe's history is challenged by the non-European, the invaders, be they the Turkish empire of yore, Islamic warriors battling Christians, nationalists of the Nazi or Cold War era, or the contemporary media. Recognizing this tie, this strategic territorialization (in Deleuze and Guattari's sense) offers a key to European consciousness and self-definition, particularly to the persistent inadequacy of designations like "Central," "Eastern," "East-Central," and other "European" entities.

Historiographically, the Balkans are the region where national narratives meet and break down as they face the resistance from a landscape that never successfully nurtured nationalist illusions of similarity and national identity, because they have perpetually been multicultural, multilingual, and shifting. In one sense, all three authors use this Balkan-Europe in the traditions of conservative humanism, but they move beyond that narrative. If one would add a text like Claudio Magris's 1986 *Danubio* to the mix, one would see the region as a different kind of test case: not, as Karl Kraus called the dying Austro-Hungarian empire, a "proving-ground for world destruction," but rather a region that puts Western identity, Europe's identity, and its political and ethical narratives, to the test. This narrative Balkans resists co-optation by other too-simple historical narratives, be they heroic, ethnic, nationalist, religious, or economic.

None of the three authors has a solution for that three-fold "problem" of the Balkans. To reclaim a region's story on the basis of an individual's experience is to deny it its voice on the international stage and its credibility as a moral agent—Handke's problem. To claim a region as damaged denies it the possibility of contributing to the dominant West—Habsburg's and Dor's problem, albeit with different contributions in mind. All three try to extend the map of Europe to include the Balkans, but they do so at the cost of exposing their own blindness about twentieth-century nationalisms, defaulting as they do to a moralistic narrative about human rights.

Handke offers the most radical solution for raising his audience's consciousness, first turning the history of the last century into a legend, and then trying to rescript history itself on new terms derived from direct experience instead of stereotypes. His resulting map of Europe, however, still counts as a *ou-topia* to the rest of Europe—a no-place. He and his companions have not yet managed to restart the conversation about Serbia's future.

The Balkan histories told here seem, ultimately, to have helped to consign Austria to the past rather than to help create a new Europe. They are part of the discourse on Europe that has been at play in Austria for at least two hundred years; they are explicitly tagged as *narratives*, each with its own program of enlightenment and its own moral purpose, and implicating an *arche* and a *telos*—a source and a goal—for its politics.

All three authors believe, moreover, that multiply told tales can foster new public discussions, directed by new narratives that are not tied to abstracts that naturalize themselves as immutable truths (abstracts like "the nation" or *das Volk*). Habsburg tells the stories in the form of the national histories that crisscross the Balkans and Central Europe, spreading competing claims for legitimacy; Handke tries to show the essential falsity of these narratives, revealed by the authority of individual experience and its compelling narrative truth; Dor points to historical continuities and shifts in the identity stories that have continued to bedevil Balkan politics.

These three essayists still maintain Austrian intellectuals' faith in public spaces for discussion and for public critique; they consider their local experiences and politics in light of Europe; and they hope to bring their audiences to reconsider the truth value of narratives inherited from a past that now looks more than a little shopworn. But trying to reclaim political agency by casting doubt on old master narratives of history and new national fictions may not be sufficient to combat the overburden of history that has kept nations away from the Europe that lies just beyond today's politics.

Afterword

Austria as Europe? The Art and Science of the Post-National Culture

The case studies presented here are by no means intended to present a comprehensive picture of how the "idea of Europe" was and is used in Austria. Both historically and methodologically, it would be a profound error to reify a trope or theme as belonging integrally to a national culture. But tracing how intellectuals closely identified with Austria and the cultural ideals appealing to its various historical incarnation none the less has value in interrogating how, in a purportedly post-national era, Europe can figure into the identity politics of nations and their citizens. The last two centuries have been declared the eras of nationalism and imperialism, and so scholars have tended to use the too-simple borders of nations to define their areas of study.

Yet the very name and public image of "Austria" calls into mind a Europe before nationalism, a Europe that has never been adequately articulated in relation to the identity claims of nation-states, singly or in the aggregate. No country in Europe has ever actually had the luxury of being a community with a single ethnic or linguistic identity, no matter how much it might have claimed the status of the kind of "imagined community" that Benedict Anderson described a generation ago. None the less, of the nineteenth-century imperial states of Europe, only Austria, in its various incarnations, more or less consistently acknowledged (albeit often grudgingly) that its territories did not all speak German and could not be forced to on a day-to-day level, and that profoundly different cultural traditions had been brought together in it.

When Austria-Hungary imagined itself in the nineteenth century, it did so without the luxury of centralization and a clear cultural mission. It could neither uniformly dismiss the various cultures that formed its nation, nor suppress them to the point of extinction (many claim it tried), nor pretend that it was monolingual, mono-confessional, or monoethnic. So this political entity, despite frequent outbreaks of untenable violence against its ethnic and national minorities, dealt with these legacies of diversity. Its army sent rabbis into the field along with priests and ministers as chaplains, and it had kosher laws. Its school laws defined and accommodated *Landessprachen* (not every language spoken in a region, but those with an associated integrated cultural community); higher education had regional quotas that guaranteed at least token representation of non-status regions in the elite schools. German was the dominant language of culture and commerce, but translations and functional multilingualism helped the modernization of other national groups within the empire[1] (preparing, however inadequately, for the Charles University in Prague to be split into a German university and a Czech one, and for a new Parliament to function in Hungarian after the 1866 Compromise). The characters in Joseph Roth's novels, looking back at Austria-Hungary, acknowledge that they had a larger field of action before national boundaries were set down on the Balkans and Central Europe, if not an easy one.

The "modern" nation-states of Europe, defined after the French Revolution and the Napoleonic era, ignored many of these challenges, or treated their internal "others" (their ethnic minorities) as problems to be eliminated, often by engaging them in the colonial enterprise and decimating their internal regional cultures, when the promising young went off to jobs in other parts of globe. The regions of the British Isles shipped out huge percentages of their laborers with the Royal Navy or merchant marine, or as economic emigrants; the rural regions of France were emptied by Napoleon's armies. The Habsburg state, however, was caught up in an on-going balancing act of interests, never able to centralize with the vehemence of France, nor to become imperial as did England with its colonial money. Its army seemed unable to win battles; it did not have the money to enforce particular ethnic and class interests, and so too often compromised with them; it accommodated— often poorly, but officially—regional interests, class mixing, religious variations, and public utilities in many regionally important cities, not just its capital. It was from first to last a compromise, a jury-rigged state destined to fail.

Even more critically, this particular cultural space was not delimited by notions of the nation-state as an ethnic unity or a financial-hegemonic center. The case studies adduced here show very much how a greater European perspective could be the reference point for

---

1   For details on how multilingualism functioned in such a state, see Michaela Wolf, *Die vielsprachige Seele Kakaniens* (2012).

the culture in nineteenth-century Austria-Hungary. The fate of Vienna and its government depended on Europe; the reference points for narrating its history are found not only in Austria-Hungary, but also in the Ottoman Empire and Poland, England and France, Italy, Spain, and Russia. There were, after all, Habsburgs who did not even speak German, spread through various capitals, and there never was a single legal framework for the nation (courts adjudicated various regions' hereditary privileges). Similarly, in the twentieth century, Austria never quite settled into a position as a nation apart from its peers in Central Europe before its (forced? willed?) absorption into Nazi Germany and its post-war neutrality. Every evidence exists that European reference points continued to figure centrally in the identity narratives for this small country—from its lobbying to become the third United Nations city in the 1970s, through its work with the legal frameworks of the European Union today.

Today's scholars cannot afford to forget that, when it did fall, Austria-Hungary did so less dramatically than it might have: it was politically dismembered on paper, not through a decisive revolution (like Russia) or by a forced devolution (like Britain's surrender of India), just at the moment when it might have modeled European federalism. Yet for today's scholars, it "crumbled" and thus could never have been a proper nation. Austria-Hungary has been eagerly studied as a declining political culture and for its germanophone culture, but also as a colonizer of Balkan, Hungarian, and Central European territories.

This myth persists today, to obscure the reality that I have been tracing here: a wealth of "Austrian" intellectuals who acted with a map of *Europe* directing their activities, rather than the map of a single nation-state.[2] The histories that would recover such projects as inherently multi- or transnational have not been written, and the guardians of political correctness still insist that national subjects' self-determination and identity politics require that a nation be a monoculture.

We are, in other words, still looking at Europe through imperialistic eyes formed in the latter nineteenth century, where Austria appeared to its imperial rivals as less a sleeping giant than a dying one. From the point of view of the twenty-first century, however, the "Austrian mind"

---

2   There is ample evidence, too, that many more such intellectuals could be recovered from the Slavic histories of Europe—those educated in Austria-Hungary but coming to maturity in its successor states—or from the histories of the refugee intelligentsia that found shelter in the United States, Canada, and Great Britain in World War II and the Cold War following it. One could be Austrian without speaking (fluent?) German. See for example the studies by Agnieszka Nance (2004), Nikola Petković (1996), and Ana Foteva (2009), who explore various Slavic identities that evolved within or in response to the legacies of the Habsburg territories (and not only in opposition to them).

and Austrian map of Europe that operates for its most visible authors and intellectuals might better be seen as the birth pangs of a multicultural Europe, as represented in a political entity that resisted ethnic nationalism. Vienna and its smaller sister cities in the empire modeled various kinds of emerging public networks and spaces functioning between center and periphery to join regional and ethnic causes to a "national cause," and they created in their inhabitants a profound sense that they had the shared civic and ethical duty to engage in public discussion and public enlightenment.

Moreover, because the region's culture was beginning to operate in networks over a multicultural, multiethnic, and multilingual region, the mass media so decried by the Frankfurt School emerged at the heart of its cultural networks and of its connection to Europe. To be sure, the theater circuit, publishing, print and newspaper cultures that constituted the mass media in the nineteenth century (and the film medium that grew up next to them in the early twentieth century, before that industry was exported to Hollywood)[3] were often commercial enterprises rather than solely state-supported and state-controlled ones. But critically, those public networks were never singular, nor under the complete control of a central entity, despite the famous censorship of Metternich's Europe, between the Congress of Vienna in 1815 and the Revolutions of 1848, and beyond. "Austria's" networks of culture, commercial, local, and regional, never were bounded by a single national culture.

Until World War II, players, authors, directors, and musicians moved between state-sponsored and commercial venues, between patronage and ticket-supported wages—and between audiences in various germanophone theaters, as well as in theaters in other languages (and in the silent films that transcended language cultures). Their jumps were facilitated by networks of translation and cross-language performance, including venues like the German Theater in Prague, where Mozart's operas premiered, or the *Theater in der Josephstadt* in Vienna, where Ferenc Molnár's plays, written in Hungarian, were and are staples of the germanophone repertoire.[4] German was the first language of government in most regions (but never the only one), and hence of the dominant (and often domineering) culture in

---

3   See Robert von Dassanowsky, *Austrian Cinema* (2005), whose work reminds us how many of Hollywood's "German" directors were actually of Austro-Hungarian regional descent. Dassanowsky and Oliver C. Speck have also edited a series of studies on the *New Austrian Film* (2011) that argue it as a transnational film project with commercial and artistic claims, not just national ones.

4   Note that several of his plays were produced on Broadway by David Belasco.

Austria-Hungary until its demise, but it was not the functional barrier to public discussion that one might assume it was today—it was one of several official languages in a culture with many functionally stable bi- or multilinguals.

At the same time, the Austrian Empire, Austria-Hungary, and Austria all were *consciously* imagined communities. The Habsburg rulers understood the politics of marriage for a millennium; hundreds of years of conscious work created illusions of Habsburg legitimacy[5] and how they might claim Vienna and other cities in the Empire as critical to Habsburg culture: Prague between the sixteenth and nineteenth centuries, Salzburg after World War I, Linz in the Nazi era, and Graz after World War II. Austrian performers and artists were well aware, in the twentieth century, that Germany constituted its largest market. No wonder, then, that Thomas Bernhard and Elfriede Jelinek take their critiques of Austrian culture to Germany—as genuine political sentiments, but also as marketing ploys, selling images of that little, backward country to a self-important Germany that considered itself key to NATO's West and to German culture. That willingness to address international markets, however, is not new: Broadway in the first three decades of the twentieth century was heavily influenced by Central Europe, as plays by Molnár and operettas by major Viennese composers like Oscar Straus, or by composers trained in Austria (Rudolf Friml, Victor Herbert, Sigmund Romberg) became great hits. Early Hollywood had as its founding moguls a group of Russian Jews fleeing pogroms (a number of whom might better be described as having roots in Galicia), but Austrian theater properties (especially operettas) and artists (both behind the scenes and on-stage, including names like Hedy Lamar) took prominent roles long before World War II forced a more elite group of artist-intellectuals into emigration. That the *Sound of Music* has forced Austria into a new round of publicity is nothing new—it is the "new" face, the new dream, that connects Austria to other worlds beyond its borders.[6]

Vienna's Dreams of Europe has therefore offered cases of post-nationalism from the nationalist era of Europe, as they were staged in a region with a pre-national political heritage. The intellectuals, writers, and public figures from many genres and political orientations shared reference points that were straightforwardly available in Vienna: maps

---

5   See Marie Tanner, *The Last Descendant of Aeneas: The Hapsburgs and the Mythic Image of the Emperor* (1993), for descriptions of this imperial self-marketing.

6   See Ulrike Kammerhofer-Aggermann and Alexander G. Keul, eds, *"The Sound of Music": Zwischen Mythos und Marketing* (2000), for the proceedings of an Austrian Symposium dealing with the international fame of the von Trapp Family.

of Europe, the necessity of considering various class and regional positions in public discussions of policy and history. Yet they also acknowledged the reality that all history is simply a set of narratives, and the fact that intellectuals have the ethical responsibility to consider the human costs of their decisions, rather than just use instrumental justifications based on abstracts. These public intellectuals were also already performing the critique of Enlightenment rationalism that we claim as the property of the late twentieth century, just as they were championing the cause of public Enlightenment through education and challenges issued to the public through the media, encouraging a kind of deliberative democracy (a twentieth-century term useful here, stressing democracy as a process rather than a norm). They understood that culture was indeed an "industry," but not necessarily one that had to be rationalized on only one pattern.

The myths of distinctions between high and popular culture predominating in today's cultural studies, derived from the era of nationalism, also fail in significant ways to describe the space in which these Austrian intellectuals worked and sometimes failed. *Official* culture never ceased to be popular, or responsive to popular taste, in this cultural space. Austrian State Theaters now include musicals in their purview (ostensibly commercial theater), and musicals incubated in them have to meet commercial standards, potentially marketable to a known international circuit of theaters staging them. These results would have surprised none of the writers addressed here, who would have seen in them principally the danger of a monoculture rather than the decline of some sort of mythical national culture—the same kinds of protests familiar from the *Wiener Gruppe* in the 1960s and 1970s.

I am by no means arguing for scholarly consideration of *Austrian* literature or culture in isolation, as was the wont of many US Germanists and historians after World War II. What I am alluding to is a different scholarly project: a consideration of how a European viewpoint persists in Central Europe's intellectual life, a cultural center that is not only germanophone but also extends far beyond the various "Germany" incarnations post-1871—a project that truly addresses Europe in Central Europe, rather than in national narratives. The cases outlined here, I believe, document the persistence of broader reference points in "Austrian" cultural production than is commonly assumed in today's scholarship; they point to moments when the national(ist) scholarship of the last century and a half have muddied awareness of widely known circuits of cultural production that extend far beyond Austria-Hungary and Austria into the anglophone and francophone worlds.

The Austrian cultural history written from the German-national point of view (or from that of other Central European states) has most often overlooked transnational and regional, community, and interest-based networks of communication above the level of the nation-state, and thus has essentialized our models for cultural production and cultural history into narratives of ethnicity and national determinism. Twentieth-century scholarship on germanophone Europe and Central Europe first valorized (in the nineteenth century), and then demonized (in the twentieth, and beyond), "official" cultures of a nationalist and imperialist Europe that probably never functioned as they were modeled. Imperial Austria did not function as did the British or German Empires; Austria has never been nationalist in the way that Germany and France were and are. These other *limit* cases of official culture and patronage under extreme conditions of nationalist imperialism and centralizing cultural identity have been taken to be the *normal* model for cultural production in Europe and its American colonies.

The traces of a European culture network that are preserved in Austria, but otherwise almost lost to history, suggest the necessity of reconsidering the Hegelian models of cultural studies (or their Marxist twins of revolution through opposition) as inappropriate, centered as they are around nation-states, rather than on a more strictly materialist vision of networks of cultural production and circulation. Directly or indirectly, taking up the project of cultural studies as a focus on cultural networks promises a yield beyond what we understand about cultures in national(ist) contexts. Michael Hardt and Antonio Negri have redefined the study of *Empire* (2000) as the study of forms of hegemony that can extend over the globe but which are not necessarily isomorphic with nation-states or with imperial holdings defined geopolitically. Austria's networks reached further and deeper than national-imperial studies tend to assume. Vienna, Prague, New York, and Hollywood were waypoints on "Austria's" vibrant transnational theater network in 1900. Berlin was added to it after the political catastrophe of 1918, as Austria-Hungary's writers and actors looked for paying work in their own language (or rather, in *one* of their languages) in a state with a broader financial base. Wider networks of practice added further connected spheres of anglophone influence once Austria's philosophers migrated to England, its musicians to the major US and Canadian cities, and major lights of its film industry to Hollywood. Such networks of cultural practice exert a cultural hegemony far outweighing the narrower cultural networks of Vienna as imperial capital, a capital lacking the financial base of its peer empires in the nineteenth century and whose influence as a node was actively denied by its non-germanophone heritors after 1918. Yet plays imported from France and England were passed on through its lens to the US and beyond—playwrights like Nestroy, Schnitzler, and Hofmannsthal, just as so many of their peer intellectuals, calculated their sources and audience more broadly in the nineteenth and twentieth centuries. "Austrian" culture connects to much more than its hereditary capital cities.

At the same time, the examples pursued here remind us that these networks are not abstracts: they correspond to the real experiences and practices of those involved in them. The *Wiener Gruppe*, like the group of political essayists treated in the final chapter of the present study, understood that they had to act locally, no matter how global or European their reference points have become. Otto von Habsburg's *Return to the Center* made that point by reenacting older historical narratives that have defined politics for a century—using local stereotypes to make a point about Europe. Peter Handke tried, probably unsuccessfully, to move beyond media stereotypes into representations of human experience that would give ethical weight to decisions made about the future of the Balkans. Milo Dor understood that he could not speak *for* Serbia, but that he had a legitimate position within Austrian history to speak *of* Serbia and his own ethical responsibility to introduce to others the voices silenced behind a wall of media. Austria extends beyond its own borders.

And with this, we arrive back at the image introducing this volume: the *Sol Austriacus*. That image reminds us of alternate globes and maps, to regions where the sun does or has not set, regardless of the political entities on which it shines. Or perhaps it simply presents a dream of an earlier millennial Vienna that can today help correct the nationalist image imposed on it—the purportedly decadent empire of the last *fin de siècle*—by twisting the globe to another orientation. The case studies presented here have tried to twist that globe within Europe to correct the scholarship based on monolingual (germanophone) nation-states and their *others* (rather than on networks possibly shared by many sites). They have tried to reduce artificial divides in scholarship between elite and popular cultures reifying class positions as strictly correlated with commercial or national cultures alone.

The intellectuals treated here give ample evidence of more concrete ways of referring to Austria and speaking to or from its platform. They choose their reference points in their own histories or in Europe and draw on tools appropriate to their addressees, whether indigenous or not; their goal is public discussion of issues. Most critically, they refuse to speak *for* anyone but themselves (or to try to do so), while allowing themselves to speak *about* anything that they can ethically authorize themselves to do—as experts and public intellectuals responsible for their speech and their publics rather than to abstract rationalities. Vienna dreams not of its "lost" nation-state (which never existed as such) but rather of a Europe with multiple public spaces, each populated with intellectuals responsible for asking questions and for showing the human costs of answers.

Bibliography

Allen, Julie Doll. *Determining Their Own Destiny: The Portrayal of Women's Emancipation In Lou Andreas-Salome's 'Fenitschka' and Arthur Schnitzler's 'Frau Berta Garlan.'* Diss., University of Washington, 1996.

Ametsbichler, Elizabeth G. "'Der Reiz des Reigens': *Reigen* Works by Arthur Schnitzler and Werner Schwab." *Modern Austrian Literature*, 31, no. 3/4 (1998): 288–300.

Andrade, Oswald de. *Cannibal Manifesto* [*Manifesto Antropófago*, 1928. Trans. Leslie Bary, 1991. Online at http://www.academia.edu/1424345/Cannibalist_Manifesto (accessed 5/4/2015).

Angress, Ruth K. "*Weh dem, der lügt*: Grillparzer and the Avoidance of Tragedy." *Modern Language Review*, 66 (1971): 355–64.

Arens, Katherine. "An Alternate Stifter: Psychologist." In *Austria and Other Margins: Reading Culture*. Columbia, SC: Camden House, 1996, 111–31.

Arens, Katherine. "Arthur Schnitzler and the Discourse of Gender." *A Companion to the Works of Arthur Schnitzler*. Ed. Dagmar C. G. Lorenz. Rochester, NY: Camden House, 2003a, 243–64.

Arens, Katherine. "Central Europe and the Nationalist Paradigm." Working Papers in Austrian Studies. University of Minnesota, March 1996, 96–1.

Arens, Katherine. "The Culture of 'Culture': The Paradox of Primacy in the Kulturwissenschaften." In *The Meaning of Culture: German Studies in the 21st Century*. Eds. Martin Kagel and Laura Tate Kagel. Hannover: Wehrhahn Verlag, 2009, 42–62.

Arens, Katherine. "*Geister der Zeit*: The Allies' Enlightenment and German Literary History." *JEGP*, 102, no. 3 (July 2003b): 336–61.

Arens, Katherine. "Eclipses, Floods, and Other Biedermeier Catastrophes: The theatrum mundi of Revolution." In *The Other Vienna: The Culture of Biedermeier Austria, Österreichisches Biedermeier in Literatur, Musik, Kunst, und Kulturgeschichte*. Sonderpublikations der Grillparzer-Gesellschaft (Wien), no. 5. Eds Robert Pichl and Clifford A. Bernd, with Margarete Wagner. Wien: Lehner, 2002, 173–88.

Arens, Katherine. *Empire in Decline: Fritz Mauthner's Critique of Wilhelminian Germany*. Frankfurt/M: Peter Lang, 2001.

Arens, Katherine. "For Want of a Word: The Case for Germanophone," *Unterrichtspraxis/Teaching German*, 32, no. 2 (Fall, 1999): 130–42.

Arens, Katherine. "The Fourfold Way to Internationalism: Grillparzer's Non-National Historial Literacy." *Aneignungen, Entfremdngen: The Austrian*

Playwright Franz Grillparzer (1792–1872). Eds Marianne Henn, Clemens Ruthner, and Raleigh Whitinger. New York: Peter Lang, 2007, 21–48.

Arens, Katherine. "Grillparzer's *Fiddler*: The Space of Class Consciousness." In *Austria and Other Margins: Reading Culture*. Columbia, SC: Camden House, 1996, 154–81.

Arens, Katherine. "Hofmannsthal's Essays: Conservation as Revolution." *A Companion to the Works of Hugo von Hofmannsthal*. Ed. Thomas A. Kovach. Rochester, NY: Camden House, 2002, 181–202.

Arens, Katherine. "Die Klassik als Tyrannei der Moderne: Wie Grillparzer Weimar widersteht." *Jahrbuch der Grillparzer-Gesellschaft*, 3. Folge, Bd. 22 (2007–8): 13–50.

Arens, Katherine. "Linguistic Skepticism: Towards a Productive Definition." *Monatshefte*, 74, no. 2 (Summer 1982): 145–55.

Arens, Katherine. "The Linguistics of French Feminism: Sémanalyse as Critical Discourse Practice," *Intertexts*, 2.2 (1998).

Arens, Katherine. "The Persistence of *Kasperl* in Memory: H. C. Artmann and Peter Handke." In *Postwar Austrian Theater: Text And Performance*. Eds Linda DeMeritt and Margarete Lamb-Faffelberger. Riverside, CA: Ariadne Press, 2002, 33–53.

Arens, Katherine. "Revolution from the Prompter's Box: Grillparzer and Nestroy in Vienna." Unpublished speech manuscript for a session sponsored by the *Grillparzer Gesellschaft*. *Modern Language Association*, San Francisco, CA, December 29, 1998.

Arens, Katherine. "Said's Colonial Fantasies: How Orientalism Marginalizes Eighteenth-Century Germany." *Herder Jahrbuch*, 7 (2004): 11–29.

Arens, Katherine. "Translators Who Are Not Traitors: Herder's and Lessing's Enlightenment." *HerderJahrbuch/Herder Yearbook*, vol. 5. Stuttgart: J. B. Metzler, 2000, 91–109.

Arens, Katherine. "Wilhelm Griesinger: Psychiatry between Philosophy and Praxis." *Philosophy, Psychiatry & Psychology*, vol. 3, no. 3 (September 1996): 147–63.

Aretin, Karl Otmar Freiherr von. "Das Josephinismus und das Problem des katholischen aufgeklärten Absolutismus." *Österreich im Europa der Aufklärung*. Eds Richard Georg Plaschka and Grete Klingenstein. Wien: Verlag der österreichischen Akademie der Wissenschaften, 1985, 509–24.

artmann, h. c. *brighella, sauer wie der mann im mond*. In *die fahrt zur insel nantucket*. Neuwied und Berlin: Luchterhand, 1969, 459–64.

artmann, h. c. *Kein Pfeffer für Czermak*. In *die fahrt zur insel nantucket*. Neuwied und Berlin: Luchterhand, 1969, 31–72.

artmann, h. c. *die liebe fee pocahontas, oder kasper als schildwache*. In *die fahrt zur insel nantucket*. Neuwied und Berlin: Luchterhand, 1969, 263–92.

artmann, h. c. *punch*. In *die fahrt zur insel nantucket*. Neuwied und Berlin: Luchterhand, 1969, 441–57.

artmann, h. c. and Michael Krüger. "Wer es versteht, der versteht es: H. C. Artmann im Gespräch mit Michael Krüger." In Fuchs and Wischenbart, eds, *H. C. Artmann*, 11–18.

artmann, h. c. et al. "Xogt, gesoggt oder gsokt: Ein Gespräch zwischen H. C. Artmann, Friedrich Achleitner, Gerhard Rühm und Oswald Wiener, moderiert von Wendelin Schmidt-Dengler." In Fuchs and Wischenbart, eds, *H. C. Artmann*, 19–36.

Auchenthaler, Karlheinz. "Nicht alles, was in deutscher Sprache geschrieben wird, ist deutsche Literatur: Die österreichische Literatur -- ein Sonderfall?" In Gratl and Morsak, eds, *Sonne über Österreich*, 174–87.

Aust, Hugo, Peter Haida, and Jürgen Hein. *Volksstück: Vom Hanswurstspiel zum sozialen Drama der Gegenwart*. München: Verlag C. H. Beck, 1989.

Bachmaier, Helmut. "Grillparzers Gschichtsauffassung." Hilde Haider-Pregler and Evelyn Deutsch-Schreiner, eds, *Stichwort: Grillparzer*. 87–96.

Bahr, Ehrhard. "Geld und Liebe im *Armen Spielmann*: Versuch einer sozioliterarischen Interpretation." In Clifford Albrecht Bernd, ed., *Grillparzer's "Der arme Spielmann*." 300–10.

Bandet, Jean-Louis. "Grillparzers *Weh dem, der lügt*." In Hans Steffen, ed., *Das deutsche Lustspiel*, 1. Teil. Göttingen: Vandenhoeck & Ruprecht, 1968, 144–65.

Barner, Wilfried. "Autorität und Anmaßung: Über Lessing's polemische Strategien, vornehmlich im antiquarischen Streit." In Mauser and Saße, eds, *Streitkultur*, 15–37.

Bauer, Roger. "Grillparzers Aufklärung." In Hilde Haider-Pregler and Evelyn Deutsch-Schreiner, eds, *Stichwort: Grillparzer*, 71–6.

Bauer, Roger. "'Luxus' in Österreich: Joseph von Sonnenfels zwischen Jean-Jacques Rousseau und Adam Smith." In Plaschka and Klingenstein, eds, *Österreich im Europa der Aufklärung*, 319–34.

Bauer, Roger. "'Volkstheater' et 'Nationaltheater': Deux variantes du 'theatre pour tous.'" In *Volk- Volksstück-Volkstheater im deutschen Sprachraum des 18.–20. Jahrhunderts*. Ed. Jean-Marie Valentin. Bern: Peter Lang, 1986, 9–23.

Bauer, Werner M. "Grillparzer und Ovid: Ein Beitrag zur Rezeption der Antike in the Literatur Österreichs." In Strelka, ed., *Für all*, 9–57.

Bauer, Werner M. "Ein ungeistlicher Tod: Arthur Schnitzlers Novelle *Sterben* und die Erzählprosa der katholischen Restauration." In Strelka, ed., *Die Seele*, 29–42.

Bäuerle, Adolf. "Die Bürger in Wien'" in Rudolf Fürst, ed. *Raimunds Vorgänger: Bäuere, Meisl, Gleich*. Schriften der Gesellschaft für Theatergeschichte, X. Berlin: Selbstverlag der Gesellschaft für Theatergeschichte, 1907, 3–92.

Baumgart, Wolfgang. "Grillparzers 'Kloster bei Sendomir': Neues zur Quellenfrage, Entstehung und Datierung." *Zeitschrift für deutsche Philologie*, 67, no. 3/4 (March 1943): 162–76.

Bayer, Konrad. *kasperl am elektrischen stuhl. Sämtliche Werke*, Bd. 1. Ed. Gerhard Rühm. Wien: Klett-Cotta, 1985, 261–78.

Bayer, Konrad. *Sämtliche Werke*. Ed. Gerhard Ruhm. 2 Bde. Wien: Klett-Cotta, 1985.

Bayerdörfer, Hans-Peter. "Vom Konversationsstück zur Wurstelkomödie: Zu Arthur Schnitzlers Einaktern." *Jahrbuch der Deutschen Schiller-Gesellschaft*, 16 (1972): 516–75.

Benda, Susanne. "Weil sie nicht gestorben ist, lebt sie noch heute." *Stuttgarter Nachrichten*, March 7, 2005, *Kultur*, 12.

Berghahn, Klaus L. "Zur Dialektik von Lessings polemischer Literaturkritik." In Mauser and Saße, eds, *Streitkultur*, 176–83.

Berlin, Jeffrey B. "Arthur Schnitzler: A Bibliography of Criticism, 1965–1971." *Modern Austrian Literature*, 4, no. 4 (Winter 1971): 7–20.

Berman, Nina. "Hugo von Hofmannsthal's Political Vision." *A Companion to the Works of Hugo von Hofmannsthal*. Ed. Thomas A. Kovach. Rochester, NY: Camden House, 2002, 205–26.

Bernd, Clifford Albrecht. "From Neglect to Controversy: Introducing a Volume of Criticism on *Der arme Spielmann*." In Bernd, ed., *Grillparzer's "Der arme Spielmann."* 1–8.

Bernd, Clifford Albrecht, ed. *Grillparzer's "Der arme Spielmann": New Directions in Criticism*. Studies in German Literature, Linguistics, and Culture 25. Columbia, SC: Camden House, 1988.

Bernd, Clifford Albrecht. "Phases of Grillparzer Scholarhip in America: 1821–1971." *Modern Austrian Literature*, 28, no. 3/4 (1995): 5–28.

Bisinger, Gerald, ed. *Über H. C. Artmann*. Frankfurt/M: Suhrkamp Verlag, 1972.

Bödeker, Hans Erich. "Raisonnement, Zensur und Selbstzensur: Zu den institutionellen und mentalen Voraussetzungen aufklärerischer Kommunikation." In Mauser and Saße, eds, *Streitkultur*, 184–93.

Bogen, Uwe. "'Von Traum und Wirklichkeit bleibt nur Kii-hii-itsch': Wie weit entfernt war die österreichische Kaiserin von Sissi? In Stuttgart haben die Proben für *Elisabeth* begonnen." *Stuttgarter Nachrichten*, January 15, 2005, Lokales, 27.

Böhm, Gotthard. "Dramatik in Österreich seit 1945." In Spiel, ed. *Kindlers Literaturgeschichte*, 477–644.

Borchmeyer, Dieter. "Stifters *Nachsommer*: Eine restaurative Utopie?" *Poetica*, no. 12 (1980): 59–82.

Bossinade, Johanna. "'Wenn es aber … bei mir anders wäre': Die Frage der Geschlechterbeziehungen in Arthur Schnitzlers *Reigen*." In Gerhard Kluge, ed., *Aufsätze und Kunst der Jahrhundertwende*. Amsterdam: Rodopi, 1984, 273–328.

Boyer, John W. *Culture and Political Crisis in Vienna: Christian Socialism in Power, 1897–1918*. Chicago: University of Chicago Press, 1995.

Boyer, John W. *Political Radicalism in Late Imperial Vienna: Origins of the Christian Social Movement 1848–1897*. Chicago: University of Chicago Press, 1981.

Branscombe, Peter. "The Beginnings of Parody in Viennese Popular Theatre." In *From Perinet to Jelinek*. Eds W. E. Yates, Allyson Fiddler, and John Warren. Oxford: Peter Lang, 2001, 23–34.

Brecht, Bertolt. *Die Dreigroschenoper: Der Erstdruck 1928*. Frankfurt/M: Suhrkamp, 2004.

Bulang, Tobias. "Die Rettung der Geschichte in Adalbert Stifters 'Nachsommer.'" *Poetica: Zeitschrift für Sprach- und Literaturwissenschaft*, 32, no. 3–4 (2000): 373–405.

Busek, Erhard, and Emil Brix. *Projekt Mitteleuropa*. Wien: Ueberreuter, 1986.

Busek, Erhard, and Martin Schauer. *Eine europäische Erregung: Die "Sanktionen" der Vierzehn gegen Österreich im Jahr 2000, Analysen und Kommentare*. Wien: Böhlau, 2003.

Carhart, Michael C. *The Science of Culture in Enlightenment Germany*. Harvard Historical Studies, 159. Cambridge, MA: Harvard University Press, 2007.

Cersowsky, Peter. *Johann Nestroy, oder Nix als philosophische Mussenzen: Eine Einführung*. München: Wilhelm Fink Verlag/UTB, 1992.

Chartier, Roger. "The Man of Letters." In *Enlightenment Portraits*. Ed. Michel Vovelle. Trans. Lydia G. Cochrane. Chicago: University of Chicago Press, 1997, 142–89.

Charue-Ferrucci, Jeanine. "Du Roman populaire au 'Volksstück': L'adaptation par Nestroy de la louelle de Michel Raymond: 'Le grain de sable.'" In *Volk-Volksstück-Volkstheater im deutschen Sprachraum des 18.–20. Jahrhunderts*. Ed. Jean-Marie Valentin. Bern: Peter Lang, 1986, 62–78.

Chilton, Meredith. *Harlequin Unmasked: The Commedia dell'arte and Porcelain*

Sculpture. New Haven and London: George R. Gardiner Museum of Ceramic Art with Yale University Press, 2001.

Chotjewitz, Peter O. "Der neue selbstkolorierte Dichter." In Gerald Bisinger, ed., *Über H. C. Artmann*, 13–31 (orig. 1966).

Codrescu, Andrei. *The Blood Countess: A Novel.* New York: Simon & Schuster, 1995.

Cohen, Gary B. *Education and Middle-Class Society in Imperial Austria 1848–1918.* West Lafayette, IN: Purdue University Press, 1996.

Cowen, Roy C. "The History of a Neglected Masterpiece: *Der arme Spielmann.*" In Clifford Albrecht Bernd, ed. *Grillparzer's "Der arme Spielmann."* 9–26.

Danto, Elizabeth Ann. *Freud's Free Clinics: Psychoanalysis and Social Justice, 1918–1938.* New York: Columbia University Press, 2005.

Danzer, Georg. *Traurig aber wahr.* ASIN B005N1PU74 (CD). Vienna: Polydor, 2011.

Dassanowsky, Robert von. *Austrian Cinema: A History.* Jefferson, NC: McFarland, 2005.

Dassanowsky, Robert von. and Oliver C. Speck, eds. *New Austrian Film.* New York: Berghahn Books, 2011.

Davies, Norman. *God's Playground: A History of Poland.* New York: Columbia University Press, 1982.

DeJean, Joan E. *Ancients Against Moderns: Culture Wars and the Making of a fin de siècle.* Chicago: University of Chicago Press, 1997.

Deleuze, Gilles, and Félix Guattari. *Kafka: Toward a Minor Literature* (1986). Trans. Dana Polan. Minneapolis: University of Minnesota Press, 1986.

Deutsch-Schreiner, Evelyn. *Theater im "Wiederaufbau": Zur Kulturpolitik im österreichischen Parteien- und Verbändestaat.* Wien: Sonderzahl, 2001.

Dittmann, Ulrich. "Stifters Dichtung im gesellschaftspolitischen Kontext ihrer Zeit." *Informationen zur Deutschdidaktik: Zeitschrift für den Deutschunterricht in Wissenschaft und Schule* 1, (2005): 12–17.

Domandl, Sepp. *Adalbert Stifters Lesebuch und die geistigen Strömungen zur Jahrhundertmitte.* Linz: Adalbert Stifter-Institut des Landes Oberösterreich, 1976.

Domandl, Sepp. "Die philosophische Tradition von Adalbert Stifters 'Sanftem Gesetz.'" *VASILO*, 21, no. 3–4 (1972): 79–103.

Donnenberg, Josef. "Pose, Possen, Protest und Poesie—oder: Artmanns Manier." In Donnenberg, ed., *Pose*, 149–80.

Donnenberg, Josef. ed. *Pose, Possen und Poesie: Zum Werk Hans Carl Artmanns.* Stuttgart: Akademischer Verlag Hans-Dieter Heinz, 1981.

Doppler, Alfred. "Das sanfte Gesetz und die unsanfte Natur in Stifters Erzählungen." *Geborgenheit und Gefährdung in der epischen und malerischen Welt Adalbert Stifters.* Würzburg: Königshausen & Neumann, 2006, 13–22.

Doppler, Alfred. "Die 'Wiener Gruppe' und die literarische Tradition." In Walter-Buchebner-Projekt, ed., *die wiener gruppe*, 60–8.

Dor, Milo. *Leb wohl, Jugoslawien: Protokolle eines Zerfalls.* 3. erw. Aufl. Salzburg: Otto Müller, 1996 [1993].

Dor, Milo. *Mitteleuropa, Mythos oder Wirklichkeit: Auf der Suche nach der größeren Heimat.* Salzburg: O. Müller, 1996.

Draudt, Manfred. "Fairgrounds and Halls of Mirrors: Arthur Schnitzler's *Zum grossen Wurstel* and Ben Jonson's *Bartholomew Fair.*" *Trivium*, 20 (May 1985), 9–32.

Düriegl, Günter. "Wien: Eine Residenzstadt im Übergang von der adeligen

Metropole zur bürgerlichen Urbanitat." *Österreich im Europa der Aufklärung.* Eds Richard Georg Plaschka and Grete Klingenstein. Wien: Verlag der österreichischen Akademie der Wissenschaften, 1985, 305–18.

Eco, Umberto. *Foucault's Pendulum.* Trans. William Weaver. San Diego: Harcourt Brace Jovanovich, 1989 [1988].

Ehalt, Gernot, Hubert Ch. Heiß, and Hannes Stekl, eds. *Glücklich ist, wer vergißt?: Das andere Wien um 1900.* Wien: Böhlau, 1986.

Ehalt, Silvia. "Wiener Theater um 1900." In Ehalt et al., eds, *Glücklich ist*, 325–42.

Ehmer, Josef. "Wiener Arbeitswelten um 1900." In Ehalt et al., eds, *Glücklich ist*, 195–214.

Eilert, Heide. "Abschied von Kythera? Zu Arthur Schnitzlers *Komödie der Verführung* und der Rokoko-Rezeption der *Fin de siècle*." *Sprachkunst: Beiträge zur Literaturwissenschaft*, 22, no. 2 (1991): 215–29.

Eisenmeier, Eduard. *Adalbert Stifter Bibliographie.* Linz: Oberösterreichischer Landesverlag, 1964.

Enklaar, Jattie, and Hans Ester, eds, with Evelyne Tax. *Geborgenheit und Gefährdung in der epischen und malerischen Welt Adalbert Stifters.* Würzburg: Königshausen & Neumann, 2006.

Enzensberger, Hans Magnus. *The Consciousness Industry: On Literature, Politics and the Media.* Ed. Michael Roloff. New York: Seabury Press, 1974.

Enzensberger, Hans Magnus. *Einzelheiten I: Bewußtseins-Industrie.* Edition Suhrkamp, Nr. 63. 15. Auflage. Frankfurt/M: Suhrkamp, 1995 [1963].

Eyck, John Robert Jerome. "The Tragedy of Sentimentalism and Politics in Enlightenment Europe." Diss., University of Texas at Austin, 1999.

Feichtinger, Johannes, Ursula Prutsch, and Moritz Csáky, eds. *Habsburg postcolonial: Machtstrukturen und kollektives Gedächtnis.* Innsbruck: StudienVerlag, 2003.

Fellini, Federico, and Bernardino Zapponi. *The Clowns.* [s.l.], Cinematheque Collection, 1970.

Ficker, Adolf. *Bericht über österreichisches Unterrichtswesen, 1. Theil: Geschichte, Organisation und Statistik des österreichischen Unterrichtswesens.* Wien: Adolf Hölder, 1873.

Fischer, Barbara, and Thomas C. Fox, eds. *A Companion to the Works of Gotthold Ephraim Lessing.* Rochester, NY: Camden House, 2005.

Foteva, Ana. *Do the Balkans Begin in Vienna?: The Geopolitical and Imaginary Borders between the Balkans and Europe.* New York: Peter Lang, 2014.

Foteva, Ana. *Fin de siècle Balkans: The Cultural Politics of Orientalist Imagination at Europe's Margin.* Diss., Purdue University, 2009.

François, Etienne. "Villes d'Empire et Aufklärung." In Grappin, ed., *L'Allemagne des Lumières*, 9–24.

Frodl, Gerbert, and Klaus Albrecht Schröder, eds. *Wiener Biedermeier: Malerei zwischen Wiener Kongreß und Revolution.* München: Prestel Verlag, 1992.

Frodl, Gerbert, and Marianne Frodl. "Das Wiener Genrebild: Gedanken zu seiner Entstehung." In Frodl and Schröder, eds, *Wiener Biedermeier*, 44–52.

Fuchs, Gerhard. "Fritz Mauthners Sprachkritik: Aspekte ihrer literarischen Rezeption in der osterreichischen Gegenwartsliteratur." *Modern Austrian Literature*, 23, no. 2 (1990): 1–21.

Fuchs, Gerhard. and Rüdiger Wischenbart, eds. *H. C. Artmann. Dossier*, Bd. 3. Graz, Wien: Literaturverlag Droschl, 1992.

Fülleborn, Ulrich. "Der Mensch und die Wirklichkeit der Welt: Grillparzers

Alternative zum neuzeitlichen Subjektivitätsentwurf." *Jahrbuch des Wiener Goethe-Vereins*, 94 (1990): 45–55.

Fülleborn, Ulrich. "Franz Grillparzer, 'Polarszene.'" *Jahrbuch für Internationale Germanistik*. 11, no. 1 (1979): 122–9.

Furst, Lilian R. "No Bed of Roses: The Women in the *Rosenkavalier*." *Jahrbuch für internationale Germanistik*, 16, no. 1 (1984): 116–60.

Fürst, Rudolf. *Raimunds Vorgänger: Bäuere, Meisl, Gleich*. Schriften der Gesellschaft für Theatergeschichte, X. Berlin: Selbstverlag der Gesellschaft für Theatergeschichte, 1907.

Gebhardt, Arnim. *Franz Grillparzer und sein dramatisches Werk*. Marburg: Tectum Verlag, 2002.

Geissler, Rolf. "Grillparzer und die Zukunft." *Jahrbuch der Grillparzer-Gesellschaft*. 3. Folge, 19. Bd (1996): 109–23.

Gordon, Kevin A. "Historical Rupture and the Devastation of Memory in Adalbert Stifter's 'Der Hagestolz.'" *Journal of Austrian Studies*, 45, no. 3–4 (Fall–Winter, 2012): 87–112.

Gordon, Mel. *Lazzi: The Comic Routines of the Commedia dell'arte*. New York: Performing Arts Journal Publications, 1983.

Gottwald, Herwig. "Adalbert Stifter Leben und Werk: Zeittafel 1805–1868." *Informationen zur Deutschdidaktik: Zeitschrift für den Deutschunterricht in Wissenschaft und Schule* 1. (2005): 9–11.

Gottwald, Herwig. "Stifters literarischer Umgang mit Emotionen: Erläutert am Beispiel der Mappe meines Urgroßvaters." *Informationen zur Deutschdidaktik: Zeitschrift für den Deutschunterricht in Wissenschaft und Schule* 1. (2005): 18–28.

Gottwald, Herwig. Christian Schacherreiter, and Werner Wintersteiner. "Adalbert Stifter [Special Issue]." *Informationen zur Deutschdidaktik: Zeitschrift für den Deutschunterricht in Wissenschaft und Schule* 1. (2005): 3–143.

Grappin, Pierre, ed. *L'Allemagne des Lumières: Périodiques, Correpondances, Témoignages*. Paris: Didier-Érudition, 1982.

Grass, Günter. *Die Blechtrommel*. Neuwied: Luchterhand, 1959.

Grass, Günter. *The Tin Drum*. Trans. Ralph Manheim. New York: Random House/ Pantheon, 1961.

Gratl, Christoph, and Louis C. Morsak. *Sonne über Österreich: Ein etwas anderer Beitrag zum Ostarrichi-Millennium*. Hall in Tirol: Berenkamp, 1996.

Gregory of Tours. *The History of the Franks*. Trans. Lewis Thorpe. Harmondsworth: Penguin, 1974.

Grillparzer, Franz. *Der arme Spielmann: Erzählung. Sämtliche Werke, 3: Ausgewählte Briefe, Gespräche, Berichte*. Eds Peter Frank and Karl Pörnbacher. Munich: Carl Hanser, 1964.

Grillparzer, Franz. *The Poor Musician*. Trans. J. F. Hargraves and J. G. Cumming. In Jeffrey L Sammons, ed., *German Novella of Realism I*. German Library 37. New York: Continuum, 1989.

Grillparzer, Franz. *Prosaschriften I: Erzählungen, Satiren in Prosa, Aufsätze zur Zeitgeschichte und Politik*. Eds August Sauer and Reinhold Backmann. = Sämtliche Werke: Historisch-Kritische Gesamtausgabe, Erste Abteilung, 13. Bd. Wien: Anton Schroll & Co., 1930.

Grillparzer, Franz. *Prosaschriften II: Aufsätze über Literatur, Musik und Theater, Musikalien*. Ed. August Sauer. = Sämtliche Werke: Historisch-Kritische Gesamtausgabe, Erste Abteilung, 14. Bd. Wien: Anton Schroll & Co., 1925.

Grillparzer, Franz. Weh dem, der lügt!: Lustspiel in fünf Aufzügen. *Sämtliche Werke—Ausgewählte Briefe, Gespräche, Berichte: 2*. Bd. Eds Peter Frank and Karl Pörnbacher. München: Carl Hanser, 1961, 183–256.

Gruber, Helmut. *Red Vienna: Experiment in Working-Class Culture 1919–1934*. New York: Oxford University Press, 1991.

Gump, Margaret. *Adalbert Stifter*. New York: Twayne, 1974.

Habermas, Jürgen. *The Structural Transformation of the Public Sphere: An Inquiry into a Category of Bourgeois Society*. Trans. Thomas Burger with Frederick Lawrence. Cambridge: Polity, 1989.

Habermas, Jürgen. *Strukturwandel der Öffentlichkei: Untersuchungen zu einer Kategorie der bürgerlichen Gesellschaft*. Neuwied/Berlin: Suhrkamp, 1962.

Habsburg, Otto von. *Friedensmacht Europa: Sternstunden und Finsternis*. Wien: Amalthea, 1995.

Habsburg, Otto von. *Mémoires d'Europe: Entretiens*. Paris: Criterion, 1994.

Habsburg, Otto von. *Die Paneuropäische Idee: Eine Vision wird Wirklichkeit*. Wien: Amalthea, 1999.

Habsburg, Otto von. "1000 Jahre Ostarrichi-Urkunde." In Gratl and Morsak, eds. *Sonne über Österreich*, 9–10.

Habsburg, Otto von. *Zurück zur Mitte*. Wien: Amalthea, 1991 = *Return to the Center*. Riverside, CA: Ariadne Press, 1993.

Hacker, Friedrich. "Im falschen Leben gibt es kein Richtiges." *Literatur und Kritik*, no. 163/164 (April–May 1982): 36–44.

Hadamowsky, Franz. "Ein Jahrhundert Literatur- und Theaterzensur in Österreich (1751–1848)." In Herbert Zeman, ed., *Die Österreichische Literatur*, 289–305.

Haider-Pregler, Hilde. "Entwicklungen im Wiener Theater zur Zeit Maria Theresias." *Österreich im Europa der Aufklärung*. Eds Richard Georg Plaschka and Grete Klingenstein. Wien: Verlag der österreichischen Akademie der Wissenschaften, 1985, 701–16.

Haider-Pregler, Hilde, and Evelyn Deutsch-Schreiner, eds. *Stichwort: Grillparzer*. Grillparzer-Forum 1. Wien: Böhlau, 1994.

Handke, Peter. *Abschied des Träumers vom Neunten Land: Eine Wirklichkeit, die vergangen ist—Erinnerung an Slowenien*. Frankfurt/M: Suhrkamp, 1991.

Handke, Peter. "Für das Straßentheater, gegen die Straßentheater." In *Prosa, Gedichte, Theaterstücke, Hörspiel, Aufsätze*, 308–13.

Handke, Peter. *Kaspar*. Frankfurt/M: Suhrkamp, 1968.

Handke, Peter. "Kaspar." In *Kaspar and Other Plays*. Trans. Michael Roloff. New York: Farrar, Straus and Giroux, 1969.

Handke, Peter. "Das Mündel will Vormund sein." In *Prosa, Gedichte, Theaterstücke, Hörspiel, Aufsätze*, 157–79.

Handke, Peter. *Prosa, Gedichte, Theaterstücke, Hörspiel, Aufsätze*. Frankfurt/M: Suhrkamp Verlag, 1969.

Handke, Peter. *Sommerlicher Nachtrag zu einer winterlichen Reise*. Frankfurt/M: Suhrkamp, 1996.

Handke, Peter. "Straßentheater und Theatertheater." In *Prosa, Gedichte, Theaterstücke, Hörspiel, Aufsätze*, 303–7.

Handke, Peter. *Eine winterliche Reise zu den Flüssen Donau, Save, Morawa und Drina, oder Gerechtigkeit für Serbien*. Frankfurt/M: Suhrkamp, 1996 = *A Journey to the Rivers: Justice for Serbia*. Trans. Scott Abbott. New York: Viking, 1997.

Hardt, Michael, and Antonio Negri. *Empire*. Cambridge, MA: Harvard University Press, 2000.

Hars, Endre, Wolfgang Müller-Funk, Ursula Reber, and Clemens Ruthner, eds. *Zentren, Peripheren und kollektive Identitäten in Österreich-Ungarn.* Tübingen: A. Francke, 2006.

Haselsteiner, Horst. "Europa rediviva?! Das Beispiel der kulturellen Vielfalt des Habsburgerreiches." In Gratl and Morsak, eds, *Sonne über Österreich,* 159–69.

Haslinger, Adolf. "Zwei Randglossen zur Textrealization bei H. C. Artmann." In Donnenberg, ed., *Pose,* 35–47.

Häusler, Wolfgang. "Adalbert Stifter und Friedrich Simony entdecken die Alpen: Die geologische Grundlegung der Geographie in Österreich." *Österreich in Geschichte und Literatur (mit Geographie),* 53, no. 2 (2009): 113–40.

Häusler, Wolfgang. "'Biedermeier' oder 'Vormärz'?: Anmerkungen zur österreichischen Sozialgeschichte in der Epoche der bürgerlichen Revolution." In Frodl and Schröder, eds, *Wiener Biedermeier,* 35–43.

Hebdige, Dick. *Subculture: The Meaning of Style.* London: Routledge, 1979.

Helmensdorfer, Urs. "Die Kunst, Grillparzer zu sprechen." In Hilde Haider-Pregler and Evelyn Deutsch-Schreiner, eds, *Stichwort: Grillparzer,* 145–52.

Hein, Jürgen. *Johann Nestroy.* Sammlung Metzler 258. Stuttgart: J. B. Metzler, 1990.

Hein, Jürgen. "Nestroy's 'Epic' Theater." In John R. P. McKenzie and Lesley Sharpe, eds, *The Austrian Comic Tradition: Studies in Honour of W. E. Yates.* Austrian Studies, 9. Edinburgh: Edinburgh University Press, 1998, 86–101.

Hein, Jürgen. "Zur Funktion der 'musikalischen Einlagen' in den Stücken des Wiener Volkstheaters." In *Volk- Volksstück-Volkstheater im deutschen Sprachraum des 18.–20. Jahrhunderts.* Ed. Jean-Marie Valentin. Bern: Peter Lang, 1986 103–26.

Heller, André, and Helmut Qualtinger. *Heurige und gestrige Lieder: Geschichten aus dem Wienerwald.* Polydor 831 290–1 (LP). Austria: Polydor, 1979.

Hellyer, Marcus. *Catholic Physics: Jesuit Natural Philosophy in Early Modern Germany.* Notre Dame, IN: University of Notre Dame Press, 2005.

Helmetag, Charles H. "The Gentle Law in Adalbert Stifter's *Der Hagestolz.*" *Modern Language Studies* 16, no. 3 (Summer 1986): 183–8.

Henn, Marianne, Clemens Ruthner and Raleigh Whitinger, eds. *Aneignungen, Entfremdungen: The Austrian Playwright Franz Grillparzer (1792–1872).* Austrian Culture, Vol. 37. New York: Peter Lang, 2007.

Herles, Helmut. *Nestroys Komödie "Der Talisman."* München: Wilhelm Fink Verlag, 1974.

Hertling, Gunter H. "Der Mensch und 'seine' Tiere: Versäumte Symbiose, versäumte Bildung: Zu A. Stifters *Abdias.*" *Modern Austrian Literature* 18, no. 1 (1985): 1–26.

Herzmann, Herbert. *Tradition und Subversion: Das Volksstück und das epische Theater.* Stauffenburg Colloquium, Bd. 41. Tübingen: Stauffenburg/Brigitte Narr, 1997.

Hertz, Deborah. *Jewish High Society in Old Regime Berlin.* New Haven: Yale University Press, 1988.

Hettche, Walter, Johannes John, and Sibylle Steinsdorff, eds. *Stifter-Studien.* Tübingen: Niemeyer; 2000.

Himmel, Hellmuth. "Grillparzers Novelle 'Das Kloster bei Sendomir': Struktur und Erzählsituation." *Grillparzer Forum Forchtenstein: Vorträge, Forschungen, Berichte* (Austria) (1976): 42–68.

Hobsbawm, Eric, and Terence Ranger, eds. *The Invention of Tradition*. Cambridge: Cambridge University Press, 1983.

Hofmannsthal, Hugo von. "Ein Brief." In *Erfundene Gespräche und Briefe (Sämtliche Werke XXXI)*. Ed. Ellen Ritter. Frankfurt/M: S. Fischer, 1991: 45–55.

Hofmannsthal, Hugo von. *Gesammelte Werke: Reden und Aufsätze I, 1891–1913*. Ed. Bernd Schoeller. Frankfurt/M: S. Fischer, 1979.

Hofmannsthal, Hugo von. *Gesammelte Werke: Reden und Aufsätze II, 1914–1924*. Ed. Bernd Schoeller. Frankfurt/M: S. Fischer, 1979

Hofmannsthal, Hugo von. *Gesammelte Werke: Reden und Aufsätze III, 1925–1929*. Eds Bernd Schoeller and Ingeborg Beyer-Ahlert. Frankfurt/M: S. Fischer, 1979.

Hofmannsthal, Hugo von. *Der Rosenkavalier*. New York: Boosney & Hawkins, 1943; rpt. In London Records, OSAL 1435.

Höller, Hans. "Zur Aktualität von Grillparzers Dramen-Sprache: Eine Interpretationsskizze zu den drei letzten Dramen." In Hilde Haider-Pregler and Evelyn Deutsch-Schreiner, eds, *Stichwort: Grillparzer*, 59–70.

Holmes, Deborah, and Lisa Silverman, eds. *Interwar Vienna: Culture Between Tradition and Modernity*. Rochester, NY: Camden House, 2009.

Holmes, Tove. "'… was ich in diesem Hause geworden bin': Adalbert Stifter's Visual Curriculum." *Zeitschrift für Deutsche Philologie* 129.4 (2010), 559–77.

Horkheimer, Max, and Theodor W. Adorno. *Dialektik der Aufklärung*. Amsterdam: Querido, 1947; Frankfurt: S. Fischer, 1969.

Huish, Louise Adey. "An Austrian Comic Tradition?" *The Austrian Comic Tradition: Studies in Honor of W. E. Yates*. Eds John R. P. McKenzie and Lesley Sharpe. Austrian Studies, 9. Edinburgh: Edinburgh University Press, 1998, 3–23.

Hüttner, Johann. "Der ernste Nestroy." In *The Austrian Comic Tradition: Studies in Honour of W. E. Yates*. Eds John R. P. McKenzie and Lesley Sharpe. Austrian Studies, 9. Edinburgh: Edinburgh University Press, 1998, 67–80.

Hüttner, Johann. *Theater als Geschäft*. Hab. Wien, 1982.

Hüttner, Johann. "Volkstheater als Geschäft: Theaterbetrieb und Publikum im 19. Jahrhundert." *Volk- Volksstück-Volkstheater im deutschen Sprachraum des 18.–20. Jahrhunderts*. Ed. Jean-Marie Valentin. Bern: Peter Lang, 1986, 127–49.

Huyssen, Andreas. "The Disturbance of Vision in Vienna Modernism." *Modernism/ Modernity*, 5, no. 3 (September 1998): 33–47.

Ireton, Sean. "Geology, Mountaineering, and Self-Formation in Adalbert Stifter's *Der Nachsommer*." In Sean Ireton and Caroline Schaumann, eds, *Heights of Reflection: Mountains in the German Imagination from the Middle Ages to the Twenty-First Century*. Rochester, NY: Camden House, 2012, 193–209.

Ireton, Sean. "Walden in the Bohemian Forest: Adalbert Stifter's Transcendental Ecocentrism in 'Der Hochwald.'" *Modern Austrian Literature*, 43, no. 3 (2010): 1–18.

Irmscher, Hans Dietrich. *Adalbert Stifter: Wirklichkeitserfahrung und gegenständliche Darstellung*. Munich: Wilhelm Fink Verlag, 1971.

Ivory, Yvonne M. "The Perils of Post-Holing: Arthur Schnitzler versus Hugo von Hofmannsthal in Carl Schorske's *Fin-de-siècle Vienna*." *New German Review* 13 (1997–8): 57–66.

Jansen, Peter K. "Johann Nepomuk Nestroys Skeptische Utopie: Märchen und Wirklichkeit in *Der Talisman*." *Jahrbuch der deutschen Schillergesellschaft*, 14 (1980), 247–82.

Jakubów, Marek. "'Kostbare Gegenstände': Zu Adalbert Stifters Umgang mit der ästhetischen Wahrnehmung." In Jattie Enklaar and Hans Ester, eds, with Evelyne Tax. *Geborgenheit und Gefährdung in der epischen und malerischen Welt Adalbert Stifters.* Würzburg: Königshausen & Neumann, 2006, 153–60.

Japp, Uwe. "Die Signifikation des Ästhetischen im Raum des Realen bei Adalbert Stifter." In Sabine Schneider and Barbara Hunfeld, eds, *Die Dinge und die Zeichen: Dimensionen des Realistischen in der Erzählliteratur des 19. Jahrhunderts.* Würzburg: Königshausen & Neumann, 2008, 95–105.

John, Johannes. "Die Historisch-Kritische Ausgabe der Werke und Briefe Adalbert Stifters." In Jattie Enklaar and Hans Ester, eds, with Evelyne Tax. *Geborgenheit und Gefährdung in der epischen und malerischen Welt Adalbert Stifters.* Würzburg: Königshausen & Neumann, 2006, 35–42.

John, Michael. "Obdachlosigkeit—Massenerscheinung und Unruheherd im Wien der Spätgründerzeit." In Ehalt et al., eds, *Glücklich ist,* 173–94.

Jones, Sheila. "Werte und Menschlichkeit in *Weh dem, der lügt.*" *Jahrbuch der Grillparzer-Gesellschaft,* 17 (1987–90): 43–51.

Judson, Pieter M. *Exclusive Revolutionaries: Liberal Politics, Social Experience, and National Identity in the Austrian Empire, 1848–1914.* Ann Arbor: University of Michigan Press, 1996.

Judson, Pieter M. *Guardians of the Nation: Activists on the Language Frontiers of Imperial Austria.* Cambridge, MA: Harvard University Press, 2006.

Judson, Pieter M. and Marsha L Rozenblit, eds. *Constructing Nationalities in East Central Europe.* Oxford: Berghahn Books, 2005.

Kammerhofer-Aggermann, Ulrike, and Alexander G Keul, eds. *"The Sound of Music": Zwischen Mythos und Marketing.* Salzburg: Salzburger Landesinstitut für Volkskunde, 2000.

Kann, Robert A. "Die historische Situation und die entscheidenden politischen Ereignisse zur Zeit und im Leben Arthur Schnitzlers." *Literatur und Kritik,* no. 161/162 (February/March 1982): 19–25.

Kann, Robert A. *A History of the Habsburg Empire, 1526–1918.* Berkeley: University of California Press, 1980.

Kaplan, Robert D. *Balkan Ghosts: A Journey through History.* New York: St. Martin's Press, 1993.

Kelemen, Pál. "The Epistemology of the Arbour: On the Intersection of Nature and Technology in Adalbert Stifter." In Judit Pieldner and Zsuzsanna Ajtony, eds, *Discourses of Space.* Newcastle upon Tyne: Cambridge Scholars, 2013, 198–225.

Kiesel, Helmuth, with Georg Braungart and Klaus Fischer, eds. *Briefe von und an Lessing 1743–1770* (= *Lessing Werke und Briefe,* Bd. 11/1). Frankfurt/M: Deutscher Klassiker Verlag, 1987.

Kilian, Klaus. *Die Komödien Arthur Schnitzlers: Sozialer Rollenzwang und kritische Ethik.* Düsseldorf: Bertelsmann Universitätsverlag, 1972.

Klingenstein, Eva. *Die Frau mit Eigenschaften: Literatur und Gesellschaft in der Wiener Frauenpresse um 1900.* Köln: Böhlau, 1997.

Koch, Hans-Albrecht. *Hugo von Hofmannsthal.* Darmstadt: Wissenschaftliche Buchgesellschaft, 1989.

Kolleth, Sabina. "Gewalt in Ehe und Intimpartnerschaft." In Ehalt et al., eds, *Glücklich ist,* 145–71.

Kompert, Leopold. "Ohne Bewillingung." In *Alt-Wiener Geschichten.* Ed. Joseph Peter Strelka. Frankfurt/M: Insel, 1984, 43–90.

Koschatzky, Walter. *Biedermeier und Vormärz: Die Kammermaler Matthäus Loder und Eduard Gurk.* Wien: Albertina, 1978.

Koschorke, Albrecht. "Erziehung zum Freitod: Adalbert Stifters pädagogischer Realismus." *Die Dinge und die Zeichen: Dimensionen des Realistischen in der Erzählliteratur des 19. Jahrhunderts.* Würzburg: Königshausen & Neumann, 2008, 319–32.

Koutek, Eduard. *Wien: Straßen, Gassen und Plätze erzählen Geschichte.* Vienna: Verlag H. Kapri, 1977.

Kovach, Thomas A., ed. *A Companion to the Works of Hugo von Hofmannsthal.* Rochester, NY: Camden House, 2002.

Krebs, Roland. "Une Revue de L'Aufklärung viennoise: *L'Homme sans prejuges* de Joseph von Sonnenfels 1765–1767." In Grappin, ed., *L'Allemagne des Lumières,* 215–33.

Krispyn, Egbert. "The Fiasco of *Weh dem, der lügt.*" *German Life & Letters,* 25, no. 3 (April 1972): 201–9.

Kristeva, Julia. *Polylogue.* Paris: Éditions du Seuil, 1977.

Kristeva, Julia. *La révolution du langage poétique: L'avant-garde à la fin du XIXe siècle, Lautréamont et Mallarmé.* Paris: Éditions du Seuil, 1974.

Kristeva, Julia. *Revolution in Poetic Language.* Trans. Margaret Waller. New York: Columbia University Press, 1984 [part 1 only].

Kuehnelt-Leddihn, Erik von. "Gedanken über eine tausendjährigen Fälschung." In: Gratl and Morsak, eds, *Sonne über Österreich,* 19–27.

Kühn, Joachim. *Gescheiterte Sprachkritik: Fritz Mauthners Leben und Werk.* Berlin: De Gruyter, 1975.

Lachinger, Johann. "Adalbert-Stifter-Bibliographie." *Adalbert Stifter Institut des Landes Oberosterreich: Vierteljahresschrift,* 39, no. 3–4 (1990): 41–86.

Lachinger, Johann, Alexander Stillmark, and Martin Swales, eds. *Adalbert Stifter Heute: Londoner Symposium 1983.* Linz: Adalbert Stifter Institut des Landes Oberösterreich and Oberösterreichischer Landesverlag, 1985.

Lang, Helmut W. "Die Zeitschriften in Österreich zwischen 1740 und 1815." In Herbert Zeman, ed., *Die österreichische Literatur,* 203–27.

Längle, Ulrike. "Die Haupt des Titus Jochanaan Feuerfuchs: Die biblische Salome Geschichte im *Talisman.*" In *Der unbekannte Nestroy.* Ed. W. Edgar Yates. Wien: WUV/Universitätsverlag, 2001, 79–97.

Laufhütte, Hartmut, and Karl Möseneder, eds. *Adalbert Stifter: Dichter und Maler, Denkmalpfleger und Schulmann—Neue Zugänge zu seinem Werk.* Tübingen: Niemeyer, 1996.

Lawson, Richard H. "The Starost's Daughter: Elga in Grillparzer's 'Kloster bei Sendomir'." *Modern Austrian Literature,* 1, no. 3 (1968): 31–7.

Leitgeb, Christoph. "Grillparzers 'Kloster bei Sendomir' und Musils 'Tonka': Ein Sprachstilvergleich." *Sprachkunst: Beiträge zur Literaturwissenschaft,* 25, no. 2 (1994): 347–71.

Leinfellner-Rupertsberger, Elisabeth. "Fritz Mauthner (1849–1923)." In M. Dascal et al., eds, *Handbuch der Sprachphilosophie,* Teil 2. Berlin and New York: Walter de Gruyter, 1992, 495–509.

Le Rider, Jacques. *Hugo von Hofmannsthal: Historismus und Moderne in der Literatur der Jahrhundertwende.* Trans. Leopold Federmair. Wien: Böhlau, 1997 [French original, 1995].

Lengauer, Hubert. "Zur Stellung der 'Briefe über die wienerische Schaubühne' in der aufklärerischen Dramentheorie." In Herbert Zeman, ed., *Die österreichische Literatur,* 587–621.

Lessing, Gotthold Ephraim. *Werke, 5. Bd.: Literaturkritik, Poetik und Philologie.*

Darmstadt: Wissenschaftliche Buchgesellschaft, 1996 (rpt. of München: Carl Hanser Verlag, 1973).

Lettner, Gerda. "Franz Grillparzer in und nach der Wiener Revolution 1848–1890." *Jahrbuch des Wiener Goethe-Vereins*, 96 (1992): 39–71.

Lobkowicz, Nikolaus. "Das europäische Menschenbild." In Prunskiene and Habsburg, eds, *Europa*, 33–44.

Lorenz, Dagmar C. G., ed. *A Companion to the Works of Arthur Schnitzler*. Rochester, NY: Camden House, 2003.

Lorenz, Dagmar C. G., ed. "Franz Grillparzer und die alten und neuen Ordnungen." *Modern Austrian Literature*, 28, no. 3/4 (1995): 29–41.

Lorenz, Dagmar C. G., ed. *Grillparzer, Dichter des sozialen Konflikts*. Wien: Böhlau, 1986.

Luft, David S., ed. and trans. *Hugo von Hofmannsthal and the Austrian Idea: Selected Essays and Addresses, 1906–1927*. West Lafayette, IN: Purdue University Press, 2011.

Lütgenau, Stefan. *Paul Esterházy 1901–1989: Ein Leben im Zeitalter der Extreme*. Innsbruck: StudienVerlag, 2005.

Magris, Claudio. *Danubio*. Milan: Garzanti, 1986 (=*Danube*). Trans. Patrick Creagh. New York: Farrar, Straus, Giroux, 1989.

Mahlendorf, Ursula. "Stifters Absage an die Kunst." In Gerhart Hoffmeister, ed., *Goethezeit: Studien zur Erkenntnis und Rezeption Goethes und seiner Zeitgenossen, Festschrift für Stuart Atkins*. Bern and Munich: Francke Verlag, 1981, 369–83.

Maier, Wolfgang. "Die Pose in ihrer edelsten Form." In Gerald Bisinger, ed., *Über H. C. Artmann*, 98–101.

Martini, Fritz. "Franz Grillparzer: *Weh dem, der lügt*, oder von der Sprache im Drama." *Lustspiele—und das Lustspiel*. Stuttgart: Ernst Klett Verlag, 1974, 198–212.

Martyn, David. "The Picturesque as Art of the Average: Stifter's Statistical Poetics of Observation." *Monatshefte*, 105 (Fall, 2013): 426–42.

Maurer, Kathrin. "Close-Ups of History: Photographic Description in the Works of Jacob Burckhardt and Adalbert Stifter." *Monatshefte für Deutschsprachige Literatur und Kultur*, 97, no. 1 (Spring, 2005): 63–77.

Mauser, Wolfram. "Identitätsbildung und Spielkonstellation: 'Der Rosenkavalier.'" In *Hugo von Hofmannsthal: Konfliktbewältigung und Werkstruktur—Eine psychologische Interpretation*. München: Wilhelm Fink, 1977, 127–37.

Mauser, Wolfram, and Günter Saße, eds. *Streitkultur: Strategien des Überzeugens im Werk Lessings*. Tübingen: Max Niemeyer, 1993.

Mauthner, Fritz. *Beiträge zu einer Kritik der Sprache*. 3., um Zusätze verm. Aufl. 3 Bde. Leipzig: Felix Meiner, 1923.

Mauthner, Fritz. *Wörterbuch der Philosophie: Neue Beiträge zu einer Kritik der Sprache*. 3 Bde. 2., verm. Aufl. Leipzig: F. Meiner, 1923–24 [1910].

Mautner, Franz H. "Johannes Nestroy: *Der Talisman*." In *Das deutsche Drama vom Barock bis zur Gegenwart: Interpretationen*. Bd. II. Düsseldorf: August Basel Verlag, 1958, 23–42.

Mayer, Matthias. *Hugo von Hofmannsthal*. Sammlung Metzler, 273. Stuttgart: J. B. Metzler, 1993.

McKenzie, John R. P. "Nestroy's Political Plays." In *The Austrian Comic Tradition: Studies in Honour of W. E. Yates*. Eds John R. P. McKenzie and Lesley Sharpe. Austrian Studies, 9. Edinburgh: Edinburgh University Press, 1998, 123–38.

McKenzie, John R. P., and Lesley Sharpe, eds. *The Austrian Comic Tradition: Studies in Honour of W. E. Yates.* Austrian Studies, 9. Edinburgh: Edinburgh University Press, 1998.

Melton, James Van Horn. "Von Versinnlichung zur Verinnerlichung: Bemerkungen zur Dialektik repräsentativer und plebejischer Öffentlichkeit." *Österreich im Europa der Aufklärung.* Eds Richard Georg Plaschka and Grete Klingenstein. Wien: Verlag der österreichischen Akademie der Wissenschaften, 1985, 919–41.

Michael, Nancy Carolyn. *Elektra and Her Sisters: Male Representations of Female Characters in Viennese High Culture, 1900–1905.* Diss., University of Wisconsin, Madison, 1991.

Montfort, Thomas van. "Das Bild im Text: Adalbert Stifter zum 200. Geburtstag." *Geborgenheit und Gefährdung in der epischen und malerischen Welt Adalbert Stifters.* Würzburg: Königshausen & Neumann, 2006, 161–71.

Morsak, Louis C. "Auf dem Weg zur Selbstfindung: 'Sonne über Österreich.'" In Gratl and Morsak, eds, *Sonne über Österreich,* 35–59.

Mullan, W. N. B. *Grillparzer's Aesthetic Theory: A Study with Special Reference to his Conception of the Drama as "eine Gegenwart."* Stuttgart: Akademischer Verlag Hans-Dieter Heinz, 1979.

Müller, Gerd. *Das Volksstück von Raimund bis Kroetz: Die Gattung in Einzelanalysen.* München: R. Oldenbourg Verlag, 1979.

Müller-Funk, Wolfgang, Peter Plener, and Clemens Ruthner. *Kakanien Revisited.* Tübingen: Francke, 2002.

Nance, Agnieszka Barbara. *Literary and Cultural Images of a Nation without a State: The Case of Nineteenth-Century Poland.* New York: Lang, 2008.

Nance, Agnieszka Barbara. *A Nineteenth-Century Polish 'Invented Community': Galicia as a Nation without a State.* Diss., University of Texas at Austin, 2004.

Nehring, Wolfgang. "Schnitzler, Freud's Alter Ego?" *Modern Austrian Literature,* 10, no. 3–4 (1977): 179–94.

"Die Nekropole." http://www.planet-vienna.com/Nekropole/nekropole.htm (accessed August 11, 2011).

Nestroy, Johann. *Freiheit in Krähwinkel. Historisch-Kritische Ausgabe: Stücke 26/I.* Ed. John R. P. McKenzie. Wien: Jugend und Volk, 1995.

Nestroy, Johann. *Der Talisman. Historisch-Kritische Ausgabe: Stücke 17/I.* Eds Jürgen Hein and Peter Haida. Historisch-kritische Ausgabe. Wien: Jugend und Volk, 1993.

Neugebauer, Klaus. *Selbstentwurf und Verhängnis: Ein Beitrag zu Adalbert Stifters Verständnis von Schicksal und Geschichte.* Tübingen: Stauffenberg Verlag, 1982.

Neumann, Gerhard. "Das Schreibprojekt des ästhetischen Historismus: Autobiographie, Restauration und Heilsgeschichte in Adalbert Stifters Erzählwerk." *Zeitschrift für Deutsche Philologie,* 123 (Supplement) (2004): 89–118.

Neumann, Gerhard, and Günter Schnitzler, eds. *Franz Grillparzer: Historie und Gegenwärtigkeit.* Freiburg im Breisgau: Rombach, 1994.

Nicoll, Allardyce. *The World of Harlequin: A Critical Study of the Commedia dell'arte.* Cambridge: Cambridge University Press, 1963.

Nölle, Volker. "Beichten und ihre 'Bruchstellen' in Erzählungen von Grillparzer, Keller und Joseph Roth." *Zeitschrift für Deutsche Philologie,* 120 (2001): 34–53.

Offermann, Ernst L. *Arthur Schnitzler: Das Komödienwerk als Kritik des Impressionismus.* München: Fink, 1973.

Otis, Laura. "The Language of Infection: Disease and Identity in Schnitzler's *Reigen." Germanic Review.* 70, no. 2 (Spring 1995): 65–75.

Pabisch, Peter. *H. C. Artmann Ein Versuch über die literarisce Alogik*. Wien: Verlag A. Schmidt, 1978.

Pargner, Brigit. "Charlotte Birch-Pfeiffer und das kommerzielle Theater im Wien des 19. Jahrhunderts." *From Perinet to Jelinek*. Eds W. E. Yates, Allyson Fiddler and John Warren. Oxford: Peter Lang, 2001, 63–78.

Pauget, Michèle. "Der Brief des Lord Chandos in seinem Verhältnis zum mythischen Denken: Seine Aktualität im französischen Sprachraum." In Sigurd Paul Scheichl and Gerald Stieg, eds, *Österreichische Literatur des 20. Jahrhunderts: Französische und österreichische Beiträge*. Innsbrucker Beiträge zur Kulturwissenschaft, Germanistische Reihe Band 21. Innsbruck: Institut für Germanistik der Universität Innsbruck, 1986, 99–114.

Pelinka, Anton. "Die Struktur und die Probleme der Gesellschaft zur Zeit Arthur Schnitzlers." *Literatur und Kritik*, no. 163/164 (April–May 1982): 59–66.

Perlmann, Michaela L. *Arthur Schnitzler*. Sammlung Metzler, Bd. 239. Stuttgart: J. B. Metzler, 1987.

Petković, Nikola. *The 'Post' in Postcolonial and Postmodern: The Case of Central Europe*. Diss., University of Texas at Austin, 1996.

Pfoser, Alfred. "Rund um den *Reigen*: Eine interpretatorische Einführung." In Pfoser et al., *Schnitzlers "Reigen."* I, 13–42

Pfoser, Alfred, Kristina Pfoser-Schewig, and Gerhard Renner. *Schnitzlers "Reigen."* Bd. 1: Der Skandal: Analysen und Dokumente; Bd. 2: Die Processe: Analysen und Dokumente. Frankfurt/M: Fischer, 1993.

Pick, Hella. *Guilty Victim: Austria from the Holocaust to Haider*. London: I. B. Tauris Publishers, 2000.

Plaschka, Richard Georg, and Grete Klingenstein, eds. *Österreich im Europa der Aufklärung: Koninuität und Zäsur in Europa zur Zeit Maria Theresias und Josephs II.* Wien: Verlag der österreichischen Akademie der Wissenschaften, 1985.

Politzer, Heinz. *Franz Grillparzer, oder das abgründige Biedermeier*. Wien, München, Zürich: Molden, 1972.

Potthast, Barbara. "'Ein lastend unheimliches Entfremden unserer Natur': Adalbert Stifters 'Die Sonnenfinsterniß am 8. Juli 1842' als Dokument einer anderen Moderne." *Scientia Poetica: Jahrbuch für Geschichte der Literatur und der Wissenschaften* 12 (2008): 114–40.

Pronay-Strasser, Inge. "Von Ornithologen und Grashupgerinnen: Bemerkungen zur Sexualität um 1900." In Ehalt et al., eds, *Glücklich ist*, 113–32.

Proß, Wolfgang. "Das Konzept des Populären in Italien und sein Einfluß auf das deutschsprachige Theater des 18. Jahrhunderts." *Volk- Volksstück-Volkstheater im deutschen Sprachraum des 18.–20. Jahrhunderts*. Ed. Jean-Marie Valentin. Bern: Peter Lang, 1986, 24–40.

Prunskiene, Kazimiera, and Otto von Habsburg, eds. *Europa, ein Kontinent gewinnt Gestalt: Die geistige Auseinandersetzung um das neue Europa*. Mainz: v. Hase & Koehler, 1992.

Raab, Riki. "Das k. k. Hofballett unter Maria Theresia." In Plaschka and Klingenstein, eds, *Österreich im Europa der Aufklärung*, 767–86.

Rausch, Mechthild. "Punch und Putschenelle." In Gerald Bisinger, ed., *Über H. C. Artmann*, 166–77.

Riccabona, Christine, Erika Wimmer, and Milena Meller. *Die Österreichischen Jugendkulturwochen 1950–1969 in Innsbruck*. Innsbruck-Wien-Bozen: Studien Verlag, 2006.

Rieck, Werner. "'Fast mit jedem Jahr wächst meine stille Bewunderung des großen

Mannes': Friedrich II. im Urteil Herders." In *Johann Gottfried Herder: Geschichte und Kultur*, ed. Martin Bollacher. Würzburg: Königshausen & Neumann, 1994, 289–302.

Rigler, Christine. *Generationen: Literatur im Forum Stadtpark, 1960–1995*. Graz, Wien: Literaturverlag Droschl, 1995.

Riha, Karl. "Ein patagonischer Aviatiker: Zu H.C. Artmanns Dramen." In Gerald Bisinger, ed., *Über H. C. Artmann*, 157–65.

Ritzer, Monika. "Lektionen in Demokratie: Adalbert Stifters politische Essays: Textstrategie und kulturhistorische Hermeneutik." *KulturPoetik: Zeitschrift für Kulturgeschichtliche Literaturwissenschaft/Journal of Cultural Poetics*, 10, no. 2 (2010): 177–98.

Robert, Adrian Clive. *Arthur Schnitzler and Politics*. Riverside, CA: Ariadne, 1989.

Robertson, Ritchie. "The Failure of Enlightenemnt in Grillparzer's *Ein Bruderzwist in Habsburg* and Goethe's *Die natürliche Tochter*." In Strelka, ed., *Für all*, 165–85.

Roe, Ian F. "The Comedy of Schnitzler's *Reigen*." *Modern Language Review*, 89, no. 3 (July 1994): 674–88.

Roe, Ian F. *An Introduction to the Major Works of Franz Grillparzer, 1791–1872, Austrian Dramatist*. Studies in German Language and Literature, vol. 7. Lewiston: Edwin Mellen Press, 1991.

Roe, Ian F. "Truth and Humanity in Grillparzer's *Weh dem, der lügt!*." *Forum for Modern Language Studies*. 22, no. 4 (October 1986): 289–307.

Roli, Maria Luisa, ed. *Adalbert Stifter: Trafilologia e studi culturali*. Milan, Italy: Cuem, 2001. Online at http://users.unimi.it/germscand/roli_stf.pdf (accessed January 2, 2015).

Rommel, Otto. *Die Alt-Wiener Volkskömodie: Ihre Geschichte vom barocken Welttheater bis sum Tode Nestroys*. Wien: A. Schroll, 1952.

Roth, Joseph. *Radetzkymarsch*. Köln: Kiepenhauer & Witsch, 1932.

Rühm, Gerhard, ed. *Die Wiener Gruppe—Achleitner, Artmann, Bayer, Rühm, Wiener: Texte, Gemeinschaftsarbeiten, Aktionen*. Reinbek bei Hamburg: Rowohlt Verlag, 1967.—"Vorwort," 5–36.

Sagarra, Edda. "Grillparzer the Catholic?" *Modern Language Review*, 97, no. 1 (January 2002): 108–22.

Schäublin, Peter. "Stifters Abdias von Herder aus gelesen." *VASILO*, 23, no. 3–4 (1974): 101–13; and 24, no. 3–4 (1975): 87–105.

Schaum, Konrad. "Grillparzers 'Kloster bei Sendomir' und Hauptmanns Elga: Ein Vergleich." *Grillparzer Forum Forchtenstein: Vorträge, Forschungen, Berichte* (Austria) (1976): 18–41.

Scheibelreiter, Georg. "Franz Grillparzer und Bischof Gregor von Tours." *Jahrbuch der Grillparzer-Gesellschaft*, 15 (1983): 65–78.

Scheible, Hartmut. *Arthur Schnitzler und die Aufklärung*. München: Wilhelm Fink Verlag, 1977.

Scheible, Hartmut, ed. *Arthur Schnitzler in neuer Sicht*. München: Wilhelm Fink, 1981.

Scheible, Hartmut. *Liebe und Liberalism: Über Arthur Schnitzler*. Bielefeld: Aisthesis Verlag, 1996.

Scheichl, Sigurd Paul. "Atalus: Ein unaufgelöster Widerspruch in *Weh dem, der lügt!*." *German Life & Letters*, 44, no. 1 (April 1991): 198–207.

Scheichl, Sigurd Paul. "*Weh dem, der lügt!*: Grillparzers literarisches Lustspiel." In Winfried Frend, ed., *Deutsche Komödien vom Barock bis zur Gegenwart*. München: Wilhelm Fink Verlag, 1988, 129–45.

Scheit, Gerhard. *Hanswurst und der Staat: Eine kleine Geschichte der Komik: Von Mozart bis Thomas Bernhard*. Wien: Deutike, 1995.

Schenker, Hansjörg. *Theaterdirektor Carl und die Staberl-Figur: Eine Studie zur Wiener Volkstheater vor und neben Nestroy*. Diss., Universität Zürich (aku-Photodruck Zürich), 1986.

Schiffermüller, Isolde. "Adalbert Stifters deskriptive Prosa: Eine Modellanalyse der Novelle *Der beschriebene Tännling*." *Deutsche Vierteljahrschrift für Literaturwissenschaft und Geistesgeschichte* 67, no. 2 (June 1993): 267–301.

Schmitz, Thomas. *Das Volksstück*. Sammlung Metzler, Bd. 257. Stuttgart: J. B. Metzler, 1990.

Schnabel, Werner Wilhelm. "*Professor Bernhardi* und die Wiener Zensur: Zur Rezeptionsgeschichte der Schnitzlerschen Komödie." *Jahrbuch der Deutschen Schiller-Gesellschaft*, 28 (1984): 349–83

Schneider, Gerd K. *Die Rezeption von Arthur Schnitzlers Reigen 1897–1994: Pressespiegel und andere zeitgenossische Kommentare*. Riverside, CA: Ariadne, 1995.

Schneider, Günter. "Grillparzer und die Spätaufklärung." In Gerhard Neumann and Günter Schnitzler, eds, *Franz Grillparzer: Historie und Gegenwärtigkeit*, 179–201.

Schneider-Halvorson, Brigitte L. *The Late Dramatic Works of Arthur Schnitzler*. New York: Peter Lang, 1983.

Schneider, Lothar. "Das Komma im Frack: Adalbert Stifter, von Hebbels Kritik aus betrachtet." In Hartmut Laufhütte and Karl Möseneder, eds, *Adalbert Stifter: Dichter und Maler, Denkmalpfleger und Schulmann—Neue Zugänge zu seinem Werk*. Tübingen: Niemeyer, 1996, 105–18.

Schnitzler, Arthur. *Briefe 1913–1931*. Frankfurt/M: S. Fischer, 1984.

Schnitzler, Arthur. *Entworfenes und Verworfenes: Aus dem Nachlaß*. Ed. Reinhard Urbach. Frankfurt/M: S. Fischer, 1977.

Schnitzler, Arthur. *Medizinische Schriften*. Ed. Horst Thomé. Wien: Paul Zsolnay, 1988.

Schnitzler, Arthur. *Marionetten: Drei Einakter (Der Puppenspieler: Studie in einem Aufzug, Der tapfere Cassian: Puppenspiel in einem Akt, Zum großen Wurstl: Burleske in einem Aktl)*. *Das dramatische Werk*, Bd. 4. Frankfurt/M: Fischer, 1978, 85–142.

Schnitzler, Arthur. *Der Schleier der Pierrette: Pantomime in drei Bildern*. In: *Das dramatische Werk*, Bd. 6. Frankfurt/M: Fischer, 1979, 111–26.

Schnitzler, Arthur. *Der tapfere Kassian: Singspiel in einem Aufzug*. In: *Das dramatische Werk*, Bd. 5. Frankfurt/M: Fischer, 1979, 57–76.

Schnitzler, Arthur. *Die Verwandlungen des Pierrot: Pantomime in einem Vorspiel und sechs Bildern*. In *Das dramatische Werk*, Bd. 5. Frankfurt/M: Fischer, 1979, 41–56.

Schorske, Carl E. *Fin de siècle Vienna: Politics and Culture*. New York: Vintage Books, 1981.

Schorske, Carl E. *Thinking with History: Explorations in the Passage to Modernism*. Princeton: Princeton University Press, 1998.

Schröder, Klàus Albrecht. "Epocheneuphorie und Epochenillusion." In Frodl and Schröder, eds, *Wiener Biedermeier*, 7–8.

Schröder, Klaus Albrecht. "Kunst als Erzählung: Theorie und Ästhetik der Genremalerei." In Frodl and Schröder, eds, *Wiener Biedermeier*, 9–34.

Schultz, H. Stéfan. "Hofmannsthal and Bacon: The Sources of the Chandos Letter." *Comparative Literature*, 13, no. 1 (Winter 1961): 1–15.

Schwaiger, Brigitte. *Wie kommt das Salz ins Meer*. Wien: Zsolnay, 1977.

316   Bibliography

Schwarz, Egon. "Milieu oder Mythos?: Wien in den Werken Arthur Schnitzlers." *Literatur und Kritik*, 163/164 (April/May 1982): 22–35.

Seibert, Ernst. *Jugendliteratur im Übergang vom Josephinismus zur Restauration, mit einem bibliographischen Anhang über die österreichische Kinder- und Jugendliteratur von 1770–1830*. Wien, Köln, Graz: Böhlau Verlag, 1987.

Seibert, Ernst. "Zur Quellenlage von Grillparzers Novelle *Das Kloster bei Sendomir*." *Jahrbuch des Wiener Goethe-Vereins*, 96 (1992): 73–89.

Seidler, Herbert. "Adalbert-Stifter-Forschung 1945–1970 (Erster Teil)." *Zeitschrift für deutsche Philologie*, 91, no. 1 (1972a): 113–57.

Seidler, Herbert. "Adalbert-Stifter-Forschung 1945–1970 (Zweiter Teil)." *Zeitschrift für deutsche Philologie*, 91, no. 2 (1972b): 252–85.

Seidler, Herbert. "Die Adalbert-Stifter-Forschung der siebziger Jahre." *VASILO* 30, no. 3–4 (1981): 89–134.

Seidler, Herbert. "Die Forschung zu Arthur Schnitzler seit 1945." *Zeitschrift für Deutsche Philologie*, 95, no. 4 (1976): 567–95.

Seidler, Herbert. "Grillparzers Lustspiel *Weh dem, der lügt!*." *Jahrbuch der Grillparzer-Gesellschaft*, 4 (1965): 7–29.

Seitter, Walter. *Unzeitgemäße Aufklärung: Franz Grillparzers Philosophie*. Wien/Berlin: Turia + Kant, 1991.

Sengle, Friedrich. *Biedermeierzeit: Deutsche Literatur im Spannungsfeld zwischen Restauration u. Revolution, 1815–1848*. 3 vols. Stuttgart: Metzler, 1971, 1972, 1980.

Sherman, Murray H. "Reik, Schnitzler, Freud, and 'The Murderer.'" *Modern Austrian Literature*, 10, no. 3–4 (1977): 163–7.

Sieder, Reinhard. "'Vata, derf i aufstehn?': Kindheitserfahrungen in Wiener Arbeiterfamilienum 1900." In Ehalt et al., eds, *Glücklich ist*, 39–89.

Sjörgren, Christine Oertel. "The Frame of *Der Waldbrunnen* Reconsidered: A Note on Adalbert Stifter's Aesthetics." *Modern Austrian Literature* 19, no. 1 (1986): 9–25.

Sonnenfels, Joseph von. *Briefe über die Wienerische Schaubühne*. Ed. Hilde Haider-Pregler. Graz: Akademische Druck- und Verlagsanstalt, 1988 (= Wiener Neudrucke, Bd. 9).

Sonnleitner, Johann, ed. *J. A. Stranitzky, J. F. Kurz, P. Hafner, J. Perinet, A. Bäuerle: Hanswurstiaden: Ein Jahrhundert Wiener Kömodie*. Salzburg: Residenz Verlag, 1996.

Spiel, Hilde. "Die österreichische Literatur nach 1945: Eine Einführung." In Spiel, ed., *Kindlers Literaturgeschichte*, 11–127.

Spiel, Hilde, ed. *Kindlers Literaturgeschichte der Gegenwart (Autoren, Werke, Themen, Tendenzen seit 1945): Die zeitgenössische Literatur Österreichs*. Zürich and München: Kindler Verlag, 1976.

Staiger, Emil. *Adalbert Stifter als Dichter der Ehrfurcht*. Zurich: Verlag der Arche, 1952.

Steinberg, Michael P. *The Meaning of the Salzburg Festival: Austria as Theater and Ideology, 1890–1938*. Ithaca, NY: Cornell University Press, 1990.

Stekl, Hannes. "Unterschichten und Obrigkeit im Wien des ausgehenden 18. Jahrhunderts." In *Österreich im Europa der Aufklärung*. Eds Richard Georg Plaschka and Grete Klingenstein. Wien: Verlag der österreichischen Akademie der Wissenschaften, 1985, 291–304.

Stern, Martin, ed. and intro. "Der Briefwechsel Hofmannsthal-Fritz Mauthner." *Hofmannsthalblätter*, Heft 19/20 (1978): 21–38.

Stiehm, Lothar, ed. *Adalbert Stifter: Studien und Interpretationen*. Heidelberg: Lothar Stiehm, 1968.

Stifter, Adalbert. *Bunte Steine: Buchfassungen*. Ed. Hermut Bergner. In *Werke und Briefe* 2, part 2. Eds Alfred Doppler and Wolfgang Frühwald. Stuttgart: W. Kohlhammer, 1982.

Stifter, Adalbert. "Die Poesie und ihre Wirkungen." *Vermischte Schriften*. *Gesammelte Werke in vierzehn Bänden*. Ed. Konrad Steffen. Basel and Stuttgart: Birkhäuser Verlag, 1972, XIV, 356–71.

Stifter, Adalbert. "Die Sonnenfinsternis am 8. Juli 1842." *Gesammelte Werke in vierzehn Bänden*. Ed. Konrad Steffen. Basel und Stuttgart: Birkhäuser Verlag, 1972, XIV, 103–14.

Stifter, Adalbert. "Vorrede" and "Einleitung." In *Bunte Steine*, 9–16 and 17–20.

Stifter, Adalbert. "Wirkungen der Schule" [1849]. *Vermischte Schriften*. *Gesammelte Werke in vierzehn Bänden*. Ed. Konrad Steffen. Basel and Stuttgart: Birkhäuser Verlag, 1972, XIV, 256–62.

Stillmark, Alexander. "Adalbert Stifter: The Eclipse of the Sun." In Karlheinz F. Auckenthaler, Hans H. Rudnick, and Klaus Weissenberger, eds. *Ein Leben für Dichtung und Freiheit: Festschrift zum 70. Geburtstag von Joseph P . Strelka*. Tübingen: Stauffenburg, 1997, 3–10.

Strelka, Joseph P., ed. *Für all, was Menschen je erfahren ... : Beiträge zu Franz Grillparzers Werk*. New Yorker Beiträge zur Österreichischen Literaturgeschichte, 2. New York: Peter Lang, 1995.

Strelka, Joseph P., ed. *Die Seele ... ist ein weites Land: Kritische Beiträge zum Werk Arthur Schnitzlers*. Bern: Peter Lang, 1996.

Stroszeck, Hauke. *Heilsthematik in der Posse: Über Johann Nestroys "Der Talisman."* Aachen: Alano Verlag, 1990.

Sugar, Peter F., and Péter Hanák, eds. *A History of Hungary*. Bloomington, IN: Indiana University Press, 1990.

Sullivan, Lawrence. "Arthur Schnitzler's *The Veil of Pierrette*." *Europa Orientalis*. 14, no. 2 (1995): 263-280.

Swales, Martin. "The Aristocratic Philanderer: Reflections on Hofmannsthal's *Der Schwierige*." In: *The Austrian Comic Tradition: Studies in Honour of W. E. Yates*. Eds John R. P. McKenzie and Lesley Sharpe. Austrian Studies, 9. Edinburgh: Edinburgh University Press, 1998, 176–84.

Swales, Martin. *Arthur Schnitzler: A Critical Study*. Oxford: Clarendon, 1971.

Swales, Martin. "Schnitzler als Realist." *Literatur und Kritik*, no. 161/162 (February/March 1982): 52–61.

Swales, Martin, and Erika Swales. *Adalbert Stifter: A Critical Study*. Cambridge and New York: Cambridge University Press, 1984.

Tabor, Jan. "An dieser Blume gehst Du zugrunde: Bleich, purpurot, weiß— Krankheit als Inspiration." In Ehalt et al., eds, *Glücklich ist*, 215–43.

Tanner, Marie. *The Last Descendant of Aeneas: The Hapsburgs and the Mythic Image of the Emperor*. New Haven, CT: Yale University Press, 1993.

Thomé, Horst. "Sozialgeschichtliche Perspektiven der neueren Schniztler-Forschung." *Internationales Archiv für Sozialgeschichte der Deutschen Literatur*, 13 (1988): 158–87.

Todorova, Maria. *Imagining the Balkans*. Updated edition. New York: Oxford University Press, 2009.

Trumpener, Katie. *Bardic Nationalism: The Romantic Novel and the British Empire*. Princeton, NJ: Princeton University Press, 1997.

Tweraser, Felix W. *Political Dimensions of Arthur Schnitzler's Late Fiction*. Columbia, SC: Camden House, 1998.

Urbach, Reinhard. *Arthur Schnitzler*. Trans. Donald Daviau. New York: Friedrich Ungar, 1973.

Urbach, Reinhard. *Schnitzler Kommentar zu den erzählenden Schriften und dramatischen Werken*. München: Winkler-Verlag, 1974.

Urbach, Reinhard. *Die Wiener Kömodie und ihr Publikum: Stranitzky und die Folgen*. Wien: Jugend & Volk, 1973.

Valentin, Jean-Marie. "J. von Sonnenfels et le peuple: Vision politique et esthetique theatrale." *Volk- Volksstück-Volkstheater im deutschen Sprachraum des 18.–20. Jahrhunderts*. Ed. Jean-Marie Valentin. Bern: Peter Lang, 1986, 41–61.

Valentin, Jean-Marie. ed. *Volk- Volksstück-Volkstheater im deutschen Sprachraum des 18.–20. Jahrhunderts*. Akten des [...] Kolloguims Nancy, November 12–13, 1982. *Jahrbuch für Internationale Germanistik*, Reihe A: Kongressberichte, Bd. 15. Bern: Peter Lang, 1986.

Venuti, Lawrence. *The Translator's Invisibility: A History of Translation*. London: Routledge, 1995.

Vierhaus, Rudolf. "Kritikbereitschaft und Konsensverlangen bei deutschen Aufklärern." In Mauser and Saße, eds, *Streitkultur*, 78–92.

Vilain, Robert. "'Stop all the Clocks': Time and Times in the 'Vienna Operas' of Hofmannsthal and Strauss." In *The Austrian Comic Tradition: Studies in Honour of W. E. Yates*. Eds John R. P. McKenzie and Lesley Sharpe. Austrian Studies, 9. Edinburgh: Edinburgh University Press, 1998, 185–201.

Wagner, Renate. *Arthur Schnitzler: Eine Biographie*. Wien: Fritz Molden, 1981.

Walla, Fred. "Johann Nestroy im Urteil und Vorurteil der Kritik." *Österreich in Geschichte und Literatur mit Geographie*, 35, no. 4 (1991): 242–62.

Wallnig, Thomas, Johannes Frimmel, and Werner Telesko, eds. *18th Century Studies in Austria, 1945–2010*. The Eighteenth Century and the Habsburg Monarchy: International Series, vol. 4. Bochum: Dr. Dieter Winkler Verlag, 2011.

Walter-Buchebner-Projekt, ed. *die wiener gruppe*. Wien: Böhlau, 1987.

Weber, D. "Mozart als Bühnenstar: Musical-Uraufführung im Theater an der Wien." *Neue Zürcher Zeitung*, October 4, 1999, 28.

Weinberger, G. J. *Arthur Schnitzler's Late Plays: A Critical Study*. Peter Lang. New York, NY, 1997.

Weinhold, Ulrike. "Arthur Schnitzler und der weibliche Diskurs: Zur Problematik des Frauenbildes der Jahrhundertwende," *Jahrbuch für Internationale Germanistik* 19, 1 (1987): 110–45.

Weiss, Gerhard H. "Johann Nestroy: The Revolution on the Stage." In *Playing for Stakes: German-Language Drama in Social Context —Essays in Honor of Herbert Lederer*. Eds Anna K. Kuhn and Barbara D. Wright. Oxford: Berg, 1994, 161–72.

West, Rebecca. *Black Lamb and Grey Falcon: A Journey Through Yugoslavia*. New York: Penguin Books, 1982 [1941, with sections from *The Atlantic Monthly* (1940)].

Whaley, Joachim. "Die Habsburgermonarchie und das Heilige Römische Reich im 18. Jahrhundert." In Wilhelm Brauneder and Lothar Höbelt, eds. *Sacrum Imperioum: Das Reich und Österreich 996–1806*. Wien: Amalthea, 1996, 288–318.

Wiese, Benno von. "Adalbert Stifter: Abdias." In *Die deutsche Novelle von Goethe bis Kafka: Interpretationen II*. Düsseldorf: August Bagel Verlag, 1962, 127–48.

Wiesmayr, Elisabeth. "Patt der Herzen: Inszenierungen der Liebe im fin de siècle." In Ehalt et al., eds, *Glücklich ist*, 133–44.

Wiesmüller, Wolfgang. "Die Europa-Diskussion im 19. Jahrhundert und der historische Roman: Zum literarischen und feuilletonistischen Kontext von

Bibliography 319

Adalbert Stifters Witiko." *'Germanistik im Konflikt der Kulturen', Band 12: Europadiskurse in der deutschen Literatur und Literaturwissenschaft; Deutsch-jüdische Kulturdialoge/-konflikte.* Bern: Peter Lang, 2007, 121–8.

Wiesmüller, Wolfgang. " Die politische Rede als Medium der Geschichtsdeutung in Stifters *Witiko.*" Études Germaniques 40, no. 3 (July–September 1985): 349–65.

Wiesmüller, Wolfgang. "Zur Krise geschichtsphilosophischer Positionen der Aufklärung bei Adalbert Stifter." In Klaus Müller-Salget and Sigurd Paul Scheichl, eds. *Nachklänge der Aufklärung im 19. und 20. Jahrhundert.* Innsbruck: Innsbruck University Press; 2008, 43–54.

Wolf, G. *Das Unterrichtswesen in Oesterreich unter Kaiser Josef II, nach einer Vorstellung von Jos. V. Sonnenfels.* Wien: Alfred Hölder, 1880.

Wolf, Michaela. *Die vielsprachige Seele Kakaniens: Übersetzen und Dolmetschen in der Habsburgermonarchie 1848 bis 1918.* Wien: Böhlau Verlag, 2012.

Wolff, Larry. *Inventing Eastern Europe: The Map of Civilization on the Mind of the Enlightenment.* Redwood City, CA: Stanford University Press, 1994.

Wolff, Lutz-W. "'Bürger der Endzeit': Schnitzler in socialistischer Sicht." In Scheible, ed., *Arthur Schnitzler in neuer Sicht,* 330–59.

Wolgast, Karin. "Die Commedia dell'arte im Wiener Drama der Jahrhundertwende." *Orbis Litterarum,* 44, no. 4 (1989): 283–311.

Yates, W. E[dgar]. *Grillparzer: A Critical Introduction.* Cambridge: Cambridge University Press, 1972.

Yates, W. E[dgar]. "'Ich will hiemit gar nicht gesagt haben, daß Herr N. entlehnt ...': Zu Nestroys Einfällen und Refrains." *Der unbekannte Nestroy.* Ed. W. Edgar Yates. Wien: WUV/Universitätsverlag, 2001, 13–33

Yates, W. E[dgar]. *Nestroy and the Critics.* Columbia, SC: Camden House, 1994

Yates, W. E[dgar]. *Schnitzler, Hofmannsthal and the Austrian Theatre.* New Haven: Yale University Press, 1992

Yates, W. E[dgar]. *Theater in Vienna: A Critical History, 1776–1995.* Cambridge: Cambridge University Press, 1996.

Yates, W. E[dgar], ed. *Der unbekannte Nestroy: Editorisches, Biographisches, Interpretatorisches.* Wien: WUV/Universitätsverlag, 2001.

Yates, W. E[dgar], Allyson Fiddler, and John Warren, eds. *From Perinet to Jelinek: Viennese Theatre in its Political and Intellectual Context.* British and Irish Studies in German Language and Literature, Bd. 28. Oxford: Peter Lang, 2001.

Yates, W. E[dgar], and John R. P. McKenzie, eds. *Viennese Popular Theater: A Symposium.* Exeter: University of Exeter, 1985.

Zahra, Tara. *Kidnapped Souls: National Indifference and the Battle for Children in the Bohemian Lands, 1900–1948.* Ithaca: Cornell University Press, 2008.

Zeman, Herbert. "Die alt-Wiener Volkskömodie des 18. und frühen 19. Jahrhunderts." *Österreich im Europa der Aufklärung.* Eds Richard Georg Plaschka and Grete Klingenstein. Wien: Verlag der österreichischen Akademie der Wissenschaften, 1985, 716–41.

Zeman, Herbert, ed. *Geschichte der Literatur in Österreich,* Bd. 7: *Das 20. Jahrhundert.* Graz: Akademische Druck- und Verlagsanstalt, 1994.

Zeman, Herbert. "'Niederländische Gemäldewahrheit': Das Genrebild in der österreichischen Musik und Literatur des Biedermeier." In Frodl and Schröder, eds, *Wiener Biedermeier,* 71–80.

Zeman, Herbert. "Die österreichische Literatur und ihre literaturgeschichtliche Darstellung vom ausgehenden 18. bis zum frühen 19. Jahrhundert." In Herbert

Zeman, ed., *Die österreichische Literatur: Ihr Profil an der Wende vom 18. zum 19. Jahrhundert (1750–1830)*. Graz: Akademische Druck- und Verlagsanstalt, 1979, 563–86.

Zeman, Herbert. "Reminiszenzen und Lesefrüchte: Zu den Stifter-Jahren 1968 und 2005: Wissenschafts- und literaturgeschichtliche Aspekte-Adalbert Stifters Weltanschauung." *Jahrbuch der Österreichischen Goethe-Gesellschaft*, 108–10 (2004–2006): 339–44.

Zieger, Wilfried. "'Doch ich vergesse mich. Wie gehört das alles zur *Zelmire*?'" In Mauser and Saße, eds, *Streitkultur*, 552–62.

Index of Names

324   Index of Names